RELICTS OF A
Beautiful Sea

RELICTS OF A
Beautiful Sea

Survival, Extinction, and Conservation
IN A DESERT WORLD

Christopher J. Norment

The University of North Carolina Press *Chapel Hill*

This book was published with the assistance of the Wachovia Wells Fargo Fund for Excellence of the University of North Carolina Press.

© 2014 CHRISTOPHER J. NORMENT

All rights reserved. Manufactured in the United States of America. Designed by Sally Scruggs and set in Calluna by codeMantra.

The paper in this book meets the guidelines for permanence and durability of the Committee on Production Guidelines for Book Longevity of the Council on Library Resources.

The University of North Carolina Press has been a member of the Green Press Initiative since 2003.

Complete cataloging information for this title is available from the Library of Congress.

ISBN 978-1-4696-1866-1 (cloth: alk. paper)
ISBN 978-1-4696-1867-8 (ebook)

18 17 16 15 14   5 4 3 2 1

Portions of Pattiann Rogers's poem, "Animals and People: 'The Human Heart in Conflict with Itself,'" have been reprinted by permission of the author from *Orion* 16(1) (Winter 1997); Pattiann Rogers, *Eating Bread and Honey* (Milkweed Editions, 1997); and Pattiann Rogers, *Song of the World Becoming: New and Collected Poems* (Milkweed Editions, 2001).

This book is dedicated to those who have worked so hard
for so long to protect the voiceless ones, the pupfish, salamanders,
toads, and their kin—too many people to name here,
but in particular, Phil Pister and Jim Deacon

Contents

Illustrations

RELICTS OF A
Beautiful Sea

Prologue

OH MY DESERT

Oh my desert. You have bred the viscid scent of creosote in the searing air, thick spines out of the arid soil, the scuttle of scorpions from the calcined ground, this thermal litany of desiccation and desire: shadscale scrub, Panamint alligator lizard, bursage, tarantula and tarantula hawk, salt-crust playa, Basin and Range, spare hills rising from their own rubble, the long view across the lost miles, a longer view down the corridors of time, a deluge of heat and light. Life takes its path; lineages of reptiles and arachnids, insects and cacti, all at home, drift down the long slope of history, eddy and course through time. The tangled bank yields to naked rock; a raven's guttural croak echoes down some dry wash; a cast snake skin, thick with keratin, lies below a drifting dune; a kangaroo rat, huddled in its burrow, shelters from the solstice sun: in this xeric world these things make absolute sense. But it is more difficult to accept—to believe in—the sweep of fins through a thin film of water, the silent sway of salamanders across moistened soil, a trill of toads in the desert night.

I walk for hours across the hardscrabble ground, beneath a sun-blasted sky, taste salt on my burnt skin. But then I am taken, suddenly, by a trace of seep willow, the rustle of cottonwood leaves, a tiny spring hidden in some rough canyon. I stoop down, cup water in my hands, feel its cool welcome on my face, and then turn a flat rock. A small creature coils, refugee from the deepest past, from another, wetter time. I catch my breath and time spirals. The day is consecrated. All the world's lost, aching beauty comes flooding in and life's long skein claims my heart.

Introduction

They are other nations, caught with ourselves in the net of
life and time, fellow prisoners of the splendor and travail of the earth.
—Henry Beston, *The Outermost House*

Relicts of a Beautiful Sea is a story about the natural world, woven out of
science, poetry, aesthetics, and personal experience. It is a tale about the
beauty of the Great Basin, its life, and my longing to belong fully to a place
and find resonance in its creatures—in other words, to locate myself in this
world and so claim a home. And in this age of extinction and collapsing
species ranges, my story also is an argument about biodiversity's inherent
right to exist. This right was codified by the 1973 federal Endangered Species Act, but many people still wonder—why should we cherish and protect
the many threads of life's deep and intricate history, and just what are all
the lonely and besieged species worth? This story and my argument are
built around six desert animals, all of them small and restricted to aquatic
habitats: a salamander, four types of pupfishes, and a toad. These animals
depend upon the same desert waters that people desire, and so they are rare
and mostly threatened. And because they are small and live in a tough and
inaccessible part of the world, they also are relatively obscure and carry little of the innate appeal associated with "charismatic megavertebrates" such
as gray wolves, polar bears, California condors, giant pandas, and whoop-
ing cranes. And yet in their own right these creatures are as stunning and
compelling as wolves and bears, and as worthy of our love and concern. The
salamander is one of only two desert salamanders in the world. The pupfishes are considered to be freshwater fish, but some of them can survive
in water twice as salty as seawater, at temperatures over 100°F. The toad
is exiled to an isolated desert valley a world away from its nearest kin. To
hold one of these salamanders or toads in your hand, or to watch a small
school of pupfish arc through a tiny pool of desert water, is to discover

3

something vital about wonder, and the tenacity of life. And because these animals are rare, and mostly isolated from their nearest kin, they also may teach us something crucial about what it is like to be alone in the world, and how to transcend this loneliness. I know that this has been true for me: living with these rare desert creatures and coming to know their stories has helped heal some of the emotional wounds that I have carried with me out of my childhood.

To fully understand any story you must begin with its setting—in this case the spare and aching Great Basin country running east from the Sierra Nevada, a land that rises and falls in an endless iteration of mountains and valleys. A march of desert, 200,000 square miles of it, backlit crenellated hills stretching north and south: a touch of trees in the high places, a drift of luminous clouds across empty territory, of lonely highways through deep and lovely valleys. A threadbare blanket of ragged shrubs draped across the land, the scent of dust and sage in the afternoon air, two or five or ten inches of rain and snow per year. Heat and light in the summer, cold and light in the winter, the waters of the land in pockets and pools, always rationed and rare, running onto salt-pan playas, disappearing into the great empty basins, draining into the gesso ground, alkaline wastes glistening beneath the noonday sun, held beneath the ragged strike and dip of the lost ranges. It wasn't always this way, though. Once there was more water: giant lakes arrayed like fingers splayed in soft sand, tracking the basins. Pinyon pine, juniper, and oak ran across the great valleys; glaciers nestled against the highest peaks; the spoor of mastodon and mammoth littered the ground. It would have been something—to stand above Death Valley and see a lake 80 miles long and 600 feet deep, cupped between the Panamint and Funeral Mountains. Lake Lahontan, Lake Russell, Searles Lake, Panamint Lake, Lake Manly: gone these last 10,000 years, gone with the giant ground sloths and saber-toothed cats, gone with the glaciers. The gulls that wheeled above the lakes, the fish that swam through the waters, the snails that crawled amid the algae and reeds—all the creatures that lived with the waters would have gone elsewhere if they were able, or perished, or followed the dying streams into springs and hidden canyons. And in these places the descendants of these refugees have lived on for generation after generation, wedded to the promise of water flowing from the mountains or rising up out of the ground, a liquid fossil drifting through thick beds of rock and time.

I am drawn to this spare country, to its broad and treeless valleys, to the mountains rising from those valleys, to the long views of empty space and the longer views of time that rise from the land like the mountains themselves. I am drawn to the tiny, scattered archipelagos of watered grace, to those refuges where life has crawled, wriggled, drifted, flown, and swam as it sought shelter from the heat and drought. For me there is something emotionally compelling about these islands of life, about the ways in which their inhabitants have become isolated from others of their kind. This ecological loneliness resonates with me in a fundamental way, and so I also am drawn to the refugees, to the species that have hitched their fates inexorably—and now perilously—to the fate of the waters. These waters pool in tinajas and cobbled creeks and wind their way through cottonwoods and willows before disappearing into sand and bedrock and huge empty basins, or before disappearing into another sort of emptiness as humans take what they believe they need and deserve. There are bulldozers and pipelines, pumps and wells, ditches and dams, lawns and lakes, fields of alfalfa and fields of houses, and the thousands and millions of people living a few miles or a few hundred miles away from the waters. We demand a tribute more than a tithe, seize what we will, and until recently have lived as though the waters are limitless, the opportunities for growth as vast and endless as the farthest horizon seen from the tallest peaks of the Basin and Range country.

Although the desert is defined by the absence of water, there is water enough in the desert if you live properly. And when I come to desert water, whether in heat or cold, in thirst or its absence, I always lift a handful to my mouth and taste what is there—sweet or salty, cool or warm, fetid or fragrant. I work the water across my tongue, contemplate its qualities and how it nourishes the living and once nourished the dead. I have held the waters' toads and salamanders in my hands, felt tiny fish nibble my fingers, squinted at minute insects and miniscule snails, listened to the celebrations of birds sung from lost gardens of cottonwood and willow. I have read, too, about the fish and frogs and snails and mice that have vanished in my lifetime, the "immortal coils" of their DNA no longer immortal, disappearing instead into the gloom of history. Lineages now lost to us, lost to the future, lost to the world like so much chaff blown free of time: Tecopa pupfish, Vegas Valley leopard frog, Las Vegas dace, Pahrump Ranch poolfish, Raycraft Ranch poolfish, Ash Meadows poolfish, Longstreet springsnail, Ash Meadows montane vole. All of them gone, and most of them gone because their waters are gone.

This book is set in the southwestern corner of the Great Basin, where it meets the Mojave Desert: an area running east from the Sierra Nevada crest through the Owens Valley and Inyo Mountains, across the Panamint Range, Death Valley, and the Amargosa Range, then over the California-Nevada border into the Ash Meadows area, with the great sprawl of Las Vegas an insistent, ominous outlier to the southeast. In this relatively small slice of Basin and Range country—10,000 square miles of it, a rough rectangle over one hundred miles on a side—lie Mount Whitney, the highest point in the conterminous United States, and Badwater, the lowest point in North America. There are conifer forests and alpine tundras, snow-fed lakes and alkaline playas, sparse, xeric scrublands and lush meadows, glacier-scoured cirques, tiny seeps and gushing springs, and creeks that in this dry country are called rivers. The region's aridity and its complex geological history and topography have divided the land and water into islands, isolated populations of plants and animals and pushed them onto their separate evolutionary trajectories. Thus, in Death Valley National Park alone there are roughly thirty-four endemic species or incipient species that occur nowhere else in the world. Perhaps this doesn't sound that remarkable, because Death Valley encompasses about 5,200 square miles and is the largest national park outside of Alaska. But leave the park head-quarters at Furnace Creek and drive east for thirty miles through a gap between the Funeral Mountains and Greenwater Range and slide down the broad alluvial fan south of the Funerals to Death Valley Junction. Then head north on California Highway 127 for six miles to the Nevada state line before turning east just past the Longstreet Casino. Another three miles or so will bring you to the boundary of Ash Meadows National Wildlife Refuge, born in 1984 out of angry resistance on the part of some and dogged determination on the part of others. Here, on only 24,000 acres—an area that would fit easily in a rectangle six miles by nine miles on a side—are (or were) twenty-nine endemic organisms, a higher density than in any other national wildlife refuge in the country, most likely more than in any other place in the United States and Canada. These species are (or were) tied to water or to moist habitats near water—to a cluster of springs that rise from the great carbonate aquifer lying north and east of Ash Meadows. This plethora of unique plants and animals is beautiful, stunning, and frighten-ing: beautiful because of the harsh land in which it occurs and the adaptive stories that it tells; stunning because of its concentration and perseverance in the face of adversity; and frightening because it is tied completely to the water that so many people would use until it is gone.

The setting for the book may be narrow but its implications are not. I write about the particulars of this Basin and Range country because I love

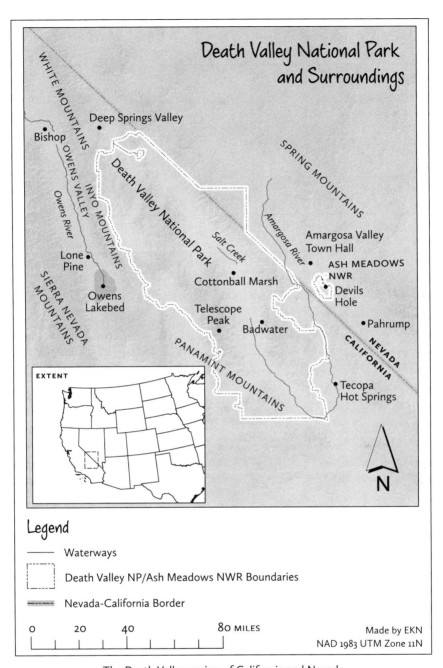

The Death Valley region of California and Nevada

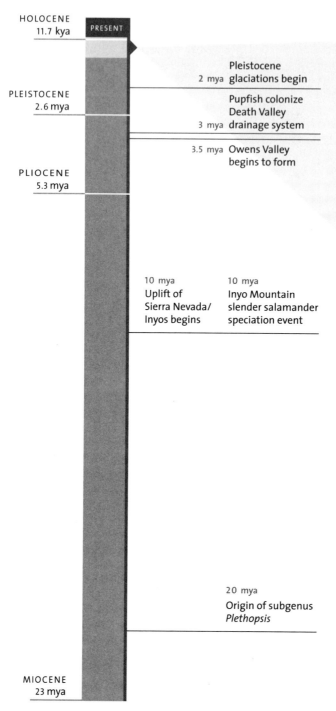

HOLOCENE
11.7 kya

PRESENT

Pleistocene
2 mya glaciations begin

PLEISTOCENE
2.6 mya

Pupfish colonize
Death Valley
3 mya drainage system

3.5 mya Owens Valley
begins to form

PLIOCENE
5.3 mya

10 mya

Uplift of
Sierra Nevada/
Inyos begins

10 mya

Inyo Mountain
slender salamander
speciation event

20 mya

Origin of subgenus
Plethopsis

MIOCENE
23 mya

Geological time scale, Miocene to Recent (all dates approximate)

7.5 kya
Holocene
warming begins

10 kya
Final disappearance
of Lake Manly

PRESENT

HOLOCENE
11.7 kya

11.5 kya
Humans colonize
Great Basin

15 kya
Retreat of
last Pleistocene
glaciers begins

5 KYA

160 kya
Amargosa River
breaches lower
end of Lake Tecopa

100 KYA

200 KYA

300 KYA

PLEISTOCENE

400 KYA

500 KYA

600 kya
Possible black toad
speciation event

600 KYA

760 kya
Long Valley
Caldera explosion

700 KYA

its spare aesthetic and have come to love the creatures that have endured in the face of so much adversity, some of it purely environmental, some of it crafted by people. And although I focus on a handful of animals, their stories encompass much of what is seductive about the country in which they live, the many reasons why we should care about all rare and endangered species, and what I call the "aesthetics of evolution": its beauty, drama, contingencies, and magnificence. In some cases their stories also tell of the difficult, frustrating, sad, and seemingly inexorable conflict between human appetite and animal (or plant) need. Our values and needs are like an avalanche of rock tumbling into water, creating giant waves that wash over the larger world—waves that have broken against so many species, in so many places. Finally, the species of my desire offer up compelling stories about the complex borderland where science and art, the personal and the collective, intersect. There are the animals themselves and perhaps they should be enough, but there are also the ways in which these creatures speak to me, of my own life and yearning, and of the sensual and sensuous world that is enhanced by, but lies partly beyond, the realm of facts and direct observation.

And yet this is a book rooted in sensory experience and data. I am a scientist and so appreciate numbers and the inductive logic of science. It is in the particulars of this world, whether in data or poetry, that I find reason and resonance, beauty and desire. The architect Ludwig Mies van der Rohe, channeling Flaubert, once said that "God is in the details." I'd add that beauty and understanding also are "in the details," as I imagine that one of my favorite poets, Kenneth Rexroth, would have argued. Rexroth lived much of his life in the West and had a keen eye for the natural world. Although he was uneven in his poetry Rexroth often was wonderful with description. One of his poems that I love most is "Toward an Organic Philosophy," which is set in the Sierra and Coast Range of California. The poem creates an ecological argument rooted in description and place, and I take as much pleasure from the following lines as from almost any of Rexroth's that I have ever read:

It is storming in the White Mountains,
On the arid fourteen-thousand-foot peaks;
Rain is falling on the narrow gray ranges
And dark sedge meadows and white salt flats of Nevada.

I love the cadence of these lines, the way in which their spare but vivid economy carries me so completely into the Great Basin. And as I pursued the ideas and experiences described in this book I walked across Rexroth's dark sedge meadows and white salt flats, climbed through narrow gray ranges to arid peaks, and sat by springs that water the canyons. In these places I watched the animals, and when I could, held them in my hands and measured them. My experiences were mostly focused on observation and being out on the land rather than on formal scientific research, but the ideas of *Relicts of a Beautiful Sea* rely heavily on the work of the scientists who have gathered so much data over so many years. I have read the technical papers and taken what stories I could from their numbers. I believe, passionately, that it is possible to use the particulars of metabolic rates, premaxillary bones, dehydration tolerance, osmotic regulation, mitochondrial DNA, and growth rates—mostly the adaptive outcomes of evolutionary processes—to help craft an aesthetic and ethical argument for the conservation and appreciation (or say it: love) of rare and beleaguered species everywhere. For as Ivan Illich wrote, "To consider what is appropriate and fitting in a certain place leads one directly into reflection on beauty and goodness."

In *Paterson* the poet William Carlos Williams makes the startling statement, "No ideas but in things." It is a long way from the landscape of Williams's urban New Jersey to the Basin and Range country of Death Valley, but his argument is also my argument: it is in the particulars of place and being that we will take our meaning, the goodness of our lives, and the lives of others. And paradoxically we are brought into the larger world through particular places, and the ideas and emotions that they propagate.

The concluding lines of "Toward an Organic Philosophy" quote the nineteenth-century English physicist and glaciologist John Tyndall, who in *The Glaciers of the Alps, and Mountaineering in 1861* wrote about the "Chamouni" region of the French Alps:

"Thus," says Tyndall, "the concerns of this little place
Are changed and fashioned by the obliquity of the earth's axis,
The chain of dependence which runs through creation,
And links the roll of a planet alike with the interests
Of marmots and men."

"The interests of marmots and men" or of pupfish and people: linked by place and need and history, all of us spinning into an uncertain future with the roll of the planet, traveling through what has been, and I hope will continue to be, the fullness of time.

Collecting the Dead

And so, for my sake
I bring them back, watching the quick cloud of vapor that blooms
and vanishes with each syllable.
—B. H. Fairchild, "Speaking the Names"

Do you ever find yourself talking with the dead?
—Abraham Lincoln

I have no sense of where species go when they disappear, entire nations of plants and animals laid to waste by human agency, the collected memory of their molecules, the intricate networks of their DNA—their *now*—vanishing into the thick haze of history. I have no idea what happens to life's lost land-scapes, or if this final form of entropic decay can be made right in any way, or forgiven, or even fully understood. The folding and faulting of time, dip and strike of life, the once-balanced equation—one death for one life, on and on, over millennia—suddenly going negative, until the last dace suffocates in a thin film of water, the last poolfish egg is shoveled into the mouth of a scav-enging crayfish, or the final vole scurries through the last, ruined patch of al-kali meadow. Everywhere on this earth is a myriad of vanished species, deaths laid at our feet, and the Basin and Range country can claim its share. In the great long valleys between the Amargosa and Colorado rivers eulogy becomes elegy and a roster of their names creates a sad and bitter lament: Longstreet springsnail, Tecopa pupfish, and Las Vegas dace. Ash Meadows poolfish, Pah-rump Ranch poolfish, and Raycraft Ranch poolfish. Vegas Valley leopard frog. Ash Meadows montane vole.

Songs forever silenced, arcs of body and fin forever stilled, certain scents never again claimed by the soft, nocturnal snuffle of a mouse in some desert meadow. . . . And I wonder. What were these animals like? Where exactly did they live and just how did they make their way through the world? I want to know the facts of their existence, and through these facts grasp something small but vital about their essence. I want to use the precise details of their lives and deaths to write their obituaries. But what I find—what we are left with—are enigmatic histories that wander through frustratingly vague recollections, short technical descriptions in scientific papers, and a few specimens preserved in jars of ethanol or on museum trays. All that remains of these creatures are scattered shards of memory, a few small caches of data, and the workings of my imagination, an impoverished inheritance of loss.

––––––––––

Pyrgulopsis sp.: the Longstreet springsnail. This tiny gill-breathing aquatic snail was collected by the malacologist and paleontologist Dwight Taylor in the late 1940s or early 1950s but was never formally described—hence the "sp." after the genus name, *Pyrgulopsis*. The species occurred only at Longstreet Spring in the northernmost part of Ash Meadows and was part of the area's rich fauna of springsnails, now comprised of at least eleven species, three of which are restricted to single springs. All preserved specimens of the Longstreet springsnail apparently vanished during the course of Taylor's peripatetic and difficult life, which was plagued by intellectual jealousies and personal strife. Almost nothing is known about this ghost species, but judging from characteristics of other Ash Meadows springsnails, its whorled conical shell would have been about three millimeters high and two millimeters wide, roughly the dimensions of a sesame seed. It would have differed from other springsnails in details of its shell and penile morphology, both of which are important characteristics used by taxonomists to classify snails. Among *Pyrgulopsis* species penises vary in pigmentation, lobe shape, ridging. About the length of a pinhead, they resemble tiny branched or unbranched horns and probably are important in maintaining the reproductive isolation of co-occurring species.

Pyrgulopsis is an old genus restricted to the North American West; its fossil evidence extends back 10 million years, into the Miocene. Although it is unclear as to how long Ash Meadows springsnails have been isolated, other *Pyrgulopsis* lineages endemic to the Death Valley region are at least 2 million years old. Whatever their history, for hundreds of thousands of years or more Longstreet springsnails, minute dark specks of shell and muscle, must have grazed aquatic plant debris and diatoms growing in the springhead pool, which now is about sixty feet in diameter and nine feet deep. This pool was their only country, and when groundwater pumping dried Longstreet Spring in the 1970s these tiny creatures lost all claim to the present and crawled into the cracked and muddy past, their lives and history no less distant from us than the farthest stars.

Cyprinodon nevadensis calidae: Tecopa pupfish. The Tecopa pupfish, a subspecies of the Amargosa pupfish, *C. nevadensis*, occurred in outflows of North and South Tecopa Hot Springs, about seven miles south of the small town of Shoshone in Inyo County, California. Tecopa pupfish were absent from the springs themselves but were abundant in the outflow channels that discharged across a "white, barren alkali flat" toward the mostly dry bed of the Amargosa River, a bit less than one mile from the springs. Tecopa pupfish were first collected on May 30, 1942, and described in 1948 by Robert Rush Miller, perhaps the greatest expert on North American desert fishes. Development of the hot springs and hybridization with nearby populations of Amargosa River pupfish following removal of barriers to upstream movement led to the extinction of the subspecies. The Tecopa pupfish was last seen on February 2, 1970; when Miller returned to Tecopa Hot Springs in 1972 the subspecies was gone. The Tecopa pupfish was the first taxon to be declared officially extinct under the 1973 U.S. Endangered Species Act.

Adult Tecopa pupfish were about 1.5 inches long—slightly shorter than an AAA battery. Like other pupfishes they would have fed on algae, small invertebrates, and microbe-rich detritus. The deep-bodied nuptial males were a vivid electric blue, with black vertical bars along their sides and a black terminal band on their tail fin. Females were duller, more slender, and more rounded in cross section. The reproductive behavior and social organization of Tecopa pupfish were never described, but their behavior must have been similar to that of other pupfishes—the male and female tiny S-shaped waves of desire, small bursts of color flashing against the gray gravel substrate, flanks flush against one another. The short dance would have ended when the male wrapped his anal fin around the female's vent and she released a single egg, which he then fertilized with his sperm. On a sunny spring day in 1942, before the subspecies fell into oblivion and other stories about the future still were possible, it would have been easy to squat down next to the outlet from South Tecopa Hot Springs and watch this intimate choreography: the sidle and weave of mates, fertilized eggs settling out of the warm and brackish water, pupfish genes drifting into the future. And just beyond the mating pupfish there would have been the white salt barrens and outflow channel's small barriers and steep gradient that gave the Tecopa pupfish their isolation and otherness.

Robert Miller found Tecopa pupfish living in 104°F springs, but they could tolerate water temperatures of almost 108°F, very near the upper thermal limit for fish. When Miller published his monograph on Death Valley fishes in 1948 he remarked that 104°F was "the second highest recorded temperature in which fish have been taken." I imagine that scientists have found a few other vertebrates capable of surviving such high water temperatures, but the thermal tolerance of Tecopa pupfish, now lost to the world, remains remarkable: tiny, iridescent slices of scale, muscle, and bone arcing through water that would kill almost all fish.

Miller included a photograph of Tecopa Hot Springs in his 1948 monograph. The photograph, taken on September 26, 1942, looks west. In the foreground are a dirt road, Miller's car, and two buildings, presumably destined to become the first bathhouses at Tecopa Hot Springs. The outflow stream is visible as a darkened channel winding through empty salt flats and past a low rounded hill, toward the Amargosa River. I visited Tecopa Hot Springs in March 2012, about forty-two years after the Tecopa pupfish went extinct, and stood at Miller's vantage point. I faced the Amargosa River and oriented myself using the distinctive rounded hill in the middle distance. Although the outlet stream was visible it now skirted several exotic palm trees and a campground filled with recreational vehicles. A paved road and asphalt parking lot had replaced the 1940s-era dirt road, and a large building now housed the baths. Just across the road from the hot springs the outlet stream emerged from a culvert and ran clear and shallow across gravel and bits of blue and white plastic. The water temperature was 105°F, near the thermal limit of Tecopa pupfish, which of course were nowhere to be seen. To the east a large white cross stood on a hill overlooking the bathhouse. The cross was a standard expression of religious belief and had nothing intentional to do with extinct pupfish. When I asked one of the workers at the hot springs if he knew anything about Tecopa pupfish he shrugged and replied, "There used to be fish right where the bathhouse is but I don't know what happened to them." One of his coworkers, a sun-bleached woman in her late forties, added as an aside, "I think they were pretty tiny, not good for much of anything. You couldn't eat them. Not like trout."

Rhinichthys deaconi: Las Vegas dace. This minnow, a member of the family Cyprinidae, occurred in Las Vegas Creek and its source springs, which also supported the Vegas Valley leopard frog. Although the first specimens of the species were collected in 1891 Robert Miller did not describe the species until 1984. Some more recent workers have classified the Las Vegas dace as a subspecies of the speckled dace, *Rhinichthys osculus.* Whatever its taxonomic status the last known collection of Las Vegas dace occurred on July 30, 1940, at Lorenzi Ranch. In 1844 the explorer John C. Frémont described the springhead for Las Vegas Creek as "two narrow streams of clear water, four or five feet deep, [which] gush suddenly with a quick current, from two singularly large springs." When the outlet springs were flowing well, at perhaps 8,000 gallons per minute, water traveled for six miles down Las Vegas Creek. In higher water runoff from the creek reached the Colorado River, providing a potential connection between Las Vegas dace populations and those of speckled dace in basins along the lower Grand Canyon. The Las Vegas dace probably persisted until somewhere between 1955 and 1957, when increased water withdrawals from the artesian basin beneath Las Vegas reduced spring flows feeding Las Vegas Creek. Once the waters of Las Vegas Creek were extinguished, so were the dace.

Miller differentiated Las Vegas dace from related populations of speckled dace based on the species' uniquely shaped anal fin; short, weakly forked tail fin; tiny pectoral fins; and relatively large scales. Las Vegas dace were small and slender; females were up to 2.5 inches long while males grew to a bit over 1.5 inches. Both sexes probably fed mostly on bottom-dwelling invertebrates. The field notes of Carl Hubbs—Miller's major professor, colleague, and father-in-law—described living fish of both sexes as having an olive background color; their backs and sides were covered with irregular black spots. Males were decorated with splotches of orange at the base of paired fins, and the anal and caudal fins. Some individuals were further brightened by a wash of red across their abdomen and an orange dot at the base of each gill opening. Now the bright colors of the Las Vegas dace—small bursts of fire—have vanished, washed from the bodies of museum specimens that float in graves of ethanol, these dead fish the last of their kind.

In the days before development began in the Las Vegas basin the source springs would have been, as Frémont noted, "a delightful bathing place." Perhaps the explorer and his men swam among the dace, fish and humans languidly floating in the 72°F water, drifting through the desert on a bright afternoon in May.

Empetrichthys merriami: Ash Meadows poolfish, also known as the Ash Meadows killifish. This species was restricted to bottom habitat in a few deep springs in Ash Meadows. The first specimens were collected by members of the Death Valley Expedition on March 3, 1891; the ichthyologist C. H. Gilbert used these fish to describe the species in 1893. The last Ash Meadows poolfish was collected at Big Spring by W. Hildeman and John Kopec on September 7, 1948. The species apparently was uncommon, at least from 1891 onward. Robert Miller wrote, "Over the 6-year period (1936–1942) during which we collected in this region, only 22 specimens have been taken, although we made special efforts to obtain greater numbers." Reasons for extinction of the Ash Meadows poolfish are unclear. Habitat alteration may have played some role, although the species vanished before the major wave of spring destruction began in the 1960s. Contributing causes probably included predation and competition by introduced crayfish and bullfrogs, which were present at Ash Meadows by at least 1937. Some authors have speculated that competition from abundant pupfish may have contributed to its rarity. Others suspect that scientific collecting of this uncommon species may have contributed to its demise, although the twenty-two specimens collected between 1891 and 1948 only could have affected a population already endangered by other factors.

The Ash Meadows poolfish was small and slender, with a broad, up-turned mouth, relatively small and narrow head, and no pelvic fins. Mature individuals ranged from about 1.5 inches to 2.5 inches in length. Ash Meadows poolfish had a discontinuous, dark lateral band that tended to disappear in older individuals. Although the color of the species appears not to have been described in the scientific literature, they most likely were similar to Pahrump poolfish: greenish brown above and silver-green below, with bright orange-yellow dorsal, anal, pectoral, and caudal fins. Spawning males probably were lightly washed with blue. The shape and size of poolfish teeth suggest that they were adapted to feeding on snails, although they probably ate a variety of animal and plant foods.

There are only two recent species of poolfish: the Ash Meadows poolfish and the Pahrump poolfish, which was native to three springs in Pahrump Valley, eighteen to twenty-five miles southeast of Ash Meadows. However, *Empetrichthys* once ranged more widely over the southern Great Basin, as fossils belonging to the genus have been identified from 4-million-year-old Pliocene sediments in Los Angeles County and more recent deposits in southern Nevada. The rarity of Ash Meadows poolfish, even when the Death Valley Expedition first encountered them, the highly restricted modern poolfish populations, and the wider distribution of the genus during the Pliocene and Pleistocene, suggest that Ash Meadows poolfish may have lost the evolutionary race even before they swam headlong into the twentieth century, the decline of their springs, and the mouths of crayfish and bullfrogs.

Imagine the last Ash Meadows poolfish patrolling the bottom of Big Spring on a warm, calm afternoon in the late 1940s: a single small arrow of silvery green meandering across patches of brilliant white sand and streamers of dark green algae, swimming through schools of *others*, mostly Ash Meadows Amargosa pupfish. Spread above the poolfish was the glistening lens of the springhead, a shimmering blue world composed of light as much as water. Big Spring would have been luminous, even as the light of the Ash Meadows poolfish disappeared with a tiny imploding flash. It might have happened in October 1948 or March 1949, but whatever the time a moment would have come when the last poolfish swam to its death, its kind having traveled too far from the things that might have saved them.

———

Empetrichthys latos pahrump and *Empetrichthys latos concavus*: the Pahrump Ranch and Raycraft Ranch poolfish. These subspecies occurred in two springs on Pahrump Ranch and one spring at Raycraft Ranch, about one-half mile north of Pahrump Ranch. A third subspecies, the Pahrump poolfish (*E. latos latos*), was confined to Manse Spring, about six miles southeast of Pahrump Ranch. The three subspecies were the only fish native to Pahrump Valley, a broad basin nested between the Spring Range to the east and the Nopah and Resting Spring ranges to the west. They were first collected by Robert Miller in October 1942 and described by him in his 1948 monograph. When Miller encountered them the Pahrump Ranch poolfish apparently was more common than the Raycraft Ranch poolfish. The Raycraft Ranch poolfish was last collected by O. Sokol in September 1953, although he was unable to find Pahrump Ranch poolfish. Habitat alteration, along with introduced carp, crayfish, and bullfrogs, may have contributed to the decline of both subspecies, but excessive groundwater pumping in Pahrump Valley led to their extinction. The two Pahrump Ranch springs failed in 1957; in the same year, after the once swiftly flowing Raycraft Spring had metamorphosed into a stagnant pool, it was bulldozed full of soil to control mosquitoes.

Agricultural development in Pahrump Valley, which emphasized irrigation of water-intensive crops such as alfalfa and cotton, peaked in the 1960s when groundwater withdrawals exceeded recharge rates by 250 percent. By 1975 Manse Spring, which in 1875 discharged about 2,700 gallons per minute, had dried completely. In the late 1960s biologists fortunately recognized that excessive groundwater withdrawals would quickly lead to the failure of Manse Spring and that the Pahrump poolfish soon would follow the Raycraft Ranch and Pahrump Ranch poolfish into extinction. In 1971 twenty-nine poolfish were rescued from Manse Spring and transplanted to Corn Creek Spring on the U.S. Fish and Wildlife Service's Desert Game Range. Additional captive populations of Pahrump poolfish were later established in White Pine County, Nevada, and at Spring Mountain State Park, west of Las Vegas. The three refuges continue to protect Pahrump poolfish, but *Empetrichthys latos* remains extinct in the wild.

The extinct Pahrump poolfish subspecies had broader heads and mouths than Ash Meadows poolfish; the lateral band of black flecks also was broader and more discontinuous in the Ash Meadows species. Miller used head shape, length and shape of the caudal fin, and distance between the base of the anal and caudal fins to distinguish between the three subspecies of Pahrump poolfish. He described the Pahrump Ranch poolfish as having a "shorter and nearly truncate caudal fin," while the head of the Raycraft Ranch poolfish was distinctively concave above the snout. All three poolfish subspecies were small, ranging in length from less than three-quarters of an inch to two inches in length—at most, the distance between the tip and knuckle of my index finger. Almost nothing is known about the ecology and behavior of the Raycraft Ranch and Pahrump Ranch poolfishes other than the most general features of where they once lived. What we are left with are a few pages of descriptions and data in Miller's 1948 monograph, mostly having to do with morphology, and several bottles of specimens residing in the University of Michigan's Museum of Zoology. Anything else that we might surmise about the extinct subspecies can only come by reference to captive populations of the Pahrump poolfish.

Pahrump Valley is separated from Ash Meadows by a low divide; Las Vegas lies forty miles to the east, beyond the Spring Range. Even though the springs that sustained the three Pahrump poolfish subspecies were no more than seven miles apart, the populations must have remained isolated from one another since the waning days of the Pleistocene. After the last glacial advance ended and whatever streams flowing through Pahrump Valley began to permanently dry, the poolfish must have retreated into Pahrump Ranch, Manse, and Raycraft Ranch springs and there fell into isolation and divergence. For 10,000 years or more the Pahrump Valley poolfish populations survived their solitude, passing from one generation to the next in a handful of small springs and wet meadows. Their largest patch of habitat was Manse Spring, which formed a pool just fifty feet wide by sixty feet long. The poolfish would have prospered or suffered as spring flows fluctuated. Perhaps conditions were hardest for them during the middle Holocene, when environmental conditions in the region were even warmer and drier than today. Small bands of Native Americans, most recently the Paiute people, must have camped by the springs, but mostly the poolfish were left alone, at least until ranchers and farmers settled in Pahrump Valley and the springs began to fail.

There now are almost 40,000 people in Pahrump Valley, all needing water in a place where there is little enough to feed their thirst. Today, when I stand at the edge of Highway 160 in the center of Pahrump, it is hard to focus on anything other than the manifestations of what humans have brought to the area: McDonald's, Wal-Mart, Albertson's, Saddle West Hotel and Casino, Kingdom Gentleman's Club, strip malls and trailer parks, subdivisions and micro-ranchettes, massively jacked 4WD pickup trucks, the scent of gasoline and fast food and Russian olive in the air. But when I look out over all of this development—say on a beautifully mild spring evening when the winds haven't kicked up too much dust—and ignore the ambience that surrounds Highway 160, I can summon some vague sense of what Pahrump Valley must have been like 150 years ago. Ten miles distant, across the vast and falling sweep of Pahrump Valley, are the arid, backlit Nopah and Resting Spring ranges; behind me, the steep forested slopes of the Spring Mountains, awash with orange-pink alpenglow in a year of heavy snows. The beautiful and wonderful space remains even as the quiet has vanished, along with several desert oases now dried into dust. It is hard to imagine what those improbable pools and channels must have been like, the sense of deliverance and wonder that they must have generated. And it is even more difficult to wrap my mind around the concept of fish in this place, and the tens of thousands of years that they survived *here*.

Small of body and almost unknown, the Raycraft Ranch and Pahrump Ranch poolfish now seem like ephemera, even less substantial than the momentary flash of grace brought on by the desert evening, which disappears as I climb into my car and drive on, toward Death Valley and into the falling dark.

———————————

Rana fisheri: Vegas Valley leopard frog. This species occurred in a few springs and short streams in upper Vegas Valley, Nevada, many of which also were home to the Las Vegas dace. The type specimen, an adult female, was collected by the Death Valley Expedition in 1891. The species was described by Leonhard Stejneger in 1893 and last seen on January 13, 1942, when

A. Vanderhorst collected ten at Tule Springs, north of Las Vegas. On May 17, 1942, Albert and Anna Wright were unable to find any frogs, although they heard several splashes of what they suspected were *R. fisheri*—perhaps the last plops of their kind, final waves of sound radiating out into the hot desert air. At the time the Wrights suspected that the Vegas Valley leopard frog was doomed: "Our *R. fisheri* may go with the old springs gone, the creek a mess." These short-legged frogs resembled the familiar northern leopard frog; they were olive green to brownish green above, sometimes brighter toward the head, with dark green spots, and an unusually large eardrum, or tympanum. Their snout-vent length, a dimension typically reported for frogs and toads, ranged from 1.7 to three inches; one would have fit easily in the palm of my hand. Although the Las Vegas Valley leopard frog was isolated from other populations of the genus occurring in the Colorado and Virgin river valleys, its evolutionary relationship with two existing frogs, *Rana onca* (relict leopard frog) and *Rana pipiens* (northern leopard frog), is unclear. *R. fisheri* had less head and back spotting than *R. onca*, which in turn has shorter legs and less spotting than *R. pipiens*. Recent molecular data based on analysis of museum specimens suggests that the Las Vegas Valley leopard frog was very closely related to northwestern populations of the Chiricahua leopard frog (*R. chiricahuaensis*), which occurs far to the south and east, along the Mogollon Rim in Arizona.

Species, subspecies, or population, the Las Vegas Valley leopard frog most likely disappeared in the 1940s due to a combination of groundwater pumping, urban development, and competition from introduced bullfrogs. The full mating call of the Vegas Valley leopard frog was never recorded. The only partial description we have is by Albert Wright, who collected six Vegas Valley leopard frogs on August 20, 1925—far outside of their likely mating season—and placed them in a bag that he carried on his belt. As he walked, the captured frogs uttered "a few semicroaks which reminded me of *R. palustris* [the pickerel frog]. Once or twice heard a very low croak."

The mating call of *Rana fisheri* is lost to us but I can imagine it, when Las Vegas Creek was still a real creek surrounded by creosote bush scrub: a guttural, purring rattle, given out as gravid females hopped and swam toward ardent males, their calls gathering into a chorus of celebration and frog-promise that graced the desert night.

Microtus montanus nevadensis: Ash Meadows montane vole. This subspecies of the widespread montane vole lived in wet alkali meadows, where it must have fed on grasses, sedges, and broad-leaved herbs. It was first collected in 1891 in "the big salt marsh below Watkins Ranch, Ash Meadows," and described in 1898. Like so many other species in the area the Ash Meadows montane vole was alone in the world. The nearest other subspecies of montane vole occurred (and still does) far to the east in Pahranagat Valley, which is separated from Ash Meadows by ninety miles of vole-killing desert. As with the other extinct species of the Basin and Range country the Ash Meadows montane vole must have claimed its isolation as the land warmed and dried in the aftermath of the last glacial advance. This relatively large "meadow mouse" averaged about 6.7 inches in length, about the distance from my wrist to my outstretched fingertips. As with other voles it was stout-bodied, with a short tail and tiny ears. E. R. Hall described the color of the Ash Meadows montane vole as "blackish, but with a few overhairs tipped with reddish rather than grayish." Although it was last located by W. C. Russell and W. B. Davis in 1933, who used "persistent trapping" to obtain a few specimens from a site 3.5 miles north of its type locality, the Ash Meadows montane vole may have survived until the 1960s, when peat mining, alfalfa cultivation, and cattle ranching destroyed thousands of acres of alkali meadows. Subsequent intensive searches have failed to find any voles, and they are almost certainly extinct.

However, there are a few people who suspect that the Ash Meadows montane vole is still hanging on somewhere in the area known as Carson Slough. Although the U.S. Fish and Wildlife Service recently embarked upon an ambitious project to restore the slough, it still bears the harsh and vivid scars of the agricultural development that ceased almost forty years ago. In 2012, when I sought out the last known locality of the Ash Meadows vole, I found ditches of clear water draining from Fairbanks, Longstreet, and Rogers springs, but nothing that much resembled a wet alkali meadow. Instead there were dry fields and flats, still ridged and furrowed, and great swatches of exotic weeds, although there also were scattered patches of native vegetation. The habitat lacked standing water and moist patches of sedges and grasses. It did not feel at all "voleish," and I could not believe that that the Ash Meadows montane vole still hung on somewhere in the broad sweep of Carson Slough. But for a moment let me assume, somewhat irrationally, that the optimists are right, even as they apparently are not for the ivory-billed woodpecker in Arkansas and Florida. I can—hope against hope—imagine using the present tense instead of the past tense when writing about Ash Meadows montane voles. I can envision searching out a characteristic network of vole runways in what remains of their wet alkali meadow habitat, the narrow paths radiating out from spherical nests of dried grass. During the day the voles would be almost impossible to see unless it was during an extraordinarily good year with high populations, and I happened to kick one up while walking. But if I searched out a series of active pathways and sat patiently in the cooling air of a late spring night, my headlamp switched to red-light mode, I might be lucky enough to spot a vole: a quick, dark stub of an animal weaving among the rough-edged grasses and rushes, a shadow snuffling through shallow water or along a muddy, scent-marked runway. It would be gone in a moment but that sudden encounter would be enough. And after the vole had vanished into the darkness I can imagine shivering slightly, smiling, and glancing up at the shadowed break of the low desert ranges to the east. Then I would inhale a deep breath of chilly riparian air, rise from my seat, and set off for camp—walking though fields of saltgrass and niterwort, beneath an avalanche of stars, and happy to have seen such a rare beast. The night would be rich and alive around me, the desert's future somehow more hopeful than it really is, here in this impoverished present.

A Cultivation of Slowness

THE INYO MOUNTAINS SLENDER SALAMANDER (*Batrachoseps campi*)

Again we live
in a time of fasting.
—Lisel Mueller, "The Need to Hold Still"

We leave the rental car at the base of an alluvial fan spilling out of the Inyo Mountains, and for an hour my son and I track a washed-out road through the usual cast of desert plants: creosote bush, barrel cactus, bursage, spiny hopsage, Anderson thornbush, Mormon tea, cotton-thorn. It is only March and yet the sun carries intimations of summer. Temperatures climb into the eighties and radiation pours from a cloudless sky. Thermal waves shimmer on the desert pavement, almost bare in this time of drought, in a place where only five inches of rain might fall in an average year. There are few flowers here and no birds sing. Side-blotched lizards scuttle for shelter; this is the land of reptiles, and of the raven pair that glide by, black wraiths riding thermals southward along the base of the mountains. We walk through a realm of light and heat as we climb the cone of debris funneling from a spare waterless canyon. Ahead is the steep western scarp of the Inyo Mountains, a treeless, turbulent jumble of basalt, limestone, dolomite, granite, and sandstone—chocolate-brown, reddish, and tan rocks, tilted skyward, vaulting into the azure day and offering up their testament to deep time. My son and I stop for a drink, our pallid eastern faces flushed and sweaty, winter bodies not yet acclimated to the assault of the desert sun.

The canyon narrows. Martin and I walk beneath steep shoulders of angular rock dotted with a scatter of small shrubs as we follow the dry wash deeper into the mountains. Harsh light bounces off the slopes and July's furnace whispers in the air. I tug the bill of my hat further down on my forehead and look up canyon; even with sunglasses on, I need to squint against the sun's intensity. At 5,000 feet we still are immersed in the desert, but ahead I spot a small cottonwood tree and cluster of willows, just now leafing out. A few more minutes brings us to a thin stream of water weaving through cobbled rock and a thin green garden. Even though our topographic map tells us that there is a spring here its presence is astonishing. Here in this arid canyon, the desert offers us the wonderful dissonance of water, as well as the pleasure of an unexpected discovery. It's like a packet of your great-grandparent's letters hidden away in some dusty attic chest, the shadow of a wolverine disappearing into a thicket of pines, or the taste of cold water on your parched tongue as the sun goes nuclear.

Martin and I begin flipping rocks near the stream and work our way into a dense thicket of willows. Nothing. To the east water tumbles down a steep slope of gray talus through patches of moss and sedge and thickets of wild rose. I trace the water into the boulders, trying to avoid the slash of thorns on my bare legs, halting wherever the habitat looks best, probing crevices, peering into cracks, gently lifting clumps of moss, prying rocks loose from the wet soil. Still nothing. I try to push discouragement from my mind even though I have traveled far from New York and have searched two other documented localities without success. I have read the sparse scientific literature on the species but have no visceral feeling for what microhabitats the animals prefer. During thirty-five years of fieldwork I have learned that written descriptions mean very little if I haven't searched out the nest or held the creature in my hand, seen and smelled and felt enough to let my senses and intuition, rather than my intellect, do the looking. Everything near the water looks possible yet at the same time nothing looks right. I have no search image and so am mostly clueless. I climb higher, taking my time. The day falls away and my world narrows to each small patch of rock and moss. The sound of falling water disappears and Martin, somewhere downslope, vanishes. And then. I roll an oblong rock about fifteen inches across, and beneath the rock is what I've come looking for: an Inyo Mountains slender salamander, genus *Batrachoseps*, species *campi*. I'm punched by a small jolt of adrenalin. The day goes electric and I shout to Martin, "*Come here!*" I reach down, pluck the salamander from the moist soil and bring it close to my face. The salamander sits in my hand, as light as a leaf. It squirms much less than most salamanders I find in the East, and for a few moments I study its features. It's about three inches long and broadheaded, its chocolate-brown back dotted with a thick constellation of silver speckles. The air buckles; I catch my breath and there's a film of water in my eyes. Silly, I think—a fifty-seven-year-old man, highly educated, with the usual collection of human baggage, so moved by this tiny creature. Although I understand something of personal pain and failure and the larger canvas of human suffering and desire, I remain a living embodiment of an effete intellectual, too damned romantic and emotional.

And yet the Inyo Mountains slender salamander offers up both lovely fact and touching metaphor. It lives on in one of the most unreasonable and inhospitable places in the world for its kind, a lungless salamander that breathes only through its moist skin, which is thin as parchment and provides almost no barrier to the evaporation of water. It is one of only two desert salamander species in the world and was not discovered until 1973. Its distribution, as far as known, is limited to about twenty rugged canyons on the eastern and western slopes of the Inyo Mountains, a desert range 11,000 feet high framing the eastern side of the Owens Valley, in the rain shadow of the High Sierra. Each population appears to be completely isolated from others of its kind, restricted by the heat and dryness of the surrounding desert, alone in a harsh and inimical land. The species has been separated from closely related salamanders for millions of years. It has survived the folding and faulting of desert ranges, volcanic eruptions, the advances and retreats of Pleistocene glaciers, and the great Holocene drought some 7,500 to 4,500 years ago. Its presence here approaches the incredible, in the full meaning of that overused word: the opposite of credible, capable of being believed. Simply put, there should not be salamanders here. Walk up a heat-soaked bajada deep into the scorched mountains and you will understand something of this anomaly and of the lovely, heart-breaking tenacity of life, its insistence and powerful presence in the world.

The Inyo Mountains slender salamander lives only in the central portion of the 110-mile-long White-Inyo Range, where its total habitat amounts to about fifty acres. To the east of the White-Inyo Range, parallel desert ranges rise from parched valleys like the fractured spines of great fossil beasts—the Panamint Range, Saline Range, Grapevine Mountains, Funeral Mountains, Eureka Valley, Panamint Valley, Death Valley, Saline Valley. To survey this country from the crest of the Inyo Mountains is to take in a sweep of space that is mostly inhospitable to aquatic life. Yes, eighteen miles to the west are the High Sierra, with their glacial cirques and mountain meadows, rising 10,000 feet above the great gulf of Owens Valley. And at the base of the precipitous canyons that slice toward the lowlands is the meandering Owens River, flowing south through desert scrub and irrigated pastures

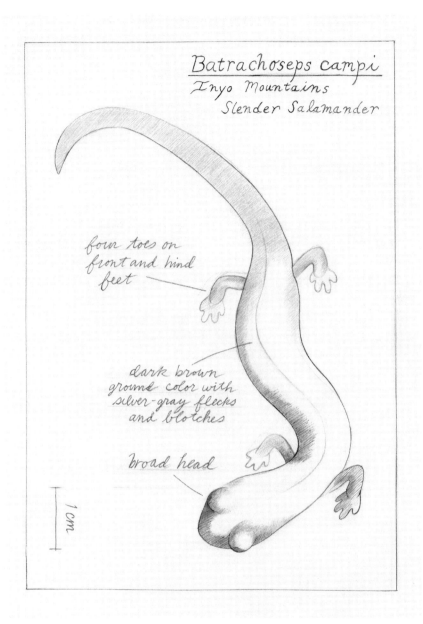

Inyo Mountains slender salamander (*Batrachoseps campi*)

before it disappears into the white salt flats of desiccated Owens Lake. But out in the Basin and Range country to the east of the High Sierra, the water mostly comes in tiny sips, the springs and small creeks hidden in the spread of sand and salt and rock. It is mostly an arid world: the canteen is empty, the arroyos and canyons and ancient lake beds mostly dry. Rain is a reluctant visitor.

And one day, after climbing to near the crest of the Inyo Mountains and absorbing as much of this country as I can, I make my slow and difficult way into a jumbled canyon where Inyo Mountains slender salamanders live—one of a handful of sites on the western side of the range, with about ten more lying east of the crest. I move carefully through rough and trailless terrain, across steep bands of loose rock and down hillsides covered with sagebrush and Mormon tea, then descend a seam spilling off a steep ridge, one that hammers my aching knees and thighs until it bottoms out in a narrow gorge. There is water in the canyon, and a ribbon of native thistles and seep willow, wildflowers and grasses. I begin flipping rocks, looking for the salamanders that shelter beneath them, carefully replacing each rock before moving on. After fifteen minutes of searching I am lucky enough to find a salamander tucked under a small rock at the edge of the water, wedged into a narrow, muddy slot. It is a big one, about four inches long from snout to tail tip, its dark brown back sprinkled with a thick band of silver-green dots. I take a few measurements, then set it down. The salamander hesitates briefly, then begins walking deliberately toward water. It travels with a slightly sinuous side-to-side motion, in the manner of a swimming fish. A running mouse or lizard moves nothing like a salamander; modifiers such as "scuttle" or "scamper" have no place in the lexicon of words we might use to describe how a terrestrial salamander travels. This aquatic pattern of movement in a terrestrial species is an essential aspect of the Inyo Mountains slender salamander's primordial nature, its life of inherited slowness.

I watch the salamander disappear into some streamside debris then briefly consider visiting another documented locality. The nearest site is only three air miles away, but it is separated from where I am by a thick corrugation of rugged, waterless ridges and canyons. It would take half a day and thousands of feet of elevation gain and loss to reach the spring. There is no easy route, and as temperatures climb into the nineties I decide to rest. I find some shade and pull a granola bar out of my pack, down some water, and think of fish and salamanders, of deep time and the isolation that holds the canyon and its inhabitants. There is the desert, but there also are the limitations of the salamanders themselves, which in the Inyo Mountains have forced them into what looks like an evolutionary dead end every bit as absolute as the waterless alcove at the head of the canyon where I sit. There is no way out of the Inyo Mountains for *Batrachoseps campi*. There are no salamander pasturelands waiting just downstream, only heat and light and dust and rock. Slender salamanders are very sedentary; the maximum extent of their home ranges over months or years may be less than fifteen yards. Their skin is extremely porous and must remain moist in order to exchange respiratory gases. Evaporative water loss from the skin of a lungless salamander is equivalent to evaporation from the surface of a shallow pool; place a wide bowl of water in the desert sun and watch the water disappear—essentially the same thing will happen to any exposed salamander. And so I wonder. I wonder how these salamanders ever found their way into the canyons of the Inyos and how they have endured, being so tied to water, so slow, and so alone in the desert world. There are other populations in the Inyo Mountains—nineteen known ones, perhaps a few others waiting to be discovered—but each must mostly drift down its own current of time. And as I shoulder my pack and hike down the jumbled canyon to the nearest road I wonder, too, how the Inyo Mountains slender salamander, which is as silent and phlegmatic as any vertebrate I have ever seen, has worked its way so deeply into my heart.

The story of the Inyo Mountains slender salamander has been crafted out of time, ecology, the genetic legacy of the salamander's ancestors, and the changing landscape of western North America. To more fully appreciate this story it is necessary to understand something of the species' traits, evolutionary relationships, and history. Slender salamanders are members of the family Plethodontidae ("many teeth"); all plethodontids lack lungs and except for the larvae of aquatic forms breathe through their skin. Fossil and molecular evidence suggest that the family arose in eastern North America about 100 million years ago, during the Cretaceous. A complex molecular analysis comparing thirteen genes from the mitochondria, the subcellular structures where most biochemical energy is manufactured, suggests that the slender salamander genus *Batrachoseps* originated some 80 million years ago. Species of *Batrachoseps* are united—in other words, they share a common ancestor, to the exclusion of other lineages—by molecular characteristics and several morphological traits. The latter include four digits on the hind feet and a large gap between the dorsal bones of the skull.

Within the genus *Batrachoseps*, which is comprised of at least two dozen species, evolutionary biologists have identified two finer divisions, or subgenera, designated as sg *Plethopsis* and sg *Batrachoseps*. Molecular evidence, particularly differences in DNA sequences that accumulate though mutation, suggests that these subgenera represent discrete lineages that went their separate ways at least 20 million years ago. Species in the larger lineage, sg *Batrachoseps,* are mostly restricted to California, from the western slopes of the Sierra Nevada to the coast. This subgenus is a complex assemblage of species with a history shaped by the constantly changing climate and geological landscape of the region. These forces have driven population fragmentation and divergence in isolation, followed by the recontact and merging of some units. In contrast the sg *Plethopsis* contains only three species and has a more northerly and inland distribution. The Oregon slender salamander (*Batrachoseps wrighti*) occurs on both sides of the Oregon Cascades from the Columbia River Gorge south into the central part of the state. The Inyo Mountains slender salamander is restricted to a single arid mountain range in east central California, while the Kern Plateau slender salamander (*Batrachoseps robustus*) occurs just to the west and south, in the southeastern Sierra Nevada. The discontinuous distribution of the sg *Plethopsis* suggests that other species and populations in the subgenus must have disappeared, tragic characters in an evolutionary drama overwhelmed by the contingencies of time, their histories and tiny, crushed skeletons now lost to us.

Molecular data, characteristics of the skull, and geographical distribution distinguish the subgenera *Plethopsis* and *Batrachoseps* from one another, but there is another easily observed difference—their build. Adult members of the sg *Batrachoseps* are mostly gracile, with thin limbs, while the three species of *Plethopsis* appear stouter, with heavier bodies and thicker limbs. The relative robustness of Inyo Mountains salamander—but can any four-inch-long creature be considered "robust"?—led the biologists who discovered the species to first suspect that they had found a web-toed salamander in the genus *Hydromantes*. In hand, an Inyo Mountains slender salamander feels more substantial than most members of the genus, an attribute vaguely at odds with the desert landscape in which it lives, which graces the species with a ghostlike aura.

Elizabeth Jockusch, who studies *Batrachoseps* evolution, feels that mutational differences in the mitochondrial DNA of the Oregon, Inyo Mountains, and Kern Plateau slender salamanders places their separation at roughly 10 million years ago. One puzzle is that although the ranges of the

Oregon and Inyo Mountains species are separated by 600 miles, while the Kern Plateau and Inyo Mountains species are isolated only by the narrow trough of Owens Valley, the genetic differences among the three species are about equal. But the view from Walker Creek where it spills from the eastern flank of the High Sierra suggests one reason for the deep evolutionary split between the species. Walker Creek is one of the northernmost localities for the Kern Plateau salamander, which occurs in patches of moist habitat to the west and south. The country adjacent to Walker Creek receives only about eight inches of precipitation per year, but there are streams in most nearby canyons, fed by snowmelt and tasting of winter, and enough pines and firs on the high ridges to make one think of the wetter, more thickly vegetated country west of the main crest. The debris cone built by Walker Creek is covered by bigleaf sagebrush, but along the stream is a luxuriant tangle of canyon oak, water birch, mountain alder, and willow—anomalous but welcoming habitat for salamanders.

From Walker Creek you can look north and east past the white waste-land of Owens Lake and the distant meander of the Owens River. Beyond the river's narrow riparian corridor are desiccated alkaline soils and grayish green shadscale scrub flats. Then come the alluvial fans that bury the lower slopes of the Inyo Mountains in several thousand feet of sediment, and steep-walled side canyons cut from a chaotic mix of igneous, metamorphic, and sedimentary rocks. As the raven flies it is only about twenty-three miles from Walker Creek to the nearest known population of Inyo Mountains slender salamanders, but as the salamander crawls it might as well be a continent away, across terrain as inhospitable as death—terrain that for a salamander is death. The genetic and temporal distance that separate the Inyo Mountains and Kern Plateau slender salamanders illustrate just how inimical Owens Valley is to these species. But even in good habitat *Batrachoseps* salamanders don't move around very much, and so the scattered populations of Inyo Mountains slender salamanders, which may be separated from one another by only a few miles of dry and rugged country, show genetic subdivisions greater than reported for any mammal species.

We know, more or less, when the lineages of *Batrachoseps* arose, but at present we can make only educated guesses about the precise ecological, behavioral, and geological forces that drove their divergence. Although there are no geological events that can be unequivocally tied to speciation events in slender salamanders, Elizabeth Jockusch says that the genus *Batrachoseps* "has inherited California's complex geologic history," a history that in the last 20 million years has been built upon intense periods of mountain building, volcanism, and glaciation. The western part of North America is a restless part of the Earth—think of the eruption of Mt. Lassen in 1915, or the Lone Pine earthquake of 1872, estimated at magnitude 7.8—and has been for many millions of years. Perhaps basalt floods and a rain of ash first divided some ancestral *Batrachoseps* population, but in the end we just do not know what forces sent the sg *Batrachoseps* and sg *Plethopsis* down their separate evolutionary paths. We gaze at life's history through a window that sometimes is remarkably translucent, and at other times frustratingly opaque. Sometimes the fossil-bearing strata that might hold the answers are eroded into oblivion. At other times they are present, and we patiently sort through tons of sedimentary rock, searching for fossils more rare than Mojave rain. And what are the odds that in all of our searching we will find the crushed skeleton of an animal no more than four inches long that lived 10 million years ago? That we find anything of these tiny creatures is a remarkable testimony to the dogged determination of those few people who have looked long and hard for their remains. Or we isolate DNA, feed it into a polymerase chain reaction machine, and automatically generate the genetic sequences that help us peer into the shadowed alcoves of evolutionary history. We wipe our collective hand across a steamy window, thick with time's moisture, and gaze at the past, looking for—what?—some hint of our own antecedents, some connection to the lives of others, something in all those years that will anchor us more firmly to the temporal world.

Large-scale uplift of the modern Sierra Nevada and White-Inyo Range probably began about 10 million years ago as crustal movements began pulling the western part of what is now Oregon northward. At the same time volcanic activity shifted from the eastern and central part of the region to the western Cascades, in the center of the current distribution of the Oregon slender salamander. To the south of the Oregon Cascades faulting and volcanic activity also increased. To the west of the Sierra Nevada shallow marine waters filled the Great Valley; these would drain some 5 million years ago. And so, somewhere around 10 million years ago, give or take a few million years, mountain building and volcanic activity divided the range of a widespread but unknown ancestral species possessing traits of the subgenus *Plethopsis*; this species subsequently disappeared from much of its range, leaving isolated populations that eventually evolved into the Oregon, Kern Plateau, and Inyo Mountains slender salamanders. Fossil trackways and skeletal material from the Sierra Nevada, dated to near the Miocene/Pliocene boundary around 5 million years ago, represent the earliest geologic evidence of *Batrachoseps* in the region, although ancestral slender salamanders must have been going about their business long before then.

The sundering of *Plethopsis* would have occurred while the present-day Sierra Nevada, Owens Valley, and White-Inyo Range remained a continuous growing mountain range. It wasn't until 3 to 4 million years ago that parallel uplifts of the eastern Sierran escarpment and White-Inyo Range and downfaulting of Owens Valley began creating the current topography of the region. In the Sierra Nevada a complex series of glacial advances and retreats, driven by fluctuating temperatures and precipitation, began about 2 million years ago, with the last major advance ending about 15,000 to 20,000 years ago. Glaciers also occurred in higher parts of the White Mountains, although not in the Inyos. During the last glacial advance, which began about 79,000 years ago, a discontinuous ice cap 250 miles long and up to 30 miles wide covered the main crest of the Sierra as far south as the current range of the Kern Plateau slender salamander. Along the eastern side of the Sierra glaciers poured meltwater into a vast basin containing ancestral lakes such as Lake Owens and Lake Manly in Death Valley. The country to the east of the highest mountains, although never glaciated, was much cooler and moister than it is today and would have nourished pine and juniper as much as cacti and shadscale scrub.

One rich source of information on Pleistocene and post-Pleistocene climates of the region comes from ancient packrat middens, which are formed from plant material collected by the rodents. If the midden is sheltered it may be preserved for tens of thousands of years by packrat urine, which the animals deposit in a less-than-fastidious manner on their gathered treasures. Given the right environmental conditions the urine eventually crystallizes into "amberat," which has the consistency of rock candy and protects the encased seeds, twigs, and leaves from decay. One publication describes ancient packrat middens as "resembl[ing] blocks of asphalt with the consistency and mass of an unfired adobe brick." Members of the Manly Party, which became lost in Death Valley in 1849, made the regrettable gastronomical blunder of mistaking amberat for food. Today paleobotanists have identified a more useful and aesthetic function for the ancient middens and use them to reconstruct Pleistocene plant communities and climates. Packrat middens in the Panamint Mountains of Death Valley, radiocarbon dated to between 19,550 and 11,210 years ago, show that woodland plants such as Utah juniper occurred from 4,000 to 5,000 feet lower than they do today; at the time precipitation may have been three to four times present values and summers 11 to 15°F cooler.

Superimposed upon the ebb and flow of the Pleistocene glaciers was a series of volcanic eruptions along the eastern side of the Sierra, which began about 3.6 million years ago and lasted until perhaps 1470 A.D. A drive up U.S. Highway 395 through Owens Valley reveals many features associated with these eruptions: rust red cinder cones, ragged black lava fields, and the pinkish tan cliffs of Bishop Tuff, formed from consolidated volcanic ash. The most impressive of the recent eruptions occurred about 760,000 years ago in Long Valley, north and west of the White-Inyo Range. This eruption blasted out about 144 cubic miles of ash and molten rock—2,500 times the size of the 1980 eruption of Mount St. Helens and 33 times that of Krakatoa in 1883. The superheated material covered 580 square miles in the upper Owens Valley and Mono Basin, burying the area in up to 600 feet of volcanic debris. Prevailing winds pushed the ash eastward to as far away as Nebraska and New Mexico. Huge amounts of it must have covered much of the Inyo Mountains slender salamander's habitat with a thick, choking blanket.

The close of the Pleistocene marked the cessation of major glaciations in western North America but not the end of environmental perturbations. The Pleistocene is arbitrarily taken to have ended, and the more recent Holocene to have begun, 10,000 years ago. Since then the climate of the White-Inyo region has fluctuated tremendously. The early Holocene generally was cooler and moister than today, while the middle Holocene, from roughly 7,500 to 4,500 years ago, was a time of higher temperatures and lower precipitation. Remains of bristlecone pines from the White Mountains, just to the north of the current range of the Inyo Mountains slender salamander, indicate that between 7,400 and 4,200 years ago the tree line was up to 450 feet higher than today, an upslope advance driven by a warm season temperature increase of around 3.5°F. In the northern Mojave Desert plants favored by increased moisture became less common, as did packrats and their middens. More recently generally cooler and moister conditions have predominated, although the climate has continued to fluctuate.

In the Sierra and Basin and Range country to the east, the dominant melody of the last 2 million years has been one of intense geologic, climatic, and ecological variability. The climate has cooled and warmed repeatedly. Glaciers have advanced and retreated, and a tremendous volcanic eruption shattered the region some 760,000 years ago, sending huge and lethal pyroclastic flows of gas, pumice, and ash spilling across the land. Across North America as many as thirty-five genera of mammals and nineteen genera of birds disappeared in a remarkably short period of time, from about 14,000 to 8,000 years ago. Among the vanished species in the Great Basin were mammoths, mastodons, camels, musk ox, giant ground sloths, horses, saber-toothed cats, and at least seven genera of birds. The incredible teratorn, a relative of vultures and condors with a wingspan estimated at seventeen feet, no longer patrols Great Basin skies. Giant short-faced bears, 30 percent larger than modern grizzly bears, no longer prowl the Intermountain West. Replacing the extinct mammals and birds were the aboriginal humans who arrived in the region roughly 11,500 years ago. They brought with them Clovis points and a hunting technology that may have contributed to the extinctions that spread across the land, foreshadowing the recent disappearances in the region, which are a product of human thirst more than hunger.

Everywhere in this land, from the Sierra Nevada east into Death Valley and beyond, into the great and lovely and empty swath of Basin and Range country, you can find evidence of impermanence, steal a glance at the great perturbations that have swept through the region. Near the town of Bishop in the Owens Valley you can climb through beds of compressed ash hundreds of feet thick or carefully pick your way through fields of razor-sharp lava. You can scramble over glacial moraines thousands of feet below the High Sierra cirques that today cup tiny ice fields. At Salt Springs in southern Death Valley you can find the bones of extinct mammoths and cradle them in your arms. In Death Valley you also can walk across ancient lake beds that once were buried beneath 600 feet of water or hold bits of crystallized packrat urine containing the fragments of plants that now grow 4,000 feet higher than they do today. You can visit Badwater, 282 feet below sea level, and look west toward the summit of Telescope Peak, 11,500 feet above you. Stand there and imagine the march of the Holocene: marshes and giant pluvial lakes shrinking or disappearing, montane woodlands retreating into the Panamints, sagebrush spreading and then receding, creosote bush and pinyon pine reaching into the region and finding their home, mammals adapted to montane habitats seeking refuge from the spreading dryness in higher areas, or disappearing altogether.

This land—it would not have been an easy place in which to survive. And yet slender salamanders did survive, and their descendants live on in a handful of canyons deep within the Inyo Mountains, members of a species that has persisted for millions of years in the face of crushing adversity. Threatened by drought, buried in volcanic ash, riding mountain uplifts, sunk deep in isolation, constrained by their own legacy—by their susceptibility to desiccation—these avatars of evolution have endured, their long history and tenacious persistence an iconic monument to life's dogged determination. It is an imperative worth considering and, more important, worth feeling.

———————————

One day in late September I drove as far as I could along a washed-out road in the southern Inyos. I then walked for ninety minutes up a dry canyon to the place where in 1973 two biologists, Ron Marlow and John Brode, stumbled across the type specimen used to describe the Inyo Mountains slender salamander. Marlow recollects that he and Brode had been searching for Panamint alligator lizards and were "just screwing around" when Brode flipped a rock and was surprised to find a salamander. Marlow told me that "the presence of a salamander in the Inyo Mountains made some sense, given the distribution of *Batrachoseps*." He was raised in southern California and during his youthful explorations found garden slender salamanders, *Batrachoseps major*, in the dry chaparral east of Los Angeles. Also, in 1969 a new species of slender salamander, *Batrachoseps aridus*, had been discovered in a small desert canyon near Palm Springs. Still, Marlow "didn't expect to find that kind of animal there," in a narrow desert canyon about 30 feet wide and 300 feet long, choked with wild rose and desert olive. When I visited the site where Marlow and Brode had found nine salamanders the thick vegetation was gone, destroyed by a flash flood in the early 1980s. The thinnest trickle of water—just enough to moisten the naked rock—ran for fifty feet through a series of small steps, then vanished into gravel. Split pieces of water pipe and an empty trough suggested that once there had been more water at the spring. But on that hot morning there was nothing in the place that spoke to me of salamanders, and I found none as I searched among a thick swarm of bees drinking from the tiny seep.

The canyon was unlike other sites in the Inyo Mountains where I'd seen salamanders—with little water and almost no moist soil or flat rocks around the tiny seep—and I wondered if the population had been destroyed by some lethal combination of over-collecting, flooding, and decreased spring flow. The ambience of the small canyon seemed completely wrong, but when I mentioned my pessimism to David Wake, Elizabeth Jockusch, and Bob Hansen, biologists who have spent decades studying *Batrachoseps*, they reassured me that slender salamanders still persisted in the canyon. Perhaps bad conditions had driven them deep underground, but they were getting through the difficult times much as they always had, wedged into moist cracks and waiting for benign respites that would bring them near to the surface to feed and perhaps mate. "It's just what they do," wrote Hansen. It's what the gregarious slender salamander, *Batrachoseps gregarius*, does every summer in the oak woodlands surrounding Hansen's house near Fresno, when intense summer heat and drought wither the grass to straw and turn the surface into a killing field for any salamander that might crawl across the burning land. And it is what the ancestors of *Batrachoseps campi* must have done 760,000 years ago when a perfect storm of volcanic ash rained down upon their mountains, or 7,500 years ago during the middle Holocene, when a millennial drought took hold and the streams and springs began to fail. The limestone and dolomite strata that comprise sections of the Inyo Mountains are riddled with solution channels, which would have provided excellent refuges for salamanders during the hardest times. The salamanders must have retreated into these deep and hidden places to where there was adequate moisture and they could drowse and wait, ever so patiently, for better times. And in their waiting they would have been favored by their evolutionary legacy, for throughout their history lungless salamanders have cultivated a certain physiological tenacity.

On a hot desert day in September when water is mostly fantasy, an Inyo Mountains slender salamander feels like the epitome of contradictions. Hold one in the palm of your hand: it seems as vulnerable as a naked, newly hatched sparrow. What is it doing *here*, among the radiant rocks and cacti, the brittle bursage and torrents of light? And yet its skin, that thinnest and leakiest of envelopes, hides a wonderful toughness, for lungless salamanders are very good at taking their time and hanging on. They need little, tolerate much, and can endure. They are a moist and living paradox in a world of heat and drought.

Although hot, dry air is absolutely lethal to salamanders, they are remarkably tolerant of dehydration. A relative of the Inyo Mountains slender salamander, the California slender salamander, can survive until water loss approaches 30 percent of its body weight. A comparative value for humans is roughly 15 percent, although severe mental and physical impairment kicks in at about 10 percent loss. While *Batrachoseps* can survive levels of dehydration that would kill most mammals or birds another general aspect of their biology must help them through the leanest times. Salamanders, including lungless species, have an extraordinarily low resting metabolic rate and need little energy to survive. Vertebrate ectotherms—animals that do not use metabolic heat production to regulate their body temperature—require much less energy than do endotherms such as mammals, which use most of their metabolic energy to generate heat. Although all ectotherms use less energy than equivalent-sized endotherms, salamanders are masters of energy efficiency. Their resting metabolic rates are about 60 percent of other air-breathing vertebrate ectotherms, and they need only one-eighth to one-thirtieth of the energy required by birds and mammals. And because ectotherms do not defend their body temperatures in the same way that endotherms do, surface-to-volume ratios are of less consequence and they can be very small. Adults of about 65 percent of all salamander species weigh five grams or less, while 20 percent weigh less than one gram. To get some idea of how insubstantial a one-gram salamander is, take two small raisins and cup them in your hand; that's roughly the mass of a species such as the California slender salamander.

Given their low metabolic rates, small lungless salamanders require very little in the way of their invertebrate prey to get by. One study estimated that a one-gram female dusky salamander needs about 1.2 grams of food *per year* to survive and reproduce. In comparison the tiniest endotherms, such as small shrews and hummingbirds, have body masses near five grams. Get much smaller than this and the surface-to-volume ratio increases to the point that heat floods from an animal's body so quickly that it cannot maintain a constant body temperature. A 3.3-gram masked shrew, one of the smallest endotherms, must consume roughly two and a half times its body mass in food per day. To feed oxygen and food to its metabolic fires requires an average pulse rate of around 780 beats per minute, which may climb to 1,200 beats per minute during heavy exertion. During their short, intense lives small shrews rarely stop their manic search for food. I have watched them forage in the woods and meadows around my home in Brockport, New York; in contrast to the measured slowness of salamanders, shrews are continuous shivers of frenetic energy as they work the ground for insects and worms. Compare this activity and voraciousness to the metabolic frugality of a lungless salamander, which may consume little more than its body weight in food in a year and carries in the tiniest of bodies a heart that thrums along at a rate of fifty beats per minute—the resting pulse rate of a young, fit marathon runner.

Finally, when faced with heat, drought, and lack of food many amphibians enter a state of decreased metabolic activity known as aestivation, when their steady-state metabolic rate decreases to about 25 percent of the normal resting rate. The low energy demands of lungless salamanders, combined with further decreases during aestivation, make them extremely tolerant of both starvation and low oxygen levels, or hypoxia. Lungless salamanders can persist for long periods without eating anything; in one lab population of *Batrachoseps* 74 percent survived at room temperature for one year without food—under warmer conditions, and thus with a higher metabolic rate, than deep in the limestone crevices of the Inyo Mountains, where slender salamanders must wait out the toughest times.

Never having adopted the need to maintain a constant body temperature, salamanders are free to use much of their food energy for growth and reproduction instead of staying warm. In vertebrate endotherms the percentage of food energy used for adding biomass is typically 0.5 to 1.2 percent, but it runs as high as 50 to 80 percent in lungless salamanders. Thus one hundred pounds of food might mean a one-pound weight gain for a human but anywhere from fifty to eighty pounds for an equal mass of salamanders. (Give humans a higher food-conversion efficiency and every last one of us would be dead in the diet waters, victims of gross obesity, diabetes, and coronary disease.) And so when long pulses of killing conditions visited the Inyo Mountains the salamanders must have retreated deep underground, where some could have survived for years. They are that slow. They would have lived off lipid reserves stored in their tails, perhaps while guarding eggs that developed directly into miniature replicas of adults. Waves of drought, volcanic ash, heat, and cold must have decimated populations and pushed refugees into tiny pockets of favorable habitat. Tightly wedged in the moist and absolute darkness of deep hypoxic cracks, bereft of all food, the salamanders—the ultimate subterraneans—would have drowsed away the days, weeks, months, years. Many would have died: a poorly chosen refuge, not enough stored energy, a world gone bad for too long. But when the world did brighten the survivors would have crawled from the rocks. Perhaps they would have surfaced along tiny streams, in the riparian sweetness of some rainy desert night. There they would have found sufficient food and enough of their kind to mate and grow the eggs that would carry the population into the future.

The Inyo Mountains slender salamanders are very good at what they do. They have gotten by for millions of years in a tough land, but there cannot be all that many of them. The Inyo Mountains are too dry, and there simply is not enough habitat for them. How many salamanders could possibly live in the fifty acres that they have, given the harshness of the surrounding desert and the isolation of their tiny habitat islands? Perhaps there were many more back in the Pleistocene, when there was more rain, when the streams and springs ran strongly and extended their reach far down lush canyons. There would have been more cottonwoods and willows, abundant leaf litter beneath the trees, and pockets of soil rich with humus and invertebrate prey. Perhaps conditions once were moderate enough so that the salamanders did not retreat as often and as deeply into their cloistered crevices to await the next respite. Although I very much doubt it, once there could have been as many slender salamanders in prime Inyo Mountains habitat as there are lungless salamanders in the deciduous woods of New Hampshire—up to 10,000 per acre. There, salamander biomass may equal that of small mammals and be two times greater than that of breeding birds. There salamanders play important roles in the ecosystem, both as highly concentrated protein packets for predators and as regulators of invertebrate populations on the forest floor.

Although I can imagine a hypothetical scenario with abundant Inyo Mountains slender salamanders and a major role for them in riparian ecosystems, it is more likely that for thousands of years they have been uncommon and ecologically "unimportant." They have remained uncommon because there is very little high-quality habitat for them. And though they are good at surviving the hardest times, they live in an arid world where the very nature of their skin—their primary means of contact with the environment—conspires against them. And curiously, perhaps their "unimportance" and slowness have been their salvation. David Wake, emeritus curator of herpetology in the Museum of Vertebrate Zoology at the University of California at Berkeley, once said something puzzling to me: "Perhaps Inyo Mountains slender salamanders have survived because they aren't very important." I was confused about his statement, but after wandering through the salamanders' homeland, spending time with them, and reading about their physiology and ecology I believe that I understand what he was getting at. Slender salamanders aren't important to Inyo Mountains ecosystems because the land offers so little to sustain them, and so they are uncommon. They also are uncommon because the physiological slowness that preserves them also makes it difficult for their populations to take advantage of favorable conditions and increase after a decline.

Rates of population increase are affected by many factors, but two of the most important are age at sexual maturity and number of young per reproductive bout. What little data we have suggest that by both measures *Batrachoseps* salamanders are not fecund. No one knows how long it takes an Inyo Mountains slender salamander to reach sexual maturity, but the smaller California slender salamander matures in three to four years and may live for eight years or more. Nor do we know how many eggs a female Inyo Mountains slender salamander lays, although clutch size in the Kern Plateau slender salamander is only four to six eggs, with no more than one clutch laid in a year. Compare these reproductive traits to those of a small endotherm such as the white-footed mouse, which reaches sexual maturity at two months of age, produces two to three litters of four young per year, and then dies after only a year or so of life. Because slender salamanders are unimportant and uncommon they can endure, and no predator can specialize on them. They are astounding misers of energy and can slip through (and into) the "ecological cracks," but they have entered into an evolutionary trade-off: slowness and survival in exchange for quickness and increase.

Inyo Mountains slender salamanders require far less than many creatures to get by, but if too much heat and drying come to their remaining habitat, individual populations could wink out or the entire species could perish. Yet the salamanders have endured much in their long history. Give them just the barest minimum of food and water in a world where there is little of either and they will get by, much as they always have. They have their physical needs, but mostly what they need is to be left alone. Perhaps this is why the Inyo Mountains slender salamander is listed only as a "species of special concern" by the California Department of Fish and Game, rather than as threatened or endangered by the state or U.S. Fish and Wildlife Service.

The character of the Inyo Mountains—little water, sparse vegetation, and apparently not much in the way of valuable mineral resources—contributes to our benign neglect of the species. In the past some of the springs and small streams that the salamanders depend upon were loci for mining and cattle grazing. But this wave of development has mostly passed by the salamanders, for the abandoned troughs and pipes, the scattered bits of lumber and rusted machinery speak of a land too spare to offer much economic sustenance. Feral burros and cattle may have grazed and trampled their way through enough mountain canyons to decrease salamander populations in some places. And perhaps illegal collectors have taken too many salamanders from the few sites that offer relatively easy road access; I suspect this about two localities but do not have enough evidence to support my pessimism. But now few burros or cattle roam the Inyo Mountains, and most of the salamander populations have become more isolated than they once were as wilderness designation and the wear of water have pushed drivable roads farther away from where the salamanders live. If rain and snow continue to fall in the Inyo Mountains—just enough to keep the springs and streams flowing—and no fools try to collect what little water does issue from these spare sources, the salamanders will endure, at least in my lifetime and my children's lifetime. The uncertain impacts of climate change and what a long-term regional drought might do to the hydrology of the Inyo Mountains offer up a more negative scenario, but I remind myself that the salamanders survived the great drying of the middle Holocene, hopefully no worse than what the anthropogenic flux of greenhouse gasses may have in store for us and the slender salamanders.

––––––––––––

It's another hot day in late September. I'm miles up a dry canyon in the Inyo Mountains, alone with a few chipping white-crowned sparrows probably down from the High Sierra's autumnal meadows. I sit beneath a shaded overhang, sipping from my water bottle and letting my body cool into stillness. The morning climbs into heat and the world is mostly quiet as the sparrows fossick in the debris beneath a lone cottonwood. I push my boot heels into the gravel and work at the pebbles and sand, carving out loops and swirls, digging out small depressions, then destroying the patterns and starting again: a physical parallel to my mental excavations. I wonder about my obsession with Inyo Mountains slender salamanders, about the combination of sensory experience, information, and predisposition that drew me toward them and into their empty hardscrabble home. I know that my heart was taken by the first ones that I found eighteen months before and that the essence of the Inyo Mountains is vital to me, that it is difficult to imagine a passion for any organism without a concurrent passion for the place in which it lives. A love of the spare landscapes of the Basin and Range country began incubating in me over three decades ago, when I studied feral burros in the Panamint Mountains on the west side of what was then Death Valley National Monument. There I wandered through knee-high forests of spiny shrubs, across the heat-soaked land, and so learned something vital about the desiccated and desolated ranges and their endless fractals of space and light and heat.

All of this makes good sense. But ornithologist that I am, why salamanders? Why not some bird of the Panamints and Inyos, like black-throated gray warblers or gray flycatchers? Years before I worked in Death Valley, and long before hearing about Inyo Mountains slender salamanders I developed an incipient fascination with several narrowly endemic western lungless salamanders: the Larch Mountain salamander of Oregon and the Jemez Mountain and Sacramento Mountains salamanders of New Mexico. I first read about these species in Robert Stebbins's *Field Guide to Western Reptiles and Amphibians* and was taken by their isolation, whether in the high hills above the Columbia River Gorge or the sky islands of the Southwest. At the time I did little with my interest except spend several rain-soaked and fruitless days searching for Larch Mountain salamanders. Yet my fascination generated in me an inclination and desire, later steeped in my professional interest in the conservation of small, isolated populations. But beyond the science and intellectual curiosity, the facts and theory, I now understand that there is something about ecological isolation itself—those small pockets of life in desert springs, or on mountaintops or islands, surrounded by inhospitable emptiness—that appeals to me on a visceral level. I wonder if the Inyo Mountains slender salamander's situation, its haunting loneliness in a landscape of adversity, is a psychological and emotional metaphor for feelings that I've carried out of childhood and into my adult years. Like the salamanders, I have my solitude. But unlike the salamanders my solitude is mostly a matter of choice, although as I age it sometimes feels more like an indelible aspect of my character.

The sparrows cease their foraging and head down canyon. I finish my water and rise to follow them toward the lowlands. It is time to leave the Inyos for a few weeks and focus on my other obsessions, desert pupfish and toads. As I walk down the eroded streambed, a crunch of gravel underfoot, my thoughts shift from obsession toward value. In my conservation biology course we discuss the value of biodiversity and the myriad reasons for preserving species and their habitats. But what makes great sense in the classroom doesn't necessarily work well out here. Textbook explanations about roles in ecosystems, potential medical value (perhaps an undescribed biomolecule for treating disease), or ecotourism dollars do not resonate all that much. Just what good are Inyo Mountains slender salamanders, hidden away in the empty country east of Owens Valley? Why should anyone concern themselves with a species that few people know about and even fewer will ever see? Why should a waitress in Bishop or a rancher in Lone Pine care anything about the salamanders that I have become devoted to? This question of worth will rise again and again as I work my way through the desert; it will nag me like the small stone lodged in my left boot, which I am too lazy to stop and remove but which gives my gait an irritating little hitch. And when I spend time with the biologists and resource managers who work with and care for the toads, salamanders, and pupfish of this country, they sometimes ask me what I think about value. As passionate as they are about conservation they also search for value, meaning, and thoughtful responses to angry or puzzled questions raised in the Wal-Mart in Pahrump, at a public meeting in Bishop, or on the editorial page of the local newspaper.

For now I am mostly perplexed about possible answers to questions of value, but a few weeks later I will sense the outline of one possible answer. One afternoon, after a long hot day in the field, I stopped at the Manzanar National Historic Site just south of the small town of Independence in the Owens Valley. Manzanar was one of ten "war relocation centers" where Japanese Americans were imprisoned during World War II. The Manzanar camp once held more than 10,000 "internees" crowded into 504 barracks. (For public relations reasons I suppose that they were not called "prisoners.") Most of the original camp structures have disappeared, but the National Park Service has renovated the auditorium as an interpretive center and erected replicas of several buildings, including barracks, a mess hall, and a guard tower. Manzanar's setting is spectacular, with the 14,000-foot peaks of the Sierra to the west and the stark, arid escarpment of the Inyo Mountains to the east. On that gracefully warm afternoon in October, Manzanar was almost deceptively beautiful: a gentle breeze, cool enough to take the edge off the afternoon heat, and a crystalline sky strewn with electric white cumulus. The weather that had plagued the prisoners—bitter winter winds, 105°F summer temperatures, and choking spring dust storms—seemed as though it was the setting for another, improbable story.

Although the armed soldiers, guard towers, and barbed wire fences are more than sixty years gone, Manzanar remains a place where the ghosts of the past wander with you, much like on the killing fields of Antietam in Maryland or the Little Bighorn in Montana. Suffering, pain, injustice, anger, death; these things were never far away as I worked my way through the interpretive center ("Japs Keep Moving This Is a White Man's Neighborhood," reads one photograph in the exhibit) or walked from the barracks to the mess hall, with its fresh pine floorboards and tar-papered exterior walls. The eddying voices of school children, "loyalty questionnaires," men and women cultivating formal gardens, the death notices that came to the families of Japanese American soldiers killed in combat, and the rage and shame bred by interment: these things were like the insistent, whispering voice of an invisible tour guide. For a while I thought about fear, racism, hatred, and man's inhumanity to man and was drawn into sadness and impotent anger. But then I happened to glance up and eastward toward the Inyo Mountains and the drainage where I'd found slender salamanders just a few hours before. Those tiny, tenacious creatures came to mind, with their patient slowness and the ways in which they have endured—and how they did so as the horrors of World War II unfolded, with one small performance of that deadly and anguished play acted out precisely where I stood.

I understood that nothing could ever repay the internees for their suffering, not even the belated 1988 U.S. Civil Liberties Act, which granted a $20,000 payment and an apology to former prisoners of Manzanar and other relocation camps. But I took some comfort in knowing that while 10,000 people were imprisoned at Manzanar the Inyo Mountains slender salamanders were going about their business, much as they have for the last 10 million years. I do not pretend to understand much about the Japanese American experience in World War II, nor can I say how victims of any terrible injustice might come into forgiveness and peace. I have not experienced anything comparable to what the internees must have gone through, but like every person in this world I have lived through my own tiny Manzanars, my small imprisonments, pain, and sadness. And for me it is of some solace to know that, beyond the reach of human folly, Inyo Mountains slender salamanders have crawled and drowsed their way through the millennia. Wonderful travelers of time, they have ridden waves of change and stasis into the present as what we now call the Inyo Mountains were buckled and lifted and eroded into being. In doing so the salamanders have carried the DNA of countless generations into this present evolutionary moment, dragging with them genetic whispers of their ancestors and, more faintly, of our own history. Such pleasure and wonder: to know that the salamanders have endured, and to hope that we shall, too, in our own haphazard way.

At closing time I left Manzanar and headed north on U.S. Highway 395, toward Bishop. The Inyos stood clear to the east, cloud capped and richly textured by the afternoon's shadow and light. And as I drove I imagined a small host of slender salamanders rousing from their sleep and preparing to crawl into the cooling desert night, the scent of water and seep willow laving the quickened air.

Surviving an Onslaught

THE OWENS PUPFISH

(Cyprinodon radiosus)

We live and die in what we have left.
—Robert Wrigley, "Skull of a Snowshoe Hare"

It is mid-September and the evening winds are up, pummeling the Owens Valley. Thick gulps of air push out of the south, kicking up small clouds of dust, hammering the bulrushes and cattails along the slough, throwing dried plants down the dirt track. Rabbitbrush stems scritch and scratch against one another, their branches a swirl of brilliant yellow flowers. Tiny bits of gravel sting my bare legs; grit settles in my hair and eddies behind my glasses. To the west the Sierra crest is a backlit serrated silhouette; to the east the full moon rises over the great arid bulk of the White Mountains. This would be a beautiful place but for the wind—well, it is a beautiful place, but the gusts push against my solitude and force me deep into myself. I am all clenched jaw and weary resignation. The spring pool that I have come to see is a chaotic ripple of waves, as opaque as sand, and so I retreat to my small car for a cold dinner of bread and cheese, and watch the moon-rich dark colonize the land. I finish writing up my field notes, switch off my headlamp, and settle into a cramped and restless sleep in the back of my vehicle, which creaks and rocks in time with the gusting beat of the wind.

I awake sometime after midnight. The winds have died away and the moon hangs in the western sky, high above the Sierra. The clear peace is warm and welcoming, immaculate. I slip on my sandals and walk down to the spring, where the moon swims in the mirrored water. A few mosquitoes whine; a lone bat flicks above the pool, and a gentle rustle of bulrushes stirs the night air. A moth struggles across the white alkaline soil and is still. I look down into the quiet water, which is about five feet deep. A thick carpet of crayfish decorates the sandy bottom. Some scout for food; others wait with outstretched pinchers, ready to embrace whatever food comes their way. Occasionally a crayfish jets backwards, impelled by a sudden disturbance to its world. Small clouds of mosquitofish swarm near the surface of the pool. And suspended between the two alien species is a scatter of the small slivers that I have come to see: Owens pupfish, *Cyprinodon radiosus*. I watch these tiny swimmers for a while, happy in their presence, then switch off my headlamp and let in the moon-struck night. Twenty minutes later I walk back to my car, less anxious and alone than when the winds were up, and sleep easily until dawn.

In the morning the waters of BLM Spring are calm. Active crayfish remain, but in smaller numbers. Carcasses of their dead brothers and sisters—some dismembered, others partly buried in sediment—lie scattered across the bottom of the pool as though it was the aftermath of a vicious nocturnal battle. Dark green strands of algae stream with the slight current, which leads out of the crescent-shaped pool and into a small channel flowing east and then south. Pupfish cluster near the craters surrounding bubbling spring vents, which spew forth roiling clouds of sand and water. From where I stand the pupfish look mostly silver, with a faint blue wash and dark vertical bands along their sides; they have little of the deep blue that marks males during the spring spawning season. Each vent seems to have its own swirling shoal of twenty to thirty pupfish circling the crater like a cloud of darting electrons. Each pupfish cloud is dominated by a large alpha male who is all perpetual motion—a constant shiver of energy chasing smaller intruders and claiming the space as his own. The dominant fish never seem to feed. Instead they relentlessly defend the scattered vent craters, which must be prized territory, swimming in staccato pulses, flashing silver, inscribing tight S- and figure-eight-shaped arcs in the clear water, which sparkles with facets of light.

The main pool at BLM Spring is about twenty feet across, sixty feet long, and five feet deep. There is an entire universe waiting in the water, and I pass much of the morning watching its form and function: the clusters of mosquitofish near the pool's surface, the patient march of crayfish, and the restless dance of pupfish. The rutted road that passes by BLM Spring remains empty, and so my attention stays focused on the fish. Occasionally, though, I glance up at my surroundings—close at hand, the quiet murmur of bulrush along the west and north sides of the spring, where common yellowthroats and Lincoln's sparrows call from the thick cover. Beyond the spring margin lies the broad swath of Fish Slough, a flat march of alkali,

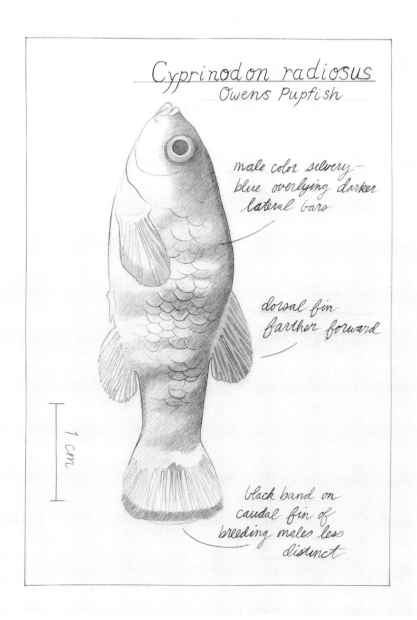

Cyprinodon radiosus
Owens Pupfish

male color silvery-blue overlying darker lateral bars

dorsal fin farther forward

1 cm

black band on caudal fin of breeding males less distinct

Owens pupfish (_Cyprinodon radiosus_)

grass, bulrush, and cattail dotted with scattered cottonwoods and willows, green streaked with equinoctial yellow. A flight of thirty white pelicans sails down valley, and ravens perch on the volcanic rocks that line the slough, black bird-dots set against the azure sky. Beyond the wetlands are the arid, shrub-dotted uplands, dun colored in the midday light, rising through brown cliffs of Bishop Tuff toward the parallel vectors of the 14,000-foot Sierra and White Mountains.

I stand surrounded by the great sweep of the Owens Valley, and yet my attention repeatedly returns to the small fish, no more than two inches long, which swim at my feet. The Owens pupfish seem healthy, vibrant, and abundant. Yet they are refugees, much like the Inyo Mountains slender salamanders that live forty miles to the south of BLM Spring. The pupfish, though, have fled not so much from the great pulses of environmental change that have swept across the Southwest during the last 20,000 years. Instead they have been forced into (or more accurately, gathered into) a handful of tiny refuges, as a way to protect them from the onslaught of humans and our surrogates. The Owens pupfish have managed to survive in spite of adversity and the perversities of chance—and on a glorious September morning at BLM Spring they swim on, as the day gathers its heat and light and their world opens before me.

The Owens pupfish that I watched at BLM Spring were forty generations or more removed from fish that, on August 18, 1969, had been rescued from a drying pool in the northwest corner of Fish Slough. There were about 800 of these survivors and they literally were the only Owens pupfish left in the world. The pupfish were being carried from their dying home in two buckets by Phil Pister, a California Department of Fish and Game biologist based out of Bishop. Pister later recalled, "I distinctly remember being scared to death. I had walked perhaps fifty yards when I realized that I literally held within my hands the existence of an entire vertebrate species. If I had tripped over a piece of barbed wire or stepped into a rodent burrow, the Owens pupfish would now be extinct." Pister released the two buckets of fish into BLM Spring, which had been cleared of all nonnative fish. At first the transplanted fish prospered, but they eventually died out, as would several subsequent populations. But the descendants of the original survivors lived on in other refuges in the area, and some would be used to reestablish the current population at BLM Spring, as well as those in four other sites in the Owens Valley.

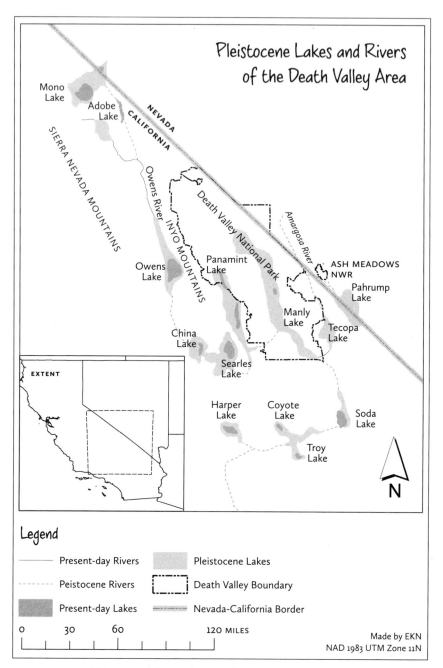

Pleistocene lakes and rivers of the Death Valley region

It wasn't always this way, though. Once, Owens pupfish were abundant along one hundred miles of the main channel of the Owens River and in backwater sloughs and marshes throughout the Owens Valley. The story of the species' near extinction, tentative recovery, and precarious existence is fashioned out of water, the West's most precious resource; the urban imperatives of Los Angeles; alien species; and the dedication and passion of a few obstinate biologists. Without their advocacy and determination the Owens pupfish may well have shared the fate of the extinct Las Vegas dace, Ash Meadows poolfish, Raycraft Ranch poolfish, Pahrump Ranch poolfish, and Tecopa pupfish. Add to these losses at least seven other fish extinctions elsewhere in the Great Basin, the widespread decline of native mollusks and aquatic insects, and the general collapse of desert fish populations—somewhere on the order of 130 species, subspecies, or important populations are threatened—and the magnitude of the collapse in regional biodiversity becomes apparent. The three main riders of this aquatic apocalypse have been the overuse of groundwater, habitat destruction, and the havoc wrought by exotic species, primarily crayfish, largemouth bass, mosquitofish, and bullfrogs. But one might more directly blame human shortsightedness, error, stupidity, cussedness, and (occasionally) malfeasance, which collectively make for a large posse of dusty and determined horsemen, riding hard in the saddle to rid the Intermountain West of its native aquatic species.

The Owens Valley lies at the extreme southwestern edge of the Great Basin. It is arid and spectacular, a great fault-block trough roughly ten to twenty miles wide running north-south from near Bishop for seventy-five miles and bordered by the parallel thrusts of the Sierra Nevada to the west and the White-Inyo Range to the east. Stand at 4,000 feet on the valley floor near the small town of Lone Pine and look west toward the main crest of the Sierra ten miles distant and 10,000 feet higher, and you will confront a visual and visceral definition of the adjective "magnificent." The Owens Valley lies in the rain shadow of the Sierra Nevada and receives five to nine inches of precipitation annually. It is Mary Austin's "land of little rain," and much of the valley floor is dominated by desert scrub vegetation, particularly plants adapted to alkali soils. Climb onto the alluvial fans spilling from the Sierra or Inyo Mountains, though, and you will find the cacti and thorny shrubs associated with images of the desert. Although much of the Owens Valley feels like desert, it once was (and locally, still is) nourished by streams draining from the Sierra Nevada, which coalesce to form the Owens River. Although the Owens Valley is by desert standards well watered, the water is unevenly distributed. Walk ten feet away from a trout-filled stream tumbling out of the mountains and the vegetation veers suddenly from verdant riparian (a tangle of water birch, willow, and aspen) to spare desert scrub (shadscale, big sagebrush, rabbitbrush, Mormon tea). The Owens River winds along the valley floor, flowing through a narrow swath of irrigated pastures and hayfields. During summer the river and its tributaries nurture a wash of vibrant green that threads through the flat browns and gray-greens of the surrounding desert. In autumn the creeks and rivers are transformed into corridors of gold by the streamside aspens, willows, and cottonwoods.

The modern-day Owens River is a small stream and by eastern standards it should be called Owens Creek. Its current annual discharge is only about 80 percent that of Cattaraugus Creek in western New York State, and most often there isn't all that much water in the main channel. For all of the ways in which it nourishes the valley, the river's hold on the land—its imprint on the surrounding desert—seems tentative. The Owens River has much less visual and emotional impact than the first feature you confront when entering Owens Valley from the south, running north on U.S. Highway 395 out of Mojave: what some maps label "Owens Lake Bed," a great white salt pan about seventeen miles long and up to ten miles wide lying hard against the eastern escarpment of the Sierra Nevada. As with all Great Basin streams the Owens River has no outlet to the ocean. What's left of it flows for 183 miles from its headwaters southeast of Yosemite National Park to a terminus in the mostly dry Owens Lake Bed just south of Lone Pine. When the frequent valley winds kick up, choking clouds of arsenic- and salt-laden dust rise from Owens Lake Bed. Recently this alkali wasteland was probably the largest single source of small aerosol particles in the United States, producing between 900,000 and 8 million metric tons of fine-grained dust per year, and it has been identified as the primary cause of the respiratory problems that have plagued residents of the southern Owens Valley. Although recent mitigation efforts have improved the area's air quality, on windy days the dust-laden air still demands one's attention—and when the skies are clear and calm the vast expanse of Owens Lake Bed's gesso ground creates an ambience that the better-watered parts of Owens Valley cannot quite dispel, an affirmation of the land's arid nature.

Once, though, there was more water in Owens Lake. During the Pleistocene it covered up to 200 square miles, but even until the early twentieth century the lake had an extent about half that of its Pleistocene maximum, with a depth of twenty-three to fifty feet. The lake also must have been either freshwater or brackish because there is an early museum specimen of tui chub, a species intolerant of high salinity, from Owens Lake. Early accounts describe an extensive lake that supported abundant flocks of migratory waterfowl and shorebirds. However, beginning in the 1860s pioneer settlement and wholesale water diversions initiated a decline in the flow of the Owens River. By 1901 there were 200 miles of irrigation ditches and canals in the northern part of the valley and 40,000 acres under cultivation. Owens Lake slowly shrank, a process hastened by the arrival in Owens Valley of the Los Angeles City Water Company, which coveted the same water that nourished the valley's farms. Los Angeles was growing rapidly—between 1900 and 1905 its population doubled from 100,000 to 200,000—and running low on water. The nearest feasible source was the Owens River; although it was 250 miles to the northeast and on the other side of the Mojave Desert, its terminus at Owens Lake was almost 4,000 feet above sea level. Gravity could pull the water to Los Angeles, and so the city began buying Owens Valley land and water rights.

The story of how the Los Angeles City Water Company, later the Department of Water and Power, or DWP, came to own most of the Owens Valley water and build the Los Angeles Aqueduct is one of subterfuge, ambition, greed, political machinations, violence, profound environmental impacts, and impressive engineering—and so a classic example of water development in the American West. It is a spectacular history, one told most notably in Marc Reisner's nonfiction book *Cadillac Desert*, and fictionally (with much dramatic license) in Roman Polanski's 1976 film *Chinatown*. I will not retell the story here, except to note its outcome: after the Los Angeles Aqueduct was completed in 1913 much of the basin's water was diverted to the subdivisions and orange groves of southern California. By 1926 Owens Lake and fifty miles of the Owens River had gone mostly dry. The valley once called the "Switzerland of America" had lost its aquatic birthright; its citizens were embittered and felt as though their lives had been destroyed by Los Angeles. Late in 1924 some Owens Valley residents used dynamite to blow a hole in the aqueduct just north of Lone Pine, and further acts of rebellion followed over the next few years. But the political, economic, and demographic advantages rested with Los Angeles. The water mostly belonged to the city, and the 6,000 or so people of Owens Valley had no hope of resisting Los Angeles's inertial power. As a regional drought continued through much of the 1920s and 1930s more and more of the valley's surface water was siphoned down the aqueduct, a process enhanced by the extensive groundwater pumping that began in 1970. And as the Owens River dried, so did many of the valley's springs. Many of the marshes and meadows that once lined the river vanished, and the Owens pupfish tracked the region's ecological and economic decline.

In 1915, before the Los Angeles Aqueduct began draining Owens Valley in a serious way, Clarence Kennedy of Cornell University collected fish and aquatic insects in the Owens River watershed. He found Owens pupfish, then classified as the desert pupfish, *Cyprinodon macularius*, "in abundance in all the shallower parts of the sloughs and tule swamps at both Lone Pine and Laws [just north of Bishop]," and in irrigation ditches throughout the valley. Kennedy wrote that the Owens pupfish "was most abundant in the edges of the large tule swamp that lies in the big bend of Owens River between Laws and Bishop," but when Carl Hubbs visited the locality in 1934 he found only a few shallow, fishless pools. Hubbs, an ichthyologist from the University of Michigan and a pioneer in the study of desert fishes, also failed to find Owens pupfish along forty miles of the Owens River south of Bishop, although pupfish did persist in two sites: Fish Slough, a well-watered, relatively undisturbed wetlands complex north of Bishop, and in a slough east of Independence. Robert Miller noted pupfish in upper Fish Slough in 1937, but when he returned in 1942 he found only introduced carp and largemouth bass. Miller, by then a graduate student at the University of Michigan, was Carl Hubbs's intellectual son and a developing expert on desert fishes. In his 1948 monograph on the cyprinodont fishes of the Death Valley system Miller described the Owens pupfish as a new species, *Cyprinodon radiosus*, based on a number of unique characters that included a very forward position of the dorsal fin and lack of a distinct terminal black band on the caudal fin of breeding males. Miller apparently believed that his description of the new species was a technical epitaph. Although scientific conservatism probably led him to write that the Owens pupfish was "rare" he believed that it was extinct, due to "the influx of exotic fishes, particularly largemouth bass and carp" and the "removal of a major part of the natural water supply of the valley."

Although Miller was pessimistic about the fate of the Owens pupfish, in 1956 Bill Richardson and Ralph Beck of the California Department of Fish and Game collected several pupfish from shallow pools on the east side of Fish Slough. The pupfish were kept for a while in an aquarium but Richardson "subsequently discarded" the fish, having no idea that the species was considered extinct. A crew of biologists were unable to find any pupfish during an intensive two-day search of Fish Slough in 1963, but on July 10, 1964, Carl Hubbs, Robert Miller, and California Department of Fish and Game fish biologist Phil Pister rediscovered the population of Owens pupfish sampled in 1956. They estimated that there were about 200 fish in a shallow pool of warm water. Most likely, these were the only Owens pupfish in the world, surviving amid competing mosquitofish and predatory largemouth bass—hanging on at what must have been the furthest, most fragile edge of their species' history.

In September 2010 I visited Phil Pister at his Bishop home on a quiet side street just off U.S. Highway 395, about twelve miles from the site in Fish Slough where Owens pupfish were rediscovered in 1964. Pister retired from the California Department of Fish and Game in 1990 after spending virtually his entire thirty-eight-year career as a fish biologist working out of the agency's Bishop office. Although in his early eighties, Pister is energetic and anything but "retired," as indicated by his cluttered office, where strata of scientific articles and books surround his computer and Post-it notes decorate every surface. On the morning when Phil and I first talked he ran through his "to-do" list, which included organizing a video conference at the National Conservation Training Center in West Virginia on restoring high mountain lakes; his work as executive secretary of the Desert Fishes Council, the scientific and conservation organization that he helped found in 1969; and a host of writing and consultation projects. Pister seems to know everyone who is directly involved with desert fishes and a host of prominent environmental philosophers and activists. Although he began his career as a "traditional" fisheries biologist, which meant promoting introduced game fishes such as brown trout, eastern brook trout, and rainbow trout in High Sierra waters, Pister eventually became one of the country's first endangered species biologists, a process facilitated by working "hundreds of miles away from the nearest administrator."

Pister's professional metamorphosis probably started before he began working in the Owens Valley region. In the spring of 1949, while an undergraduate at the University of California at Berkeley, Pister took a course from A. Starker Leopold. Leopold asked his students to read a draft of his father's as-yet-unpublished book, A Sand County Almanac, a lyrical and prescient articulation of the modern conservation ethic. Although Aldo Leopold's book would become a classic in environmental literature, Pister says that it did not affect him much at the time. However, A Sand County Almanac's central message—that humans are citizens of what Leopold termed the "land community" and have a responsibility to maintain its health—must have laid the groundwork for his later conversion. Pister revisited A Sand County Almanac during the summer of 1964, when it "had more impact on me," but his conservation epiphany came after Carl Hubbs and Robert Miller stopped by the California Fish and Game office and asked Pister to help them search for any surviving Owens pupfish. Pister requested a day off from his normal duties, and on July 10 the trio drove out a dirt track along the east side of Fish Slough to the marshy meadow where Richardson and Beck had found pupfish eight years before. It was a typical Owens Valley summer day, cloudless and hot, and shortly after they waded out into Fish Slough Pister had his desert moment, "like Saint Paul on the road to Damascus." Hubbs glanced down into the water and shouted, "Bob [Miller], they're still here!" Hubbs and Miller "were like kids, very excited and happy." For Pister, seeing living Owens pupfish for the first time and knowing that those few fish and their ancestors somehow had swum through the gauntlet of Los Angeles's thirst, the depredations of largemouth bass, and human neglect was "like a flash of blinding light." He had been given the purpose that would guide the rest of his professional career: "At that instant, I dropped everything I had been working on and never picked it up again."

Hubbs, Miller, and Pister agreed that the Owens pupfish could be saved only if the surviving fish were placed in a refuge to protect them from exotic predatory fishes and competition from mosquitofish. Fish Slough was the ideal location for the preserve, and in 1968 the California Fish and Game Commission approved establishment of the Owens Valley Native Fish Sanctuary, although the area was not fully protected until 1982, when Congress authorized a land swap between the U.S. Bureau of Land Management and a developer who owned land in the drainage. The best site for the pupfish refuge was in the northwestern part of Fish Slough, where two springs provided sufficient water for a large pool. Ironically the land and water were owned by the DWP, which provided engineering and design assistance for the project. The 5.6-acre refuge, with an outlet structure to control water levels and a barrier to prevent exotic fishes from migrating into the main pool, was finished in October of 1969, three months after the last Owens pupfish population had, once again, come perilously close to extinction.

The rediscovered Owens pupfish had been included in "The Class of 1967," the first list of vertebrates classified as threatened by extinction under a new federal law, the Endangered Species Preservation Act. Because of inadequacies in the 1967 law and its 1969 amendment, Congress passed the completely rewritten Endangered Species Act of 1973, which was signed into law by that archdruid President Richard Nixon. Under the 1973 law, an amended version of which remains in effect today, the Owens pupfish was classified as endangered, or "in danger of extinction throughout all or a significant portion of its range." This definition accurately described the species' plight, in spite of efforts begun by Phil Pister to reintroduce Owens pupfish to suitable sites around Bishop. Most of these populations failed to thrive, and by the summer of 1969 the only surviving Owens pupfish were confined to a single, room-sized pool below the northwestern springs in Fish Slough, where they awaited completion of their new refuge home. Unusually high precipitation had fallen in Owens Valley throughout the winter of 1968–69, which should have guaranteed a strong flow from the springs supplying the pool. However, the springs' flow declined during the following summer, perhaps due to luxuriant riparian growth nourished by the increased precipitation, which probably led to increased transpiration of water from the flourishing plants.

And so it was that in August Bob Brown, a graduate student working for the Department of Fish and Game, burst into Pister's office and announced, "Phil, if we don't get out to Fish Slough immediately, we are going to lose the entire species!" Pister, Brown, and another Fish and Game employee raced out to the refuge, rescued 800 pupfish from the drying pond, and placed them in hastily constructed cages in the channel of Fish Slough—but in eddies away from the main current. Pister then sent his companions back to Bishop for dinner but decided to take one last and fortunate look at the channel before heading home. There he saw many of the rescued fish languishing from insufficient dissolved oxygen and lots of "white bellies floating in the warm water." Phil knew that he "damned well better move fast" if he was going to save the last Owens pupfish, and so he ran back to his truck, retrieved two buckets, aerators, and a dip net and returned to the slough. He placed the survivors in well-oxygenated water, carried the buckets back to his truck, and carefully drove the pupfish to BLM Spring, which had been treated with calcium hypochlorite to kill any nonnative fish. There the pupfish would, for a time, persevere.

For the second time in less than a decade the Owens pupfish, the oldest lineage among the four species of Death Valley pupfishes, had directly confronted extinction. Although the species had been abundant throughout the Owens Valley in the early twentieth century, by the 1960s it had been nearly destroyed by human-induced "drought" and exotic fishes. But in the most recent moments of the Owens pupfish's history, the dedicated actions of a few biologists had rescued it from oblivion. Or think of it in this way: in the 1950s and 1960s the 3-million-year-old vector of the species' trajectory was plunging toward extinction, toward a universe in which it would be possible to speak of the species only in the past tense. But the Owens pup-fish lineage continued into the present, into a different world in which the future remained a wonderful possibility. The disappearance of the Owens pupfish—the loss of its essence in the world—would have been a tragedy, but to comprehend the full magnitude of the loss it is necessary to travel back more than 4 million years into the Pliocene, to explore pupfish evolu-tion and the chronicle of the Great Basin's lost landscapes.

————————

Everywhere in this country of light lie the shadows of time: in the sharp thrust of fault-block ranges and their deep alluvial graves; in the bands of shoreline sediments resting hundreds of feet above the valley floors, relics of vanished waters; and in the thick beds of Bishop Tuff, thrown forth from the Long Valley Caldera 760,000 years ago. There are shadows of time, too, in the genes of pupfish and springsnails and amphipods, the species whose fates have tracked the history of the Great Basin's lakes and rivers—the history of waters that have ebbed and flowed through intervals of tectonic thrust and subsidence, episodes of drought and flood. Crest the southern end of the Inyo Mountains on California Highway 190 and ride the long fall-ing slide of the land northwest, and there confront the expanse of Owens Lake Bed and the 10,000-foot-tall scarp of the Sierra. Climb a steep slope above Mormon Point at the southern end of Death Valley and contemplate ancient Lake Manly's graveled strandline, 400 feet above the valley floor. Look up at the cliffs of Bishop Tuff above BLM Spring and consider the terrible onslaught of killing ash that must have blanketed and sterilized the land. Glance down at a shoal of small fish shining with iridescent blue light in some desert springhead or pluck a tiny snail no bigger than a sesame seed from a pool of thick brine, and confront animals isolated from others of their kind by an ocean of years, as well as by the dry and deathly sweep of creosote bush and sand. Everywhere in the Great Basin, in all of its places and in all of its creatures, is time's magnificent legacy, a story spread across the lovely spatials of the Basin and Range country, full of subtle hints and dramatic declarations about the world that once was, played forward into the world that now is our world and our children's world.

I stand on a Pleistocene lake bed and gaze down some long valley, my view funneled by the astonishing boundaries of two parallel desert ranges. The waters have vanished but I am swept along the dry drainage by a cur-rent of time, its constant flow spilling out of the deep past, filling the basin and running into the future. In the world of human experience and in the history of the world that we study with scientific methods, the physical passage of time is essentially invariant. But our view of time's long flood and the legacy that it has bequeathed to the present is muddied and imperfect, limited by the disparity between the length of our own lives and the great swath of years that extends into the furthest depths of the Precambrian. Scientists search for fossils, analyze sediment cores from ancient lakes, track strata of volcanic deposits, sequence strands of DNA, measure the polarity of ash beds, and determine isotope ratios of carbon-14 to carbon-12. They collect information like bees collect pollen on a warm summer day: obsessively, patiently, and persistently—as in one recent scientific paper that summoned "lithologic, chemical, mineralogic, geophysical, and paleontological data" to discern the Pleistocene history of Owens Lake. Sometimes the data are clear and unambiguous and we are able to build a cairn at a precise location along time's path, as with the explosion of the Long Valley Caldera 760,000 years ago. In some instances our view of time is less sharp, although there still is a single viable hypothesis most strongly supported by the data—as with the sediment layers and isotopic signatures that support highstands, or deep-water events, in the lakes of the Owens River system some 185,000 to 130,000 years ago. In other cases the data are fragmentary or contradictory and no clear answer to an important question is evident—for example, the timing and route by which the ancestors of today's Death Valley pupfishes, including the Owens pupfish, arrived in the region, an event which may have occurred as recently as 2–3 million years ago, or as long as 11 million years ago.

In reading about the geologic and biotic history of the region I am struck by the profusion of qualifiers that populate technical papers—"probably," "perhaps," "may have," "appear to have," "plausible," and "hypothetical." These terms are common to all scientific disciplines; they articulate the constraints imposed by rules for evaluating evidence and testing hypotheses, and by an emphasis on provisional rather than absolute truths. But there is another reason why scientists who study the geological and biological history of the Great Basin must deal in qualifying terms: the manner in which evidence of the past has been weathered and metamorphosed by the flow of years. There is a single story out there, a particular sequence of events leading out of the deep past and into the present, but our telling of it is tentative. We use sophisticated state-of-the-art technologies and traditional approaches to understand a past that in the case of pupfishes extends across roughly 11 million years, from the middle Miocene to the last 11,000 years of the postglacial Holocene. The effort, skill, and devotion dedicated to unraveling the evolution of the Great Basin and its life is impressive, the data generated on this one subject overwhelming in its abundance, detail, and beauty. We understand enough about the Great Basin's history to create a convincing overview of the plot but remain uncertain about some important parts of the narrative. What we have is a scumbled sense of time's passage and its products, much like the bleached view across an alluvial fan on a hot summer day. The immediate foreground is distinct, and in the distance is the outline of a desert mountain range with its particular geometry of rock and canyon, cliff and scree. But the shimmering waves of infrared radiation that rise through the creosote bush scrub create a measure of visual noise, a slight distortion of the landscape, and we sense that our perception of the world is provisional, our place in it less certain than we desire.

Taxonomic experts generally recognize four species of the pupfish genus *Cyprinodon* in the Death Valley region: the Owens pupfish, *C. radiosus*; the Salt Creek pupfish, *C. salinus*; the Devils Hole pupfish, *C. diabolis*; and the Amargosa pupfish, *C. nevadensis*. Among Death Valley pupfishes the Owens pupfish is the most intrepid wanderer, with the westernmost distribution. The Salt Creek pupfish is restricted to the Salt Creek and Cottonball Marsh area in Death Valley, a few miles northwest of the park headquarters at Furnace Creek, while the Devils Hole pupfish occurs only at Devils Hole, an isolated pool near Ash Meadows in the Amargosa River Basin, thirty-five miles east of Furnace Creek. The Amargosa pupfish, with five extant and one extinct subspecies, occurs at scattered localities in the Amargosa River Basin from the southern end of Death Valley National Park north and east into Ash Meadows National Wildlife Refuge. The disjunct distribution of Death Valley pupfishes is compelling, particularly when viewed against the spectacular backdrop of the region's geological history. How have Great Basin landscape change, pupfish biology, the contingencies of probability, and human intent and ignorance interacted to carry pupfish to where they are today, living in isolation at the edge of time, surrounded by an inhospitable world of salt, sand, and rock? Although we have a good understanding of the evolutionary relationships among these species—what Darwin termed "descent with modification"—we are less clear on what the data suggest about when and how ancestors of the current pupfish species arrived in the area and the timing and routes of their dispersal and isolation. Just what is their story, which in recent years seems to have led mostly to retreat, death, and what I think of as a kind of biotic loneliness?

Our understanding of evolutionary relationships among pupfishes is based mostly upon DNA sequences, supplemented by data for thirty-two proteins. The methods used to obtain and analyze these data involve a complex stew of sophisticated biochemical techniques and arcane statistical analyses, spiced with assumptions about how to interpret molecular genetic data and determine evolutionary rates and relationships. It would require a book to describe in detail the methods used in studies of molecular evolution, or systematics. Explaining even the "Methods" section of a paper such as "The western North American pupfish clade (Cyprinodontidae: *Cyprinodon*): mitochondrial DNA divergence and drainage history," by Anthony Echelle, would require a similar treatment, but the basic approach is as follows. Begin by collecting tiny snippets of pupfish fin tissue and then release the donors to swim and spawn another day. Isolate pupfish DNA from the small set of genes in the mitochondria, which replicate independently of the cells where they reside. Mitochondrial DNA (mtDNA) has been particularly useful for evolutionary studies for two reasons. First, it is more abundant than individual nuclear genes and therefore more accessible for sequencing. Second, mtDNA has a relatively rapid mutation rate, which means that differences among lineages may accumulate quickly.

Once the mtDNA is isolated researchers use automated technology to sequence the necklace of nitrogen-containing base pairs that carry information in the gene of interest. Each of these base pairs (adenine, guanine, cytosine, and thymine) is part of a different nucleotide, four of which comprise the building blocks of mtDNA. The sequence data can then be used to construct phylogenetic trees, or evolutionary histories, using one of two basic approaches. In theory these approaches could produce different trees but in practice they typically show close agreement. The first approach assumes that evolution follows the principle of parsimony: the phylogenetic tree or hypothesis of relationships requiring the least number of mutations (substitution of one of the four nucleotides for another) is more likely to represent the "true" tree than any alternative. This fundamental scientific principle originated with the fourteenth-century English friar William of Ockham. According to "Ockham's razor" one should accept the simplest possible hypothesis unless there is compelling information to the contrary. The second approach incorporates models of nucleotide substitution (how one nucleotide replaces another in DNA sequences) and then finds the tree that maximizes the probability of fit between the dataset and the hypothesis of relationships. In considering all of this it is important to note the operative word, "hypothesis." Accumulating more data from different nucleotide sequences or a new technology may either support a working hypothesis or lead to its revision in favor of a more promising alternative.

So far, so good; this method of reconstructing evolutionary histories makes sense, even if my last course dealing with this exponentially growing discipline came in graduate school over twenty years ago. A problem with molecular methods becomes apparent, though, when we are interested in the precise timing of small-scale events—when and where species or populations diverged from one another and established separate evolutionary paths. Timing these events relies on what's known as a molecular clock, which basically is another assumption. (Any scientific analysis has its full complement of assumptions, as do basketball, economics, NASCAR, religion, political discourse, plumbing, driving, and other organized human endeavors. In the case of science a good assumption is strongly supported by data, a relationship that often does not hold for the ideological assumptions often applied to economic or political analyses.) The basic assumption of a molecular clock is that differences in the same gene among species or populations accumulate at a predictable rate over time. Count up the number of nucleotide differences in the same mtDNA sequence of two *Cyprinodon* species, apply the appropriate nucleotide substitution rate (number of substitutions per unit of time), and calculate divergence time.

Molecular clocks may sound relatively straightforward but there are many potential problems with actually applying them. These include calibrating the clock with a precisely dated fossil or geological event; differences in nucleotide substitution rates among organisms and even genes within a single species; a nonlinear relationship between substitution rate and time; hybridization events; and what's known as incomplete lineage sorting, which occurs when some forms of a particular gene in an ancestral population are not present in all of the descendant lineages. While systematists have developed methods to at least partially account for these problems molecular clocks do not work with the same implacable consistency as do atomic clocks. And so estimates of evolutionary divergence times based on molecular clocks are "squirrely" and often carry large confidence intervals—which mean that it may be impossible to completely resolve the timing and sequence of events in the evolution of closely related species.

Back to the Death Valley pupfishes. (Remember them?) A fossil pupfish from the Funeral Mountains in Death Valley National Park indicates that *Cyprinodon* was present in the region from at least the late Pliocene (3 million years ago), although the specimen's uncertain stratigraphic position might also support an earlier (late Miocene) arrival. The mtDNA data and molecular clock analyses for *Cyprinodon* suggest that the western lineage of pupfish, which extends from northern Mexico and the Rio Grande River northwest to Death Valley, diverged from other North American pupfishes 5.4 to 6.3 million years ago, give or take roughly 3 million years. The Owens pupfish, which appears to be the oldest extant species among western pupfishes, probably swam down its own evolutionary stream between 2.7 and 3.8 million years ago, give or take another 1.5 million years.

Either of these divergences, or speciation events, would have required two important things. First, an ancestral population would have had to establish itself somewhere in a drainage system of connected lakes and streams. Second, the incipient species must have become reproductively isolated from its close relatives due to a tectonic event, drying river or lake, change in drainage patterns, or a host of other causes. And here is the basic problem with figuring out the history of Death Valley pupfishes: while the *sequence* of evolutionary divergences (who is most closely related to whom) appears relatively clear cut, the genetic data on divergence times do not agree very well with the geological data. The geographically closest extant relative to the Owens pupfish is the desert pupfish, which occurs in the lower Colorado River system in California, Arizona, and Mexico. However, there are no geological data supporting a direct connection between the Owens River and Colorado River systems within the last 2 to 3 million years, although there is evidence of a connection between the Death Valley region and the Colorado River that lasted from more than 11 million years ago until its "defeat" around 6 million years ago. A further complication is that mtDNA data for springsnails of the Death Valley region, which like the pupfishes are restricted to aquatic environments, yield evolutionary histories generally consistent with a separation of Death Valley and the Colorado River during the Pliocene (5.3 to 2.6 million years ago), rather than earlier.

Whenever ancestors of the Owens pupfish reached the Owens River drainage, genetic evidence indicates it is the oldest and most divergent species in the western pupfish lineage and that its descendants have remained isolated from other pupfish populations for millions of years. Although the Owens River may have been connected with other parts of the Death Valley drainage system as recently as 70,000 years ago, pupfish are not good at swimming upstream. They usually live on valley floors and are less likely than many other fishes to disperse across mountain divides, a process known as "headwater capture." Because the probable connections between the Owens River and other parts of the Death Valley system during the Pleistocene apparently involved precipitous elevation changes, it is unlikely that other pupfish species ever managed to reach the Owens River system by ascending drainages from ancient Lake Manly in Death Valley and its major source, the Amargosa River.

Implications of the molecular data and uncertainties about changes in drainage patterns in the Owens River region have created what Anthony Echelle terms a "biogeographic enigma" involving the relationship of Owens pupfish and other *Cyprinodon* in the Colorado River system and Guzmán Basin of northern Mexico. But whatever the actual history of the Owens pupfish, the species—like the Inyo Mountains slender salamander— has persevered in an environment convulsed by intense and repeated bouts of climate and geologic change. The Owens Valley formed by downfaulting along the eastern side of the Sierra Nevada and west side of the White/ Inyo Mountains, precipitation peaked and declined numerous times, rivers and lakes repeatedly spread and retreated, and connections among drainages came and went. Some drainage systems even reversed their direction of flow: within the last 2 million years water from Mono Basin, which currently has no outlet, spilled north into the Walker Lake drainage or south into the Owens Lake drainage. And 760,000 years ago the Long Valley Caldera exploded with a cataclysmic force that must have devastated much of the nearby country. One paper on the Mono Basin/Owens River region speculates that this event was so catastrophic that "it seems unlikely that fishes [in the current Owens River system] could have survived such chaos." But somehow Owens pupfish did survive—at least until the twentieth century, when they swam headlong into *Homo sapiens* and a host of exotic species, an event that from the perspective of the pupfish rivaled the destructive impact of the Long Valley cataclysm. In place of incandescent ash and pumice, the pupfish faced an apocalypse that included the Los Angeles Aqueduct, agricultural development, largemouth bass, mosquitofish, crayfish, and cattails. By the evening of August 18, 1969, these forces had pushed the Owens pupfish into what could have been its final home: the two buckets that Phil Pister carried from Fish Slough. Forty-five years later the prognosis for the Owens pupfish is slightly more hopeful, even as its survival remains threatened by nonnative species and an inadequate water supply, and its persistence depends mostly upon the energies of a few determined biologists.

The Bishop offices of the California Department of Fish and Game are housed in an unassuming single-story, pinkish tan stucco building that resembles a recycled 1950s-era motel. I first met Steve Parmenter there on a warm day in early October of 2010. Steve came to the Owens Valley in 1988 and eventually inherited both Phil Pister's position with the Department of Fish and Game and his passion for protecting the Owens pupfish, which is listed as endangered under the California Endangered Species Act as well the federal law. Steve was about 5'11", lean, with glasses, sandy red hair, and a standard-issue field biologist's beard, flecked with gray. He exuded a quiet but intense passion for his work, and less than five minutes after meeting him I already understood that he had too much to do—always had, always will. His office was a clutter of field equipment and stacks of journal articles, while his dual computer screens symbolized what I took to be his penchant for multitasking. Our first conversation lasted for several hours, and despite the arrhythmic quality of our discussion, which was punctuated by numerous incoming calls on both his cell and office phones and passing questions from colleagues, we covered a wide range of topics centered on protecting endangered desert fish. It was an entertaining talk spiced by Steve's insistent laugh and his fondness for aphorisms, like his description of one official whom he deals with regularly: "I love him when I don't hate him," or, "I'm sure it would take more than one can of Tecate to get me to give you an incendiary quote."

What came across most in our first conversation, besides Steve's dedication to his job, was the never-ending difficulty of securing a safe future for the Owens pupfish. In the parlance of evolutionary ecology the Owens pupfish is a typical *r*-selected organism: small and short lived, devoting much of its energy to reproduction and less to long-term survival. When conditions are good the population of an *r*-selected species can increase rapidly, but when things go bad—as they generally have for the Owens pupfish during the last one hundred years—their numbers can plummet quickly. Steve and Phil Pister estimate that there are about 10,000 Owens pupfish left, where there once were hundreds of millions. And while a population of several hundred million provides a resilient surplus large enough to survive a catastrophe, 10,000 pupfish might not be sufficient to ensure their continued persistence. The world is too variable and unpredictable, too full of adversity. Environmental change roils over the Basin and Range country like frontal clouds spilling over the crest of the Sierra on a winter day, and nothing in this ecological and evolutionary world is guaranteed. Springs dry, alien predators reach a supposedly secure refuge, or cattails overwhelm good habitat. If things go bad desert fishes can disappear quickly; one small refuge population of another endangered fish, the

Owens tui chub, vanished after someone moved a hose a few inches and a fast-growing cottonwood root subsequently blocked water flowing into the pool. Only four weeks passed between Steve's visits to the refuge, but in the interim the pool dried and the chub were gone.

The surviving Owens pupfish live in five refuges scattered around Owens Valley. All are descended from the stock in Phil Pister's two buckets, but when I asked Steve about the history of these fish it became obvious that they represent a complex story. His database contained records of 32,071 pupfish handled during eighty-three separate transplants. When I thought about those repeated transplants, which also imply repeated failures, I imagined standing on a hill overlooking a huge metropolis at night, its giant basin of lights like a crowded galaxy of stars, or like the hundreds of millions of pupfish living along the Owens River, circa 1850. I pictured the lights as they began to go off—at first slowly and then, in the early twentieth century, in one rapid pulse of falling dark. Soon, only a handful of scattered lights remained. Each lonely light shimmered in that vast, eerie bowl of night for a few moments and then was gone: a flash and sudden vanishing, followed by another flash from somewhere across the darkened valley, and yet another vanishing. The dance of lights went on, populations winking on and off; the pupfish endured, but it was not an easy or certain process. As we examined the database that told how refuge populations of Owens pupfish had repeatedly revived and collapsed, and I thought about disappearing lights, Steve glanced up at me. For a moment tiredness supplanted his enthusiasm and he said, "It's like a shell game, keeping these fish going. It has taken so much work."

The existing patches of good pupfish habitat are all manmade, their residents descendants of a pupfish diaspora exiled from sloughs and marshes along the Owens River. It's instructive to think of these pupfish homes as islands-in-reverse, a tiny archipelago of dispossessed populations effectively as isolated from one another as St. Helena is from the coast of Africa. Each Owens pupfish refuge population has a life expectancy of five to ten years before it becomes, in David Quammen's words, "rare unto death." The habitat goes bad as cattails crowd out other plant species, invade open water, and provide a welcoming home for the crayfish that gobble up pupfish eggs and, sometimes, pupfish. A well-meaning public lands manager posts a "No Swimming" sign at BLM Spring and within a week some angry miscreant plants twenty-seven largemouth bass in the main pool. ("Take that, you bastard pupfish!") Steve managed to kill all of the adult bass, but not before they spawned; the following year sixty-one bass, which are to pupfish like lions are to Thompson's gazelles, consumed all of the pupfish in less than three months. After the bass were gone and a newly designed fish barrier was installed below the main pool, pupfish were reintroduced to BLM Spring and thrived once more, but another guerilla bass or two, if unnoticed for a few years, again could decimate the population. No wonder Steve stores snorkeling equipment and a spear gun in a corner of his office.

A visit with Steve to Warm Springs, about ten miles southeast of Bishop, provided a sobering illustration of the frustrating nature of Owens pupfish protection and how conservation operates in the borderlands between politics, bureaucracy, and science. The Warm Springs site consists of two spring-fed manmade pools totaling about one-half acre; the water rights and surrounding land are owned by the Los Angeles DWP and leased to a local ranching family. Warm Springs once was a pupfish refuge, but the population in the main pool has crashed three times since the fish were introduced in 1970, most recently in 2006—although until recently a small population persisted in an irrigation ditch below the pools that supply pastures east of the Owens River. The usual suspects were responsible for the disappearance of pupfish from Warm Springs: cattails, plus nonnative mosquitofish, crayfish, and bullfrogs. Although the latter species eat or compete with pupfish, Steve believes that preventing cattail establishment and invasion is the key to maintaining pupfish populations because the cattails provide critical shelter for their nemeses. What's missing from the cycle of pupfish population growth and extirpation is a disturbance event such as flooding, which once created and maintained natural habitat along the Owens River. Mechanical removal of cattails can act as an alternative to natural disturbance events, but it's a time- and labor-intensive process made more difficult by chronic funding and personnel shortages. What Steve has done is develop a management approach that produces an alternative climax plant community of native wetland plants, resistant to cattail invasion and capable of perpetuating itself on the site with minimal assistance. He has been working on this project for more than ten years—experimenting, observing, slogging through marshes, and killing cattails with his weapon of choice, a wicked-looking, curve-bladed rice knife—and his persistence, along with the help of able seasonal employees, finally paid off.

But beyond the impact of alien species lies another set of problems that has prevented Warm Springs from remaining a haven for Owens pupfish: short-sightedness, intransigence, the energy-sapping complications of state and federal environmental laws and regulations, and the conflicts inherent in dealing with a variety of stakeholders, each with their own interests and values. In the case of the Warm Springs pupfish the stakeholders include the U.S. Fish and Wildlife Service, California Department of Fish and Game, the U.S. Bureau of Land Management, Los Angeles DWP, national and local conservation groups, the leaseholder who runs cattle on land adjacent to Warm Springs and uses the spring's outflow for irrigating pastureland, and locals who in the past have used the ponds for swimming. This tangled human nexus has been almost as deadly for Warm Springs pupfish as are the largemouth bass that can undo years of patient conservation work almost as efficiently as a Coast Range wildfire, pushed downslope by autumnal Santa Ana winds, can burn through a chaparral-covered hillside or subdivision of Malibu homes.

Upper Warm Springs is a delightful place on a mild October day—a clear pool of 72°F water surrounded by concentric rings of vibrant green three-square bulrush and bright yellow rabbitbrush. Three-square bulrush is a wetland species as good for pupfish as cattails are bad, because it grows thickly and provides a steep edge to the shoreline, which robs cattails of the germination sites they need. A rustle of cottonwood leaves, the gentle murmur of water falling through a control structure into the pool below: it feels like a good place. Steve has spent a lot of time here during the past ten years, repeatedly rolling Sisyphus's stone uphill, trying to ensure that Warm Springs will become a self-perpetuating model ecosystem that supports pupfish for longer than the five-year half-life possessed by most Owens Valley refuges. But it has not been an easy process, and a less dedicated and driven man would have given up long ago. I know that I would have been emotionally pole-axed by the sheer intractability of the problem. To quote one individual who has been deeply involved with the Warm Springs pupfish issue, "I'm not much of a drinking man, but after going through all of this, I just might become one."

The first Warm Springs pond was built in 1970 by the DWP at the request of Phil Pister, who was looking to create additional pupfish refuges outside of Fish Slough. Because the transplanted pupfish originally did well in the upper pond, Pister later asked the DWP to construct a second pond immediately below the first, just above the Owens River floodplain. To do this work required permission by the leaseholders, Gary Giacomini and his father-in-law. Giacomini once told me that he and his father-in-law "naively" agreed to the second pond, with the understanding that they could continue to use the ditch draining Warm Springs. Because the ditch tended to become choked with cattails and bulrush, which interfered with water flow to his grazing land, Giacomini used a backhoe to clean it every few years, a scouring process that continued for more than ten years after construction of the lower pond. The small population of Owens pupfish in the ditch didn't seem to mind the periodic disturbance, which prevented emergent vegetation from overwhelming the habitat, and Giacomini could deliver water to his livestock: pupfish happy, cattle happy, rancher happy, biologists happy.

But suddenly, in March of 1995, no one was happy. And fifteen years later they still weren't—or if they had become at least moderately happy, they also were very tired. For many years the ditch wasn't cleaned, and so the pastures and cattle didn't get enough water. After a long decline the pupfish population in the ponds died out during the winter of 2006–7, leaving one less refuge for the fish. Although by 2010 there were plans to reintroduce pupfish to the Warm Springs ponds and Giacomini was again cleaning out his ditch, little hilarity had ensued. It had been an arduous, frustrating, and painful time, leavened with anger and mistrust. The process was one more suited to hard liquor than light beer, and Gary Giacomini told me about it one day in October of 2010.

———————

When I drive up to Giacomini's house just south of Bishop three friendly dogs greet me in the yard—a bandy-legged Corgi, a huge Pyrenees, and a standard-issue cow dog. Gary and I shake hands and he ushers me into his kitchen, where we sit and talk for three hours. He looks to be in his late forties or early fifties, of medium build, fit after years spent outside. He is soft spoken and affable, with a mild drawl and good sense of humor. He is wearing jeans and a long-sleeved western shirt, and dressed much more neatly and cleanly than I am after a month in the field. At first I am a bit nervous and absent-mindedly finger my left earlobe, from which I've removed my earring. I am hoping for an open, free-ranging conversation and do not want Gary's initial reaction to me to be based on the small piece of metal that I usually wear.

Gary was born and raised in the Central Valley of California, attended California Polytechnic State University in San Luis Obispo, then earned a master's degree from Kansas State University. He taught for six years at Fresno State University and Reedley Community College before asking himself the question: "More school and a PhD, or Bishop?" Although he liked teaching he chose Bishop, where his wife was born and raised as part of a ranching family with Owens Valley roots extending back into the 1800s. Their kids—one son and two daughters, now in their twenties—represent the sixth generation of a family that has made its living from the meadows and high desert country around Bishop.

Gary and his wife's family run 1,800 head of cattle, using summer range in the Sierra and winter pastures that include the Warm Springs area. They lease 45,000 acres from the Los Angeles DWP, plus additional land from the Bureau of Land Management and Forest Service. The DWP lease carries an annual allocation of five acre-feet of water on each irrigated acre. Like all ranchers in the region his cattle operation depends upon irrigation, and like many it has been affected by endangered aquatic species—in his case, Lahontan cutthroat trout, tui chub, and the Owens pupfish at Warm Springs. Without water from sources such as Warm Springs Gary would not have a cattle business, and without enough water in the right places the Owens pupfish would have no home. At least potentially the situation is a classic case of conflict over a limiting resource, which could be reduced to an oversimplified dichotomy: "pupfish or people?"

It does not take long to figure out that Gary's views on environmental issues are complex and not easily categorized. Some of his comments suggest that he is pretty conservative politically, and early in our conversation he describes many environmentalists as "zealots." Even though I partly agree with him (after substituting "some" for "many"), I still wonder if I am going to be subjected to an anti-environmentalist rant. And then he says that diversion of water from the Los Angeles Aqueduct for environmental purposes is "usually justified," which he follows with a comment that formal reconciliation efforts between stakeholder groups with very different views on endangered species issues can work well, even if the process is "a little huggy-huggy for me." (Note to self: DO NOT embrace Gary when I leave.)

About one hour into our conversation, Gary's father-in-law, Bud Cashbaugh, walks into the kitchen and sits down at the table. He's eighty-nine years old, short, with gnarled but still-strong hands. He's wearing a large straw cowboy hat and sunglasses and looks as though he has been marinated in the Owens Valley sun for his entire life—which he has. He's one of only a handful of Owens Valley residents who were alive when the DWP began large-scale diversion of Owens River water in the 1920s, and he lived through the tough times of the Depression, when many ranching families survived by using a barter system of agriculture. Gary introduces us and says only, "We're talking about the pupfish." Bud glances at me, pauses for a second, and gruffly says, "Don't get me started." Gary then launches into his version of the Warm Spring story, which is long and complicated. I sit back and mostly listen as Gary talks, with Bud offering up an occasional sardonic comment along the way.

When Gary's father-in-law bought the ranch in 1985 he reinstituted a system of borders and checks below Warm Spring so that he could irrigate nearby pastures. Gary and Bud agreed to Phil Pister's request for a second pond at Warm Springs because they were assured that they could use a backhoe to clean the ditch below the spring every two years, to prevent cattail and bulrush from blocking water flow to their pastures. In spite of the periodic disturbance—or more accurately, because of it—pupfish thrived in the ditch. But after Gary had given the ditch its semiannual scouring in March of 1995, he was confronted by a California Department of Fish and Game warden, who asked if Gary had been working on the ditch. When Gary admitted that he had cleaned it a few days earlier the warden replied, "I could take you to jail for that"—"that" being the supposedly unauthorized backhoe work. In the language of endangered species regulations Gary's actions amounted to "incidental take," which the California Fish and Game Code defines as "take incidental to otherwise lawful development projects," with "take" being to "hunt, pursue, catch, capture, or kill, or attempt to hunt, pursue, catch, capture, or kill" any species listed under the California Endangered Species Act. In the view of the State of California (and presumably the federal government) Gary's actions, although otherwise lawful, violated state law because they may have killed Owens pupfish—although a backhoe is a poor device for catching pupfish and Gary's work actually maintained good pupfish habitat in the ditch.

Gary smiles ruefully and continues his narrative. "From that point on I needed a permit to clean the ditch. I tried to get one from the state two years later, but the application was complicated by my lessee [from the DWP] status. Then the Army Corps of Engineers got involved because the ditch was considered a 'navigable waterway.' [*For what?* I think.] The mess dragged on for three or four years. The DWP finally got a permit to clean the ditch but the Army Corps told them that the material had to be put on the uphill side of the ditch or hauled away, because the meadow we had created was considered a wetland. I felt that dumping the fill on the uphill side of the ditch would damage the desert but I was not allowed to give anyone any input. And my poor cows just wanted a bite to eat."

Gary abandoned the ditch-cleaning process around 1998. During the following ten years he could not effectively irrigate the meadows below the ditch because the reestablished cattails and bulrushes partially blocked water flow. Around 2005 he thought about getting another permit, "but by then I'd lost the fire. Such a debacle." The regulatory situation involving the DWP, U.S. Fish and Wildlife Service, California Department of Fish and Game, and U.S. Army Corps of Engineers was just too complicated and frustrating. Meanwhile the pupfish population in Warm Spring was declining due to exotic species, cattail invasion, and neglect. Gary says, "The pupfish didn't have a chance. We protected them into oblivion."

Bud, who has been listening quietly, adds, "Them fish just needed a place to spawn."

Steve Parmenter began his active involvement with Warm Springs around 2000, after Gary had become fed up with the regulatory mess. Steve wanted the DWP to clean cattails out of the Warm Springs ponds, but the DWP said it would not do the work unless the California Department of Fish and Game did something for its lessee, Gary. And so the state issued Gary an incidental take permit allowing him to clean his ditch—once—as long as the DWP mitigated the action by cleaning the ponds, which it did at great expense.

When I hear all of this, I quietly sigh. Ecological succession and regulatory inertia being what they are, a one-time permit for the ditch was a completely inadequate solution and would only perpetuate conflict. Steve recognized this and initiated direct contact with Gary. Steve felt "guilty" because the pupfish were dying out, and the State of California and other regulatory agencies had made such a mess of the situation. At first, though, Gary was mistrustful of Steve: "I was hostile. I felt that I had gotten whacked over the head to no advantage to the species. I was so disgusted with the whole process and the total disregard for how it affected everything else, and what it did to the environment." But Steve was patient, and he and Gary eventually established a good, respectful working relationship. Steve rescued the few surviving pupfish from the ditch, and Gary was given permission to do maintenance work under the California Department of Fish and Game's existing authority. So Gary got out his backhoe and, according to Steve, "cleaned the shit out of that ditch."

By the time that I first visited Warm Springs the U.S. Fish and Wildlife Service, California Department of Fish and Game, and DWP had successfully completed a cooperative project to rebuild both dams, the lower pond, and the ditch. The Department of Fish and Game had assumed responsibility for pond maintenance and had through Steve's determined work removed the cattails and established favorable bank vegetation. Both ponds were primarily open water and, according to Steve, "at a steady state with respect to succession for the first time in their existence." Warm Springs once again was ready for pupfish, but as of late 2012 there still were none in the ditch or ponds because in 2010—for the first time ever—the DWP placed a condition upon pupfish reintroduction. The DWP wanted legal assurances that it could continue to maintain and operate its facilities at Warm Springs. Steve would like to apply for a recovery permit from the Fish and Wildlife Service allowing repeated bouts of incidental take during periodic ditch-cleaning operations, then instruct Gary, "Do what's best for you." However, it's been difficult for the State of California to "get its mind around the issue," and Steve thinks that a long-term agreement allowing ditch maintenance "will happen about the time that cold fusion happens."

What the ditch, Gary, DWP, and Owens pupfish need is a "Safe Harbor" agreement. These agreements allow nonfederal property owners to contribute to the recovery of endangered and threatened species in return for formal assurances that "if they fulfill the conditions of the Safe Harbor Agreement, the [U.S. Fish and Wildlife] Service won't require any additional or different management activities by the participants without their consent." Although the U.S. Fish and Wildlife Service sees the benefit in this approach and has prepared a draft Safe Harbor Agreement for the Warm Springs pupfish, a similar deal with the State of California also would be necessary, and there currently is no provision for such an arrangement under an antiquated state law. Basically, the Owens pupfish's status as a "fully protected" species in California currently means that only the Department of Fish and Game can undertake the "incidental take" actions needed to maintain channels for transporting water, even if the maintenance also enhances pupfish habitat. This means that if pupfish disappear from a DWP site through no fault of anyone at the agency, some of DWP's maintenance issues also disappear. As someone familiar with the issue once told me, "it's not that anyone at the DWP dances a happy little pupfish-dead-and-gone-jig, it's just that their lives suddenly become easier."

Bud gets up from the kitchen table and wanders off, and I ask Gary how he would feel if the Owens pupfish went extinct. He considers my question for a moment and then quietly responds, "On a personal basis, I wouldn't feel good. I don't want to see the pupfish go extinct because of something I did. I don't think that the economy or the landscape would be worse off, but it would not be a conscionable act to kill the pupfish. I believe this because the idea of stewardship is in the Bible, and we live that. I consider myself to be an environmentalist."

Gary and I make small talk for a little while, but I know that we've spent enough time discussing pupfish and I should go. I genuinely like the guy and believe that I could work with him on issues such as protecting the Owens pupfish, although I also suspect that there's much that we would disagree on, from religion to politics to endangered species protection and resource use. For instance, I dislike what cattle grazing has done to some rangeland in the West. Although I hope that family ranches remain viable and believe that ranching can be done in a way that is compatible with environmental protection, I also have seen public lands that have been severely "cowed" and need stronger grazing regulations. I also am a strong believer in state and federal endangered species protection and feel that the problem lies not so much in the laws and regulations themselves, but in their inflexible implementation. There is a certain type of bureaucratic intransigence that, well meaning or not, makes life more difficult for all of us, including Owens pupfish, Gary Giacomini, and Steve Parmenter. I think that the U.S. Fish and Wildlife Service has recognized the desirability of working with private landowners more cooperatively, as evidenced by "Safe Harbor" and "No Surprises" regulations, which are meant to introduce more flexibility into the process. However (at least in the case of the Owens pupfish) this desire seems more ideal than actuality; on-the-ground progress is precluded by the incompatibility of the landowners' needs with an inflexible and poorly designed state law.

I rise from the table and thank Gary for taking the time to talk with me, at length and openly. He walks me out to my car and by way of parting smiles and says, "Come back to visit us, and if you do, you can leave your earring in." I realize that he has, quietly and with good humor, pointed out my own stereotype—the intolerant and conservative rancher—which makes me feel a bit ashamed. I suggest that when I return to Owens Valley we could meet at Warm Springs, on a day when Gary is cleaning that damned ditch and the pupfish are going about their business. If so, I'll leave the earring in.

———————

Conversations with Phil Pister, Steve Parmenter, Gary Giacomini, and others involved with the Owens pupfish always mention the Los Angeles Department of Water and Power, the agency that I learned to dislike, heartily, after reading *Cadillac Desert* and seeing the highly fictionalized film *Chinatown*. Yet DWP machinery and its money helped restore the springs at Fish Slough and built the ponds at Warm Spring and other pupfish refuges, all of which are filled with water owned by the City of Los Angeles. Although the bad old days of unethical water-rights purchases and armed conflict over the LA Aqueduct are past and the Owens Valley region now delivers only 30 percent of Los Angeles's water, instead of the 75 percent that it once did, the DWP remains an active and highly visible presence in the area. The agency owns 315,000 acres in the valley, some of which it leases to Gary Giacomini and other ranchers. Every issue of the local paper, the *Inyo Register*, seems to carry at least one article on DWP activities. Visit Carl's Restaurant in Lone Pine at noon on almost any weekday and you will find a DWP crew eating lunch there. DWP trucks are everywhere in the Valley, and on the drive up U.S. Highway 395 the long concrete slash of the LA Aqueduct is a constant companion. And the lower Owens Valley is the site of two major environmental restoration efforts funded by Los Angeles, the Owens Lake Dust Mitigation Project and the Lower Owens River Project. These two court-mandated programs are the result of decades of litigation and involve more than sixty miles of the Owens River drainage and thirty square miles of Owens Lake Bed. The legal settlements reduced excessive groundwater pumping and particulate-matter pollution and will cost the City of Los Angeles well over a billion dollars.

Although the DWP was late in coming to environmental protection and seems to have done so mostly because of court mandates, it is an important and (now) mostly positive player in the conservation of Owens pupfish and other state- and federally listed threatened and endangered species. Because I wanted to get the DWP's perspective on conservation issues I met with Dave Martin, a PhD ecologist with the department's Water Resources division. Dave works in the DWP office in Bishop, which is much nicer, larger, and more modern than the California Department of Fish and Game's facilities—just one indication of the important role that the City of Los Angeles plays in the valley. Dave's main task is to supervise preparation of a seven-species habitat conservation plan to mitigate DWP-related impacts on federally listed threatened and endangered species, especially through habitat loss. Dave's team is determining points of conflict between the DWP's directive, which is to deliver water to Los Angeles, and the goal of protecting listed species, and how to best increase habitat for these species. Dave admitted that the habitat conservation plan is "not a voluntary effort" because it resulted from court decisions in the 1990s and a subsequent 1997 memorandum of understanding between the DWP, Inyo County, the California Department of Fish and Game, and three other stakeholders. Still, he believed that the U.S. Fish and Wildlife Service will be "very happy" with the final Habitat Conservation Plan. During our discussion I got the sense that it generally was easier to work with federal agencies than with the State of California, which Dave felt was less flexible and had "onerous" regulations and requirements mandated by the state's Natural Communities

Comprehensive Planning program. Like Steve Parmenter, Dave believed that California needed a Safe Harbor program similar to the one administered by the U.S. Fish and Wildlife Service.

I asked Dave if he ever felt conflict between his values and training as an ecologist and his role as a DWP employee. He replied that he had not, and that his employer is "trying to do the right thing" in terms of conserving rare species, even if much of this motivation has been generated by legal action. But the DWP continues to be viewed with great suspicion by some residents of the Owens Valley, as well as by conservation organizations and (sometimes) by the Inyo County government. One local conservationist told me that the DWP is trying to do the "minimum possible" for conservation and is at best a reluctant participant in environmental-restoration efforts. Whatever the current attitudes and actions of the DWP, its role in Owens Valley is much different now than it was several decades ago, and it can no longer act with impunity. Gary Giacomini says that the agency has "changed a lot" and that owner/leaseholder relations are now more difficult and less flexible than they were twenty-five years ago: "The DWP has been boxed into a corner, and much of what it now does is because of fear of legal action."

Ultimately, much of the environmental conflict in Owens Valley is about attitudes toward ownership of its water—not just legal ownership, but also ethical views about what constitutes "best use" of a limited resource. This point was made to me by Ceal Klingler, current president of the Owens Valley Committee (OVC), "a non-profit citizen action group dedicated to protection and sustainable management of the natural resources of the Owens Valley." The OVC is one of the stakeholders in the 1997 memorandum of understanding with the DWP, and it has been a tenacious critic of the agency's activities in the region. Ceal was trained as an ecologist and evolutionary biologist, but she gave up a prestigious National Science Foundation predoctoral fellowship to move to the Owens Valley, where her husband practices medicine. She traded a life in academia for one in a beautiful part of the world, where she spends her time engaged in natural history work, running in the High Sierra, and advocating for environmental protection. Slight and articulate, she projects an aura of thoughtfulness and enthusiasm, and a quiet but passionate intensity about the Owens Valley and its environmental issues, including water allocations. According to Ceal, "If the presumption is that that the LA DWP has the right to remove all of Owens Valley's water, then it becomes very easy to say that Los Angeles is being generous to provide almost 200,000 acre-feet of water [to the valley]. In fact, all that LA DWP is doing is allowing that portion of water to remain in the valley, whereas the valley ecosystem used much more than that before. Depending upon which way you look at it, either the LA DWP is generously allowing some water to remain on the East Side [of the Sierra], or LA DWP is driving off with the lion's share of the water and watching the valley die in its rearview mirror."

The DWP legally (if not always ethically) purchased the rights to much of its Owens Valley water early in the twentieth century, but people disagree, sometimes bitterly, over how much of that water should be sent down the LA Aqueduct. Western water laws, which are based on the doctrines of prior appropriation and "beneficial use," tend to protect the rights of purchasers such as the DWP. However, there's a tension in the legal system that is every bit as strong as the stress that episodically builds along the Lone Pine fault, because environmental laws and court decisions also mandate that ecosystems and species such as the Owens pupfish must be supplied with enough water to maintain their health. The questions then become: "What is 'enough'?" and "What is 'health'?" Should there be "enough" water simply to maintain the status quo and prevent the ecosystems and species of the Owens Valley from disappearing entirely? Or should there be "enough" water to return the same ecosystems and species to some semblance of their condition prior to 1904, when William Mulholland and Fred Eaton—head of the newly formed DWP and mayor of Los Angeles—first visited the Owens Valley, and the city began buying up the water rights of local landowners?

Of course the definition of "enough" depends on who you are: another manifestation of the "same planet, different world" phenomenon. If you are Dave Martin, "enough" might be the roughly 200,000 acre-feet of water that the DWP planned to provide for Owens Valley during the 2011–12 runoff year, which extends from April to March—more than twice the 91,000 acre-feet of groundwater that it anticipated pumping during the same period. If you are Ceal Klingler of the Owens Valley Committee, "enough" might not include all or even most of the 387,000 acre-feet of water that the DWP planned to export to Los Angeles from Inyo and Mono counties during the 2011–12 runoff year. However, it would include much of the 91,000 acre-feet removed via groundwater pumping, a value that exceeds recharge rates by about 21 percent. For Dave Martin the DWP's water export and mitigation policies represent an attempt to "do the right thing"; for Ceal Klingler the logic of the DWP's policies is a bit like saying, "We anticipate removing about four pints of your blood. That is less than the six pints of blood we are allowing you to keep in your body." Different world views, different values: Karl Marx versus Adam Smith, Thomas Hardy versus Jane Austen, Wayne Newton versus Henry Rollins, the Department of Water and Power versus the Owens Valley Committee. And value-driven disagreements about the best use of water in the arid West have a disturbing tendency to morph into questions such as, "What are you going to put first, humans or a fish? Are you picking a tiny little fish that you can't hardly see, let alone eat, over the best interests of people?" But as Ceal Klingler observes, few people ever ask, "Are you going to put golf courses, fountains, and the water amusement park first, or the quiet little endemic fish that doesn't make a profit?"

It might be easiest, and intellectually and emotionally comforting, to frame debate over Owens Valley water allocations as an "either/or" question. But the type of polarizing polemic that casts arguments in terms of "putting X or Y first" often represents a false dichotomy and overly simplified view of the world, as did George H. W. Bush's 1991 statement advocating for oil development in the Arctic National Wildlife Refuge: "I'll go with the people; let them [the 'environmentalists'] go with the caribou." What Bush Sr. (and Jr., for that matter) probably never bothered to consider were possible ways in which the interests of "the people" and the Porcupine caribou herd might be similar. Escaping from the tyranny of characterizing arguments in the simplest black-and-white terms doesn't necessarily mean compromise—*just a little bit of drilling on the Arctic Coastal Plain*— but rather a willingness to think about problems and solutions in different ways. Still, such dichotomies are powerful epigraphs, convenient symbols of our tendency to compartmentalize and caricature complex issues: either you are "pro-choice" or "against women"; "for America" or "against America"; for pupfish or for people. On and on.

After talking with Dave Martin at the DWP office I drove south toward Big Pine, then turned east on California 168 toward Deep Springs Valley. As I crossed what was left of the Owens River I thought about the complexities of water issues in the Owens Valley and how the Owens pupfish is affected by so many different human perspectives and actions. It would be wonderful if the Owens River were free flowing and much like it was 150 years ago, but barring the decline and fall of Los Angeles, that will not happen. Economics and southern California's thirst being what they are, the DWP will stay in Owens Valley and continue to send surface flow and groundwater south, as it can deliver LA Aqueduct water for about $75 per acre-foot, while Colorado River water costs between $300 and $700 per acre-foot, and desalinated seawater runs to about $1,400 per acre-foot. And although the past actions of the DWP have negatively impacted native species and habitats, its presence in the Owens Valley has had an unintended benefit because the resultant lack of water and the agency's land holdings have limited development. The Owens Valley remains mostly empty and full of open space. It could be worse, after all. Ranchers still run their cattle in riverside meadows and pastures, and the Owens River is not lined with housing developments, strip malls, golf courses, and trailer parks, all of which would have hammered Owens pupfish and other endangered species even more than the DWP's actions once did. As Phil Pister told me, "The only thing worse than the DWP in Owens Valley would be no DWP."

Beyond the Owens River, Highway 168 climbed the western slope of the Inyo-White Range toward Westgard Pass, through rabbitbrush scrub and pinyon-juniper woodland. To the west the snow-covered eastern scarp of the Sierra stood clear. So much country, and lost in all of that space a few Owens pupfish, under assault and still only hanging on, in spite of the efforts of folks like Phil Pister and Steve Parmenter. I thought of Gary Giacomini, whose "poor cows just wanted a bite to eat," of the DWP and thirsty Southern California millions, of crayfish and largemouth bass and cattails, of Warm Springs and BLM Spring, and of the Endangered Species Act and Safe Harbor agreements. I imagined the glacial waves that spilled out of the Sierra during the Pleistocene, the advance and retreat of ancient Lake Manly, the deathly rain of ash and magma that once spilled forth from the Long Valley Caldera, and considered how one small but beautiful line of life came perilously close to extinction back in 1969—those two buckets, actual and metaphorical. But mostly I thought of Steve Parmenter's work: the constant tension of living with and caring deeply about a species hovering at the edge of extinction, of 32,071 pupfish handled during eighty-three separate transplants. There were the never-ending management tasks, regulatory intransigence and political wrangling, thoughtless actions and reactions, and inadequate funding from the budget-impaired State of California, which for a while demanded that Fish and Game employees take three unpaid days off each month. Is it worth it, this constant shuffling of fish, this persistent, never-ending defensive action against cattails and crayfish, this unrelenting vigilance? Later, when I asked Steve about the value of protecting Owens pupfish he said that if the species disappeared, "It would have no possible significance, ecologically or economically, because its numbers are so low." Yet he doggedly continues his pupfish work because he "can't imagine a world without them. When a population is ailing and veers toward extinction, it's like having a very sick child. You are afraid, and you grieve, and you ask yourself, 'what more can I do?' And if a population or species does vanish, I mourn the lost potential, what was, but what will never again be."

And I thought about a day back in October of 2010, when Steve and I were driving into Bishop after visiting Warm Springs and the site at the White Mountain Research Station where a misplaced hose had led to the death of a carefully nurtured population of endangered Owens tui chub. As he talked about the small but tragic accident I realized that there was something unspoken in Steve, something connected to his work—perhaps a sense of weariness hidden beneath the surface of his determined and impassioned activity, a loneliness nurtured by the lack of sufficient resources and the frustration of dealing, often on his own, with the same issues again and again and again. But this sense of weariness came across most when I asked him if he had thought about retirement and getting out of the endangered species protection business. He glanced over at me, smiled ruefully and said, "If I left, no one would be there to pick up my work."

Early October, Mule Spring, western edge of the Inyo Mountains, seven miles southeast of Big Pine, elevation 4,078 feet. I sit at the edge of a small artificial pond of about 0.01 acre, another created Owens pupfish refuge. This one was stocked with fish in 1995, courtesy of the Bureau of Land Management, which owns the property and built the pond. There are hundreds of pupfish in all size classes patrolling the shallow pool, representing perhaps one twenty-fifth of all the Owens pupfish in the world. The pupfish dart and swarm, sticking close to the bottom, occasionally rising to the surface to feed. One takes a winged ant and several nip at a drowning bee, although none swallow it. I see no signs of mating behavior, and few pupfish show much of the deep blue color characteristic of breeding males—just a series of dark lateral bars along their flanks. After a few minutes of observation I notice a behavior that I've seen before in other pupfish populations, but only from a distance, and never so frequently—a curious "hopping" motion mostly performed over a horizontal stick, sometimes above a hummock of algae or a large rock. During this hopping, which Robert Miller and Phil Pister describe in their 1971 paper on Owens pupfish as "leapfrogging," one or more pupfish rise vertically, flip onto their side as they approach the stick from a perpendicular position, then sink to the far side of the object. I am reminded of a high jumper approaching, rising, and rolling over the bar, but in the case of the pupfish each jump is punctuated by a flash of silver as they expose their flank and belly. As many as four fish, but sometimes only one, are simultaneously hopping over a single piece of vegetation, but this behavior is going on all over the pool and so there are these bright winks of silver light sprinkled everywhere, flashing on and off against the rich green background of algae.

I focus on single fish and see that some individuals do only two or three hops before swimming off, while others take as many as thirty-two sequential leaps. Sometimes the pupfish swim beneath the stick in a circular motion before hopping again, but mostly they simply reverse course. I have no idea what the function of the behavior is. I don't think that it is related to mating because it's not the right time of the year and solitary fish often hop. Miller and Pister did not speculate as to the function of the "leapfrogging," and although I've described the behavior to a number of fish biologists I've never received a convincing explanation. Perhaps the dancing, leaping pupfish are cleaning parasites from their sides, but I cannot tell if they actually are scraping against the sticks as they cross over them.

Whatever the function of the behavior, I am fascinated and watch the pupfish hop and leap for more than an hour. At first I am aware of the soothing sound of falling water in the background, the faint scent of rabbitbrush in the air, the brush of wind against the willows, and the gray, overcast sky, but then the world beyond the pond falls away and there are only the pupfish, forty generations or more removed from Phil Pister's two buckets, carried forth into the future by their own tenacity and the perseverance of a few people. The fish dance on and on and for me there is only this pond and these fish, the entire existence and history of a species, its millions of years, narrowing to this one moment. And then I glance out across the Owens Valley, with its gray-green swatches of saltbush and shadscale scrub, past the willows and cottonwoods lining what's left of the Owens River and toward the High Sierra, already blanketed with snow in this year of early storms. I swing my gaze up valley and in the distance see two radio telescopes at Cal Tech's Owens Valley observatory pointing skyward like giant white desert primrose blossoms—sounding the heavens, testing the formation of stars and planets, scanning millions of light years of time and distance. And this juxtaposition of pupfish and planets, of the infinitely large and the minute, takes my heart and brings to mind William Blake's "Auguries of Innocence": "To see a world in a grain of sand / And a Heaven in a wild flower, / Hold Infinity in the Palm of your hand / And Eternity in an hour." I have come to this particular point in time, my gaze focused on the small particulars of existence, on a cluster of fish dancing in a tiny pond, a pond sunk deep in the sweep of the Owens Valley, but at the same time I am pulled toward the dance of solar systems and galaxies, the great vastness of time, a universe racing deeper into infinity, if such a thing can in any way be comprehended. And although it seems counterintuitive—What difference does one tiny fish species, with perhaps no more than 10,000 survivors, make when balanced against the infinite sweep of time and space?—there is something in this wonderful dichotomy of scale that makes protecting the Owens pupfish a task of upmost importance. The time and effort (so much) and money (not so much, really) are an offering of sorts, an apology, promise, and acknowledgement: all of us, fish and humans, planets and stars, are traveling on the deepest currents of time, swimming out of the past and into an uncertain future, and it is right and fitting that all should persevere. To protect these fish is an act of hope, a sacrament and celebration.

I glance back down at the pupfish, who continue their dance, leaping through the water, small points of light shining out into the early evening as darkness claims the sky.

Some Fish

THE SALT CREEK AND COTTONBALL MARSH PUPFISHES *(Cyprinodon salinus salinus and Cyprinodon salinus milleri)*

> I shivered in those solitudes
> when I heard
> the voice of
> the salt
> in the desert.
> —Pablo Neruda, "Ode to Salt"

Mid-September on the floor of Death Valley: at 200 feet below sea level the air is still, the sun ascendant. I park my car and step into a crucible of heat and light. I am dressed for the day, with a wide-brimmed hat, lightweight long-sleeved shirt, long pants, and sunglasses. I carry only a notebook, binoculars, digital thermometer, and two quarts of water. I follow the deserted boardwalk, which shimmers in the noonday heat. Salt Creek, which in winter and spring carries water, is nothing but baked gravel and sand. The blond, weathered boards wander among low hills of dun-colored eroded lake sediments through a spare and waterless pasture of salt-tolerant plants. After ten minutes of brisk walking I leave the boardwalk and track footprints and coyote scat north and west, toward McLean Spring. The ground is crusted with salt; the hills are devoid of vegetation, a bare patchwork of tiny, dendritic drainages and sensuous, rounded ridges. The day drowses. A horsefly hoping for a blood meal buzzes around my head, its attention momentarily distracting me from the heat. An emerald green damselfly clings to a saltgrass stem, as still as the air. The drainage begins to narrow. I jump a white-faced ibis, which rises with a guttural croak and flies upstream. Ever the empiricist, I stop and take an air temperature reading while shielding the probe with my body: 105°F in the shade, with a ground temperature of 133°F. My initial disdain for the heat ("It's not so bad") evaporates with the sweat that disappears from the corners of my eyes. I take a long drink from a small bottle in my field vest, but the water already has reached a temperature of 100°F and does little to slake my thirst.

Finally there are thin pools a few inches deep, lined with muck and crusted salt. Mats of brownish algae float in the slimy water. A male red-winged blackbird clucks twice and rises from the water's edge. I scan several pools, searching for motion, but see nothing. And then a sudden flurry of movement as a shiver of pupfish slips through the water. The fish are hard to see, more shadow than substance, and vanish beneath a sheet of floating scum. I squat and take a water temperature—91°F—then scoop a handful of the warm water and bring it to my mouth. I let the fetid stuff sit on my tongue for a moment, swirl it around to appreciate the delicate blend of sodium and chloride ions, silicates, and boron. The water tastes of undrinkable, salty bitterness. I spit it out and continue walking upstream, checking for pupfish, then climb a short steep slope to view the bleached, sun-struck landscape. In the foreground lies Salt Creek, a series of narrow pools ringed by scraggly garlands of pickleweed and saltgrass. Low hills of whitish gray sediment line the small drainage; beyond, the chocolate-brown slopes of the Panamint Mountains track the western edge of Death Valley. I squint into the sun, work the dusty soil with my boot, and consider that during the Pleistocene, camels and mastodons, horses and giant cats roamed this country. The great beasts must have drunk from streams and lakes filled with pupfish, but now dryness permeates the land and the waters are mostly gone, or turned to salt.

On the floor of Death Valley the desert pounds away at me. It sinks into my core and I feel intoxicated, giddy: give me this aching sun, this noonday furnace, this scorched earth. The air smells of burnt salt and drought, and the presence of fish seems like an improbable fiction. But in what's left of Salt Creek the pupfish live on, isolated from others of their kind, freshwater fish swimming through a world of heat and brine.

It is a wonder that they are here.

———————

The first specimens of what eventually would be identified as Salt Creek pupfish were collected in April of 1917 by Joseph Grinnell, the founder of the Museum of Vertebrate Zoology at the University of California at Berkeley.

In 1943 Robert Miller described *Cyprinodon salinus* as a new species, based on its distinctive morphological traits, including a very slender body, small scales, a dorsal fin situated closer the tail than in most pupfish, and a prominent ridge on the outer face of the tricuspid teeth. Miller wrote that "nearly the entire fish population" occurred along a two-mile-long section of Salt Creek. The small stream runs southeast from its source at McLean Spring before disappearing in the desiccated wastes leading toward Badwater, thirty miles to the south, although Salt Creek's above-ground flow varies during the year. In the winter and spring reduced evaporation and transpiration (water lost from plant tissues) allows free-flowing water to reach the gap where the drainage slices through low hills and finds the open alluvial slopes north and east of Cottonball Marsh. In the summer, though, Salt Creek retreats toward McLean Spring; the pupfish either follow the water or die. Miller believed that the Salt Creek pupfish was an extreme and distinctive isolate, and that the nearest pupfish population in the Death Valley area, identified as Amargosa pupfish, *Cyprinodon nevadensis*, lay about seventy-five miles to the south along the lower Amargosa River. In between Salt Creek and the lower Amargosa River was the wasteland at Badwater, a killing ground of salt and heat, seemingly impossible for fish to survive in.

When I park at the start of the Salt Creek interpretive trail on a mild March day and stroll a few yards up the boardwalk, I find free-flowing water, alive with pupfish. In choice spots along the periphery of the creek territorial males guard their mating spaces and try to court receptive females, while large schools of pupfish patrol slightly deeper waters in midstream. Here, among the braided channels of fine sand and gravel, conditions for the pupfish seem almost benign: the glint of sunlight on the clear water, mild temperatures, a chaotic swirl of mating fish. Still, a taste of Salt Creek reminds me how the stream got its name, as the salinity is about 50 percent that of seawater, depending upon temperature and flow—nearly 17 parts per thousand of total dissolved solids. And I know, too, that the assault of summer will come. Then the channel before me will become a pupfish graveyard as the waters vanish and Salt Creek withdraws toward McLean Spring. Summer salinities in some parts of the stream may exceed twice that of seawater, and it is remarkable that a freshwater fish could survive in such a hostile brew.

Yet the loveliness of the spring day is seductive, and in spite of Salt Creek's very position in the world—sunk so deeply in Death Valley's arid expanse—it is possible to accept the presence of pupfish in this place. But if I follow Salt Creek a few hundred yards downstream, to the point where the waters emerge from the shallow gorge cutting through the Salt Creek Hills and vanish into alluvial sediments, it is easy to understand why Miller believed that the Salt Creek pupfish were so isolated from other pupfish. The view south, into the heart of Death Valley, incorporates nothing but a wasteland of bare rock and sand. It is the worst (or the best?) that the desert has to offer, and there is absolutely nothing in the prospect that hints of fish. And yet. About six miles away, in the heart of the salt pan, lives another subspecies of pupfish, *Cyprinodon salinus milleri*, the Cottonball Marsh pupfish. Cottonball Marsh is a glaring world of salt-crusted ground and hypersaline water with up to two and one-half times as much salt as seawater. Air temperatures during the summer often surpass 120°F, and the biologists who first described the Cottonball Marsh pupfish characterized its environment as perhaps "the most extreme fish habitat in North America in terms of temperature and salinity." If the existence of the Salt Creek pupfish seems improbable, then that of the Cottonball Marsh pupfish is ludicrous. No fish should, under any circumstance, live in Cottonball Marsh. And yet they do.

The three species of pupfishes occurring in the present-day Amargosa River Basin form what systematists term a monophyletic group, representing all lineages descending from a common ancestor. The phylogenetic tree depicting evolutionary relationships among the Salt Creek/Cottonball Marsh pupfish, ten populations of the Amargosa pupfish, and the Devils Hole pupfish shows a clear and tightly clustered series of nodes, representing events that divided lineages and propelled them down their separate evolutionary pathways. Although we have a pretty clear idea of the general sequence of steps leading to the current distribution of the three Amargosa River Basin pupfish, it is unclear whether the closest relative of these species is the Owens pupfish or *Cyprinodon fontinalis* from the Guzmán Basin of northern Mexico.

A synthesis of studies suggests two separate pupfish invasions of the Owens Valley/Amargosa River region. An initial invasion, probably from the Colorado River, was followed by geologic events that fragmented the population into two segments, one that evolved into *C. radiosus* in Owens Valley and another that occupied the Amargosa River Basin. This scenario is supported by a 1993 study on allozymes, variants of proteins produced by a single nuclear gene. Their distribution in pupfish populations suggests that the Owens pupfish is the closest relative of the Amargosa Basin pupfish. Analysis of mtDNA sequences, however, indicates that *C. fontinalis* is the closest relative. There are various ways to reconcile these conflicting results, but the more plausible hypothesis seems to be that the initial pupfish occupation of the Amargosa River Basin preceded invasion by a more distant relative carrying the mtDNA of *C. fontinalis*. This led to hybridization and eventual replacement of the original Amargosa River Basin mtDNA by that of the *C. fontinalis*-like pupfish. Such replacements following hybridization seem to have occurred repeatedly in the evolution of pupfishes, as well as in other groups of fishes.

As with the evolutionary history of the Owens pupfish, conflicts between molecular clock and geological data make it difficult to determine when the Amargosa River Basin pupfish lineages split. The molecular data suggest that the Salt Creek pupfish diverged about 1 million years ago, followed by a split between the Devils Hole and Amargosa pupfish some 500,000 years ago. However, dating of lakeshore features, and muds and salts found in a core sample taken from a hole 600 feet deep in Badwater Basin, indicate that potential connections between pupfish species in the Amargosa Basin were not completely severed until Lake Manly entered its final stage of retreat 10,000 years ago. Lake Manly reached its maximum extent between 180,000 and 128,000 years ago, when conditions were wetter and April-May temperatures were 18 to 27°F cooler than today. During this period the ancient Owens River probably flowed through Searles and Panamint Lakes into Death Valley. Between 170,000 and 150,000 years ago the Amargosa River, which previously had terminated in ancient Lake Tecopa, breached the lower end of the lake and also flowed into Lake Manly. It's difficult to believe from a contemporary view—say from the alluvial fans spilling out of the Funeral Mountains a few miles east of Salt Creek—that the combined flow of the two rivers created a freshwater lake up to one thousand feet deep and one hundred miles long, extending from north of present-day Salt Creek to the lower end of Death Valley. Pupfish, perhaps descended from Owens River pupfish, must have swarmed through the shallower parts of giant Lake Manly, forming a random breeding population. Although it probably was impossible for pupfish to migrate up the precipitous route leading west to the Owens River, they could have dispersed freely throughout much of the Amargosa River Basin, from Salt Creek to Ash Meadows.

Lake Manly disappeared around 120,000 years ago, as drier (but generally still cool) conditions prevailed. This temporarily would have isolated some Death Valley pupfish populations, although they again could have dispersed and intermixed between 35,000 and 10,000 years ago, when Lake Manly reappeared. During this more recent period of cold, wet conditions, the lake was up to 300 feet deep, with salt concentrations about one-tenth or less that of seawater. Lake Manly disappeared again about 10,000 years ago, at the end of the Wisconsin glaciations, as the climate warmed and dried. Mudflat or saline-pan environments similar to those of present-day Death Valley persisted, although pollen diagrams, carbon-14 dating, and marsh and dune stratigraphy suggest that shallow aquatic habitats on the floor of Death Valley again may have been connected about 3,600 and 300–400 years ago.

It is likely, then, that the ancestors of *Cyprinodon salinus* retreated into Salt Creek within the last 10,000 years, as the waters of Lake Manly disappeared, although the Cottonball Marsh and Salt Creek subspecies may have been connected as recently as 300 years ago. Rare spring floods in Salt Creek, such as one in 1969, may also facilitate gene flow by washing pupfish southward into temporary pools that connect to Cottonball Marsh. Whatever the connection between Salt Creek and Cottonball Marsh, individuals from these two populations show a complete lack of mtDNA variation. This suggests that the population underwent one or more historical bottlenecks, in which numbers were drastically reduced and much of the ancestral population's genetic variation was lost. Such an event could have occurred during the mid-Holocene drought, from 7,500 to 4,500 years ago. Given the lack of mtDNA variation in *Cyprinodon salinus*, and the small amount of time since separation of the Salt Creek and Cottonball Marsh subspecies, it is remarkable that there are persistent heritable differences in their morphology. James LaBounty and James Deacon, who in 1972 described the Cottonball Marsh pupfish as a separate species, *Cyprinodon milleri*—later downgraded to subspecies status because of its genetic and morphological similarities to Salt Creek fish—noted many differences between the two populations. Subsequent research also suggests that Cottonball Marsh pupfish have evolved the ability to tolerate even higher salt concentrations than Salt Creek pupfish. These recently derived, genetically influenced traits point to another impressive feature of pupfish— their ability to evolve very rapidly. In New Mexico, genetically controlled morphological, and perhaps behavioral, differences occur in wild pupfish populations isolated for only thirty years, while Amargosa pupfish from populations separated for as little as 400 years show genetically mediated differences in aggression and neural pathways in the brain.

In trying to understand what molecular data suggest about the evolutionary history of the Death Valley pupfish, I am reminded of the King

James version of 1 Corinthians 13: "for now we see through a glass, darkly." Although there are several plausible hypotheses about divergence times and the most recent common ancestor of the Death Valley pupfish lineage, at present we do not have enough information to determine which is correct. Some scenarios appear more plausible than others, but our view through history's glass remains partially obscured; there are too many bubbles and striations, too much discoloration. This is both the beauty and frustration of science. Even though we know much more about pupfish evolution than we did forty or fifty years ago, our knowledge remains imperfect. But I have faith; the winnowing effect of persistent research will smooth and polish history's glass, remove its worst imperfections. In one decade, or perhaps ten, we shall tell a more complete and accurate story about the history of the Death Valley pupfishes. In the meantime we are left knowing that the Cottonball Marsh and Salt Creek pupfish share a remarkable ability to withstand conditions that would kill most fish, and that they are mostly alone in the world. During the summer Salt Creek pupfish occur only in the permanent flow of Salt Creek, which is about one mile long, while the Cottonball Marsh pupfish is limited to a sparsely distributed set of pools and springbrooks scattered through an area roughly one mile long by 300 yards wide. In both places it is clear that these little fish are held to the fundamental truths of heat and salt and isolation.

Even in mid-March the light on the Death Valley salt pan is blinding. Steve Parmenter, my friend Ralph Black, and I are plodding south from Salt Creek toward Cottonball Marsh, each of us with a full pack holding two gallons of water. We begin our walk by cutting through the Salt Creek Hills, then head southeast, directly toward a shimmer of water in the midst of the playa. At first we walk through an area with scattered shrubs, across soft ground covered with a thin crust of salt—just firm enough to support our weight for a moment before collapsing. Beyond this we leave the vegetation behind, and our route takes us into terrain latticed with an intricate network of brine-filled channels. It is difficult to stick to a bearing and after an hour of hot, tedious wandering, during which the glistening illusion of water seems to grow no closer, we turn southwest toward Salt Springs and our planned campsite at the base of an alluvial fan spilling from the massive bulk of Tucki Mountain.

We slog through a chaotic wasteland of slabs, cups, and pustules of gypsum and sodium sulfate salt. The slabs are as much as eighteen inches high, off-white and marbled with gray-brown soil, rough-edged, with the tensile strength of low-fired clay pottery. They are tilted at crazy angles and arranged in irregular rows separated by shallow troughs. The pustules, for which Cottonball Marsh was named, are six to twelve inches across and look a bit like cauliflower heads or those marshmallow-covered Hostess "snowball" cakes that I loved when I was a kid. When I examine one I find that they are about one-quarter to one-half inch thick, partially hollow, and filled with a latticework of salt crystals. There are patterns to the salt formations but they are mostly small-scale, while the larger landscape is a muddled confusion of form and texture. Walking through this harsh, salt-plagued terrain is hard on my feet and ankles and harder on my mind: all herky-jerky motion, up and down over slabs and into troughs, the ground sometimes very hard and tearing at my boots, at other times soft enough to *almost* hold my weight before it gives way. I feel as though I'm trudging through jumbled piles of shattered roofing tiles. It is impossible to find any rhythm. The walk bears more resemblance to an atonal stumble than a melodic stride, its soundtrack more John Cage than J. S. Bach. The gathering frustration of the hike pushes me deeper into myself. I grow quiet and veer away from Ralph and Steve. As much as I want to see Cottonball Marsh pupfish, at the moment there is only the shattered ground at my feet and this aggravating walk. I sink into my silence, cultivate an irrational anger consistent with the texture of this saline landscape, and think only of the immediate goal: firmer ground beyond the salt, and a flat place to rest and lay my sleeping bag.

Ninety minutes later we've found a camp south of Salt Springs, sorted out sleeping sites among the desert holly and alluvial debris, and downed some water and food. Steve, a gracious companion, surprises Ralph and me with a six-pack of cold beer, a perfect antidote to the weariness induced by our slog. The afternoon breeze dies away and the scent of brine drifts up from the salt pan. A lone black-throated sparrow sings, then quiets. The evening falls toward night, and across the valley the desiccated peaks of the Funeral Mountains slip into darkness. The lights of Furnace Creek come on, and even though the park offices, campgrounds, inns, golf course, curio-plagued shops, RVs, and tourists are only seven miles away, our little camp feels almost as isolated as any I've ever had in the lower forty-eight states. There is something about the nature of this place—at the edge of Death Valley's salt pan, hundreds of feet below the surface of Pleistocene Lake Manly—that creates a profound sense of solitude. The salt and its very hostility to most life has imbued the land with an extraordinary distance and depth, which transcends even the massive physical scale of the Basin and Range country. It's what a biologist who once spent ten consecutive days at Cottonball Marsh understood when he told me, "The place lays your soul bare."

In the morning we head east for a mile toward the heart of Cottonball Marsh, tracking a shallow meandering stream that forms a series of connected pools only an inch or two deep. The mineral deposits along the margins of the stream are smooth and almost as hard as cement, and the walking is easy. The scattered stands of pickleweed and saltgrass growing near the alluvial fan fall away and soon there is only salt and brine, and the brilliant gesso ground. Given the textbook definition of a marsh, "an emergent wetland dominated by herbaceous, non-woody vegetation," the "Marsh" in Cottonball seems like a surreal joke. In this postapocalyptic landscape no life should endure—not "herbaceous, non-woody vegetation," and certainly not fish. Yet we find spiders beneath hemispheres of salt, a shorebird nest with three speckled eggs, tiny snails at the water's edge, and then, in a set of small pools impounded by mineral terraces, the Cottonball Marsh pupfish, *Cyprinodon salinus milleri*. And even though I have read the scientific papers and talked to biologists who have studied Cottonball Marsh pupfish, I feel a visceral jolt when I first see them, and a small stab of joy. Their presence here, in this aquatic habitat unlike almost any other in North America, is bizarre, unexpected, and beautiful.

We leave our packs on a mound of upthrust salt near an expanse of shallow water that glistens in the blinding light and spend the next several hours watching the pupfish. They are swimming in pools about three to six inches deep, which are filled with grayish green algae; some fish are solitary, others cluster in small schools. Many pluck away at the algae, while a few try to ascend a small race of water about one inch high, like miniature salmon climbing a fish ladder. The tiny stream falls from a terraced pool, and the fish struggle repeatedly with the current before they reach their goal, a visible reminder that pupfish are not good at swimming upstream. Most of the fish look to be less than one and one-half inches long and have the vertical bars characteristic of Death Valley pupfish, which extend down their sides from their backs to their belly. It's too early in the year for the males to have their bright blue nuptial colors, and they look pale and washed out, as if the salt has leached the color from their scales.

I take off my boots and wade into the water. Below the algal mat is a salt shelf—hard, but not strong enough to support my weight. My legs break through the crust, scrape against the jagged edges, and sink into fine black muck, which stinks of sulfur. I reach down, take some water into my palm, and bring it to my lips. It is unbelievably bitter, even more so than the Salt

Creek water I'd tasted in September. It tastes of death, even as pupfish swim around my calves, presumably content in their pupfish kind of way. Once, when Phil Pister and I were talking about Cottonball Marsh pupfish he commented that "most fish would be more at home in battery acid." Phil has a gift for hyperbole, but out on the salt pan his picturesque description seems apt. Just what are the Cottonball Marsh pupfish about? What is their story and what are they doing *here*? What would their world be like on a summer day, when air temperatures break 120°F and salinities in some of these pools are more than twice that of seawater?

I think about the hostility of this place then segue to Robert Miller, who spent his career studying desert fishes and advocating for their conservation. When Miller wrote his classic 1948 monograph, *The Cyprinodont Fishes of the Death Valley System of Eastern California and Southwestern Nevada*, he was unaware of the existence of the Cottonball Marsh pupfish, although he had studied Salt Creek pupfish. The first mention of Cottonball Marsh pupfish in the scientific literature that I have found came in 1966, in a monograph on the Death Valley hydrological basin: "Perennial pools of water in Cottonball Marsh contain a considerable population of desert fish of the same species . . . that are found in . . . Salt Creek." Charles Hunt, the primary author of the report, must have stumbled across the pupfish between 1955 and 1957, when he did much of his fieldwork on the salt pan. Had Hunt heard about the existence of pupfish at Cottonball Marsh prior to his fieldwork? Did he communicate with Miller, and did Miller ever visit the site? And what would Miller have thought if he could have stood where I was and seen pupfish in such an otherworldly place?

As I focus on the water at my feet and consider the pupfish and their pools, and Robert Miller's passion for desert fish, the rest of Death Valley disappears—the sunlight and gathering heat, the scabrous surface of the salt pan, a small and solitary mound of pickleweed in the middle distance, the rough bounds of the Funeral Mountains to the east and Panamint Mountains to the west. I squiggle my toes in the rich muck, feel pupfish bump against my calves, and watch as they swim in and out of the algae, inches from the thick crust of salt lining the pool where I stand. I wonder if it's appropriate to use the word "magnificent" when describing a creature little more than one inch long, but that's one adjective that comes to mind, along with "bizarre" and "incredible." But then sudden a noise makes me glance up. When I do, I am seized with a short snap of vertigo as my sensory world suddenly expands and rushes out into the distance: these pupfish, swallowed by so much salty space, pushed into Cottonball Marsh by the vagaries of time and time's contingencies, such aloneness in a place not meant for fish.

———————

To comprehend one fundamental environmental problem confronted by Salt Creek and Cottonball Marsh pupfish, mix up a solution as saline as seawater by dissolving thirty-five grams (roughly 1.5 tablespoons) of table salt in a liter of warm tap water. Take a small mouthful—you don't need much—and taste the awful saltiness. Swirl it around on your tongue for a few seconds and imagine that you have nothing else to drink. Dehydration would kill you quickly, although the Salt Creek and Cottonball Marsh pupfish continuously consume a similar solution without much stress. Now, double the amount of salt in the solution, to three tablespoons per liter. Take another sip, trying not to gag, and consider that Salt Creek and Cottonball Marsh pupfish regularly tolerate such wretched water, even though they carry the genetic heritage of freshwater fish. But what's even more impressive is that the same fish, if acclimated, can live quite nicely in fresh water; they are a perfect example of what environmental physiologists term a euryhaline species. Like salmon or eels, *Cyprinodon salinus* can osmoregulate, or maintain the composition of its body fluids, in a wide range of salinities. And, as is true with other aspects of pupfish biology, understanding their physiological capabilities also means understanding something of the evolutionary history of the genus.

Mitochondrial DNA evidence suggests that *Cyprinodon* arose in the Late Miocene, 7–9 million years ago, on the Mesa del Norte of Mexico, south of the Rio Grande. From their center of origin ancestral pupfish spread into western North America, southern Mexico, and the Gulf Coast/Atlantic Coast region. Coastal pupfish inhabit estuaries that experience a wide range of environmental conditions, including large fluctuations in salinity. The sheepshead minnow, *Cyprinodon variegatus*, which lives along the Atlantic Coast as far north as Massachusetts, has been called the "toughest fish in North America" because it tolerates salinities ranging from fresh water to 142 parts per thousand (four times that of seawater), adjusts to temperatures from just above freezing to 111°F, and survives in oxygen-poor environments. Other genera in the killifish family Cyprinodontidae, which includes *Cyprinodon*, even those typically inhabiting fresh water, also can adjust to a wide range of salinities. Thus the evolutionary heritage of *Cyprinodon* has imbued the genus with a physiological hardiness enabling it to inhabit severe and variable environments, from estuaries and saltwater marshes to desert salt pans. This legacy allowed ancestors of the Cottonball Marsh and Salt Creek pupfish to survive periodic bouts of drying and warming during the last several million years—most recently less than 10,000 years ago. As the Pleistocene glaciers completed their final retreat and the heat grew and Lake Manly evaporated, Death Valley's pupfish would have found themselves swimming through waters that were blossoming into brine.

Mammals maintain water balance primarily by means of their kidneys. Through filtration and reabsorption mammalian kidneys produce hypertonic urine, which has less water and higher concentrations of solutes (salts and the byproducts of protein metabolism, primarily urea) than in blood plasma. Maximal urine concentration in mammals varies with habitat. Beavers, which never have to worry about water loss, can only produce urine with a urine-to-plasma concentration ratio of 2:1, while several species of desert-dwelling Australian hopping mice can concentrate their urine at an amazing 25:1 ratio. Humans fare poorly in the urine-concentrating game, as their kidneys can only manage a 4:1 urine-to-plasma ratio—one reason among many why free-ranging hopping mice never drink water, while a free-ranging biologist trudging around Cottonball Marsh on a warm March day requires at least one gallon of liquids per day to stay hydrated. The extraordinary urine-concentrating ability of some desert rodents also means that they can survive by drinking water with the same solute concentration as seawater, while a biologist forced to do the same thing would suffer a net loss of one-third liter of water for every liter of seawater he consumed. His death would follow quickly.

Although mammal and bird kidneys produce hypertonic urine, those of other vertebrates, including fishes, cannot. From a pupfish's perspective this is not a problem in fresh water, as excess water flows into its plasma, where it is at a lower concentration than in the environment. But because the concentration of solutes is about 15 parts per thousand in pupfish plasma and close to zero in the surrounding water, a freshwater fish must hang on to ions such as sodium and chloride, which tend to flow out of the body. So instead of conserving water and expelling salts, as does a desert mammal, a freshwater fish flushes excess fluids and the toxic products of protein metabolism from its system, and concentrates salts. It does this by producing dilute, or hypotonic, urine, while its gills use energy to take up the extra salts needed to counter passive outflow. No worries, then, for a fish in freshwater, but what about one living in the ocean or Cottonball Marsh, which must fight the ineluctable loss of water and influx of salt?

Fish are constrained by their evolutionary history, and none has a kidney than can concentrate urine. Instead, their gills function as salt-secreting organs. Salt Creek and Cottonball Marsh pupfish drink salt water because they must, then use energy to pump excess salt from specialized chloride cells in their gills.

Pupfish survive high salinities by tolerating increased solute concentrations in their blood and increasing metabolic rates to facilitate salt excretion by their gills. In one experiment Cottonball Marsh pupfish collected in water with a salinity of about 60 percent that of seawater and maintained at 77°F could tolerate salinities as high as twice that of seawater, while some survived in water three times as salty as the ocean. Pupfish surviving in the most extreme salinities tolerated a 67 percent increase in plasma solute concentration over values maintained in fresh water. In comparison, consider that humans can tolerate increases in plasma solute concentration of only 3 percent before suffering headaches, reduced alertness, and difficulties in concentrating, while an increase of around 26 percent causes death. Apparently, increased water temperatures help pupfish adjust to higher salinities. Experimental Salt Creek pupfish survived nicely in water with one-half as much salt as seawater—about the concentration in Salt Creek during the spring—at acclimation temperatures from 59 to 86°F, and did so without increasing their plasma solute concentration. However, pupfish survived salinities 1.5 times greater than seawater only at 86°F, because regulating plasma solute concentrations at high salinities evidently requires a faster metabolic rate, which pupfish can maintain only at high water temperatures.

The experimental responses of Cottonball Marsh and Salt Creek pupfish to changes in salinity and water temperature relate nicely to seasonal fluctuations in their environment. Salinities and water temperatures are lowest from the late fall through the early winter, when air temperatures are cooler and there is more surface water. Salinity values at Salt Creek during this time of the year typically are around half that of seawater, while those in Cottonball Marsh are roughly equal to seawater. As surface flow decreases during the hottest months, salinities and water temperatures rise. A comprehensive study by Don Sada and Jim Deacon found Cottonball Marsh pupfish present in sites with summer water temperatures of 100°F and salinities of up to about 1.3 times that of seawater; corresponding values at Salt Creek were 85°F, with salinities twice that of seawater.

Pupfish show a remarkable ability to acclimate to high salinities, but they also are among the most heat-tolerant of all fish. In the wild, some pupfish tolerate water temperatures up to about 107°F, in contrast to salmon from cool Pacific Northwest waters, which may have upper lethal temperatures of only 70°F. Experimental laboratory studies that acclimated Cottonball Marsh pupfish to warm water demonstrated that they can survive temperatures of 110°F, while desert pupfish tolerate water temperatures of 112°F. Pupfish also can survive water temperatures as low as 35°F and adjust well to the large daily and seasonal fluctuations in their thermal environment characteristic of habitats along the Amargosa River and Salt Creek. The ability to tolerate high water temperatures and a broad range of thermal conditions is characteristic of all pupfish life-history stages, from eggs to juveniles and adults. Experimental studies and field observations suggest that juvenile pupfish can even tolerate water several degrees warmer than adults, which may allow them to exploit shallow-water environments with fewer predators and more food due to reduced competition from other fish.

In addition to temperature acclimation, pupfish employ a sophisticated set of behaviors to control their body temperature and take maximum advantage of their thermal environment. An example of this precise regulation occurs in Amargosa pupfish living in Tecopa Bore, a small artesian spring near the Amargosa River. Water issues from the ground at 117°F, too hot for even the toughest pupfish, but rapidly cools to 96°F in the small stream below the springhead. Pupfish reach their maximum density between 90 and 97°F, but may follow the 107°F isotherm along the stream edges, while only inches away is water beyond their upper thermal tolerance. Pupfish living in shallow pools and marshes also show consistent daily movement patterns in response to changes in their thermal environment. They may spend the night in cool, shallow water, perhaps as a way to save energy by reducing their metabolic rate. At dawn they move to deeper, warmer water, before transitioning to shallower water that has warmed to their preferred temperature. If the shallow water becomes too warm, the pupfish retreat to deeper water, but return to shallower water when it cools to an optimum temperature. Finally, as the water continues to cool, the fish sink to the bottom of the shallow pools, where they spend the remainder of the night.

Although pupfish from all Death Valley populations acclimate to a wide range of water temperatures—even those living in a constant thermal environment such as Devils Hole or Saratoga Spring—experiments show that adaptive change has occurred in response to local thermal conditions. The thermal tolerances of Amargosa pupfish were compared for populations from Big Spring at Ash Meadows (constant water temperature of 81°F) and the Amargosa River (fluctuating seasonal thermal environment, from near 33 to 104°F) about forty miles to the south. Researchers hatched fertilized eggs from the two populations in the laboratory and raised them under identical conditions, removing any possible differences due to development in different environments. Fish from the Amargosa River population displayed small but consistently greater tolerances to hot and cold conditions than the Big Spring fish, demonstrating genetic divergence in populations that have been isolated for only 400 to 4,000 years.

Organisms are very sensitive to their thermal environments because high body temperatures cause shape changes in proteins such as enzymes, which are necessary for proper body function. Enzymes work only if their complex configuration precisely matches that of their target, or substrate. A classic demonstration of how shape change, or denaturing, affects a protein occurs when egg whites are cooked, which turns the albumen from liquid and translucent to solid and white. Protein denaturing is why a rise in body temperature of only a few degrees above normal can be life threatening. And given the temperature sensitivity of many organisms, populations should display genetically mediated adaptations that allow them to deal effectively with the thermal conditions they normally encounter. Differences in thermal tolerance among pupfish populations of the same species, or among any group of species, may be due to a number of physiological and biochemical factors, including heat shock proteins. Heat shock proteins serve as "molecular chaperones" and help prevent various types of stress, such as high temperatures, toxins, low oxygen levels, and strenuous exercise, from negatively affecting protein structure and function. Although the specific relationship between heat shock proteins and thermal tolerance has not been studied in pupfish, Amargosa pupfish do produce them in response to stress. However, the adaptive—read evolutionary—basis of population-level differences in heat shock proteins has been studied in a related species, the common killifish (*Fundulus heteroclitus*), which occurs along the Atlantic coast of North America. In this species, the abundance of several heat shock proteins is correlated with differences in the thermal tolerance of northern and southern populations. Fish from these populations also show a small but consistent differences in the amino acid sequence of one heat shock protein known to affect their thermal tolerance. In another genus of distantly related desert fish, the topminnows (*Poeciliopsis*), the thermal tolerance of Mexican desert species and populations is related to the abundance of particular heat shock proteins and the water temperatures at which they were produced. Interestingly, high levels of heat shock proteins are found in the gills of some euryhaline fish, suggesting that they may also facilitate the remarkable ability of Salt Creek and Cottonball Marsh pupfish to tolerate wide fluctuations in salinity.

––––––––––

It is another warm spring day in Death Valley and I am back at Salt Creek. I park my car and walk up the boardwalk, which teems with people, while the temporarily watered channel along the boardwalk teems with pupfish. But instead of continuing toward the source of Salt Creek I reverse direction, ford the stream's braided channel, and walk south across an alluvial plain dotted with a wash of scraggly creosote bushes, their leaves curled and branches stripped of flowers in this year of drought. Beyond the plain I climb into the Salt Creek Hills, up a series of rounded slopes devoid of vegetation, the ground a stone-and-sand mosaic whose texture reminds me of photographs of the Martian landscape taken by the Mars Rover. From a high point on the ridge 200 feet above the valley floor I can look back toward Salt Creek, which runs southeast from McLean Spring, its course bounded by hills to the east, brown and chalky yellow. Directly to the north is a series of deeply eroded gullies cutting through sediments fading from gold to yellow, blonde, and sand. To the south lies the heart of Death Valley, the salt pan a dirty white, the sky thick with a haze of dust and heat. I scan this arid garden through my binoculars and catch what I take to be a thin seam of water in Cottonball Marsh, which glistens faintly in the afternoon sun.

I take a map from my pack and mark my position and the range of *Cyprinodon salinus*, with its two isolated populations. The nearest Amargosa pupfish population lies forty miles to the south: closer than Robert Miller once thought, but still a world of salt and brine away. Beyond this it's almost thirty-five miles to Saratoga Springs and the next pupfish population. *Cyprinodon salinus* is so very alone in the world. One of its subspecies is restricted to a thin bead of water a few miles long in the best of seasons, the other exiled to a universe of less than one-half square mile. But measurements—"a few miles long," "one-half square mile," "forty miles to the south"—do not adequately describe the isolation of *Cyprinodon salinus*. To grasp this solitude it is necessary to sit on a ridge above Salt Creek and look down the long, broad spread of Death Valley, the bounding march of the Panamint and Amargosa ranges plundering the miles, and consider what it means to be so lost in the great sprawl of the Basin and Range country, to have swam into such an aching solitude, the years and sand and salt and vast distance spiraling away from your only home, like the land itself. As with the Inyo Mountains slender salamander, these small fish have retreated into an evolutionary cul-de-sac. As wonderfully adapted as the Salt Creek and Cottonball Marsh pupfish are, if the waters ever fail—if the Great Basin descends into a drought worse than that of the mid-Holocene or groundwater pumping dries the feeder springs supplying Salt Creek and Cottonball Marsh—they will have nowhere else to go. In such a case, and if we care enough, we could rescue the survivors and maintain them as pets in artificial refuges, but they would be done for in the wild.

For now though, the pupfish are safe, protected by the National Park Service and the isolation and harshness of their environment. Unlike the Owens pupfish, there are no exotic species to harry *Cyprinodon salinus* toward extinction. There are no crayfish, bass, sunfish, mosquitofish, or bullfrogs to compete for food or gobble pupfish and their eggs. There are no invasive plants pushing against what remains of pupfish habitat, providing refuges for predators or simply overwhelming the waters. Even nonnative tamarisk, the scourge of so many riparian ecosystems in the arid West, is absent from Salt Creek and Cottonball Marsh. Although tamarisk trees shade the resort and campgrounds at Furnace Creek, just a few miles to the south, they cannot survive the rigors of the environment where the pupfish live. Salt Creek and Cottonball Marsh remain essentially pristine, undisturbed by the multitude of factors that have affected almost every aquatic habitat in the conterminous Unites States.

However, there are thirsty humans and the thirsty plants valued by humans. Because the water that feeds Salt Creek most likely originates in places protected by the National Park Service (the Panamint Range and Last Chance Range to the northwest) or in basins to the north without current plans for large-scale groundwater development, Salt Creek and its pupfish probably are safe for now. Still, Las Vegas hopes to begin mining underground reservoirs in northern and central Nevada around 2020. And although the National Park Service certainly has sufficient concern for the safety of the pupfish and controls groundwater originating in the Panamints and Last Chance Range, it does not have as much say about what transpires elsewhere in the region. Beyond Death Valley National Park's boundaries, other value systems and concerns—such as those of Las Vegas—may prevail. Some models suggest that unsustainable groundwater pumping in Nevada could affect the water table in Death Valley, which might affect spring flow in the Salt Creek area, and so the pupfish. And there is always the possibility that climate change and a general drying of the region will impact Salt Creek.

In the Salt Creek Hills, as I imagine the dying of pupfish in the bleak light of tomorrow, I confront the same question that perplexed me below a small seep in the Inyo Mountains when I considered the value of desert salamanders. Las Vegas or no Las Vegas, why should we concern ourselves with the Salt Creek and Cottonball Marsh pupfishes? As lost as those creatures are, confined to an aquatic system whose waters disappear into a purgatory of salt and heat, why should we care, any more than we should care about the Inyo Mountains slender salamander or the Owens pupfish? Why should the tourists getting ripped off for bottled drinks and turquoise jewelry at the Furnace Creek general store abandon their golf carts, recreational vehicles, minivans, motorcycles, hybrids, or SUVs for few minutes, stroll along the Salt Creek boardwalk, and by encountering the pupfish, come into some state of compassion and concern? Or why is preserving the pupfish of Cottonball Marsh, which only a few handfuls of people will ever see, of some critical importance to us all?

The text that I use in my conservation biology class enumerates many arguments for preserving species and their ecosystems; as applied to *Cyprinodon salinus*, some of them make sense and others do not. Their direct use value—economic benefits due to harvesting—obviously are nil, even if the Park Service did allow such a thing. There wouldn't be much of a meal in even two dozen of the biggest Salt Creek pupfish, which run to less than two inches in length, although Native Americans once gathered them with porous baskets and tule brooms. Instead, perhaps we should protect the Salt Creek and Cottonball Marsh pupfish for what we might learn about the heat shock proteins that undoubtedly help them survive the thermal and saline rigors of their habitat. Therapies based on heat shock proteins, including those isolated from pupfish tissues, might be used to delay cell death, increase the effectiveness of cancer vaccines, or act as direct anticancer agents. Or maybe we should be most concerned with the "ecosystem services" provided by pupfish; after all, they are the top predators and herbivores in their relatively simple aquatic habitats. Without them the Salt Creek and Cottonball Marsh ecosystems might function differently, and in a less healthy way. But—I am thinking selfishly here—these ecosystems are small and isolated, and they provide nothing of material value to humans. And as with all Great Basin drainage systems their surface waters flow nowhere, except into the ground—in this case, ground that has been poisoned by the salt that has accumulated over tens of thousands of years, as the waters of Death Valley repeatedly retreated and dried.

Perhaps, though, we (I) do not know enough. Perhaps if we study Salt Creek pupfish sufficiently we will come to understand how their absence would have profound ecological effects—not only on isolated bits of aquatic habitat but also, via unforeseen ripple effects, on the larger world. As John Muir wrote, "When we try to pick out anything by itself we find it hitched to everything else in the Universe." Although Muir was in the most general ecological sense correct, his statement has been overused (as well as misquoted) to the point where it has become a truism. Yes, all organisms are in one sense connected to one another, but the degree of their interaction varies tremendously, as do their roles in energy flow, nutrient cycling, and the population dynamics of other species. Remove a keystone species— gray wolves from Yellowstone, sea otters from Alaskan coastal waters, black-tailed prairie dogs from the high plains, salmon from the rivers of the Pacific Northwest—and the entire ecosystem can be profoundly disturbed, in ways that negatively affect humans. And although our knowledge of the Salt Creek and Cottonball Marsh pupfishes is inadequate, I believe that their disappearance due to a falling water table would have minimal large-scale ecological effects—ignoring for the moment the fundamental issues of the region's carrying capacity for humans and unsustainable growth in desert environments, the constant search for new water sources that inevitably will be overexploited, and the environmental impacts caused by regional ground- and surface-water depletion.

So, none of the immediate ecological arguments for preserving the Salt Creek and Cottonball Marsh pupfishes (and Inyo Mountains slender salamander) make much sense, although they certainly do for many other species, in many other places. I am not even convinced by arguments about the potential medical value of pupfish as it relates to heat shock proteins. It is true that "elements" of biodiversity (populations, species, communities) have what environmental economists call an option value: their potential worth based on future needs and the probability that people will want to "use" the element in the future. Option values are very difficult to quantify; how do we anticipate future need and value, based upon what we don't yet know? But it also is true that exciting and useful discoveries have come from unexpected places. One example: basic research on naked mole rats, those nearly blind and bald, sausage-shaped rodents from eastern Africa, has revealed that they can live for more than twenty-eight years, an age unknown for such a small mammal, or even for much larger mammals such as sheep, pigs, and dogs. Naked mole rats also do not develop cancer, at least in part because their cells show extremely high levels of contact inhibition, a property lacking in malignant cancer cells. The implications are obvious; understand the nature of naked mole rat cell contact inhibition and then apply our knowledge to the treatment of human cancers. Determine how naked mole rats can live as long as they do and use this knowledge to slow down the aging process in humans, even if such a thing might not be the best idea on an already overcrowded earth. Perhaps, then, the Salt Creek and Cottonball Marsh pupfish carry heat shock proteins that could provide the basis for innovative medical therapies. But very similar molecules also occur in humans, and these would be more easily adapted for therapeutic use. And even in the unlikely case that *Cyprinodon* heat shock proteins did prove to be of superior medical quality, more abundant species like the sheepshead minnow also tolerate very high temperature and salinities, and most likely produce heat shock proteins of equal or greater option value, whatever that might be.

So—away with the Salt Creek and Cottonball Marsh pupfishes. Off with their fins. To hell with them; we have plenty of sources for heat shock proteins and extinction of the two populations would have no important ecological consequences. Humans and their world would get on perfectly well without *Cyprinodon salinus salinus* and *Cyprinodon salinus milleri*, and no one's material life would be affected by their disappearance. Tourists walking along the Salt Creek boardwalk would no longer see pupfish, but remove the interpretive signs and most would never notice their absence, just as I am certain that very few patrons of the small resort at Tecopa Hot Springs understand that an endemic subspecies of the Amargosa pupfish, *Cyprinodon nevadensis calidae*, once swam in the waters below the spring-head. Although the Tecopa pupfish is extinct—and let's face it, this would not make great advertising copy ("Visit Tecopa Hot Springs, Former Home of the Extinct Tecopa Pupfish!")—why should extinction interfere with a long, hot, and blissful soak? Still, I wonder if anyone who slips into the mineral baths at Tecopa Hot Springs ever contemplates what it means to have forever lost the Tecopa pupfish. Was there anything vital about this tiny fish, once tied to a few hundred yards of outflow channel below Tecopa Hot Springs? And is there anything truly important about the Salt Creek pupfish, committed as it is to an inconsequential trickle of water, which in turn is hidden in the wastes of Death Valley? And as far as the Cottonball Marsh pupfish goes almost no one, except for a few addled biologists, will ever take the trouble to slog out to the heat-ravaged salt pan and search for *Cyprinodon salinus milleri*. The pupfish swim on, unknown to most people, utterly useless, lost to any right-thinking economist's cost-benefit spreadsheet, and also undoubtedly lost to Felecia Nimue Ackerman, professor of philosophy at Brown University. In a letter to the *New York Times Book Review*, Ackerman responded to a review of James Prosek's *Eels: An Exploration, From New Zealand to the Sargasso, of the World's Most Amazing Fish* by writing, "Isn't it time we recognize that, in view of our limited resources, there are higher priorities than eels and their ilk?"—the phrase "their ilk" certainly including species such as *Cyprinodon salinus*.

And yet there also is the argument of intrinsic value, which insists that all species have a right to exist, independent of human utilitarian concerns and needs. As I interpret the concept, intrinsic value argues that human agency should not be the cause of a species', subspecies', or even population's extinction. To destroy the essence of a lineage—its history, its place in the bright light of evolution—is to participate in a tragedy. The concept of intrinsic value is the ethical foundation of the U.S. Endangered Species Act, and I subscribe to it, more or less: hence this book and one of its central arguments. (But what about the causative agent of malaria, the single-celled protist *Plasmodium falciparum*, or the one hundred plus species of *Anopheles* mosquitoes that transmit the disease?) I doubt, though, that the concept of intrinsic value would resonate well with folks who rarely concern themselves with environmental issues. It probably would not do much to convince my archetypal waitress in Bishop, a rancher in Lone Pine, or a gambler in Las Vegas. It probably would not do much to assuage Dr. Ackerman's disdain for eels or to moderate the sentiments of Glenn Woiceshyn, who wrote in *Capitalism Magazine* that "anti-human sentiments are logically consistent with environmentalism's 'intrinsic value' philosophy."

I also suspect that intrinsic value would do little for Dr. Rob Roy Ramey II, a former curator of vertebrate zoology at the Denver Museum of Science and Nature. Ramey, who now heads his own consulting firm, is a wildlife biologist and vocal critic of the current version of the Endangered Species Act, which he feels is too focused on protecting the "little twigs" at the end of the "big branches" of the biodiversity "tree"—the "big branches" being species such as the California condor and bighorn sheep. (Although I wonder if Dr. Ramey has ever considered that a tree without its twigs and leaves is nothing but a dead or dying skeleton, incapable of photosynthesis and transpiration.) Ramey's tree metaphor might be an inappropriate one to use in defense of his position, but he has argued against recognizing and protecting taxa such as the federally listed Preble's meadow jumping mouse in Colorado and Wyoming, a subspecies of the much more widely distributed meadow jumping mouse (*Zapus hudsonius*). Given Dr. Ramey's attitudes, I would imagine that he also would view the Cottonball Marsh and Salt Creek pupfishes as "little twigs" not worthy of protection, in part because they might hypothetically waste "conservation resources at the expense of the big branches."

Finally, intrinsic value, as a basis for conservation decisions, does not even impress Lynn Maguire and James Justus, academics with expertise in environmental decision analysis and environmental ethics. Maguire and Justus write that "intrinsic value is a vaguely formulated concept and not amenable to the sort of comparative expression needed for conservation decisionmaking." Perhaps, but then again the seven virtues—love, hope, faith, prudence, justice, restraint, and courage—also are "vaguely formulated concept[s] and not amenable to the sort of comparative expression needed for conservation decisionmaking."

But even if we ignore the critics of intrinsic value and grant that most environmentalists accept and are motivated by the concept, it is an argument that works best with the converted. I desire something more, something other than a truism ("everything is connected to everything else") or wishful thinking, even if it might eventually come to pass ("someday those Salt Creek pupfish heat shock proteins might help us treat cancer"). I am also leery of arguments for conserving biodiversity that rest primarily on monetization, because any cost-benefit analysis—which is what economics is all about—can be manipulated in so many ways, and to whatever end. As Richard Leakey and Roger Lewin have written, "Ecologists have largely allowed economists to set the terms of the debate over the value of biodiversity. The danger is, that having accepted the invitation to enter the lion's den, they are likely to end up as the lion's dinner."

Perhaps it's a bit odd, but what I keep returning to as I consider the value of pupfish are the data—particularly those facts about thermal and salinity tolerances. I love their precise detail, the ways in which they grant the pupfish a distinct context that helps me understand their beautiful uniqueness. In thinking about wild geese flocking over an Oregon field Kathleen Dean Moore, channeling the poet William Carlos Williams ("No ideas but in things"), writes "Maybe it's not what the facts of the world point to, but the facts of the world themselves that should entrance me." Precisely, but it's not the facts alone that move me. Rather it's the combination of facts and experience, the numbers when considered—and felt—in the context of place. *There*: parts per thousand, degrees Celsius, and mtDNA while standing on a salt-shattered plain, lost in the Basin and Range vastness and watching the shadows of tiny fish cut through a pool of brine.

Here, metabolic rates and plasma osmotic concentrations while plodding into the headwaters of Salt Creek on a brutal September afternoon, a shiver of fish in a pool of stagnant water, pickleweed and saltgrass for their garden. In *Charlotte's Web*, Charlotte the spider spins the message "SOME PIG" to save Wilbur from the cleaver. With the help of the numbers—numbers steeped in Death Valley's heat and light and salt and space—the pupfish become all the more remarkable. Here in the Salt Creek Hills, cradled between the Panamint and Amargosa Ranges, I can come as close as I ever will to glimpsing something of *Cyprinodon salinus*'s essential nature. And it is here, in this sere and searing landscape, that I know, both intellectually and viscerally: *some fish*.

Charles Darwin wrote that the ways in which "the innumerable species inhabiting this world have been modified, so as to acquire that perfection of structure and coadaptation . . . most justly excites our admiration." But for me it's more than admiration and intellectual curiosity alone that are excited by the pupfish. It's love, passion, and—here's my contribution to arguments about the value of conserving biodiversity—empathy. The Salt Creek and Cottonball Marsh pupfish are so damned tough. They are tougher than any cliché, certainly tougher than nails, which will corrode and disappear in the salty waters of Cottonball Marsh. And this pupfish resilience comforts me; it gives me hope and grants me a measure of strength and peace.

Like any adult I have seen my share of anguish—less than many, perhaps more than some. I have felt the dark brush of death and tasted the bitterness of isolation. I have been betrayed, but far worse, I have betrayed others too easily and too often, and strayed into lies and deceit. And I have sat with a group of men and listened as they told their stories, terrible and horrific, of being sexually abused when they were young, just as I told my story to them. For me, it was my stepfather; for others in the group it was a father, an uncle, a Catholic priest, a family "friend," a brother, or the perfect storm of a stranger. Whatever the particulars, which are in no way the subject of this book, both the listening and the telling always left me dejected, morose, and nauseous. After a particularly draining session I would walk out into the night air of Rochester and glance up at the stars (or more likely, a blanket of clouds) and just feel stunned. And sometimes, when the weight of our collective experiences seemed almost too much to accept, I was dogged by depression, and for a while lost to the world. Ultimately, though, the process of telling and listening buoyed me up and gave me strength: to *know* how much people have endured and struggled against, and fallen and then risen up and carried on.

In a like manner, to understand something of the Cottonball Marsh and Salt Creek pupfish, to know their history and grasp the essence of their toughness, encourages me. They are the embodiment of tenacity and strength, as so are many of the other living things that I have watched and studied: an American pipit hunkered down on her nest and riding out a summer snowstorm high in the Beartooth Mountains; for three years running the same banded Harris Sparrow returning to the same stunted spruce in the Canadian arctic, after a 1,600-mile migration through the Great Plains and boreal forest; a slender salamander peering out from a muddy crevice in a desert canyon of the Inyo Mountains, living on in a place where no salamander should ever be; a scraggly pinyon pine, growing out of a crack on a north-facing slope some 2,000 feet below its normal range.

And so this is what I would ask of someone strolling along the boardwalk at Salt Creek: watch the pupfish intently, for an hour or so. Stand somewhere, quietly and patiently, with the sun hard upon your back. Try to ignore the chatter of passersby and focus on the fish. Watch the shoals darting through the braided channels, or a female spawning in the sandy shallows, an iridescent male cupped against her quivering flank. Note the vibrant blue brilliance of the male, the soft and subtle tones of the yellowish brown female. And while watching the pupfish consider the salt and the heat, the way in which summer forces the water and the fish upstream, into a hard and stagnant world. Think of the repeated births and deaths of Lake Manly, the breadth and depth of time, of the forces that pushed life—Fish, for god's sake!—into such a place as Salt Creek. Think about how resilient the pupfish are, and what they have endured, and then contemplate, gently, your own struggles and what you have endured. For all of us, at some time or another, this can be a dogshit world, unbelievably cruel and sorrowful and painful. I do not pretend to know much about dealing with the adversity that strikes us all, sometimes with a force that dwarfs anything I have experienced. I have nothing to suggest by way of easy pop-psychology remedies; I would never be so arrogant or condescending. But I will say this: that in my own life I have been consoled and heartened by the strength of pupfish and salamanders, in spite of their otherness, and the 300 million years or more of time that separates my evolutionary lineage from theirs. I value these creatures for their own sake, but also for the ways in which they reassure and comfort me. They and their ancestors have persevered in places that are inimical to so much of life, and I pray that we always will grant them the water and deference they need to survive. They have come so far, through so much. Their presence in the world, their insistent example, helps me to endure and go on, too.

After sitting above Salt Creek for two hours and considering Death Valley, *Cyprinodon salinus*, and my life—all of *this*—I rise, smiling, and make my way back to the car, once again thinking: *some fish*.

A Fragile Existence

THE DEVILS HOLE PUPFISH

(Cyprinodon diabolis)

Under the stone sky the water
waits.
—W. S. Merwin, "The Well"

To come upon Devils Hole is to approach a well of time, an anomaly, and a symbol. On a brilliant March morning I park along the dirt road that runs north and east from Ash Meadows, skirt a locked gate, and walk west for 200 yards. The dirt access road cuts across several small drainages—mere traces cutting through a thin wash of creosote bush and bursage—toward a rugged hill of layered limestone. To the east are more desert hills, trailing south, probing the great spaces, built from brown and orange-gray rock, rough to the touch and sharp enough to slice open a hand or knee. There is a sprinkle of birdsong in the air, and after a winter with sufficient rain, a scatter of wildflowers across the desert soil. But my attention is drawn away from the ground before me and into the great opening distance to the west and southwest, where the country slopes toward Ash Meadows and the Amargosa Valley, then rises into the Funeral Mountains and Greenwater Range. The far country is mostly an arid spread of sand and rock, fading to bleached browns and tans in the ascendant light. But there are gray-green swatches of leatherleaf ash and mesquite surrounding Ash Meadows' springs, and to the north, just out of sight, the emerald geometries of the Amargosa Valley, where fossil groundwater is pumped onto fields that see no more than four inches of rain per year.

There is water out there, but close at hand it is all hardscrabble desert soil—and before me, a chain-link fence crowned with barbed wire. The fence encloses an area roughly 150 yards on a side, hard up against the hill, where the topography of slope turns to plain. (Imagine that lovely point of inflection on the human body, where the neck's sinew and muscle curve toward the bony shelf of the clavicle, and you'll have the fence's position.) In the empty desert the fence looks misplaced, AWOL from its regular duty at a medium-security prison. Inside is a small solar array and weather station. There are no buildings within the fence, but near its western boundary there is a cavity in the desert's surface, a gaping hollow perhaps ninety feet long and eighty feet wide edged by orange and pinkish gray rock. I track the southern end of the fence, turn right into a tunnel of black fencing, and walk onto a wooden platform where I can look into the earth. About fifty feet below the desert's surface—so oddly and unexpectedly, like sudden rain in a time of drought—is a small rectangular pool of water surrounded on two sides by vertical cliffs; to my left is a sloping shelf; before me, a steep gully, partly filled by limestone blocks. The pool looks to be about ten feet wide, sixty feet long, and shallower at the southwest end. Along the right side of the pool, just above the water, is a series of wires leading from instruments that hang suspended in the water. I bring my arms up to the fence and grasp the wire, focus on the water, and the day drops away—the birdsong, the scent of creosote bush, the huge play of distance directly behind me, even the bright sun. From my vantage point I cannot see much detail in the pool, although I understand that there is a small pocket of life down there: algae and snails and beetles and flatworms, a refuge of the most absolute kind, and the only home of the Devils Hole pupfish, *Cyprinodon diabolis*. The tiny fish are not much more than one inch long and live mostly in the top one hundred feet of the pool—the smallest range of any vertebrate species in the world. Below them are caverns of water, mostly unexplored, an abyssal world extending deep into the earth, in the same way that space spreads outward from the place where I stand, clutching the wire.

For the moment there is no legal way down into Devils Hole, and so I turn to the west. As I do I notice a tiny gully that begins on a small shoulder a few yards beyond the fence and leads into Devils Hole. Beyond the shoulder there are a few dry channels too shallow and narrow to be called arroyos. They drain toward Ash Meadows and the springs that spill from the ground less than a mile away, some of which nourish their own populations of Amargosa pupfish, *Cyprinodon nevadensis*. Close enough, I think, but then I begin walking, at first tracking one of the thin channels, then cutting northwest across the lay of the land toward School Spring, where the nearest other pupfish live. The spring lies about one-half mile from

Devils Hole and my walk takes only twelve minutes, slicing across a gently dissected alluvial fan and descending through white clay deposits. In most places the ground is a pavement of chipped gray limestone peppered with grayish green desert holly and a light wash of spring annuals; just ahead is the grove of mesquite and ash nourished by the waters of School Spring. The hike is pleasant: the downhill slope, easy warmth, and intoxicating light, the Funeral Mountains and great sprawl of space that marks the Amargosa Desert. But the walk is also a puzzle because it confirms what I've read in the technical papers: that there are no Pleistocene lake deposits here, like those that mark the shores of Lake Manly in Death Valley, no eroded channels that in wetter times could have taken a few pupfish, against a current, into Devils Hole.

How *Cyprinodon diabolis* reached Devils Hole is a beautiful enigma. But regardless of how pupfish got into Devils Hole, the most important thing to understand about the species is that it survives only in this one place, where it confronts starvation, anoxia, and extinction. In Devils Hole it also swims against one of the strongest tides of human desire, which is our craving for water. And although this flood has pushed the Devils Hole pupfish to the edge of existence, there is another stream of desire in the desert, which insists that the Devils Hole pupfish is worth protecting and preserving. This stream has carried scientists into patient and detailed technical studies, and as deep as one can safely go into the depths of Devils Hole— just as it has carried lawyers to the U.S. Supreme Court, the federal government into elaborate and sometimes controversial management programs, and environmentalists into stubborn resistance to the idea that growing alfalfa is the best use for the desert's water. And so, when I reach School Spring and turn to look back toward Devils Hole, I think of those tiny fish— *down there, alone and surrounded by a landscape of drought*—and an eddy of this same compelling stream carries me into wonder, into something that I might describe as reverence.

On December 23, 1849, the Death Valley forty-niners entered Ash Meadows and camped at Collins Spring. In his journal one member of the party, Louis Nusbaumer, recorded the first known description of Devils Hole, which was less than one mile from the expedition's camp: "At the entrance to the valley to the right is a hole in the rocks which contains magnificent warm water in which Hadapp and I enjoyed an extremely refreshing bath." Although Nusbaumer did not mention swimming with pupfish, thirty-nine years later William Manly recalled that "on the second or third night we camped near a hole of clear water which was quite deep and had some little minus [*sic*] in." Descendants of these "minus" were first collected in 1891, during the Death Valley Expedition of the U.S. Biological Survey. Charles Gilbert, who described fishes collected during the expedition, identified specimens from Devils Hole as *Cyprinodon macularius*, the desert pupfish. Although what we now call *C. macularius* occurs far to the south of Ash Meadows, the species once occupied much of the lower Colorado River drainage and Río Sonoyta in Sonora. But the fate of *C. macularius* illustrates the history of range collapse so common in desert fishes. Most populations of this once "remarkably abundant" fish vanished as their habitat was destroyed by water-diversion schemes, pollution, and invasive species, and the desert pupfish now occurs only in a few scattered sites, from the Salton Sea to the Colorado River Delta and Organ Pipe Cactus National Monument.

Gilbert, one of the founders of modern American fisheries biology, thought that his *C. macularius* were immature pupfish: "Ten young specimens from the 'Devil's Hole,' Ash Meadows, are all without ventrals [pelvic fins], and further collections from this locality would be of interest." In 1930 Joseph Wales classified pupfish from Devils Hole as a new species, a conclusion confirmed in 1948 by Robert Miller. Wales and Miller based their diagnoses mostly on meristic characters—the number and placement of body parts such as scales and fins—rather than on the DNA sequences used in modern systematic studies. Miller's monograph is filled with data on the 10,000 or more fishes that he collected, plus many other museum specimens—at least forty-four measurements and counts *per fish*, of characters from number of anal scales and lateral line pores of the head to total body length and dorsal fin basal length. This must have been mind-numbing work: the smell of formalin and ethanol, repetitive counts, and measurements taken to the nearest 0.1 millimeter on fish less than two inches long. Miller recorded and summarized over 440,000 pieces of data in an era before computers simplified information storage and analysis. Based on his painstaking analysis, Miller noted that *C. diabolis* was a "dwarfed species . . . exceptional in *Cyprinodon* for the lack of pelvic fins. . . . The head and eye are very large." There were differences in coloration, too: mature female Devils Hole pupfish lacked the vertical side bars found in other Death Valley *Cyprinodon* and a spot at the base of the dorsal fin. Miller also noted—correcting Gilbert's conclusion that pupfish collected from Devils Hole in 1891 were juveniles—that "a number of the characters of [adult] *diabolis* are juvenile features and that dwarfing is probably also a retention of juvenile traits."

The location of Devils Hole and the distinctive morphology of *C. diabolis* led Miller to conclude that it had been isolated for much longer than other pupfish populations in the Amargosa River basin. Miller's conclusions about the unique morphology of the Devils Hole pupfish and its small population eventually helped secure its listing under the U.S. Endangered Species Preservation Act of 1966, which led to its protection by the much more powerful Endangered Species Act of 1973. Although Miller determined the distinctiveness of the Devils Hole pupfish, it was Joseph Wales who suggested a fascinating possibility for the population. Wales noted the morphological differences between Devils Hole pupfish and those from nearby "King's Spring" in Ash Meadows and then wrote: "It might be argued that the fish [in Devils Hole] are dwarfed directly by certain environmental stimuli . . . [if] it were proven that the offspring of King's Spring fish, when kept in Devil's Hole, were essentially like the fish now living there, then the population would be known to be a physiological race, not a distinct species." In other words, perhaps the environment makes the fish: it might be possible to place pupfish from another population in Devils Hole and after a few generations get something that closely resembled resident fish. Wales's prescient suggestion foreshadowed by seventy years research on what now is termed "phenotypic plasticity" in *Cyprinodon* and raised a complicated issue that is much more than a matter of arcane academic interest. What Wales was considering in his speculation about the relationship between an organism's phenotype, or form, and its environment was really the question, "What is a Devils Hole pupfish?" Although the answer to this question appears straightforward—a Devils Hole pupfish is one that lives in Devils Hole—this question of identity is deceptively complex and has major implications for the conservation of Devils Hole pupfish, our understanding of evolutionary processes, the statutory protection of all endangered species, and water-rights issues in the Southwest.

Devils Hole began its journey into conservation prominence on January 17, 1952, when President Truman declared it to be part of Death Valley National Monument, in order to preserve "the unusual features of scenic, scientific, and educational interest therein contained." Truman's proclamation was the culmination of a dedicated campaign begun by Carl Hubbs, at the time professor at the Scripps Institution of Oceanography. Hubbs began his studies of desert fishes in 1915, as an assistant on a Stanford University expedition to Utah; later, as curator of the fish division at the University of Michigan's Museum of Zoology, he made a number of ambitious collecting trips into the Great Basin. Hubbs convinced some well-placed people in the U.S. Department of the Interior that the zoology, hydrology, and geology of Devils Hole were unique, which led to Truman's executive order and protection for the forty-acre outlier of National Park Service property, one-quarter mile on a side and thirty air miles east of the Monument headquarters at Furnace Creek.

Between 1938 and 1942 Miller made six visits to Devils Hole and counted between 50 and "at least 400" fish, values that roughly agreed with an estimate made in 1939 by Sumner and Sargent, who wrote that "the entire existing population of this form can hardly exceed a few hundred individuals." Although formal counts of Devils Hole pupfish would not begin until 1972, Miller's population estimates, his work on pupfish taxonomy and evolution, and surveys of springs in Ash Meadows, demonstrated one irrefutable fact: there were very few Devils Hole pupfish, and all of them lived in one tiny place. Subsequent studies of the geology and ecology of Devils Hole would reveal its unique characteristics, as well as reasons for the unusual morphology and behavior of its pupfish, and its vulnerability to environmental change, particularly the groundwater pumping that began at Ash Meadows in 1968.

———————————

I first climbed down into Devils Hole in March 2009. It was late morning, and although the desert was full of bright sun, the bottom of Devils Hole was shaded, the air cool. From my perch I could see scores of pupfish swimming above the algae-coated ledge at the southwestern end of the pool, a choreography of tiny, swirling bodies darting through the shallow water. It was a year before I began reading intensively about pupfish and Great Basin aquatic ecosystems and talking to the biologists and managers who worked with *C. diabolis*. I hadn't yet encountered Miller's 1948 monograph on the cyprinodont fishes of the Death Valley region, or met Jim Deacon, Kevin Wilson, Darrick Weissenfluh, Sean Lema, or Zane Marshall—just a few of the people who would help me understand something of Devils Hole and its pupfish. But even then I saw that there were three keys to understanding how the ecosystem worked: the subterranean water from the deep underground aquifer, the light that drove the ecosystem, and the rock that embraced Devils Hole.

The rock: mostly marine carbonate, limestone and dolomite formed from the shells of invertebrates, shades of pink, orange, and gray, harsh and sharp-edged in the hills above Devils Hole, but on the apron above the pool smoother and more welcoming. The sediments that formed the rocks were deposited some 570 to 225 million years ago, above older layers that formed what hydrogeologists once called an aquitard—impermeable material that impedes the flow of water. Beginning 70 to 80 million years ago, these layers were alternately uplifted, deformed, and pulled apart during periods of mountain building and crustal thinning. As the Basin and Range topography blossomed, block-faulting created a complex of interconnected fissures and joints, subterranean passages for the water that percolates downward from the land's surface—small amounts in the lowlands, more in the higher country, particularly the almost 12,000-foot-high Spring Mountains, which lie about thirty miles east and southeast of Devils Hole. Hydrologists know that water flows north and northeast through these fractures, running downhill from the Spring Mountains before arcing around their northern terminus and turning southwest through a "high-transmissivity zone" of carbonate rocks to Devils Hole and Ash Meadows. Here, along a front trending north-northwest to south-southeast, the water encounters a hydraulic barrier faulted up against deep carbonate rocks. This front, known as the Gravity Fault, is in some places more or less impermeable to water, which wells to the surface in a ten-mile-long series of brilliant blue springs. These springs, plus their associated alkali meadows and "capillary fringe discharge areas," form the Ash Meadows oasis, home to an astonishingly rich assemblage of organisms. The isolation of these springs—locally from one another, regionally from other water sources—explains the stunning endemism of Ash Meadows, which supports or (given three documented historical extinctions) once supported twenty-nine plants and animals that occur nowhere else in the world.

Think of it: snow falling in the highest reaches of the Spring Mountains during the Pleistocene, perhaps on the alpine tundra of the range's highest summit, 11,915-foot Charleston Peak, and melting into the ground. The water, acidic at first, slips into the thin soil and follows gravity deeper into limestone channels, spreads through rocks hundreds of millions of years old, growing more alkaline as it reacts with calcium carbonate. A counterclockwise drift and spiral, the Pleistocene waters flowing underground, coalescing, moving through Frenchman Flat, a slow gathering together of subterranean pools from the Pahranagat Range, Tikaboo Valley, Yucca Flats, and Emigrant Valley, all of that lovely Basin and Range emptiness. The flow then curves southwest through the deep carbonate aquifer, moves toward Devils Hole and the necklace of springs that mark Ash Meadows, where it is pushed to the surface by impermeable rocks and faulted barriers from the basement of time. The water is almost murderously low in oxygen and high in temperature when it finally flows into light and life eight thousand years or more after falling in the Spring Mountains, as it carries calcium carbonate and heat out of the deepest darkness and rises into the province of aquatic bugs and beetles, algae and cyanobacteria, diatoms and flatworms, pupfish and people. . . .

The rocks, though, are more than a passage for groundwater. They also form the structure of Devils Hole, defining the habitat available to *C. diabolis* and other aquatic organisms, and—crucially—the amount of direct sunlight entering the ecosystem. On that March day when I first stood at the edge of the Devils Hole pool, I was shaded from the sun by a pit that formed about 60,000 years ago, when the ceiling of the Devils Hole fissure collapsed. At its northeastern end the rectangular pool was sheltered by an overhang, the roosting place of owls and bats. Just above the pool was a faint ring of whitish gray minerals, a legacy of higher water levels. To my right, near the base of an overhang, were several metal rods drilled into the rock, a series of wires, a white PVC tube, three video cameras, and a collection of instruments that hung suspended in the clear, still water. To my left was a sloping shelf of bare gray limestone, streaked with white, trending vertical toward the overhang. Directly in front of me was the crucial shallow shelf, formed from a block of bedrock, about 8.5 feet wide by 20 feet long: 170 square feet of prime pupfish (not to mention Amargosa springsnail and Devils Hole warm springs beetle) habitat, and the place where most of the action in the ecosystem occurs. Without this shelf, and at least eight inches of water above it, there would be little photosynthesis to support the food web upon which the pupfish depend, and almost no pupfish spawning habitat. And so, within the miniaturized range of the Devils Hole pupfish there is an even tinier bit of space, roughly the area of a small bedroom, that means life or death for the population. Without the shallow shelf the uniqueness of the Devils Hole pupfish, its story in such an unexpected place, would vanish.

Over the last few years I have been lucky enough to spend several days by the edge of the pool, watching and thinking. In the spring the pupfish are active: a constant sinuous weaving of bodies, none much more than one and one-half inches long. Most of the iridescent males do not defend territories, unlike those in most Ash Meadows pupfish populations. The males are like beads of darting blue light, patrolling large swatches of ground, some chasing females down the entire length of the shelf. Chases usually end when the grayish blue female swims off and the male wheels away, or veers toward another female. Occasionally, though, something else occurs:

the male sidles up against a female's flank and in that moment, pupfish flesh against pupfish flesh, an egg is laid and sperm released. Afterwards the two may repeat their fleeting dance, or they may swim away from one another and across the shelf, which is streaked with algae: patches of deep forest green woven into a carpet of lighter green, dotted with a host of tiny snails, set against rock coated with delicate deposits of white calcium carbonate. Beneath the desert's surface the day drowses and the pupfish go about their business. Sunlight slides down the northwestern slope of Devils Hole, moves onto the pool, lingers for a short while, and then is gone. A slight wind stirs and pushes mats of algae across the pool. A few drowned bees drift by and three rock nettle leaves swirl in the delicate current, meager gifts of energy for the system.

The Devils Hole ecosystem is constrained by the amount of energy that reaches the water—and this quantity, like the quality of the water, is a consequence of the rocks. This energy may be in the form of the light that photosynthetic organisms—mostly filamentous cyanobacteria and diatoms, plus some green algae—transform into organic molecules, or as bits of animal and plant carbon that get blown or washed into Devils Hole, which limnologists term "allochthonous inputs." (A rush and clatter of muddy rivulets during an August cloudburst, flushing old mouse turds, the skeletons of desert trumpet, and sprigs of bursage into Devils Hole; a quick squirt of guano as a Townsend's big-eared bat skitters into the soft desert night; a struggling moth drowning in the moonlit water.) At summer solstice direct sunlight falls on the pool for only four hours per day; it is gone by late November and does not return until mid-February, a desert analog of the darkness that comes to the high arctic each winter.

The meager light energy that reaches the surface of Devils Hole at winter solstice is only 4 percent of that which nourishes the system six months later. And the catchment basin for Devils Hole is tiny, the rain that flushes organic material into the pool rare. The desert winds, although common and often brutally strong, can carry only so many insects or tiny bits of leaf into the water. The rocks surrounding Devils Hole isolate its waters from the rich pulses of light and nutrients that microbes, plants, and animals need to flourish, and the total energy budget of this ecosystem is only 20 percent that of Tecopa Bore, a desert spring near the Amargosa River. And so the ecosystem in Devils Hole is impoverished: a collection of mostly undescribed microbes; a few dominant photosynthetic species; three common "collector/ gatherers," including an amphipod, a springsnail, and a beetle; a predaceous diving beetle; and at the top of the food chain the

Devils Hole pupfish, all one inch and 0.5 grams of it, although its diet is mostly cyanobacteria, diatoms, and green algae, augmented by the occasional invertebrate.

Beyond the precious shallow shelf the waters slip into the earth along a fault line that falls away like a great staircase. The rock-bound fissure leading into the depths of Devils Hole is slanted down to the southeast, and about 6 to 12 feet wide and 130 feet long. It falls seventy-five vertical feet to a sheared-off slab, Anvil Rock. Below Anvil Rock is a cave system more than 430 feet deep. Divers descending into Devils Hole have a ceiling over their heads as they sink toward Anvil Rock; from the bottom of the slot they can look up to the surface through the clear, intensely blue water. Below them, the light quickly attenuates. For Alan Riggs, who first dove into Devils Hole in 1976, swimming down through the fault line was "like being the first person to enter a freshly opened Egyptian tomb." For Jim Deacon, who pioneered detailed ecological research on Devils Hole, sinking into the water was like "going back into the womb."

Although I never have dived into Devils Hole I can imagine hanging suspended in its bathlike waters near Anvil Rock: I feel as though I am floating in air, the water still and warm, part of a great liquid world that spreads down and outward, into the deep carbonate aquifer. Rock surrounds me; below, the beam from my diver's light shines out into the darkness, then dies away into utter blackness. Here, at the fading edge of light, the walls of Devils Hole are coated with translucent, ghostly white layers of mammillary calcite—calcium carbonate precipitated from the supersaturated solution that surrounds me. These layers are up to sixteen inches thick and look like tooth enamel, and the amount of oxygen-18 isotope they contain provides a continuous climate record for over 500,000 years of the Pleistocene—a record ending about 60,000 years ago, when Devils Hole opened to the surface of the world. Submerged in time, I glance upward through the fissure; the surface glimmers, a thumb-width slot of beckoning light. There almost never are any pupfish at this depth, and so I begin the slow ascent, stopping every now and then to decompress and search for pupfish, which I first encounter about sixty feet below the surface. Higher up, many of the fish are plucking at strands of algae with tiny, back-and-forth darting motions, tails angled upward as they lunge and recoil, spitting out tiny clouds of debris with each nip. About ten feet below the surface there is a narrow cavern beneath the spawning shelf. Suppressing a small jolt of claustrophobia, I swim into the chamber, past schools of three to five pupfish. I probe the tightening space, pivot awkwardly and swim back into a widening world, then rise to the surface along the southeastern edge of Devils Hole, loafing quietly in the water, waiting for the danger of decompression sickness to pass, eyes closed, thinking about rock and water and fish, and where I have just been.

The status of the Devils Hole pupfish as the most restricted, smallest vertebrate population in the world, its protection under the U.S. Endangered Species Act, and groundwater exploitation in the nearby Amargosa Valley have pushed the National Park Service into an extensive research and management program. Because the fundamental issue for any at-risk species is population size, the Park Service has developed a careful protocol for counting Devils Hole pupfish and evaluating the health of their habitat. The semiannual pupfish surveys, which last for two days, occur during the spring and fall. Each survey attempts to tally all adults in the population and requires three counts, two on the first day and one on the morning of the second day. The process involves four divers and three people working simultaneously on the surface of Devils Hole. I observed a survey in late September of 2010, when daytime temperatures were still above 100°F and sleepy summer heat permeated the air. Down in Devils Hole, though, only about two hours of direct sunlight reached the pool, and there always was shade near the water. It was a comfortable place to watch the counts, visit, and think about pupfish:

The underwater crew consists of two research divers: Stan Hillyard, a physiologist at the University of Nevada, Las Vegas, and Zane Marshall, head of Environmental Management for the Southern Nevada Water Authority, plus two safety divers. They work in teams of one research diver and one safety diver; each team counts pupfish independently, using a standardized methodology designed to minimize disturbance. Between them, Stan and Zane have over thirty-two years of experience surveying Devils Hole pupfish and are highly competent at cave diving, which is much riskier than open-water diving. The surface team is composed of three National Park Service biologists, Kevin Wilson, Bailey Gaines, and Linda Manning; their jobs are to assist the divers and count fish on the shallow shelf. The first survey begins after Kevin and Bailey install four sections of a portable aluminum monitoring platform over the spawning shelf, supported by horizontal metal poles slotted onto metal braces drilled into the rock just above the waterline; this allows the divers to access the pool without disturbing the fish or shallow shelf, and the surface counters to easily search for fish.

The team prepares for the count just outside the fence surrounding Devils Hole, long shadows laid across the desert in the early morning light, temperatures already in the eighties. Equipment is placed carefully on a large canvas tarp, tanks and regulators checked, everything disinfected to prevent contamination. There is a quiet excitement in the air and an easy banter among the divers, the relaxed talk of people who know each other well, love their work, and are good at it. Once the divers are ready they descend the access ladder through the narrow slot leading to Devils Hole, climb down a series of ledges to the monitoring platform, and enter the water at the far end of the shallow shelf. After slipping on their fins they assemble along the eastern end of the wall; for a few minutes they quietly talk of safety and the count, and then are gone, trailing bubbles of spent air. Much later Zane told me that descending through the extension fault "is like swimming into the stillness of an underground lake; you're literally inside the aquifer, bathed in warmth, looking up toward the light, through the intensely blue water." I think of the caving I've done, how the rock sometimes closes in on me and steals my breath, and ask Zane about claustrophobia, but he said that he never feels it, or perceives what he's doing as dangerous: "The NPS trains its cave divers in northern Florida, where it's a much more challenging situation."

The protocol calls for the divers to descend slowly to Anvil Rock. The second team then ascends to a point fifty feet above Anvil Rock while the first team begins its search by moving laterally for about seventy-five feet, toward what's called the Flat Room. The research diver takes the lead, probing crevices and scanning the walls; the safety diver remains about two body lengths behind, watching. Once the first team returns to Anvil Rock and begins counting fish nearer to the surface, the second team moves down to Anvil Rock and starts their count. The count that I am following takes fifty minutes, and when Zane and Stan rise to the surface they have tallied seventy and sixty-one fish, respectively—pretty close, I think, given the wealth of hiding places, the constant movement of the fish, and the fact that their quarry is so small. Larval Devils Hole pupfish are visible to the unaided human eye when they reach 4 millimeters in length—about as long as the tip of a chopstick is wide—but in practice, the underwater and surface researchers tally fish ranging from 12 to 40 millimeters long, which is as big as Devils Hole pupfish ever get.

As the divers go about their business Kevin, Bailey, and Linda count pupfish on the rock shelf. They divide the shelf into three imaginary zones, kneel on the platform, perform a practice count, and then make three counts in quick succession—each a rapid sequence of bobbing bodies, sweeping heads, pointing fingers, and clipped talk about fish moving from one zone into another. The average of the three morning surface counts is fifty-five; added to the sixty-one to seventy fish found by Zane and Stan, this means that in September 2010 there are about 120 Devils Hole pupfish in the world. Given that a twenty-five-millimeter-long pupfish weighs roughly 0.5 grams, there are roughly sixty grams, or two ounces, of pupfish in Devils Hole. To sense what this weight means, its reality in the context of the world's vastness, count out about 120 medium-sized raisins. Cup them in your hands and think: you are holding, ever so gently, a weight equivalent to all of the Devils Hole pupfish blood, flesh, and scale that exists. There is no more.

I spend the morning watching the count and talking mostly with Kevin and Bailey about pupfish and conservation. Kevin has a PhD from the University of Toronto—a long, long way from the Mojave Desert—and is the lead aquatic ecologist in Death Valley National Park, where there's a surprising amount of water to study, worry about, and manage. He is stocky, energetic, and talkative, looks to be in his mid-thirties, and is an expert on the Devils Hole ecosystem. Bailey is an NPS fisheries technician, with a master's degree from Texas Tech University. He is younger than Kevin, taller and leaner, quiet. As we wait for the divers I ask about pupfish research and management, and how the Devils Hole ecosystem works, and then pick a quiet moment to ask my companions about their emotional responses to Devils Hole. The three grow collectively, almost uncomfortably, silent—a reaction that at first surprises me. But as I would discover, many of the people who study and care for the ecosystems and endangered species of the Death Valley region have trouble articulating what motivates them, and the importance of their work. This reticence is not about lack of passion, knowledge, or commitment; just about every one of the professionals I have met embodies these traits, sometimes to the point of obsession. Instead, I think it has more to do with personality. Many scientists and resource managers seem, by inclination, introverted and not given to emotional displays; collectively, they would make lousy guests on an *Oprah*-like talk show: "So, Fred, tell me how you *feel* about those cute little pupfish." But down in Devils Hole I press my question about emotional reactions and finally get some short answers; Bailey mentions "complexity and humility," while Linda finds the pupfish world "stunning." Interestingly, Kevin talks of his sense of "ownership"—not in terms of physical possession, but as a form of moral responsibility. Kevin has invested years of his life in these fish and their world; as a master's student he studied the intricacies of energy flow and nutrient cycling in Devils Hole, and he later came into a job demanding that he grant his full attention to *Cyprinodon diabolis* and its sister species.

Good science—the careful crafting of a study, attention to detail, repetition, focused concentration, and search for patterns—can be understood as a form of right practice, or what the Buddhists call *dharma*. And out of *dharma* comes devotion and compassion, even if many scientists have trouble articulating such things. Through their work, Carl Hubbs, Robert Miller, and Jim Deacon must have developed close emotional ties to pupfish, just as Kevin (and Bailey and Linda) also must have. And as a corollary to this connection, I imagine that Kevin must carry the visceral sense that if the species perseveres and prospers, it will be under his watch. And if the Devils Hole pupfish were to disappear, he will be there when it happens, and so—whether justified or not—will feel in some way responsible for its fate.

Our discussion about emotional responses is briefer than a desert thunderstorm and we soon switch back to science, where the terrain is more comfortable. Kevin recounts the recent history of Devils Hole pupfish populations. At the start of monitoring in 1972, which was triggered by the collapse of pupfish populations due to groundwater pumping and declining water levels in Devils Hole, the minimum count was only 127. From the mid-1970s through the mid-1990s, rising water levels allowed the population to increase, although there were poor years and flush years—but by 1994, minimal population sizes were more than 300, with maximal counts of over 550 during good autumns. But then, in the late 1990s, something happened, and the population again decreased. The full explanation for this decline remains unclear. Hypotheses include inbreeding depression, decreased nutrient inputs, a shift in the algal community, and loss of a key invertebrate prey species from the primary feeding area, although the accidental death in 2004 of one-third of the population in larval traps did not help. The traps had been stowed within the Devils Hole drainage by a careless university researcher—against regulations—and were washed into the pool by a flash flood. Whatever the constellation of causes responsible for the decline, the April 2006 count yielded only thirty-eight adult pupfish, many of which looked "emaciated." This crisis stimulated a burst of research and management activities, including installation of an automatic feeder. These actions helped the population increase to around 120 adults by the fall of 2010—only to have it again fall into the thirties by the spring of 2013. The dog days of 2006 and 2007 had returned and now it would not take much to kick the Devils Hole pupfish into oblivion, to join the ranks of the region's other recently extinct fishes: Las Vegas dace, Ash Meadows poolfish, Pahrump poolfish, Raycraft Ranch poolfish, and Tecopa pupfish.

Active management of Devils Hole began in 1952, when it was included in Death Valley National Monument. In 1956, the U.S. Geological Survey installed a water-gauge recorder in the pool; shortly thereafter, the National Park Service restricted public access by installing a locked gate in the slot leading into Devils Hole. Following the drowning of two young divers in 1965—their bodies were never found—the Park Service became more concerned with security and erected a chain-link fence around Devils Hole. The population collapse during the late 1960s and early 1970s, and the listing of the species under the Endangered Species Act, led to the first research on Devils Hole, which has metamorphosed into a program costing $390,000 per year. William Manly's 1849 "hole of clear water which . . . had some little minus" has become an enclave, protected by barbed wire and a chain-link fence and filled with an array of scientific instruments and surveillance cameras. The pupfish are carefully counted twice each year and receive supplemental feeding. The National Park Service has instituted an intensive long-term ecological monitoring plan and supported research on everything from energy and nutrient flow to counting methods, population modeling, and larval pupfish ecology. Devils Hole (and its pupfish) is now a place that we will not, or perhaps cannot, leave alone.

The divers and surface counters repeat their protocols during the afternoon of the first day and again the following morning. I tag along in the only way that I can—as a bystander, taking notes and watching. During the third set of dives, after Kevin, Linda, and Bailey finish their surface counts, Kevin lets me don a mask and poke my head underwater, which is as close as I ever will get to following Louis Nusbaumer's 1849 lead and swimming in Devils Hole. I lie on the monitoring platform, my body extended over the far end of the shallow shelf, and gently slip my head into the warm water. There is a sudden luminosity, an opening up of the underwater world: a shimmering, pulsing dance of electric blue water and darting pupfish, a rich yellow-green tapestry of algae on the western wall and slash of white rock rising to the east. Sunlight glistens on the backs of diving beetles and on the tiny particles that fall through the water like a fine, misting rain. Pupfish pluck at the algae, darting back and forth, spitting out tiny clouds of debris after each bite. I see a few hither-and-yon chases, as males pursue females, but the pupfish mostly ignore each other and go about the business of feeding; there is none of the pugnacious behavior that males in other populations display, no aggressive guarding of space. Pupfish peace, or at least its illusion, reigns. To my right is a cylinder containing instruments for measuring dissolved oxygen, temperature, pH, and conductivity. Below me, a black sleeve housing a fiber optic cable slides down the fault and vanishes beneath an overhang. Pulses of bubbles—I think of them as schools—rise from the invisible divers, create tiny ripples as they break the surface of the pool, and mix with the small waves that I generate each time I raise my body to breathe. And after each breath I return to the color and light and warmth, to the water that disappears into the great depths of rock, and the fish and beetles that swirl around me.

After the next day's morning count Kevin allows me to remain in Devils Hole while everyone eats lunch above. I recline on the observation platform and close my eyes; Devils Hole is quiet and I am left with the track of sunlight on the rocks above, and the tracks of fish in the water below. Pupfish swim through my mind and I try to recreate the course of their lives, their feeding and mating, the ways in which they cope with their demanding environment, even the vocalizations that they must make, as do other pupfish: high-pitched, far beyond the range of human hearing, clicks, snaps, and what sound to my ear like squirrels gnawing on walnuts. I consider what I have seen over the previous two days and imagine climbing out of Devils Hole and looking west toward the nearest other pupfish populations. The sheer improbability of fish in this place strikes me viscerally. Just how did the ancestors of the fish swimming a few inches below me get here, and when did this happen? Pupfish colonists probably arrived within the last 60,000 years, after the ceiling of Devils Hole collapsed, a date based on the end of mammillary calcite precipitation, which does not accumulate in the open air. There are five hypotheses for how the ancestors of *Cyprinodon diabolis* reached Devils Hole: via lake, stream, underground passage, transport by bird, or transport by humans. Among these scenarios, underground colonization and avian transport seem far-fetched. Any underground fissures connecting Devils Hole to other pupfish populations would have been too hot and deep, and too oxygen poor, to allow colonists to survive. Transport by an aquatic bird, such as a duck, seems equally unlikely, a result of a more-than-fortuitous sequence of events: eggs or fish somehow stuck to the feathers of a duck dabbling in a nearby spring; the adventurous duck then searching out Devils Hole and deciding to visit what would be unattractive duck habitat; and the fishes (at least one pair, or fertilized eggs) somehow surviving long enough to be deposited, alive, in the welcoming water.

Colonization by surface water is more plausible. Back in 1948 Miller and Hubbs proposed that the Devils Hole pupfish were isolated about 10,000 years ago, as the giant Great Basin lakes retreated. However, there were no large lakes present in the Ash Meadows area during the Pleistocene, unlike Lake Tecopa further down the Amargosa River drainage. Sedimentary clays indicate that there were shallow-water habitats near Devils Hole, but these clays were not deposited in a shoreline or deep-water environment, and date to some 2.4 to 3.2 million years ago. In terms of a possible stream connection to nearby Ash Meadows springs, calcite deposits suggest that water levels in Devils Hole have not risen high enough to overflow the cavity in at least 116,000 years. There also is no evidence of a stream breaching the lip on the downhill side of Devils Hole. And so we are left with one hypothesis, which has its own problems: transport by early Native Americans sometime before 1849, when the Manly party visited Devils Hole. Because the oldest widely accepted archaeological evidence places human settlement of the Great Basin at no more than 11,500 years ago, humans could not have brought pupfish into Devils Hole much before the end of the Pleistocene. Devils Hole remains culturally important to the modern Timbisha Shoshone people, and this significance, coupled with the mystery of the place, its compelling ambience even in the face of Park Service fences and scientific equipment, makes it possible to understand possible motivations of early Native Americans. It would have been easy to capture pupfish in a nearby spring and carry them to Devils Hole in a clay pot or tightly woven basket. And as the colonists were dumped into the pool, I imagine that there would have been ceremonial prayers, perhaps a mythical nod toward the "water babies" said to lurk in Devils Hole, waiting to swallow anyone who lingered too long in the water.

The puzzling thing about the hypothesis of human agency is that molecular analyses, based on mitochondrial DNA sequence divergence and a molecular clock, suggest that the Devils Hole pupfish split from its closest ancestor, the Amargosa pupfish, between 200,000 and 600,000 years ago—which conflicts with the 60,000 years-before-present date for the opening of Devils Hole. However, as Alan Riggs of the U.S. Geological Survey and Jim Deacon of the University of Nevada, Las Vegas, explain, "Dating recent [speciation] events using DNA is extremely difficult because the DNA records divergence of molecules, not necessarily divergence of species . . . [and]

molecular divergence always precedes species divergence." What Riggs and Deacon imply is that divergence estimates based on molecular data most likely overestimate the timing of pupfish colonization of Devils Hole. The disparity between the geological data and mitochondrial DNA sequence data has been explained by a process termed "lineage sorting," in which divergent mitochondrial DNA lineages existed prior to the time when pupfish reached Devils Hole, but this is only a conjecture. And so, round and round I go, trying to make sense of the hypotheses on how pupfish first reached Devils Hole. What I am left with is a beautiful mystery that someday might be resolved, given the right tools and enough persistence.

All of it—the physical setting of Devils Hole, the ways in which it is colonized by water and light, the history and precarious life of its pupfish— makes me feel as though I am lying in the waist of an hourglass. For such a small space, the surface of Devils Hole opens up into stunning vastness: the immaculate blue sky above, spilling into the huge desert distance, the great blue pool of rock-bound water spreading below and running deep underground into the Basin and Range emptiness. And then there is the vast temporal stream that carries me along its current: water flowing from the Spring Mountains, 10,000 years or more old; the calcite strata that coat the chambers of Devils Hole, with their 500,000 years of layered time, spread across the rocks like fine sheaths of living tissue; and the limestone and dolomite formed from creatures that died 570 million years ago—rocks that carry the waters that flow beneath the desert. And then there are places where these subterranean waters climb into the light of the present, and grace those small pockets of the arid world where pupfish find their homes, such as the one that shelters me on this fine and glorious afternoon.

One paper describes Devils Hole as "a skylight to the water table (and beyond)," and it is easy to understand why ecologists and geologists have been drawn to Devils Hole, its pupfish, and their scientific stories. As I lie in the quiet warmth and consider what I have seen and felt during the last two days, I can even grasp something of the motivation (if not the logic) of people who have been attracted to Devils Hole for reasons most charitably described as "odd." Charles Manson supposedly believed that Devils Hole was a portal to an underground world where he and his "family" could wait out the coming apocalypse before emerging as leaders of a purified world. And a quick search of the Internet using the proper terms can dredge up websites with stream-of-consciousness riffs on Devils Hole, conversations with dolphins, pupfish ("fishy fishy little devils"), and Wilhelm Reich's "orgone" theory of cosmic energy.

It's one thing to channel Wilhelm Reich, another to consider pupfish and the ways in which Devils Hole, for all of its subterranean connections to aquifers and faults, draws us into the lovely spatial geometries of the Great Basin, its complexities and temporal vastness. The geological and evolutionary history of the world, or at least this part of it, spins outward from where I doze, the metal grating of the monitoring platform rough against my skin. I hear nothing from any dolphins, just the faint hum of a hovering bee, the *churr* of a rock wren, and the whisperings of the deepest past. "Our blood is time," writes Anne Michaels, and pupfish blood, too, is time: the blood of the magnificent blue fish swimming a few inches beneath me, the legacy of countless generations, individual lives lived out in this one place only, lives spawned in isolation, each at most spanning twelve months, the thousands and millions of years of ancestral pupfish history rising to this one point of the present, with its warming climate and groundwater pumping and drying springs and extinctions and human thirst and people struggling to make sense of who they are, where their responsibilities lie, and where each species, human and animal, will go.

For the Devils Hole pupfish the constraints of its ecosystem mean that there isn't much to eat. Yet the consistently high water temperatures, which average 92°F but may rise to 100°F when direct sunlight floods the rock shelf during the summer, push the fish toward an unsustainably high metabolic rate. High water temperatures, combined with low levels of dissolved oxygen, also result in correspondingly low oxygen saturations, creating an environment potentially detrimental to successful egg production and embryonic development. Other species of *Cyprinodon*, and presumably *C. diabolis*, are remarkably tolerant of hypoxic conditions and decrease their metabolic rates in oxygen-poor water. Although the low oxygen levels, high water temperatures, and low amounts of available energy during the winter undoubtedly stress Devils Hole pupfish, a casual observer, unschooled in fish ecophysiology, might view the remarkably constant aquatic environment of Devils Hole as more welcoming than it actually is. The reality is that the sheltered, bathlike waters of Devils Hole probably are more stressful to pupfish than the hypersaline and often warmer waters of Salt Creek and Cottonball Marsh. These places, pummeled by the worst salt and heat that Death Valley can offer, look like killing fields for fish. But *Cyprinodon salinus*, whether swimming through some fetid Salt Creek pool on a beastly August day or bathed in the brine of Cottonball Marsh, retains the typical adult morphology found in other members of the genus, while the Devils Hole pupfish does not. The small size, relatively large head and eyes, lack of pelvic fins, and extremely long anal fin of adult Devils Hole pupfish are characteristics normally present in juvenile pupfish, but which usually disappear as individuals grow and develop into sexually mature adults. The retention of juvenile traits, termed paedomorphosis, is uncommon in fish but occurs in some salamanders inhabiting high-elevation lakes and ponds with very short growing seasons and low nutrient levels.

The stressful environment might also explain the lack of aggression in Devils Hole pupfish, which intensively court females but never defend territories. This behavioral docility might be adaptive; either there are too few nutrient-rich pockets of space in Devils Hole and too many pupfish clustered on the shallow shelf, or prudent males should not devote too much energy to the constant chasing and nipping necessary to defend mating territories. Or perhaps the explanation is more mechanistic; the nutrient-poor, stressful environment of Devils Hole affects the neural and hormonal mechanisms that control aggressive behavior in male pupfish, rendering males less prone to attacks on fellow males.

All that we know about fish ecology and physiology suggests that Devils Hole pupfish confront a harsh, demanding world, where they persist at the very edge of life. As with the Salt Creek and Cottonball Marsh pupfishes, *Cyprinodon diabolis* evokes a reaction of wonder and disbelief: "Some fish, in some place"—but there are so few Devils Hole pupfish, so little to their only home, and so much in their natural environment to threaten them. A litany of potential disasters could shift the balance of energy flow from barely positive to strongly negative, so that the amount of food the pupfish assimilate is insufficient to fuel all the things that fish must do: feed, swim, grow and develop, maintain homeostasis in the face of inimical environmental conditions, mate, and spawn. A prolonged drought could end the unpredictable deluges that wash precious nutrients into Devils Hole, such as the thunderstorm of September 3, 2001, which brought more carbon into Devils Hole in one hour than usually occurs over an entire, floodless year. Or another unexplained transition could occur, like the one that happened between the late 1960s and 1990s, when the main primary producers shifted from the green alga *Spirogyra* to filamentous cyanobacteria, with a corresponding decline of an ostracod, a minute crustacean which sheltered in *Spirogyra* and was an important pupfish prey item. Or most devastating of all, the fissure that forms Devils Hole widens enough to dislodge the shallow shelf. A severe earthquake could do the job, even though moderate or distant tremors may be ultimately beneficial because they flush accumulating debris from the shallow shelf and "reset" the ecosystem. Such an event happened on March 20, 2012, when a magnitude 7.4 earthquake in Oaxaca, Mexico, generated waves that washed four or five feet up the rock walls of Devils Hole.

To watch a video of the event and consider that the waves were produced by an earthquake 2,000 miles away, at a depth of twelve miles, is to understand something of the earth's connectivity and the ways in which the fates of the water and pupfish in Devils Hole are tied to the rocks and to circumstances beyond human control. The effects of the Oaxaca earthquake on Devils Hole, the shift in algal community composition during the last forty years, or the impact of a single storm on the ecosystem demonstrate that even if humans left them alone, the Devils Hole pupfish would have a tough, unpredictable go of it. But of course, we have not left them alone. We have counted and measured them, swum with them, carried them to refuges, and tried to protect them with fences, barbed wire, and surveillance cameras. All of these things may have been necessary, and although some have had unintended and harmful consequences—those larval fish traps accidently washed into Devils Hole, possible reductions in inputs of carbon and nitrogen caused by the fencing, perhaps increased inbreeding due to removing fish from the population—I believe that the balance sheet has been positive. Some of us have meddled with Devils Hole because we are drawn to its mystery and improbable beauty, but also to protect one of the rarest, most vulnerable species on earth. We have studied the Devils Hole pupfish, tried to shelter it from harm, and sometimes stumbled along the way. But others have tried to take the desert's water—the pupfish's water—and in doing so, pushed the species to the edge of oblivion. We have argued and fought over this water, and continue to argue and fight over it. And some of us have honored and loved the Devils Hole pupfish for what it is, what it symbolizes, and what it has meant for disputes over the desert's water, while others have come to hate or at least resent the Devils Hole pupfish for much the same reason.

There should be a plaque at the capped wellhead less than a quarter-mile east of Devils Hole, just beyond the boundary of the National Park Service inholding: something to commemorate the incongruous and rusted metal tube, about three feet high, that stands among scattered creosote bushes and a denuded plane of decades-old bulldozer scrapings. The plaque would bear the inscription, "On this spot in 1976, the thoughtless use of western water began to die." The well, numbered 36dd in a 1976 U.S. Geological Survey report, was drilled in October 1966, around the time that a corporate farm, Spring Meadows Inc. began acquiring land in Ash Meadows, including 5,000 acres from the U.S. Bureau of Land Management. Spring Meadows planned to irrigate over eighteen square miles of desert, mostly to grow water-intensive alfalfa in an area that averages less than four inches of rain per year. The corporation obtained some water rights when it purchased 7,000 acres of private land; the rest came from wells and springs on property owned by the U.S. Bureau of Land Management. Although 36dd was never used as a production well, water levels in Devils Hole dropped immediately when it was tested in 1968, a situation exacerbated by pumping from production wells located between 1.25 and 2.5 miles southeast of Devils Hole, in the Point of Rocks area. By September 1972 water levels in Devils Hole had fallen by almost 2.7 feet, exposing about 87 percent of the rock shelf crucial to pupfish spawning and feeding, and portending extinction of the pupfish if the declines continued.

Fortunately—if not for Spring Meadows Inc. then certainly for the Devils Hole pupfish—since 1968 some tenacious people had understood the threat posed by water withdrawals. In November of 1969 biologists and resource managers concerned about native fish in the Amargosa River drainage, including the Devils Hole pupfish, met at Furnace Creek to devise a plan for "circumventing [federal and state] agency inertia and thereby starting a movement to preserve endangered desert ecosystems and their associated life-forms." The meeting led to the establishment of a private technical advisory group, the Desert Fishes Council, with Phil Pister of the California Department of Fish and Game as its chairman; creation of the federal Pupfish Task Force, which included representatives from the U.S. Bureau of Land Management, Fish and Wildlife Service, National Park Service, and Geological Survey; and several hydrological studies, which determined that irrigated agriculture and healthy natural habitats at Ash Meadows were incompatible, and that continued groundwater pumping would cause further water level declines in Devils Hole. A public constituency supporting protection for the Devils Hole pupfish also was developing, driven by activists from the Desert Fishes Council and conservation organizations as well as increased media publicity. Major newspapers such as the *New York Times* and *Wall Street Journal* covered the controversy, and both NBC and ABC produced television documentaries featuring pupfish. The hour-long NBC documentary on water pollution, *Timetable for Disaster*, which included a fifteen-minute segment on the Devils Hole pupfish, won an Emmy Award as the best television documentary of 1970 and may have had a particularly large effect on public opinion.

However, growing concern about the fate of the Devils Hole pupfish did not translate into a voluntary reduction of groundwater pumping by Spring Meadows. And so, in August 1971, the U.S. Department of the Interior filed a complaint in U.S. District Court in Las Vegas seeking to prevent Spring Meadows from pumping groundwater from three wells identified by the U.S. Geological Survey as having large effects on water levels in Devils Hole. Although uncontrolled water withdrawals were doing very bad things to aquatic ecosystems and vulnerable species throughout Ash Meadows, weak federal laws and agency recalcitrance made it impossible to pursue a broader suit. The Endangered Species Act of 1973 was not yet law, and the Bureau of Land Management had different institutional values and less regulatory authority than the National Park Service, and so litigation focused only on Devils Hole and its pupfish. Although the suit caused Spring Meadows Inc. to shut down the offending wells, any positive effects were short lived, and continued pumping from other wells pushed water in Devils Hole toward historically low levels. In June 1972 the federal government reactivated its suit, arguing that it had the right to reserve sufficient water, which under western water law belonged to Nevada, to protect Devils Hole National Monument and its beleaguered pupfish. The government's assertion was based on the U.S. National Park Service Organic Act and the implied reservation doctrine, which had been established for surface water by a 1908 U.S. Supreme Court decision, *Winters v. United States*. Although the implied reservation doctrine did not yet extend to groundwater, in June 1973 the district court issued a preliminary injunction requiring Cappaert Enterprises, the corporate child of Spring Meadows, to cease withdrawing water from wells, aquifers, and springs within 2.5 miles of Devils Hole.

Water levels in Devils Hole began to rise, but Cappaert Enterprises appealed the decision to the Ninth U.S. Circuit Court of Appeals, which in April 1974 upheld the district court's ruling. Cappaert appealed again, this time to the U.S. Supreme Court, which in its unanimous June 1976 *Cappaert v. United States* decision ruled in favor of the federal government: "We hold, therefore, that as of 1952 when the United States reserved Devils Hole, it acquired by reservation water rights in unappropriated appurtenant water sufficient to maintain the level of the pool to preserve its scientific value." The court also held that Devils Hole pupfish were "objects of historic and scientific interest" and worthy of protection. Cappaert's wells had been effectively capped, and the Devils Hole pupfish rescued from its immediate peril. *Cappaert* was a momentous decision; in combination with *Winters*, it affirmed the right of the federal government to reserve surface water and groundwater, as part of an interrelated hydrological network, for environmental management purposes specified by law and regulation. Devils Hole (and eventually, Ash Meadows) could be protected from uncontrolled water withdrawals. *Cappaert*, along with the newly enacted Endangered Species Act of 1973, gave the federal government the authority required to protect rare aquatic species and habitats in the southwestern United States.

Reaction to *Cappaert* varied, depending on one's political and environmental attitudes. Conservationists and biologists rejoiced. After Jim Deacon called Phil Pister with the news—"We won!"—Pister hung up the phone and "cried out of relief." Since 1964, when he helped Carl Hubbs and Robert Miller rediscover the Owens pupfish, Phil had become increasingly involved in work to save desert aquatic ecosystems. He knew that a negative decision on *Cappaert* would doom the Devils Hole pupfish to extinction and make it impossible to protect other aquatic species on federal lands. Pister told me that *Cappaert* and the Devils Hole pupfish—all 200 or so of them at the time—"had begun the whole thing" relative to western water law and protecting endangered species. In 1977, Robert Abrams, writing in the *Environmental Law Reporter*, predicted that "conservationists will find the doctrine [of reserved water rights articulated in *Cappaert*] a potent weapon in attempts to ensure a secure water supply for federal enclaves established with the purpose of preserving natural amenities." Abrams also understood that *Cappaert* would exacerbate conflicts over water, as "state law water appropriators find their rights jeopardized by possible federal reservations of unknown magnitude slowing to some extent future non-federal water dependent economic development in western states." But if conservationists and biologists were ecstatic over *Cappaert*, some Nevadans were less than sanguine about protecting pupfish and the implied reservation doctrine. Nye County commissioner Robert Rudd produced a KILL THE PUPFISH bumper sticker in response to a SAVE THE PUPFISH bumper sticker promoted by the Desert Fishes Council, and on March 8, 1976, the editor of the *Elko Daily Free Press* fulminated against the "coalition of preservationists and federal agents" who were conspiring to usurp state water rights in order to protect "the 200 little fish nobody can ever see." The editor had the solution, though: "There is an insecticide on the market called rotenone which has been used successfully to eradicate 'problem' fish. . . . This substance holds the key to resolving the 'Pupfish Caper' before any more governmental time and money are wasted on this fraudulent attempt to establish federal authority as being greater than Nevada's jurisdiction of its own state water rights. An appropriate quantity of rotenone dumped into that desert sinkhole would effectively and abruptly halt the federal attempt at usurpation."

Rotenone, which is extracted from the roots of several tropical plants in the pea family, is a potent insecticide and fish poison. In 1962 rotenone had been used to poison "trash" fish along 420 miles of the Green River in Wyoming and Utah, including many native suckers and chubs, supposedly to allow planted rainbow trout and kokanee salmon to flourish in several reservoirs. Over a three-day period, about 20,000 gallons of rotenone were dripped into the Green River and its tributaries, with no thought to its effects on aquatic ecosystems, including native fish. Rotenone killed a lot of fish along 420 miles of the Green River, and it certainly would do the job on pupfish living in the 170 square feet of Devils Hole, the little bastards.

In addition to upholding the federal government's right to reserve groundwater for environmental protection, the Supreme Court also directed the district court to establish a final minimum water level for Devils Hole. In 1977 the court set this value at 2.7 feet below a copper washer set in the east wall of Devils Hole, a level that can be adjusted up or down, based upon scientific evidence. This "line on the rock" represented the water level that would cover roughly 40 percent of the shallow shelf. Water levels in Devils Hole first climbed above this critical value in 1978 and continued to increase until 1988; since then, they have fluctuated between 2.3 to 1.8 feet below the all-important copper washer. As water levels in Devils Hole recovered, so did the pupfish. By 1977, counts before and after the reproductive season had reached 198 and 553, respectively, and the species' immediate future seemed safe, if not entirely secure.

The court-mandated cessation of groundwater pumping within 2.5 miles of Devils Hole had averted extinction of *Cyprinodon diabolis*. But the plunging water levels and small pupfish populations of the late 1960s and early 1970s emphasized the precarious nature of the species' situation. It wouldn't take much—a reversal of *Cappaert* or some angry fool armed with rotenone and a copy of the *Elko Daily Free Press* editorial—to destroy the species. Aside from the problem of maintaining adequate water levels, the main issue was that all of the Devils Hole pupfish in the world resided in one small and vulnerable place. For many people working on pupfish conservation in the early years, securing the future of the species meant establishing additional populations, and so Devils Hole pupfish were transplanted into four natural springs, two aquaria, and an artificial refuge near Hoover Dam. Most of the fish transplanted to natural springs quickly disappeared, while a population at Purgatory Spring, Nevada, was destroyed when biologists noted that descendants of the original colonists were misshapen and "larger than the maximum natural size for this species." Populations at the Steinhart Aquarium and Fresno State College also failed, and although fish at the Hoover Dam refuge initially flourished, they eventually disappeared, an event that foreshadowed later problems in other refuges.

The Hoover Dam population was founded in 1972, after substrate and invertebrates from Devils Hole had been added to a nineteen-foot-long by nine-foot-wide cement "pond," dimensions approximating those of the rock shelf in Devils Hole. Although the twenty-seven colonists founded a population that survived for fourteen years, the project was troubled by problems that persisted through numerous extinctions, subsequent transplants, and three major renovations. Flash floods destroyed pipes that regulated the pond's water temperature by controlling flow from natural hot springs, and by 1977 descendants of the colonists no longer looked exactly like Devils Hole pupfish; they were larger and their body proportions had changed. After the surviving pupfish were removed from the refuge in 1986, it underwent a major overhaul. Separate stocks of thirty and ten fish from Devils Hole were introduced in 1988 and 1989, but both efforts failed. The refuge was renovated twice more in the 1990s, and restocked three times. The first two transplants failed, once due to water-supply issues, and once because the pupfish did not reproduce. The third transplant, which was made in 1998, used descendants of Devils Hole pupfish reared in refuges. It produced a population that fluctuated between 7 and 105 fish; the last of these eventually were transferred to another fish hatchery at Willow Beach, downstream from Hoover Dam, where they failed to reproduce and died out.

Two refuges with dimensions similar to the Hoover Dam pond were built at Ash Meadows, and both also failed to produce self-sustaining populations of Devils Hole pupfish. The first was constructed in 1973 near School Spring, and the second in 1990 near Point of Rocks. The population in the School Spring refuge, aka Amargosa Pupfish Station, first collapsed during the 1970s, but a second population begun in 1980 with twenty-five pupfish survived until 2003, when a pump failure killed the last survivors. During its thirty-year history, the Amargosa Pupfish Station was plagued by neglect, power and pump failures, corroded pipes, stuck water valves, poor reproductive performance by the pupfish, and genetic bottlenecks caused by small populations. In 1991 a new refuge at Point of Rocks was stocked with sixteen pupfish from the Amargosa Pupfish Station, but by May 1992 only a single individual remained; another transplant of fish from the Amargosa Pupfish Station in July 1992 resulted in a population that eventually climbed to 149. These results were encouraging, until researchers noticed that by 2000 pupfish from the Point of Rocks refuge were larger and deeper-bodied than those from Devils Hole, with 48 percent exceeding the maximum length of wild fish. Male fish also displayed none of the pacifism of Devils Hole pupfish; they were highly aggressive and defended mating territories. It only had been eight years since the Point of Rocks refuge was restocked with pupfish, but their descendants already were substantially larger and more combative than "wild" Devils Hole pupfish, as had happened at Purgatory Springs and the Hoover Dam refuge. To use a roughly appropriate primate analogy, wild Devils Hole pupfish are to nearby populations of the Ash Meadows Amargosa pupfish, *Cyprinodon nevadensis mionectes*, as bonobos are to chimpanzees: smaller and less aggressive. However, refuge experiments suggested that if Devils Hole pupfish were transferred to a new environment—even one meant to roughly mimic conditions in their natural habitat—the resultant population would shift toward the "chimplike" larger size and more aggressive behavior of Ash Meadows Amargosa pupfish.

These environmentally induced changes, or "phenotypic plasticity," were very bad news for the Point of Rocks refuge population and the entire Devils Hole pupfish refuge concept—an outcome made worse by the discovery that refuge fish probably had hybridized with Ash Meadows pupfish. In 2003 a graduate student, Abraham Karam, found one pupfish from the Point of Rocks refuge with minute pelvic fins, although wild Devils Hole pupfish always lacked them. By 2005, 23 of 110 fish from the refuge had pelvic fins, which led to a decision to abandon the site. A subsequent molecular genetics study by Andrew Martin and his colleagues indicated that between 1997 and 2003, several Ash Meadows pupfish somehow evaded fish exclusion devices and colonized the refuge. Alleles diagnostic for Ash Meadows pupfish had increased rapidly in less than nine years, suggesting that Devils Hole pupfish had been at a strong competitive disadvantage with their larger, more aggressive relatives. The Devils Hole and Ash Meadows pupfishes were not cooperating with efforts to establish a viable refuge population; to quote one dolphin-conversing, orgone-dispensing Wilhelm Reich disciple: "fishy fishy little devils."

Although Devils Hole pupfish had persisted in artificial refuges, maintaining these populations had required extraordinary efforts—partly due to repeated equipment failures, but also because the fish often did not thrive. Even in aquaria, where environmental conditions could be precisely controlled, Devils Hole pupfish sometimes spawned and produced larvae, but the larvae almost always died before maturing. By the mid-2000s, the collective experience with artificial populations in aquaria, natural springs, and refuges had clearly shown that the species is much more difficult to raise than other *Cyprinodon*, and that it has a strong tendency to undergo morphological and behavioral shifts outside of its native habitat. All of the transplanted populations had failed, and more than thirty years after the first Devils Hole pupfish refuge was built, there still was only one viable population, just as there had been in 1971. Although the 1980 recovery plan for the Devils Hole pupfish stipulated that two refuge populations should be established, so that a disaster would not lead to extinction of the species, the sole population of *Cyprinodon diabolis* lingered on in its natural habitat just east of Ash Meadows—small, isolated, and vulnerable to an unpredictable world.

The intractability of the Devils Hole pupfish—its failure to thrive in captivity and frustrating plasticity in refuges—raise three important, interrelated questions about the conservation and evolution of *Cyprinodon diabolis*. The first question is, just what is a Devils Hole pupfish? The second question follows from the first: is the Devils Hole pupfish, whatever it might be, distinct enough from other *Cyprinodon* to warrant protection under the federal Endangered Species Act? And given the conclusion that the Devils Hole pupfish is worth saving, the third question becomes: what can we do to protect it, other than preserving the health and integrity of the Devils Hole ecosystem?

The answer to the question of identity seems simple, but tautological: a Devils Hole pupfish is one that lives in Devils Hole. Data on three regions of mitochondrial DNA, as well as "hypervariable" regions of nuclear DNA called microsatellite markers, do demonstrate that Devils Hole pupfish possess unique genetic information found nowhere else in the pupfish world, and that the population has been following its own evolutionary path for perhaps 20,000 years. Genetic studies also have identified the Amargosa pupfish, *Cyprinodon nevadensis*, as the Devils Hole pupfish's nearest relative; another way of saying this is that the two species share a common ancestor. However, the data are not adequate to resolve evolutionary relationships among subspecies and populations of Amargosa pupfish and the Devils Hole pupfish. A further complication is that the Devils Hole pupfish and populations of the Amargosa pupfish do not display what is termed "reciprocal monophyly," a failure that some systematic biologists view as equivalent to a mortal, rather than a venal, sin, given the traditional designation of *C. diabolis* as a separate species.

To understand how reciprocal monophyly relates to the identity of the Devils Hole pupfish, begin by imagining an unwieldy dinner fork with ten tines. Each tine represents a distinct pupfish population; nine of the tines are for populations of the widely distributed Amargosa pupfish, and one for the Devils Hole pupfish. Now: hold the *Cyprinodon* fork in a vertical position, as if examining it for crusted debris, and notice that it has another impractical feature. Each tine is a different length; some are quite long, but others are so short as to be useless for impaling food. Not only are the tines different lengths, but some are branched, while others are not. The fork, which was designed by a committee of antisocial culinary engineers, may be useless for eating, but it could be used to depict evolutionary relationships among pupfish in the Ash Meadows/Amargosa River region. The left-right arrangement of adjacent tines and their relative lengths represent, respectively, the sequence of evolutionary events (founding of new lineages) and the degree of differentiation between related lineages. Figuratively speaking, the "cleanest" ten-tined *Cyprinodon* evolutionary fork would be one that had the deepest tine to one side, followed by a stair-step sequence of progressively shorter tines. If the *Cyprinodon diabolis* tine were furthest to the left, and all the *Cyprinodon nevadensis* tines were clustered to the right, the fork would depict an evolutionary history in which a split in one ancestral population gave rise to two lineages, one leading to the Devils Hole pupfish, and one to all of the Ash Meadows Amargosa pupfish populations. This arrangement would support the traditional designation of *C. diabolis* and *C. nevadensis* as separate species. We would have RECIPROCAL MONOPHYLY, and the people who study pupfish evolution and classification would drink beer and be happy.

The problem is that the Devils Hole pupfish tine is not the one furthest to the left. Examine the fork again (chip off that crusted egg first), and notice that the *C. diabolis* tine is a short one in the middle of the fork, nested within *C. nevadensis* tines of various lengths. What this means, in terms of evolutionary history and pupfish classification, is that the Devils Hole pupfish lineage arose from *within* the Amargosa pupfish lineage. Another way of saying this is that at some point during the Pleistocene, a population from within the Ash Meadows Amargosa pupfish lineage was isolated in Devils Hole and began swimming down its own evolutionary path. However, the path may not be long enough, and the resultant differences great enough, to warrant designation of *C. diabolis* as a separate species; perhaps instead it should be considered a subspecies of *C. nevadensis*.

Although reciprocal monophyly may seem like a term best relegated to cloistered molecular genetics laboratories (deep-six that silly *Cyprinodon* fork), it has an important bearing on the issue of the Devils Hole pupfish's identity and reasons for protecting the population. To understand why, consider the federal law that protects the Devils Hole pupfish and about 1,433 other plants and animals in the United States: the Endangered Species Act (ESA). The law is not called the "Endangered Population Act," although the ESA's legal definition of a species does include "any species or subspecies of fish or wildlife or plants, and any distinct population segment of any species of vertebrate fish or wildlife which interbreeds when mature." Given that the U.S. Fish and Wildlife Service has defined a distinct population segment as a "subdivision of a vertebrate species that is . . . separable from the remainder of and significant to the species to which it belongs," the Devils Hole pupfish should qualify for protection under the ESA. It is separable from other pupfish (recall the unique genetic markers and absence of pelvic fins, at least in wild populations), and it is wonderfully "significant to the species [or genus] to which it belongs." Assuming that some future administration, hostile to endangered species protection, does not press Congress or the U.S. Fish and Wildlife Service to amend the legal definition of a species, the Devils Hole pupfish's legal standing should remain secure, even if its specific taxonomic status is uncertain.

And yet in considering the nature of pupfish species, subspecies, and distinct population segments, there is the reality of *Cyprinodon* biology and the manner in which pupfish defy our attempts to classify and organize nature. There is the understandable human desire to simplify and describe, to partition the world and its creatures into clearly defined and labeled categories, such as species: *Cyprinodon radiosus*, the Owens pupfish; *Cyprinodon salinus*, the Salt Creek/Cottonball Marsh pupfish, with two subspecies; *Cyprinodon nevadensis*, the Amargosa pupfish, with five extant subspecies; and *Cyprinodon diabolis*, the Devils Hole pupfish. This issue also bedevils arguments about many other creatures listed under the Endangered Species Act, and whose protection has major economic implications, such as Preble's meadow jumping mouse (*Zapus princeps preblei*) and the coastal California gnatcatcher (*Polioptila californica californica*). Both of these subspecies occur where humans want to build their houses and shopping malls—the jumping mouse along the eastern side of the Front Range in Colorado, the gnatcatcher in southern California coastal sage scrub—and both have been the subject of bitter fights about their validity as distinct populations worthy of protection under federal law.

And beyond the Endangered Species Act and scientific or political arguments about taxonomic validity there is the actual world, resistant to easy scientific categorization, the messy and confusing and beautiful world in which pupfish (and jumping mice and gnatcatchers) populations live and die, and make their way through the vagaries of their harsh and unforgiving environments, such as the hot, oxygen-deprived, light-limited, nutrient- and energy-poor pool of Devils Hole, with its miniscule 170 square feet of decent spawning and feeding habitat. And it is foolish to think of pupfish environments only in terms of the present-day Mojave Desert, with its annual two to five inches of precipitation, creosote bush scrub, and scattered, precious oases of perennial water. Instead, we must take the long view, the one that encompasses the millions of years since the first ancestral pupfish colonized the Death Valley region, the great temporal reaches of the Pliocene and Pleistocene, with their droughts and deluges, glaciers and ephemeral lakes, ebb and flow of plants and animals, the ways in which the world has changed, and will continue to change.

One strategy for surviving and prospering in such an unpredictable world would be to incorporate morphological, biochemical, and behavioral flexibility into your nature—not unlike the adaptability that humans ideally should show to economic, political, and environmental uncertainty. This is what many pupfish·populations in the Death Valley region have done, hence the response of Devils Hole pupfish to refuge habitats. Although the refuges were designed to roughly replicate environmental conditions in Devils Hole, they often experienced increased fluctuations in water temperatures and generally higher, less variable levels of dissolved oxygen and algal biomass. Refuge populations responded to these environmental differences, and after only a few generations they looked and behaved differently than wild Devils Hole pupfish.

This remarkable phenotypic plasticity may have evolved in response to the variable environments of many pupfish habitats, and it has been studied in controlled laboratory settings by Sean Lema of California Polytechnic State University in San Luis Obispo. Lema's research expertise involves endocrinology and how animals respond to their environments. One of his most interesting studies demonstrated that in less than 4,000 years, Amargosa pupfish populations have evolved genetically mediated differences in aggressive behavior, although these differences are also affected by rearing environment: take the offspring of pupfish from a less aggressive population and stick them in an environment similar to one inhabited by more aggressive fish, and the experimental fish become more aggressive, and vice versa. But the experiment most relevant to the Devils Hole pupfish story involved rearing Amargosa River pupfish (*C. nevadensis amargosae*) under several food and temperature regimes. Amargosa River pupfish raised in a food-limited environment grew more slowly and shifted toward the juvenile morphology of adult Devils Hole pupfish: they had a proportionately larger head and eyes and a smaller body depth, and many failed to develop pelvic fins. Fewer fish also developed pelvic fins when reared in warmer water, a phenomenon noted by Robert Miller, who found some Amargosa River pupfish without pelvic fins in an isolated population subject to high water temperatures. Lema elucidated the mechanism responsible for the slower growth and morphological shifts in food-restricted pupfish: lower levels of the thyroid hormone thyroxine, which mediates the transition from juvenile to adult morphology. Because these changes had arisen within a single generation they were not due to selection for particular genotypes in the experimental environments. Instead, the Amargosa River pupfish possessed the same phenotypic plasticity present in Devils Hole pupfish. Although the experimental Amargosa River pupfish did not look exactly like Devils Hole pupfish—their heads were relatively smaller, and many had pelvic fins—after only one generation in the right conditions they had lower levels of thyroxine and looked much more like *C. diabolis* than their wild-caught parents.

If refuge populations are needed to secure the Devils Hole pupfish's future, but the morphology and behavior of *Cyprinodon* is extremely sensitive to environmental conditions, the solution seems to be to create a state-of-the art refuge in which crucial environmental variables can be precisely and accurately controlled. And so the Ash Meadows Fish Conservation Facility was built near the failed Amargosa Pupfish Station at School Spring. Completed in the autumn of 2012 at a cost of $4.5 million, it is a logical and technological extension of earlier refuge efforts, designed to simulate the ecology and environment of Devils Hole, with the promise that a captive, self-perpetuating population of Devils Hole pupfish finally will be established. The facility has a 100,000 gallon concrete tank with the same dimensions as the upper levels of the Devils Hole pool. The orientation and shading of the tank, which is surrounded by adobe-brown walls of concrete blocks and topped with a louvered roof, will control insolation, while a complex water treatment system will create aquatic conditions almost identical to those in Devils Hole. During a tour of the facility, Darrick

Weissenfluh, the manager, explained that before well water is pumped into the fish tank, it is shunted through a mechanical filter, acid injector (to lower pH), sand filter, biofilter, ultraviolet light cleaner, chiller (to cool the water if necessary), vacuum degasser (to lower dissolved oxygen), tank heated by a ground-source heat pump (to warm the water if necessary), and aeration head tank (to add oxygen to the water if need be). These treatments will generate the same warm, oxygen-poor, alkaline waters that wild Devils Hole pupfish experience, but which also are stressful to them. The irony here is obvious; as one biologist commented, "The point is to build a really crummy fish habitat." There is a back-up diesel generator in case of power failures, and an automatic alarm to notify personnel in Pahrump and Ash Meadows of equipment failures. The system is monitored via computers (also backed up); a click of a mouse and the lavender glow of the monitor reveals a flow chart displaying each element in the system, with current pH, temperature, and dissolved oxygen readings. Darrick was clearly excited about the technology and proud of his ability to get the system running, although he freely admitted that "we are never going to exactly recreate Devils Hole."

Once the system is fully operational and water conditions are set, the plan is to inoculate the tank with photosynthetic cyanobacteria, algae, and a range of invertebrates from Devils Hole—although other uninvited colonists could drift or fly in via the louvered roof. After the producers and consumers have established healthy populations, Devils Hole pupfish will be added to the mix, creating an artificial but self-sustaining ecosystem. In this idealized ecosystem each generation of Devils Hole pupfish, raised under the same controlled, food-limited, warm, and oxygen-poor conditions as in their natural environment, will produce another generation of pupfish with the same juvenile-like traits as their wild brothers and sisters: peaceful, small of body and large of head and eye, and without pelvic fins.

This is the hope, if not the current reality. Although the Ash Meadows Fish Conservation Facility was operational by March 2013, when the population of Devils Hole pupfish hovered around thirty-five fish, the cooperating agencies—the U.S. National Park Service, U.S. Fish and Wildlife Service, and Nevada Department of Wildlife—had not agreed upon when, or even how, to move Devils Hole pupfish into the refuge. The major concern is with the vulnerability of the natural population: can it stand to have any fish removed to found a refuge population, and if so, how many of which age class should be selected as the lucky colonists? Several biologists involved with the facility estimate that it is at least five years away from becoming an operational refuge supporting Devils Hole pupfish. There is too much bureaucratic inertia and uncertainty: to act is risky, and the litany of failed Devils Hole pupfish transplants mandates a cautious approach, even in the face of the species' continued vulnerability.

When I toured the Ash Meadows Fish Conservation Facility I was impressed by its spare, engineered brilliance—the intricate nexus of pipes and tanks, valves and gauges; the array of computers monitoring water conditions; and the attempt to accurately mimic the dimensions and annual pattern of insolation of the Devils Hole pool. The design team had even shaped the artificial shallow shelf so that it exactly replicates the irregular topography of the crucial rock ledge in Devils Hole: a pattern of grooves and slopes that I thought of as representing contours of hope—the hope that enough attention to detail will mean success for the refuge and its pupfish. The facility speaks to our technical capability, even if one of its engineers commented, "I don't understand why they're spending so much money on a fish that doesn't benefit anybody, not like hatchery trout." His sentiments mirrored those of the woman at Tecopa Hot Springs who said of the extinct Tecopa pupfish, "I think they were pretty tiny, not good for much of anything. You couldn't eat them—not like trout." They also represent the opinion of many people in the region who remain either hostile or indifferent to endangered species protection. But my values are not those of the engineer or Tecopa Hot Springs fisherwoman, and so in spite of its problems I see the Ash Meadows Fish Conservation Facility partly as a testament to what's best in our nature: the desire to make amends for past sins; our willingness to protect the vulnerable, not only of our own kind, but of other species as well; our inclination to cherish the creatures of this earth, in all of their magnificent wildness and adaptive beauty; our technological creativity; and our insistence that the worth of some things cannot be measured in money alone.

And yet I am not certain that the Ash Meadows Fish Conservation Facility is the right way to protect the Devils Hole pupfish, as much as I want it to succeed. I am not certain on scientific grounds, just as I have my ethical and emotional reservations. I want to say to the people who built the facility, and to those who are arguing about transplanting Devils Hole pupfish and how best to ensure survival of the species (or subspecies or population): "I have sat and watched *Cyprinodon diabolis* swim and spawn and feed, and followed the sun's track across Devils Hole. I have walked through the desert that envelops their home, read the scientific papers, and thought long and hard about the pupfish. I am haunted by their story, by their singularity and fragile existence and aloneness. I hope that my children's children will have the opportunity to see them in the wild, and so I want to like the Ash Meadows Fish Conservation Facility. I want it to work. So, forgive me if I have my doubts. Convince me that I am wrong."

One scientific reason for my skepticism is that the reluctance of the Devils Hole pupfish to thrive in captivity may have less to do with equipment failure, hybridization, or refuge habitats and more with the genetic health of the wild population. Andrew Martin's research suggests that the inability of the Devils Hole pupfish genotypes to compete successfully with Ash Meadows pupfish genotypes in the Point of Rocks refuge have been less a matter of "selection based on adaptive differences between *C. diabolis* and *C. nevadensis*" and more about "selection resulting from viability differences (genetic load) between the two species." In other words, the history of the Devils Hole pupfish—perhaps a population founded by a few individuals, a series of bottlenecks in which the population was reduced to a few individuals, and chronically low population sizes—has resulted in the accumulation of harmful mutations. As one of Martin's collaborators, Anthony Echelle, told me, the Devils Hole pupfish may have undergone a "mutational meltdown." To determine if the Devils Hole pupfish is saddled with a high genetic load, Martin and his colleagues suggest a controlled study in which the "abundance and magnitude of deleterious alleles in *C. diabolis*" would be examined in the offspring of a cross between parental Devils Hole pupfish and Ash Meadows pupfish. Such an experiment would be useful if it "becomes necessary to perform a specific set of crosses as a means of restoring the fitness of *C. diabolis*."

Martin's hypothesis is not only a matter of disagreement over competing hypotheses—adaptation versus genetic load—it also raises important questions about the best approach to managing and restoring Devils Hole pupfish. If his genetic hypothesis is correct then no refuge will work well, even one with the technological sophistication of the Ash Meadows facility. If the only goal for the new refuge is to create an artificial habitat that perfectly mimics that of Devils Hole, and so provide the fish with an environment that suits their "adaptive landscape," the outcome inevitably will be compromised by the poor genetic health of Devils Hole pupfish. Instead, it might be necessary to counteract the negative consequences of inbreeding and genetic bottlenecks. Such an effort would involve an initial cross of Devils Hole and Ash Meadows Amargosa pupfish, followed by a series of backcrosses with Devils Hole pupfish. If the fish cooperated, the program could produce almost "pure" Devils Hole pupfish, but with more variation and a lower genetic load, and consequentially an increased ability to flourish in Devils Hole and refuges. Or such would be the hope, controversial as it is.

At a recent scientific meeting of the Desert Fishes Council in Death Valley, Andrew Martin gave a talk outlining his views on genetic rescue of the Devils Hole pupfish. He argued for an approach much like that used with the Florida panther. The 1995 translocation of eight females from a different subspecies in Texas restored the genetic health of the ailing population, which had been reduced to less than twenty-five individuals and was suffering from high levels of inbreeding. Infusion of new genetic material helped increase survival and reproduction in the Florida panthers, and by 2003 there were at least ninety-five adults. After his talk, Martin was asked how something similar might be done with Devils Hole pupfish. He paused, and for a moment looked reluctant to respond, as if he was weighing his options: sidestep the question and avoid controversy, or provoke a reaction? And then it was as if Martin decided, "What the hell." He replied that he would introduce a single, marked adult female Ash Meadows Amargosa pupfish into Devils Hole, let her mate, and then pull her out. Her progeny would outcompete other pupfish in Devils Hole; the population would increase rapidly, and "although there would be some *Cyprinodon nevadensis* genes in the population, it still would be a *diabolis* phenomenon." Martin was immediately challenged by Kevin Wilson, who protested that "we want pure Devils Hole pupfish," and by Christopher Martin (no relation), a PhD candidate at the University of California, Davis, who argued that the conservation goal should be to "protect the purity of the lineage." It was obviously an emotional issue; Wilson and Christopher Martin both looked upset, and during their exchanges with Andrew Martin others in the audience were shifting in their seats and murmuring—some out of disapproval, a few (perhaps) in agreement with Andrew Martin's proposal.

What Andrew Martin had done, in a public setting, was to question the basic premise of the Ash Meadows Fish Conservation Facility. He was arguing that recent declines of the Devils Hole pupfish were more about genetics than ecology, that a state-of-the-art refuge and manipulations of the Devils Hole ecosystem would never restore the Devils Hole pupfish. Martin's proposal, though, carried its own set of risks; it was an experiment without possible replication and demanded an absolute commitment to an unproven hypothesis, even if there were some good data indicating that the Devils Hole pupfish were highly inbred. Once that single female had been placed in Devils Hole, there was no going back. Later, Martin and I talked about his exchange with Kevin Wilson and Christopher Martin. He felt that "the National Park Service, Fish and Wildlife Service, and Nevada Division of Wildlife have never seriously entertained all hypotheses. When they [the U.S. Fish and Wildlife Service] built that thing [the Fish Conservation Facility], they made a final statement about the path the program would take." When I asked if establishing a healthy refuge population could provide a reliable way to supplement the Devils Hole population, he replied, "I don't think we have time for that. The population could be extinct in ten years, although I could be surprised."

Martin said this when we were sitting outside the meeting venue, and in spite of the glorious and welcoming sun of a mid-November day and the beautiful ambience of Death Valley, he seemed deflated and fatalistic. The decision had been made: the plight of the Devils Hole pupfish had more to do with ecology than with genetics, and management would proceed accordingly. The issue of inbreeding would not be addressed; genetic purity had become the ultimate conservation goal, an attitude that had its roots in the 1990s, when molecular genetics techniques began to dominate the thinking of conservation biologists.

The Desert Fishes Council meetings left me more puzzled than ever about the Ash Meadows Fish Conservation Facility and Devils Hole pupfish, although my main scientific concern did not (and still does not) involve the different management approaches suggested by the adaptive and genetic-load hypotheses. Instead, it has more to do with the issue raised by Sean Lema's research on environmentally induced phenotypic plasticity in pupfish and the related question of identity—just what is a Devils Hole pupfish? Given the ways in which the behavior, morphology, and physiology of pupfish are affected by their environment, it is difficult to conceive of *Cyprinodon diabolis* except in the context of where it lives, what Lema terms "the organism-environment interdependency." He explained to me that, "essentially, this means that you cannot really separate the organism from its environment; they interact with, and affect, one another. In the case of the Devils Hole pupfish, the issue [of a refuge population] is about the connection of the population to its unique environment."

The implications of Lema's organism-environment interdependency are profound. Although it might be prudent to grow Devils Hole pupfish in a refuge, to protect the lineage from extinction, and a captive breeding program designed to restore their genetic health might be a good idea, don't be fooled: take Devils Hole pupfish out of Devils Hole, place them in any facility, no matter how well it emulates the species' natural environment, and you will grow something else. For Lema, "it's the fish in the habitat," and what kind of a fish you want—pure *Cyprinodon diabolis*, or something with a few *Cyprinodon nevadensis* genes—is "a matter of ethics."

We should remember, too, that organisms and their environments are not static. Not only have numbers of what we call the Devils Hole pupfish fluctuated across the seasons, years, and millennia; their morphological, behavioral, and physiological characteristics have undoubtedly done so, too. And neither has their environment remained stable. Some of the post-1966 changes in Devils Hole are due to human action, such as the decline in water levels that began in the late 1960s, as Spring Meadows worked to transform Ash Meadows into an agricultural wasteland. However, the causes of other recent changes are unclear, including the transition from an ecosystem based on photosynthetic energy produced by green alga to one dependent on cyanobacteria, and the habitat shift by an ostracod that once was an important pupfish prey item. And then there are the 500,000 years of water-level fluctuations depicted by the layers of mammillary calcite, the ebb and flow of groundwater that has responded to the beat of rain and snow across the great pluvials and droughts of the Pleistocene. Lema thinks that no matter how hard we work to recreate Devils Hole in an artificial environment, the captive pupfish "are going to move phenotypically. The focus is on stasis, but the system is moving all of the time."

In spite of our best intentions, which are to protect a species that we have helped endanger, it may be that in building the Ash Meadows Fish Conservation Facility, we are chasing a ghost. We are trying to preserve a snapshot of the Devils Hole pupfish and its habitat taken at one point in time. We have assembled all of the requisite pieces—well water, filters, aeration tank, temperature and pH controls, a pool with the dimensions of Devils Hole, the correct insolation, a representative collection of invertebrates and photosynthesizers—which in our technological pride and hope we believe will allow us to produce fish with morphological, genetic, and behavioral characteristics very similar to those in Devils Hole. But what we actually have created is a simulacrum, one which might (just add fish) produce something that resembles a Devils Hole pupfish (circa 2013), but which is not exactly one. Why? Because the population carries the evolutionary legacy of *Cyprinodon*, which is in part about phenotypic plasticity, and because fish produced by the Ash Meadows Fish Conservation Facility would not live and feed and spawn and develop in Devils Hole, whether or not they contain any "foreign" Amargosa pupfish genes. Call it the "Quasi-Vermeer Effect": a paint-by-numbers scheme, no matter how minute and exact the guiding pattern of paint and polygon, will never recreate *The Milkmaid*. It will never capture the play of light on the softly roped muscles of the milkmaid's left forearm, the gleaming pitcher and thin strand of milk, the glistening loaf of bread, the young woman's focused, downward glance, the soft and haunting luminosity of the room where she stands.

Perhaps it would have been better (and cheaper) to admit that we never could create an artificial ecological and evolutionary system with dynamics that closely parallel those of Devils Hole. Instead, perhaps we should have followed Abraham Karam's advice, which was outlined at the conclusion of his insightful study on the history and ecology of Devils Hole pupfish refuges: "Short term use of artificial refuges (several years) should be considered as an option for temporarily protecting species while their natural habitat is secured . . . but managers must make every effort not to allow those refuges to persist as static populations and instead allow them to partake in evolutionary processes important to their life history." Although I doubt that Devils Hole ever can be completely "secured," I do think that we could have learned from our mistakes with the Hoover Dam, School Spring, and Point of Rock refuges. We could have designed and built simpler but reliable systems, inoculated them with small numbers of larval Devils Hole pupfish collected during the spring population peaks, before mortality took its toll, even in the face our ignorance about the species' larval ecology. We could have grown several populations of pupfish with the genetic heritage of Devils Hole pupfish and introduced some Ash Meadows Amargosa pupfish genes into the mix, while acknowledging that time and habitat always would have their due. Although there undoubtedly would be some morphological and genetic shifts in the population, we could have produced a healthy, more genetically robust population than the fish living in Devils Hole. Perhaps. Or perhaps the National Park Service is right and it's more about habitat: get the Ash Meadows Fish Conservation Facility just right, figure out how to restore the ecosystem health of Devils Hole, and *Cyprinodon diabolis* will flourish.

But in thinking about the Devils Hole pupfish and our dedicated if not always successful efforts to preserve the species, I sometimes wonder if we are meddling too much, if it would be better to let *Cyprinodon diabolis* do what it will, without our earnest attempts to help it along. In spite of our past sins, particularly early collecting and uncontrolled groundwater pumping, and our complicity in the species' fate, perhaps we should stand back and leave Devils Hole more or less alone. Maintain the fence, even if it gives Devils Hole the ambience of a small zoo, to prevent uncontrolled and harmful access—by misguided souls with orgone generators, bitter states-righters with rotenone, careless tourists with trash, swimmers who leave tracks across the spawning shelf, divers with contaminated equipment. Place a few instruments in the water to monitor the ecosystem; conduct surface counts each autumn, and underwater counts less frequently. There are many situations involving rare and endangered species in which I think intervention is a very good thing and should be pursued with all of the heart, soul, science, and money we can spare, as with the Owens pupfish and the Ash Meadows Amargosa pupfish. I am not advocating for some noninterventionist, endangered species version of the 1930s-era America First Committee. But I just do not understand how to best protect the Devils Hole pupfish, which is something that I never would have said before I began my project—or even before I began writing this chapter. My concerns are certainly not about money. At present it costs about $390,000 per year for the National Park Service to run its Devils Hole program; the U.S. Fish and Wildlife Service will kick in another $250,000 annually for the Ash Meadows Fish Conservation Facility. Compared to the cost of a single B-2 Stealth bomber, which runs to about $2.1 billion, the Devils Hole pupfish cost us next to nothing. Hell, if it would make any real difference I would devote the annual salaries of twenty members of the U.S. Congress—currently $174,000 each—to conservation of the species. Neither are my fundamental concerns primarily about research and monitoring efforts prescribed in the Devils Hole Long-Term Ecosystem Monitoring Plan, or even about attempts to propagate pupfish in captivity and proposals to restore genetic health to the species. And they are certainly not about groundwater reservations, which make perfect sense: may the *Cappaert* decision always stand. Instead, I sometimes feel that we simply are too involved in the lives of those little fish, as if by our very concern for their well-being we have perpetuated an invasion that began with museum collections in the 1890s and groundwater pumping in the 1960s—even if our scientific and management incursions have been made with the best intentions, and we feel as though we have no choice but to become enmeshed in their lives.

As I circle round this problem of intervention and try to make sense of my ambivalent emotions, the word that I keep coming back to—unexpectedly—is sadness. Sadness that humans once took so much of *Cyprinodon diabolis*'s water and were willing to destroy the species and its beautiful world, but sadness, too, that we have needed to, or felt the need to, become so intimately involved in the life of the Devils Hole pupfish, sadness that we believe we can master the natural world enough to control the fate of the species.

It's the type of sadness captured by Pattiann Rogers in her haunting prose poem, "Animals and People: 'The Human Heart in Conflict with Itself'":

> And as long as we are not
> seriously threatened, as long as we and our children
> aren't hungry and aren't cold, we say, with a certain
> degree of superiority, that we are no better than
> any of them, that any of them deserve to live
> just as much as we do.
>
> And after we have proclaimed
> this thought, and by doing so subtly pointed out
> that we are allowing them to live, we direct them
> and manage them and herd them and train them and follow
> them and map them and collect them and make specimens
> of them and butcher them and move them here and move
> them there and we place them on lists and we take
> them off lists and we stare at them and stare
> at them and stare at them.

And one time, after staring and staring at *Cyprinodon diabolis*, my friend Ralph Black and I went out into the desert north and east of Devils Hole, into a long valley lined by limestone mountains, in the manner so characteristic of the Basin and Range country, mountains which funneled the lovely space into the clean and exquisite distance. We camped at the head of the valley, and in the night I lay in my sleeping bag and thought of pupfish in the warm and quiet water, a scatter of electric blue points in the dim light, making do with what they have in their close and limited world. I pictured them slowly swimming through their vulnerable home, past the objects of our affection and concern, the sensors and feeding tube, video cameras and wires, a staccato chorus of ultrasonic *Cyprinodon* clicks and rasps in the indigo pool, creatures protected, as best we can protect them, by laws and regulations, by boundaries and fences and a thirty-five-year-old Supreme Court decision. I thought of science and our halting attempts to comprehend the Devils Hole pupfish, to describe their world of rock and light and water, to raise them and make them safe, to control them in ways that seem antithetical to their very nature. I thought of all these things, and had no clear answers to my questions. And as I drifted off to sleep beneath a halo of stars, I knew only that in Devils Hole the pupfish were going about their business much as they always had, much as I hoped they always would.

And in the morning Ralph and I walked out into the desert, where he showed me an old bore hole that he had found the night before—a relict, perhaps, of Spring Meadows Inc. and its vanished dreams of cows and alfalfa. It had been a very dry winter; the land felt as though "The structure of every living thing / Was praying for rain," and so when Ralph dropped a stone into the darkness, we expected a quick "thunk" as the stone hit dry ground. Instead, there was a much longer fall, followed by a soft "plunk" when the stone plunged into water. And then came an eerie bass reverberation, a hollowed-out echo that climbed back up the hole and into the light: a haunting pulse traveling out of the vast continent of water that flows beneath the desert, water that falls out of the Spring Mountains and sweeps through the great plains of rock beneath the long dry valleys as it drifts toward the Amargosa Desert. The water rises to the surface at Devils Hole, where it sustains the pupfish and is transformed into something other than molecules of hydrogen and oxygen: a motion and a spirit that carry what we cannot quite grasp—the absolute isolation of *Cyprinodon diabolis*, the ways in which the species has sunk so deeply into a single desert pool, the legacy of 10,000 pupfish generations or more trailing away from the first colonists, swimming through time itself, swimming into our consciousness, responsibility, and painfully imperfect care.

Swimming from the Ruins

THE ASH MEADOWS AND
WARM SPRINGS AMARGOSA PUPFISHES

(Cyprinodon nevadensis mionectes
and *Cyprinodon nevadensis pectoralis)*

Thousands have lived without love, not one without water.
—W. H. Auden, "First Things First"

I awake at five. A mourning dove calls from somewhere below my bivouac spot, which is nestled on a small saddle in the mountains just east of Ash Meadows. The waning moon falls toward the distant mountains and the day climbs into light. Ash Meadows' palette of colors reveals itself, pulled out of darkness by the dawn: powdery white beds of clay; grayish yellow desert shrubs, a pointillist scatter of bursage and desert holly dotting the dark gray and brown alluvial fans; the anomalous glacial blue of Crystal Reservoir; a light gray-green mix of mesquite and leatherleaf ash surrounding the springs, which rise from the desert in a nine-mile-long string of thin oases. Further out, swatches and streaks of tawny yellow grass and sedge mark Carson Slough and the wetlands nourished by the springs. Beyond the slough is the broad sweep of the Amargosa Desert and Death Valley's mountains, the Greenwaters, Funerals, and Panamints, crowned with a shifting stratigraphy of color, purple and rose and orange light layered above the arid ranges. As morning breaks over the desert the scattered lights of the lowlands wink out: close at hand, the Ash Meadows Fish Conservation Facility at School Spring and the Fish and Wildlife Service compound near Crystal Spring; farther off, the Longstreet Casino and Amargosa Valley area, with its symmetrical green fields of alfalfa, its irrigated feedlot dreams.

Ash Meadows rises into the day and I think of the life that has sheltered there: at least twenty-nine species, subspecies, or varieties—three of them now extinct—found nowhere else on earth, within an area of thirty-six square miles. Below me, by and in its islands of water, are all of the surviving Ash Meadows endemics, a litany of enchanting names: Ash Meadows Amargosa pupfish, Warm Springs Amargosa pupfish, and Ash Meadows speckled dace; the Ash Meadows naucorid and Devils Hole Warm Springs riffle beetle; the elongate-gland springsnail, Point of Rocks tryonia, and Ash Meadows pebblesnail; the spring-loving centaury, Amargosa niterwort, and Ash Meadows blazing star; and fifteen others, all of them refugees, all of them clinging to water, or to watered ground. Below me, too, there once were Amargosa montane voles, Longstreet springsnails, and Ash Meadows poolfish, but they are gone now, dead to the world. And below me, thankfully, there now is a wildlife refuge, created in 1984—too late to save the Amargosa montane vole or Ash Meadows poolfish, but a protected place for the survivors. Ash Meadows National Wildlife Refuge has a density of endemics replicated nowhere else in Canada or the United States, one matched by few places in the world. The ecological and evolutionary home of these endemics is formed by the springs of Ash Meadows, but their legal home has replaced a fantasy, one that insisted that any patch of land in the arid Southwest can be something other than desert. This fantasy once claimed Ash Meadows as its own, and the protection granted the National Wildlife Refuge and its native species has been built upon the ramshackle debris of a delusion constructed from irrigation ditches, springhead pumps, and the maps of a planned development, where the streets fronting the "estates" were to have the names of water-loving plants: Ivy, Hibiscus, Ficus, Azalea.

At 6:10 the first sunlight hits the Greenwater Range, southwest of Death Valley Junction. A lone black-throated sparrow divides the stillness with his whistled song, and a rock wren follows from the cliffs above my perch. I shift in my sleeping bag, prop my back against a limestone boulder, and feel the rough touch of Paleozoic rock through my jacket. I brew a pot of tea and let my stove fall silent. The day comes on and the desert comes to me, its colors and scents, sounds and textures as rich as the hot and bitter taste of tea on my tongue. As I drink my tea I collect as much of the morning as I can and consider what I have seen of the Basin and Range country these last three years: Deep Springs Valley, Owens Valley, the Inyo Mountains, Salt Creek, Cottonball Marsh, the Panamint Range, Tecopa Hot Springs, Las Vegas, and Ash Meadows. And it seems that in this place,

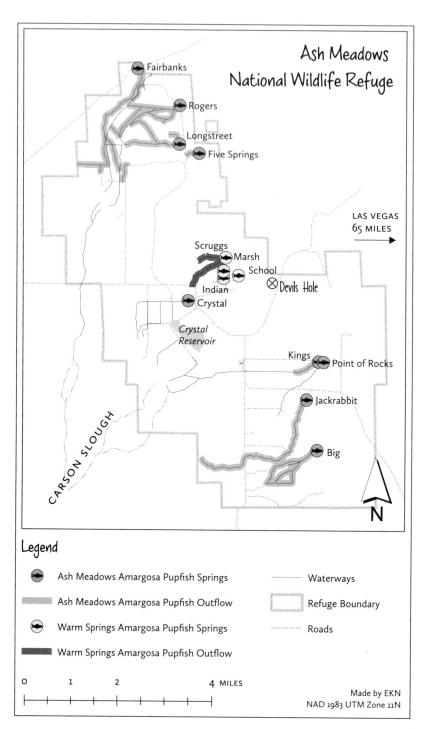

Ash Meadows National Wildlife Refuge and vicinity

which lies both physically and metaphorically just to the west of Nevada's Last Chance Range, all of the themes of my journey are drawn together. At Ash Meadows it is possible to understand something of isolation and evolution, islands and sanctuaries, the harmful press of exotic species, habitat destruction and restoration, the ebb and flow of Pleistocene waters, extinction and resilience, the misguided use of the desert's water, and how a few dedicated people can put things right.

The air is still this morning, still and rich and rising into warmth, alive with the colors of the day and the great breadth of the Amargosa Desert. Sunlight breaks across Ash Meadows, shines upon the world of pupfish and pebblesnails, niterwort and naucorids, leatherleaf ash and screwbean mesquite. I rise, pack my gear, and descend the steep slope below my camp, headed toward water and the islands of life that grace this desert world, wanting nothing more than to tell this story, and to believe—*to know*—that all that lies before me will endure.

<hr>

It's mid-March when I pick up a rental car in Las Vegas and flee north and west, away from what the city and Clark County are now (an inertial flood of 2 million people in a desert where the annual precipitation averages four inches), and the memory of what they were 150 years ago ("The Meadows," a watering place along the Old Spanish Trail, home to the extinct Vegas Valley leopard frog and Las Vegas dace): past the great sandstone scarp fronting the eastern edge of the Spring Mountains, then over Mountain Springs Summit and down into Pahrump Valley, its broad basin falling westward into the spare distance, toward the crenellated ridges of the Nopah Range. I track Nevada Highway 160 north and west, cutting across the great sprawl of alluvial fans that spill from the Spring Mountains and hurry past Manse Spring, where the Pahrump poolfish used to live. Seventy-five minutes of driving brings me to Pahrump, a 40,000-person confusion of strip malls, trailer homes, subdivisions, fast food restaurants, tattoo parlors, and "gentleman's" clubs, the perfect advertisement for unregulated growth. It was here, decades before Pahrump became what we now think of as Pahrump, when there were just a handful of ranching families in the valley, that Robert Miller discovered two new subspecies of poolfish. The Raycraft Ranch and Pahrump Ranch poolfishes were confined to several small springs and their outlet ditches supplying ranch homes and hayfields. People often say of a small town (such as Pahrump in the 1950s), "blink and it's gone," but you could say the same thing about the Pahrump Ranch and Raycraft

Ranch poolfish, because only a few years after Miller described the subspecies in 1948, groundwater pumping, habitat destruction, and introduced species obliterated them.

I gas up in Pahrump, drive north for three miles, and turn onto West Bell Vista Avenue, which on some maps also is called the Bob Rudd Memorial Highway. I do not know if naming the highway leading past Ash Meadows after Rudd was an act of unintended irony or purposeful resentment, but either way its name symbolizes the conflict engendered by federal endangered species management, because Rudd was the Nye County commissioner who ordered up those infamous "Kill the Pupfish" bumper stickers at the height of the Devils Hole pupfish controversy. I follow Rudd's Pupfish Highway for eighteen miles, across a low divide separating the Pahrump and Amargosa valleys, to South Springs Meadows Road, which runs north into Ash Meadows National Wildlife Refuge. Another five miles of dirt road brings me to a graveled parking lot at the Point of Rocks interpretive trail, and when I step from the car, I have entered another world. Emotionally, aesthetically, and ecologically, Ash Meadows is as far removed from the urban world of Clark County as my home in western New York is from the Yukon Delta National Wildlife Refuge in Alaska, where in some years I help the Fish and Wildlife Service survey nesting waterfowl. To travel in early June to the wild edge of the Bering Sea is to transition from the riotous, summer green world of a suburban college town to a landscape just emerging from winter, where ice still covers many tundra ponds, the nearest village is one hundred miles away, and the air is filled with a chorus of goose calls. At Point of Rocks there are stillness and birdsong and empty space, and a spring-fed stream nourishing a mesquite bosque. Las Vegas, with its cacophony of noise and lights, its casinos and freeways, feels as though it is part of an alternative universe composed of spiritual antimatter.

I grab my binoculars and follow the boardwalk and interpretive trail through the leafless mesquite and ash, past stands of seep willow, to a basin of brilliant aquamarine water. Kings Pool is about thirty feet long and fifteen feet wide, ringed by a garland of three-square bulrush; beyond it is a semicircular shelf of travertine, capped with mesquite, and then a world antithetical to water: dry desert ground, saltbush and bursage, a naked slope climbing to the Point of Rocks ridgeline. There's a thin, broken layer of bird noise in the air: Gambel's quail call from the scrub; a solitary Bewick's wren buzzes for a second; a small flock of black-tailed gnatcatchers scold me briefly and then are gone. My attention returns to Kings Pool, which is alive with Ash Meadows Amargosa pupfish. Bright blue males patrol choice bits of space above small outcrops of algae-covered rock, chasing intruders. A male occasionally sidles up to a passing female, but the females seem unreceptive and I see no spawning. Other pupfish cluster near the outlet, working the shallows and fighting the current, which is something that pupfish most often avoid; at Ash Meadows they prefer quiet water and leave the faster reaches to another federally endangered fish, the Ash Meadows speckled dace, a small minnow not much more than three inches long. I dip my hand into Kings Pool, which feels nearly as warm as Devils Hole, and bring a taste of it to my mouth: tepid and slightly alkaline, but certainly palatable.

I follow the pupfish for an hour, grow drowsy in the soft spring warmth, and sink into the quiet. Eventually I rouse myself and continue wandering the boardwalk, listening to birds and watching bees feed on the blossoms of leatherleaf ash. The boardwalk meanders through mesquite, then climbs a gentle slope and crosses several small streams spilling from a beige mound of travertine rock. I trace one of the small streams to a springhead—a small cavity in the rock and below it, a narrow sluice box less than one foot wide. I squat down, reach into the slot, and pick up a small submerged rock. On its underside are minute black springsnails, maybe three millimeters long, one of two springsnail species that occur nowhere else in the world beside the Point of Rocks area, not even in other springs at Ash Meadows. I rise and survey the view, which stretches to the west and south, into the Amargosa Desert, and contemplate pupfish and springsnails, the twenty-nine organisms endemic to Ash Meadows, the ways in which a multitude of histories—geological, hydrological, biological—have created such a rich pageant of life. This small rise is a good place, I think, as I glance behind me, toward a set of cylindrical holes drilled into the travertine. Each is about six inches in diameter and eighteen inches deep, and was made by Native Americans as they ground mesquite pods into flour. How many generations would have kneeled on these rocks and looked out across the same mesquite bosques, toward what we now know as Death Valley? What drew the Southern Paiute and Western Shoshone people to Ash Meadows was its water, and the bountiful life gathered in and around the springs, just as ranchers, developers, biologists, and ultimately the U.S. Fish and Wildlife Service, later would be attracted to the same area.

Ash Meadows National Wildlife Refuge is located in southern Nye County, Nevada, about ninety miles northwest of Las Vegas and thirty miles west of Pahrump. By National Wildlife Refuge standards it is moderately sized, and its 24,000 acres are substantially smaller than the nearby

1.6 million acre Desert Wildlife Refuge. Not all of the land within Ash Meadows' boundaries belongs to the Fish and Wildlife Service; there also are 676 acres of private inholdings, which present a management challenge because the interests of private landowners, such as the zeolite processing plant in the southern part of the refuge, are not those of the Fish and Wildlife Service. Finally, along the east-central boundary of the refuge are the forty acres surrounding Devils Hole, which are part of Death Valley National Park and are managed by the U.S. National Park Service. Although the Devils Hole inholding accounts for only 0.2 percent of the refuge's acreage, its importance far outweighs its size, for two reasons. First, there is the U.S. Supreme Court decision of *Cappaert v. United States*, which determined that the federal government could reserve groundwater rights in order to maintain water levels in Devils Hole. Because Ash Meadows and Devils Hole are part of an interrelated hydrological network, *Cappaert* also protects Ash Meadows from uncontrolled water withdrawals. Second, the federal Endangered Species Act protects the Devils Hole pupfish, mostly by guaranteeing adequate water levels in Devils Hole—which by proxy also protects federally threatened and endangered species in Ash Meadows. No wonder that Sharon McKelvey, manager of Ash Meadows National Wildlife Refuge, refers to Devils Hole as the "Mother Hole."

If location is everything, then Ash Meadows National Wildlife Refuge is sited in an excellent place. Although the refuge lies in the Amargosa Desert just a few miles east of the waterless, sandy channel of the Amargosa River, Ash Meadows is blessed with almost fifty perennial seeps and springs. Most of these discharge along a line just east of the Gravity Fault system, which runs northwest to southeast through the eastern part of the refuge, paralleling a series of low limestone mountains. The waters move south and west from their springheads and either sink into the desert soil or flow into Carson Slough along the western boundary of the refuge. The springs are nourished by the same system that feeds Devils Hole, which drains southwest through the Amargosa Basin, carrying groundwater gathered from the Spring Mountains, Sheep Range, Tikaboo Valley, Emigrant Valley, and Yucca Flat. These waters, which are part of the Death Valley regional flow system, may travel one hundred miles or more across numerous basins, following gravity through the deep carbonate aquifer and into the Amargosa Desert hydrographic basin, which includes Ash Meadows. The waters of the central Death Valley flow system may also travel across great swaths of time, as the groundwater discharging from the springs of Ash Meadows may be up to 30,000 years old, the result of rain or snow that fell during the Pleistocene.

Some springs in Ash Meadows, such as those at Point of Rocks, discharge directly from outcrops of deep carbonate aquifer, while others, such as Jackrabbit, Big, and Crystal springs, discharge from shallow valley-fill aquifer, although the ultimate source for these waters is the same deep carbonate rock. But whatever the geological setting for Ash Meadows' springs, the important point is that their waters are old, and gather from a large chunk of Basin and Range country. They move into the Amargosa Desert basin through fissures in the deep carbonate aquifer, beneath mountain ranges that block the movement of surface water, a process termed interbasin transfer. The waters discharging from Ash Meadows' springs represent a very small portion of the Amargosa Desert basin's groundwater capital, which accumulated during the Pleistocene, but it is these waters that sustain the refuge's astounding biodiversity. Ash Meadows has been well watered since at least the mid-Pliocene, some 3.2 million years ago, when the area was covered by marshes, playas, and shallow ponds, and springs were more abundant than today. The ancestors of many of the refuge's endemic species must have colonized the region at that time and undergone repeated bouts of isolation and range expansion as the climate alternated between pluvial and dry periods. But with the great drying that began after the Pleistocene, species with poor dispersal abilities, such as pupfishes and springsnails, would have been restricted to Ash Meadows, or even to one or a few spring systems within the area. Genetic evidence suggests that the Amargosa pupfish (*Cyprinodon nevadensis*) lineage, which includes the Devils Hole pupfish, diverged from its nearest relative, the Salt Creek pupfish, about 1 million years ago, but that further diversification occurred within the Amargosa pupfish lineage during the last ten to twenty thousand years, due to a declining water table. The resulting isolation, which is a function of elevation more than distance between springs, has produced populations with unique genetic markers, and two recognizable subspecies of pupfishes: the Ash Meadows Amargosa pupfish (*Cyprinodon nevadensis mionectes*) and the Warm Springs Amargosa pupfish (*C. n. pectoralis*), both of which are listed as endangered under the federal Endangered Species Act.

The Ash Meadows Amargosa pupfish is the more widely distributed of the subspecies, inhabiting twelve spring systems along a nine-mile line from Fairbanks Spring in the north to Big Springs in the southeast; all of these have at least intermittent water connections with Carson Slough, and constant water temperatures ranging from 65 to 89°F. Robert Miller, who described the Ash Meadows Amargosa pupfish as a new subspecies, distinguished it based on its characteristically short, slab-sided, and long-headed body, with relatively low scale and fin-ray counts. The Warm Springs Amargosa pupfish is more narrowly distributed than its sister sub-species and occurs only in six small springs in the Warm Springs complex, in the east-central part of the refuge: North and South Indian, North and South Scruggs, Marsh, and School springs. These springs are tightly clustered in an area of less than one square mile, and all have flows of less than 1.5 gallons per second. As their collective name suggests, all are warm, between 82 and 93°F—an indication of how closely their discharge is tied to the deep carbonate aquifer. Outflow from the Warm Springs complex disappears into the desert a short distance below the springheads, which means that under conditions that have existed for much of the past 10,000 years, Warm Springs Amargosa pupfish must have remained isolated from other Ash Meadows pupfish, hence their unique genetic markers and morphology.

Miller distinguished the Warm Springs subspecies primarily based on the high number of pectoral fin rays—the cartilaginous elements that support soft tissue of the fin. The Warm Springs Amargosa pupfish is also small; many are little more than one inch long and show a tendency toward reduction and loss of pelvic fins, as in Devils Hole pupfish. The small size of the Warm Springs Amargosa pupfish once was brought home to me at Marsh Spring, when I found a one-and-one-half-inch-long giant water bug grasping an inch-long pupfish between its legs, with its proboscis inserted deep into its prey, like a scene out of *Alien*. The isolation of the Warm Springs complex also has given rise to three endemic invertebrates: the median-gland Nevada springsnail, Devils Hole Warm Spring riffle beetle, and Warm Springs naucorid, or creeping water bug. All three are less than six millimeters long; they spend their entire lives in the water, and so are as tied to the springs as is the Warm Springs Amargosa pupfish.

All of the springs in the Warm Springs complex have source pools less than about six feet in diameter and four feet deep, and outflows often not much more than one foot wide. To track the course of one of these systems is to confront the isolation that embraces the Warm Springs endemics: the bath-temperature water bubbling up at the tiny springhead; perhaps a short cascade through bands of travertine rock; the thin, wandering outflow, sometimes hidden beneath a narrow riot of sedges and rushes; an overhanging canopy of mesquite and leatherleaf ash; water flowing for four or five hundred yards before disappearing into a terminal band of marsh, which grades into the great austerity of the surrounding desert, into an arid ocean that represents death for a Warm Springs Amargosa pupfish, Warm Springs naucorid, or median-gland Nevada springsnail. Aquatic habitats in the Warm Springs complex are almost completely isolated from other aquatic habitats, the only potential contact being with Crystal Spring, which lies about one-half mile downstream from where water from the Warm Springs complex disappears. But even within the Warm Springs complex the springs and aquatic species they support are generally isolated from one another. There is little connectivity among them except in times of extraordinary rainfall, an isolation reflected by the genetic structure among the populations of Warm Springs Amargosa pupfish.

The small extent of Warm Springs' aquatic habitats means that its pupfish and endemic invertebrate populations also must be small and vulnerable. Pupfish populations in several of the springs are estimated at less than one hundred, and the one in South Indian Spring went extinct around 1998, probably due to colonization by nonnative crayfish. Mexican Spring once contained one of the smallest self-sustaining vertebrate populations in the world, about twenty to fifty pupfish, but in 1973 uncontrolled growth of water-loving plants dried the spring, and the population disappeared. This extinction event was in keeping with the disassembly of aquatic ecosystems being undertaken at the same time by Spring Meadows Inc., as it worked to drain the springs of Ash Meadows and turn much of the area into an alfalfa monoculture.

As I watch pupfish at Ash Meadows, I am struck by how distinct the behavior of pupfish populations can be, an observation in keeping with Sean Lema's research on phenotypic plasticity in Amargosa pupfish and other studies on the variable mating behavior of pupfish in the region. Devils Hole pupfish are more docile than other pupfish, never defend mating territories, and usually project an air of passivity. In contrast, male Ash Meadows Amargosa pupfish in Kings Pool or Jackrabbit Spring often guard mating territories and are larger and more pugnacious than Devils Hole pupfish. Both the Kings Pool and Jackrabbit springheads are large; the latter, which is located about one mile southwest of Kings Pool, is particularly distinctive—a cone of aquamarine water twenty-five feet in diameter surrounded by a flat pan of white desert soil. Jackrabbit's breeding males are like a scatter of animated sapphires in the water; in the right season, many defend territories up to one foot across, each patrolling space around a clump of electric green algae. Territorial males pursue males that intrude into their space, but the aggression seems measured and controlled, as if the fish are conserving energy for the real work of spawning. A survey of

Jackrabbit males often shows that some are relatively still and rarely attack intruders, while others are more insistent on defending their space, even though their aggression seems to wax and wane with the day.

In contrast to pupfish in Kings Pool and Jackrabbit Spring, Warm Springs pupfish are small and frenetic; to spend an afternoon watching them is to undertake a study of piscine attention deficit disorder. The outflow below School Spring is one of the best places to observe pupfish, which are everywhere—along the riffles and runs, as well as in the shallow pools. Although coloration of breeding Warm Springs males has been described as "similar to the Ash Meadows pupfish," those that I have watched during the mating season appear muted, a trait somehow in keeping with their small size and hyperactive behavior, which may involve as many as sixty chases in a three-minute period. The pupfish of School Spring always seem to be moving, constantly inscribing figure eights, zigzags, and irregular ovals in the water. Pursuits last for a few seconds at most and then are quickly broken off; fish wriggle through the bottom sediments, tug at algae, rise to the surface, then hover in the water column, their pectoral fins a constant flutter. What's interesting is that the behavior and morphology of the pupfish varies along the outflow and seems correlated with microhabitat. Fish in faster water are smaller, with less blue, and their interactions appear to be more about feeding than mating, while those in quiet water are larger, more brightly colored, and more interested in reproduction. There are intense pockets of activity in some of the pools, often centered on areas with sticks, rocks, and mats of algae. Some fish defend fixed pockets of space for a few minutes but then abruptly switch to a different section of the pool before resuming attempts to repel the swirl of intruders. And so, in moving from spring to spring, or riffle to pool along a single springbrook, I am fascinated by the pupfishes' variability, and how it is concealed by a desert landscape that to a first-time visitor might appear monotonous and unchanging.

———————

I first visited Ash Meadows in March of 2009, when I was considering the sabbatical project that became the focus of this book. I sat beneath a veranda by the refuge headquarters with two Fish and Wildlife Service biologists, Cristi Baldino and Darrick Weissenfluh, and for an hour we talked of research ideas that I might pursue at Ash Meadows. But at the time my attention was drawn westward, to Death Valley, the Inyo Mountains, and the Owens Valley, partly because so much of my previous desert experience had occurred in those places, and partly because of the region's spectacular topography. I was (and still am) in love with the Panamint Mountains, where I spent two years studying feral burros, still entranced by the great rise and fall of Death Valley's arid ranges. Ash Meadows seemed flat and less compelling scenically—but its startling endemism intrigued me and I began spending more time there, watching pupfish, wandering across the desert, talking to people who knew the place, thinking, and reading. And the more that I learned about Ash Meadows, the more experience that I had with its springs and species, the more I thought about variability: the behavioral and physical differences among and even within populations of Ash Meadows pupfish; the thirteen species of springsnails that occur nowhere else, many of these restricted to just one or a few springs; the ways in which one species of springsnail transitions to another along a few feet of stream, in concert with changes in the channel's substrate; or the subtle morphological differences between the two species of creeping water bugs at Ash Meadows, the Warm Springs and Ash Meadows naucorids.

Naucorids are small, predaceous, flightless insects; the two species at Ash Meadows, along with a third species restricted to one Death Valley spring system, occur only in fast-flowing, warm water near springheads. When I am fortunate enough to hold a Warm Springs naucorid (*Ambrysus relictus*), there isn't all that much to see without a magnifying lens: it is only about five millimeters long, a bit less than the width of a standard-issue no. 2 pencil, ovate in outline, brownish yellow in color, with the very short forewings characteristic of flightless species. To the untrained eye it looks much like the Ash Meadows naucorid (*Ambrysus amargosus*), but it differs from its sister species in details of the external structures associated with the male and female genitalia. In the right habitat naucorids can be fairly common, but their restricted distribution, small size, and cryptic habits make it unlikely that many people will ever see a Warm Springs or Ash Meadows naucorid, let alone figure out how to identify either species. A technical paper distinguishes the Warm Springs naucorid as follows: "the male process is absent, with the sixth male tergite [hardened body segment of the abdomen] differently formed, having no angle or posterior protuberance as in *amargosus*; the female subgenital plate is almost symmetrical, versus quite asymmetrical in *amargosus*, and is notched apically as in *amargosus*, but with a slightly different shape along the posterior margin."

Although the arcane nature of the characteristics that distinguish the species and the technical language (tergite, subgenital plate, male process) are difficult for anyone but a specialist to grasp, the implications should not be: these flightless insects live in spring systems separated from one another by two and one-half miles of open desert and many thousands of years of evolutionary time. Once the Warm Springs complex became isolated from the Point of Rocks spring system, genetic changes accumulated in each naucorid population, and these changes eventually manifested themselves in morphological differences in the species' reproductive organs. To consider this process and its outcome (two tiny, cryptic insect species) is to confront, again, the issue of value, and what a naucorid species might be worth in any cost-benefit scheme. In this case the issue arises partly because the Ash Meadows naucorid was the first aquatic insect protected under the federal Endangered Species Act, an action prompted by destruction of its very limited natural habitat by agricultural development in the 1970s. Given the Warm Springs naucorid's restricted distribution and the recent extinction of several of its populations, it also should be protected, although it has not been proposed for listing under the Endangered Species Act. However, the third naucorid species in the Amargosa River drainage, the Nevares Spring naucorid, *Ambrysus funebris*, is a candidate for listing because water withdrawals for Furnace Creek in Death Valley represent "high magnitude" and "imminent" threats to its population.

While aquatic insects act as umbrella species for conserving aquatic ecosystems in places like Ash Meadows, the question of "why bother?" protecting naucorids (or pupfishes or riffle beetles or springsnails) remains. One answer is that by protecting naucorids we are protecting the springs, and by protecting the springs we are protecting the water that people need. Don Sada, a biologist who once worked for the Fish and Wildlife Service, described to me how he answered hostile questions about National Wildlife Refuges and endangered species when standing in front of audiences in places like Pahrump. Sada, an expert on the ecology and biogeography of springsnails, said that he rarely mentioned the tiny snails that are one of the passions of his life: "I didn't talk about springsnails; I talked about springs. If there's enough high-quality water, you can use it for many things, including humans—and if you take too much water, it will hurt people, as much as snails and fish."

Don Sada's argument is important. Perhaps it is even the crucial one in the arid Southwest, but I am seeking a justification beyond his utilitarian rationale. Since the great drying that followed the Pleistocene the two naucorid lineages have gone their separate ways, as have other populations at Ash Meadows, such as the Devils Hole, Warm Springs, and Ash Meadows Amargosa pupfishes. To understand this is to appreciate something of what comes from isolation by time and distance and to encounter, as is so often the case for aquatic ecosystems in the Death Valley region, the essence of what it means to be alone in the great world. It is this animal solitude that is so compelling to me, for aloneness also is one pervasive characteristic of the human condition—my condition, most everyone's condition. And although I do not quite understand the psychology of it, phenomena like the Ash Meadows and Warm Springs naucorids offer up a reassurance to me, a sense that aloneness can be endured, maybe even transcended. Wherever I go in the Basin and Range country, whenever I see a creature like the Warm Springs naucorid at a place such as School Spring, I feel as though I have encountered life's insistent tenacity, and all the justification needed for Ash Meadows National Wildlife Refuge, which came into being in 1984 after so much struggle and (I am sure) so much anger.

When the Manly party passed through Ash Meadows in December of 1849, on their way to misery and loss in Death Valley, they found "a beautiful valley considerably lower than we had been before and quite a warm region so that we encountered flies, butterflies, beetles, etc." By the 1890s "the beautiful valley" had been surveyed and its abundant water had attracted a number of pioneering families. Biologists from the Death Valley Expedition spent several weeks in March of 1891 camped near Carson Slough and encountered marshbirds, shorebirds, and waterfowl "in marshes along the irrigating ditches, and by the larger springs, in which places fish were abundant." Although early ranchers undoubtedly affected Ash Meadows, and clay mining began there in 1917, most endemic aquatic species probably maintained healthy populations until the 1960s. Photographs of Kings Pool taken in 1939 show an apparently undisturbed spring ringed by lush emergent vegetation and mesquite, and when Robert Miller studied fish in the area during the 1940s, he found good numbers of most native species— except for the soon-to-be-extinct Ash Meadows poolfish, which already was "rare." Until the 1950s the de facto protection afforded to Ash Meadows was based mostly on poor access and the lack of large-scale development. This quasi-protection would vanish in the 1960s as industrial agriculture came to Ash Meadows, in concert with similar changes in Pahrump Valley.

Major agricultural development at Ash Meadows began in the early 1960s when a local rancher, George Swink, drained a large part of Carson Slough and mined peat for three years, until the supply was exhausted. In 1967 Swink sold his property to Spring Meadows Inc., which was acquiring land in Ash Meadows, including 5,000 acres from the U.S. Bureau of Land

Management. Spring Meadows planned to irrigate over eighteen square miles of desert, mostly to grow alfalfa for livestock feed, and it needed to monopolize existing wells and drill new ones, reroute natural watercourses, and install water-control devices and pumps in the most productive springs. The company obtained some of the necessary water rights by purchasing private land, but much of the water came from state-owned groundwater or springs owned by the Bureau of Land Management. Beginning in 1961, ten production wells for irrigation were drilled in Ash Meadows; high-volume pumping from several of these would affect Devils Hole and trigger the cascade of legal actions that resulted in the 1976 *Cappaert* Supreme Court decision, which affirmed the right of the federal government to withhold surface and groundwater rights for environmental management purposes.

Most agricultural development occurred in the Point of Rocks, Crystal Pool, and Carson Slough areas, near production wells and high-volume springs. To stand above Kings Pool in 1969 and look west toward Death Valley was to survey a devastated landscape that had been transformed into something alien, something other than pupfish and naucorid habitat: a bulldozed swath of alkali soil scraped clean of all vegetation, the mesquite and leatherleaf ash bosque decimated, the springhead pool enlarged and blocked by two concrete water control structures. Jackrabbit Spring, home to Ash Meadows speckled dace and Ash Meadows Amargosa pupfish, had been similarly ruined. The native vegetation surrounding the spring had been replaced by a ghostlike wreath of bare gesso ground, the outlet channel ditched and straightened. An irrigation pump and generator were suspended above what was left of the beautiful spring, which had shrunk from a crystalline blue pool to a small sump at the bottom of a bare hole, the resident pupfish and dace sucked into a postapocalyptic agricultural void.

Not only were many of the springs of Ash Meadows being destroyed, but groundwater pumping was well in excess of recharge rates. In 1971, the U.S. Geological Survey estimated that overdrafts from hydrological units surrounding Point of Rocks represented a "9-percent additional load on the total discharge from the Ash Meadows ground-water system." However, the report cautioned that "because of the liberal estimates of salvage [mostly from clearing away moisture-loving natural vegetation], the overdraft might have been twice that amount." The report also noted that some Ash Meadows water used for irrigation was of low agricultural value. Even though pumping was sometimes driving Jackrabbit Spring's discharge rate to zero, its water was classified as "very high salinity—moderate sodium," which should "be used to a limited degree" for crops, while water from another impacted source, Big Spring, was classified as "high salinity," which should only be used to irrigate salt-tolerant crops such as Bermuda grass.

Alfalfa and cattle were overwhelming and devouring Ash Meadow's ecosystems. In 1970 Clinton Lostetter, an endangered-species specialist with the Fish and Wildlife Service, conducted a reconnaissance of seventeen Ash Meadows springs and reported that several populations of the Ash Meadows Amargosa pupfish and Ash Meadows speckled dace had disappeared. Lostetter wrote that, "It is increasingly evident that the pupfish species [at Ash Meadows] will most assuredly become extinct if subsurface waters continue to be overdrawn." By the time that Ash Meadows National Wildlife Refuge was established in 1984, Don Sada estimated that pupfish habitat and dace habitat had decreased from 600 acres prior to 1950, to 7 acres and 1 acre, respectively. However, the damage described by Lostetter and Sada was not confined to aquatic systems; the unique terrestrial flora of the area also was impacted severely, as described by Dr. Janice Beatley, an expert on Mojave and Great Basin vegetation: "Most areas of botanical interest . . . have now been totally destroyed by an out-of-state conglomerate's attempts to establish a beef-cattle feeding operation, and much of what remains of the Government and private lands is extremely intensively grazed . . . and trampled by unconfined livestock. Biological catastrophe and tragedy have come to this unique oasis in the Mojave Desert. All rare and strictly endemic plant and animal species are critically endangered in Ash Meadows." For biologists who cared about such things, Ash Meadows in the early 1970s must have been a place of gut-wrenching despair.

When I walk out into the desert near Point of Rocks, Crystal Pool, or Carson Slough, I still can find evidence of the havoc wrought by Spring Meadows Inc.: concrete-lined irrigation ditches, abandoned water-control structures, and former fields marked by symmetrical lines of furrows and ridges, now sheltered beneath revitalized stands of mesquite or overgrown with exotic weeds. Given what we know about the ecological harm that comes from growing water-intensive crops in the desert and how unsustainable the practice is, it's easy to ask the question, "What was Spring Meadows' corporate brain thinking?" The actions of the Bureau of Land Management also are a puzzle, because a federal land-management agency acted as an enabler for Spring Meadows, selling land and acquiescing to the destruction of pupfish habitat on its property. But in the 1960s and 1970s answers to questions about the wisdom of agricultural development in the desert were not necessarily clear, and one's response would have been predicated on values, just as it is today. Forty or fifty years ago the legal and regulatory environment also was very different. The Endangered Species Act did not become law until 1973 and the Supreme Court's *Cappaert* decision was not made until 1976, the same year that the BLM Organic Act was enacted in an attempt to turn the agency into something other than the Bureau of Land Mismanagement. Still, someone contemplating the wisdom of irrigated agriculture in Ash Meadows might have looked thirty miles to the south, where agricultural development in Pahrump Valley was undergoing a classic boom-bust cycle, driven by unsustainable exploitation of its water.

Beginning in the late 1950s agricultural interests in Pahrump Valley began mining groundwater in a big way, mostly to irrigate alfalfa and cotton. As irrigated land increased from 1,000 acres in the 1940s to 8,100 acres in 1968 (only two-thirds of the irrigated acreage planned for Ash Meadows), groundwater withdrawals increased to an estimated 48,000 acre-feet per year, far in excess of the basin's estimated sustainable water yield of 19,000 acre-feet per year. (The acre-foot is a standard unit of water measurement in the American West; it is defined as the amount of water needed to cover an acre one-foot deep and is equal to almost 326,000 gallons, or roughly one-half of the volume of an Olympic-size pool.) The water table sank rapidly and wells and springs went dry; these included Manse Spring, which had discharged over 1,400 acre-feet per year; two Pahrump Ranch springs; and the once swiftly flowing Raycraft Spring, which was bulldozed full of soil to control mosquitoes after it metamorphosed into a stagnant pool. The poolfish subspecies endemic to Manse Spring was rescued by biologists in 1971, who transplanted it to an artificial refuge before the spring dried completely. However, poolfish subspecies endemic to springs at Pahrump and Raycraft ranches were lost, as was irrigated agriculture, which was driven almost to extinction by the same uncontrolled groundwater extraction that doomed the poolfish, and by rapidly increasing residential development: *Sic transit gloria agricultūra*, at least in Pahrump Valley.

Industrial agriculture was having a terrible effect on aquatic ecosystems throughout the area, but many of the organizations that were working tirelessly to defend Devils Hole also were trying to protect the threatened species and springs of Ash Meadows. The goal of the Desert Fishes Council was to preserve the native fishes of the Amargosa River drainage by undertaking hydrological and ecological studies, establishing transplant sites and refuges, pursuing legal action, and preventing the further sale or exchange of public lands in Ash Meadows. The Secretary of the Interior,

Walter Hickel, endorsed the federal interagency Pupfish Task Force, and in June of 1970 stated that "the Interior Department will vigorously oppose adverse water use which would endanger the continued existence of these surviving species of fish." Although most of Interior's agencies supported efforts to protect the pupfish, the Bureau of Land Management did not. According to Phil Pister, the BLM Las Vegas district manager vigorously defended the Ash Meadows development and said that it was a shame to interfere with it "just to save a few worthless fish."

Notwithstanding the Bureau of Land Management, the 1976 *Cappaert* decision, which prohibited water withdrawals from within 2.5 miles of Devils Hole, effectively prevented Cappaert Enterprises, the corporate offspring of Spring Meadows, from continuing its agricultural operations. Cappaert Enterprises offered to sell its water rights and land to the U.S. Fish and Wildlife Service, but unbelievably the regional director of the Fish and Wildlife Service in Portland, Oregon, turned down the offer, in part because the Ash Meadows Amargosa pupfish and Ash Meadows speckled dace were not yet listed under the 1973 Endangered Species Act. According to Jim Deacon, the University of Nevada, Las Vegas biologist who was very active in pupfish research and conservation, the regional director felt that "the safety of the Devils Hole pupfish was assured by court decisions and that other endemic species were not USFWS responsibility."

As the cliché goes, the Fish and Wildlife Service's decision to abandon Ash Meadows had snatched defeat from the jaws of victory, and in 1980 Cappaert Enterprises sold its water rights and land to Preferred Equities Corporation, a development company based in Pahrump. Preferred Equities and its president, Jack Soules, hoped to build "Calvada Lakes," a desert community of more than 30,000 water-loving residents. Preferred Equities acquired 4,600 more acres of private land and proceeded with its plans, which included 33,636 residential parcels, a lake for anglers and water skiers, and associated commercial/agricultural/industrial development. In terms of environmental impacts and unrealistic attitudes toward water use, Calvada Lakes was an über Spring Meadows, which if fully realized might have required 370 percent of the total water discharged annually by Ash Meadows springs. Preferred Equities continued to farm some of the agricultural lands developed by Spring Meadows, but its main focus was on promoting its development fantasies. The company built new roads, altered spring outflows and pools, and sold a handful of lots, even as the Nature Conservancy was actively working to purchase the land and water rights forsaken by the Fish and Wildlife Service.

Four years would pass before a deal was consummated between Preferred Equities and the Nature Conservancy—a period filled with legal wrangles, political and financial machinations, the involvement of Senator Paul Laxalt of Nevada, and repeated breakdowns in negotiations. Eventually, though, on February 7, 1984, the Nature Conservancy acquired Preferred Equities' Ash Meadows properties for $5.5 million cash, plus a five-year loan of $1 million at 5 percent interest. The Conservancy's plan was to hold the property for an interim period and then transfer it at cost to the U.S. Fish and Wildlife Service, through a federal appropriation secured by Senator Laxalt. Although title issues and an attempt by Nye County to block the purchase delayed the final transfer, Ash Meadows National Wildlife Refuge was finally created in June 1984.

———————

When I read stories about Ash Meadows between 1976 and 1984, I am amazed that the vision of a national wildlife refuge in the Amargosa Desert ever was realized. In 1976, when the political and financial situation was favorable, the recalcitrance of the Fish and Wildlife Service prevented the land acquisition. Jim Deacon told me that the agency "had to be dragged kicking and screaming into the idea of having a refuge," and once Ronald Reagan became president in 1981 there were far fewer opportunities for adding to the nation's public lands than during the Carter administration. The Sagebrush Rebellion, with its antipathy toward federal lands protection, had gained ascendancy in the Intermountain West, and James G. Watt was Reagan's pro-development Secretary of the Interior. Watt, who once said, "We will mine more, drill more, cut more timber," was notoriously hostile to environmental protection. He hoped to eliminate the Land and Water Conservation Fund, which is used to acquire environmentally valuable land for National Fish and Wildlife Refuges, resisted new endangered species listings, and sold off public lands when he could.

Ronald Reagan and James Watt may have been antagonistic toward public-lands acquisition, but the relatively new Endangered Species Act was having major impacts on development projects like Calvada Lakes. If Preferred Equities were to move forward with plans to build its 30,000-person City in the Desert, which at the time would have made it the third-largest municipality in Nevada, it would have had to contend with several federally protected species, including the Devils Hole pupfish and Warm Springs Amargosa pupfish, which had been listed under the predecessor of the Endangered Species Act in 1970. And surprisingly—almost bizarrely—in May of 1982 James Watt authorized emergency listing of the Ash Meadows Amargosa pupfish and Ash Meadows speckled dace as endangered, which promised further headaches for Preferred Equities. The fate of Ash Meadows' endangered species and the schemes of Preferred Equities were tied to the fate of Ash Meadows' water, and the legal and regulatory advantage lay with the pupfishes, a situation which in 1984 resulted in the creation of Ash Meadows National Wildlife Refuge—"a phoenix rising," as it were, even if it would rise from the remains of leatherleaf ash trees destroyed by Spring Meadows, Cappaert Enterprises, and Preferred Equities, rather than from the ashes of a literal conflagration.

Ash Meadows National Wildlife Refuge came into being only because the Nature Conservancy and a few dedicated individuals kept fighting for its creation. Dave Livermore was the Nature Conservancy's newly hired Nevada and Utah Great Basin field representative when he became involved in efforts to purchase Preferred Equities' Ash Meadows properties. And although he has spent over thirty years with the organization, Livermore still recalls Ash Meadows as "one of the most memorable projects that I have ever worked on, in its own way as magnificent as the Galapagos Islands, in terms of its biodiversity and importance for understanding evolutionary processes." And yet the difficulty and complexity of the negotiations, and the dogged effort to bring together all of the involved parties—Preferred Equities, the U.S. Fish and Wildlife Service, Congress, and Nye County—at times made it seem to Livermore "like a huge hill to climb, an impossible dream."

Livermore shuttled back and forth between the stakeholders and tried to craft a deal with Preferred Equities, but Soules was difficult to deal with, fickle and full of bluff and threat. Livermore recalls him as someone who projected "the classic image of a shady real estate developer, with the demeanor of a slick salesman, a tough guy." During one memorable visit Livermore and his colleague Steve McCormick presented Soules with an offer based on an appraised value of $5 million for Preferred Equities' properties. Soules, who believed the properties were worth $20 to $25 million, literally threw the offer at the duo and shouted, "You don't know a fucking thing about appraisals!" In spite of Soules's response, the Nature Conservancy continued to negotiate with him, while others promoted the benefits of protecting Ash Meadows, particularly the biologists Jim Deacon and Don Sada, whom Livermore calls "the patron saints of Ash Meadows."

Jim Deacon was easy to track down, and I had several good conversations with him about Devils Hole and Ash Meadows, but Don Sada was harder to corner. I wasn't able to talk with him face to face until the Desert Fishes Council meetings at Furnace Creek in November of 2012. When we finally do meet up it's at Point of Rocks, and I am immediately struck by his enthusiasm and drive. Even though Don is in his early sixties he still has the build and energy of the long-distance runner that he once was, and a focused intensity that must make him a formidable advocate for desert aquatic ecosystems and organisms. Don began working for the Fish and Wildlife Service in 1979, and in his early years with the agency he spent a lot time at Ash Meadows. When he first arrived, "it was devastated; no semblance of its natural character remained. There was a ring of artificial ponds surrounding what was left of the Point of Rocks springs, domestic geese in the water, alfalfa and cattle everywhere."

As we meander along the boardwalk and Don reminisces about Ash Meadows in the early 1980s, it's difficult to believe that he is describing the same place—so much has changed. We stop above Kings Pool, near the set of cylindrical holes in which Native Americans once ground mesquite pods, where a small runnel of spring water slices through the travertine rock. Don explains that we are standing exactly where Jack Soules told him that he would like to build a house, with the spring source and grinding rock as the centerpieces of his living room. Sada pauses, kneels down by the water, and picks up a piece of limestone covered by a green iridescent scrim of algae. The algae is peppered with the tiny dark dots of Ash Meadows peb-blesnails, one of two snail species endemic to Point of Rocks, and as Don holds the rock he mutters, "Soules was a slimebucket, and he was having fun letting me know about his house plans." He shakes his head and gestures out toward the luxuriant mesquite stand that surrounds Kings Pool: "The place was so ugly, and so hideous. I remember leaving Ash Meadows once and heading north on Highway 95, toward Reno." He stops, a slight catch in his voice, before continuing, "I still get emotional about this, but I thought that I never wanted to see Ash Meadows again. It was that bad."

Yet Sada kept coming back, working on springsnails and pupfish, fighting Jack Soules and Preferred Equities. He'd go out for long morning runs and keep track of the destruction he saw, "dodging the PE security men in their bright yellow pickups." Don knew that he needed to get more influential people involved in the fight to protect Ash Meadows, and so he "put on a pair of epaulettes and took everyone that I could around the place— government biologists, congressional aides, conservationists. I'd take a day, and point out how amazing the place was." Jim Deacon was doing much the same thing, and Don's ex-wife even tried to recruit Ed Abbey to the cause.

Abbey had spent time in the area in 1966–67 and had composed the final chapter of his masterpiece, *Desert Solitaire*, "in the corner of a bar serving a legal house of prostitution at Ash Meadows, Nevada, where I waited each day with my little yellow school bus (I was the driver) to pick up children from Shoshone High School for transfer to the village of Furnace Creek in Death Valley." Although Abbey was sympathetic to Sada's cause, he sent back a postcard declining the request to get involved: "All I can say is, keep fighting, and if necessary, call in the Monkeywrench Gang."

Ultimately, though, eco-saboteurs were not needed to protect Ash Meadows; the Endangered Species Act and the dogged persistence of the Nature Conservancy did the job. Shortly after James Watt authorized list-ing of the Ash Meadows Amargosa pupfish, Sada was "standing near what was left of Kings Pool with a PE guy, and I saw dead pupfish scattered on the ground. So I brought a Fish and Wildlife Service law enforcement offi-cer with me and went to see Soules in Pahrump. The officer told Soules that the pupfish and Ash Meadows speckled dace were protected by federal law and that Preferred Equities would have to 'cease and desist' its activities." Sada's confrontation with Soules happened in May of 1982, and although it would take two more years to create the National Wildlife Refuge, "Calvada Lakes" was effectively defunct—for it depended on the same water as did the pupfish and dace, which were protected by the Endangered Species Act. Soules would bluff and stall, raise his asking price, and even sell a few lots in the moribund development, but he must have known that Calvada Lakes was dead in the proverbial water (or rather, lack of it). Don recalled the day in June of 1982 "when it all broke" and he knew that Preferred Equities would lose. "I came down to meet with Soules and Senator Laxalt's aide, Ace Robinson. We went into a room where there was this huge, 3-D model of the development on a table, lit up with lights. Soules described his vision for Calvada Estates and then he took us on a tour of Ash Meadows in his silver Lincoln. When we got out of his car at Marsh Spring, Soules dropped his bombshell: 'Ace, I want to get out of this. It's just not going to work.'" As he tells this part of the story Don smiles and adds, "And that was that."

Although Jack Soules died of a heart attack on a Pahrump golf course in 1983, "that" would take two more years to accomplish. As Dave Liver-more recalls, "The whole thing was a dance. We lobbied Congress and the Fish and Wildlife Service, even Nye County politicians. We didn't want to shove it down anyone's throat." Senator Laxalt's office was supportive of the negotiations, partly because of Laxalt's deep family roots in Nevada and his pride in the state having such a unique natural feature. According to Livermore, "Laxalt was sincerely interested in places like Lake Tahoe and Ash Meadows and supportive of efforts to protect them." Although the Reagan administration was notoriously hostile to federal land acquisition the government eventually would buy Preferred Equities' holdings from the Nature Conservancy. When Don Sada met with Craig Potter, the assistant secretary for Fish and Wildlife, Potter told him, "You know what's going to happen? We're going to rant and rave and say we don't want to do this. But then we're going to buy the property." When the deal was finally consummated Ash Meadows National Wildlife Refuge consisted of 36.6 square miles, including 19.7 square miles of Preferred Equities land, property owned by the Bureau of Land Management, and 2.4 square miles of private inholdings, "to be purchased as available."

Ash Meadows and its wonderful collection of endemic plants and animals had been saved—sort of. The U.S. Fish and Wildlife Service had been given a new refuge, but it was one that peat miners, Spring Meadows, and Preferred Equities had laid bare and stripped of its integrity. As Don Sada describes it, in 1984 Ash Meadows was "ugly" and "hideous." Its springs were ruined, exotic species were everywhere, and many endemic species, including federally protected ones, were ailing. Ash Meadows' new owner, the U.S. Fish and Wildlife Service, had been a reluctant partner in the acquisition process. In the mid-1980s many of the agency's administrators, particularly in the Refuge branch, were "hook and bullet" types, and the service's mindset about refuge management was oriented more toward its original mission, which was to conserve migratory waterfowl, rather than endangered species protection. The agency also was chronically short of money, particularly during the Reagan years, and the regional office that oversaw Ash Meadows was in Portland, Oregon, far from the Amargosa Desert. Don Sada thinks that this physical separation explained much of why Ash Meadows was neglected, because "they [the regional administrators] did not understand desert ecosystems. After the *Cappaert* decision and Ash Meadows had been purchased from Preferred Equities, they thought the problem was solved." There would be little agency money for maintenance, still less for ecosystem recovery. The first refuge manager was not appointed until the early 1990s, and when the current manager, Sharon McKelvey, arrived in 2003 the refuge office was housed in a trailer and the dial-up internet connection was shared with the phone line. Sharon had come to the Fish and Wildlife Service via the U.S. Forest Service, and her former employer had even given her a box of copy paper "because they knew where I was going": an isolated backwater, ignored by its own agency. Given the condition of Ash Meadows in the 1980s and early 1990s and the chronic lack of resources, trying to manage the refuge well was like bringing a badly injured person into an emergency room, dumping them on a gurney, and telling the staff, "Make him better, but don't spend any money doing it."

As I hear Don Sada's stories about the early years at Ash Meadows—the damage done, the long struggle to establish the refuge, and the benign neglect of some in the U.S. Fish and Wildlife Service—it's difficult to believe that so many of the springs have been restored, that there are healthy populations of pupfishes, springsnails, naucorids, and niterwort, and that instead of fields of alfalfa and cattle rolling off into the distance, there are groves of mesquite and leatherleaf ash. And so, when I stand at Point of Rocks on a warm November day and see that Ash Meadows has been transformed into something more than a bad and bitter memory, it's impossible to disagree with Don when he looks out over Kings Pool and says, "It feels pretty good to come up here now. It's quite overwhelming."

And as he says this, I notice another catch in his voice, but I know that now it's one of joy rather than sorrow.

Ecological restoration is an act of faith and hope, as well as contrition. In a place like Ash Meadows it is as much a process as an outcome because it is difficult to predict exactly how ecosystems will respond to restoration efforts. The goal of restoration sounds straightforward: to the greatest degree possible, recreate conditions prior to the time that humans began disturbing the system in major ways. But this goal conceals two important questions: which humans, and at what time? In the case of Ash Meadows the temporal restoration target presumably would be prior to the mid-1800s, before ranchers and miners moved into the area, even if the later actions of Spring Meadows and Preferred Equities had damaged native ecosystems the most. There is a value judgment here, though: the belief that impacts of Native Americans, circa 1850, were less harmful than those of later Euro-American settlers and their figurative descendants. And it is undoubtedly true that for many reasons—cultural traditions, low population density, less invasive technologies—the Western Shoshone or Southern Paiute people who lived in Ash Meadows during the 1800s and early 1900s would have affected the area less drastically than the pumps, bulldozers, cattle, and nonnative aquatic species that followed them. Yet no one knows exactly what Ash Meadows was like in the late 1800s: the particular characteristics of the vegetation surrounding each spring, the precise structure and function of the refuge's aquatic ecosystems, and the distribution of its endemic species. There are a few early descriptions and scientific records, such as those of the 1891 Death Valley Expedition and Robert Miller, but they only can tell us so much about how "things used to be." And landscapes, ecosystems, and species are dynamic in space and time, and culturally conditioned—not in any postmodernist sense, but because they are strongly affected by human actions. Simply put, natural systems change, and in the slightly modified words of Thomas Wolf, you can't (quite) go home again: whatever the outcome of a restoration, it will be only broadly analogous to presettlement conditions. Rob Andress, an ecologist who has worked on most of the Ash Meadows restorations since 2004, says that "what we create is definitely not what was there before it was disturbed by Euro-Americans, but it's about the best that we can do, given our resources and knowledge."

There are myriad historical uncertainties, as well as the future ones: how will species and their habitats respond to manipulation? Consider the restoration of a damaged spring and what must be done to recreate its "historic" condition: first, eradicate all exotic fish (mosquitofish, sailfin mollies, largemouth bass, green sunfish); bullfrogs; red swamp crayfish; an aquatic snail, the red-rimmed melania; introduced plants, including salt cedar; and invasive native plants, including cattails, which may choke waterways and destroy native fish habitat. Eradication of the introduced aquatic species requires temporarily redirecting spring flow, which necessitates removing and safeguarding protected populations of native species while water is diverted from the system. Natural patterns of water flow also may need to be reestablished in springbrook systems that were developed for irrigation.

Once nonnative and invasive species have been eradicated; the springhead and channel restored; and the appropriate substrate, gradient, and pools, runs, and riffles created, water will be returned to the system. Native aquatic plants and animals then can be reintroduced, and vegetation planted in disturbed areas, perhaps nurtured with a drip irrigation system. The surrounding landscape must also be managed to allow for exchange of genetic material among appropriate populations, and adequate water supplies for the spring system secured. Finally, and in perpetuity, the restored system must be monitored and adaptively managed to prevent reinvasion by nonnative species, ensure that target species maintain themselves, and identify any necessary corrective actions. And even if experience and research suggest the best approaches to restoring an ecosystem, consider how a changing, unpredictable environment could affect a restoration: droughts or floods, poor reproductive years for target species, good reproductive years for pest species, the chance dispersal of a previously eradicated nonnative species, decline in output from a spring after its flow has been temporarily redirected, and the sheer cussedness of a natural world that often behaves as it will, rather than as we want it to. Restoration is hard, unpredictable work, and it requires money, which Ash Meadows National Wildlife Refuge typically has had little of.

And yet many of the spring systems at Ash Meadows have been restored. Many of the exotic species are gone, replaced with natives, and springs and springbrooks run well and free. In places there still are testaments to how Ash Meadows was just forty years ago—scars of abandoned roads and agricultural fields, concrete irrigation ditches, rusted well heads, old bore holes, scattered bits of rusted barbed wire and corrugated roofing, crayfish and sunfish. But these things are annals of a former world. The alfalfa and cattle have disappeared, along with Spring Meadows and Preferred Equities, and to visit Jackrabbit Spring or Kings Pool is to step into a landscape and ecosystem that resembles, even if it does not replicate, what existed 150 years ago. Now there are healthy populations of Ash Meadows naucorids, Warm Springs riffle beetles, Warm Springs Amargosa pupfish, Ash Meadows pebblesnails, and Ash Meadows gumplants where they should be, and this small bit of the world is a much better and happier place than it was in 1970.

But restoration is not cheap. Rob Andress estimates that the contractor's compensation for each completed spring and stream project at Ash Meadows has run between $250,000 and $650,000, with resources provided directly by the Fish and Wildlife Service and its partners, and volunteer labor representing an additional 25 to 50 percent of the contractor's costs. Surprisingly, the Fish and Wildlife Service's endangered species recovery program has provided little money for restoration—a frustrating situation for refuge staff. Instead, much of the funding has come via the Southern Nevada Public Land Management Act (SNPLMA), a 1997 law that allows the Bureau of Land Management to sell public land within Clark County for private development. A small percentage of the revenues is split between the Nevada General Education Fund and the Southern Nevada Water Authority, but 85 percent of the proceeds are placed in a fund administered by the Secretary of the Interior for projects such as land acquisition, creating parks and trails, and ecological restoration.

The first restoration project at Ash Meadows occurred between 1997 and 2001 at Point of Rocks and Kings Spring, using volunteers and refuge maintenance resources; a beautiful picnic area and interpretive boardwalk later were completed with the help of SNPLMA funds. The restoration involved reconstructing the main spring pool and portions of the outflow channel for Kings Spring, which had been severely damaged during the 1960s and 1970s. Local rock was used to create spawning and foraging habitat for the Ash Meadows Amargosa pupfish, and the outflow channel was integrated with an adjacent alluvial fan to provide coarse bottom substrate for the Ash Meadows naucorid. Other, smaller springs were restored and the area surrounding the springs replanted with native plants. Restoration of Jackrabbit Spring and its outflow channel followed from 2006 to 2009, before the focus shifted to the Warm Springs complex and Fairbanks Spring at the northern end of the refuge. School Spring was rehabilitated between 2007 and 2010, and North Indian Spring and South Indian Spring between 2008 and 2011, with restoration of North and South Scruggs springs beginning in 2013. Because of the small and isolated nature of springs in the Warm Springs complex, it has been possible to eradicate crayfish and mosquitofish by draining each system prior to beginning rehabilitation work, although the tactic has not worked with the red-rimmed melania.

But to describe a restoration in a few words (create habitat, integrate with adjacent alluvial fan, replant with native species, restore channel) is to say little about the care, science, and effort devoted to a project such as eradication of exotic red swamp crayfish from the Warm Springs complex. Introduced crayfish have been implicated in the loss of native freshwater biodiversity in Europe and North America; the red swamp crayfish has been present in the Death Valley drainage system since at least the 1930s and may have been partially responsible for the extinction of the Ash Meadows poolfish and disappearance of pupfish from South Indian Spring in the 1990s. Red swamp crayfish prey on native fish and invertebrates and compete with them for food, and they are tough. Although dependent on aquatic habitats, red swamp crayfish can withstand long periods of desiccation by burrowing into moist soil and can migrate between habitat patches. Because red swamp crayfish are so hardy, removing them from a spring involves diverting water for a year or more to expose them to desiccating summers and cold winters. In turn, this requires capturing as many of the native fish and invertebrates as possible and either nurturing them in captivity or transplanting them to other nearby springs. It is relatively easy to trap pupfish—just bait a small cylindrical wire funnel trap with dry cat food, and place it in a likely spot—but it also is important to save endemic invertebrates, which means painstakingly picking out what Rob

Andress calls "microstuff" from substrate samples: naucorids, riffle beetles, and springsnails, a process that might take three people three full weeks to complete at a single spring. But controlling crayfish is not only a matter of desiccation; it also means preventing them from searching out other springs. And so the Fish and Wildlife Service, with labor provided by the Nevada Conservation Corps, has built over three-quarters of a mile of strategically placed "crayfish fencing"—fourteen-inch-high metal flashing, buried four to six inches below ground—around and between water sources in the Warm Springs complex.

When I began working at Ash Meadows I did not comprehend the effort and care devoted to restoration, and the degree to which many spring systems had been transformed. The stark differences between the current condition of Jackrabbit Spring, School Spring, and Kings Pool, and what photographs suggested about these places in the 1960s and 1970s, told only part of the story. To fully understand the process, I read the technical documents that specified construction sequences and best management practices, studied the history of specific springs, and spent time with people involved in restoration. Take, for example, Jackrabbit Spring, the second major restoration project undertaken at Ash Meadows. Jackrabbit Spring had been home to Ash Meadows Amargosa pupfish and Ash Meadows speckled dace, but they disappeared when the spring was pumped dry in the 1960s. By the early 1980s pupfish had returned to the Jackrabbit system, along with a few dace, but habitat loss and exotic continued to repress pupfish and dace populations. The decline of dace in the Jackrabbit Spring system was particularly worrisome as they had been even more impacted by human-wrought changes than pupfish. Don Sada's surveys showed that by 1990 Ash Meadows speckled dace had disappeared from nine of the fifteen springs they once occupied, and by 2006 largemouth bass had eliminated the thriving population in Big Spring, about one mile south of Jackrabbit Spring.

I first visited Jackrabbit Spring in October of 2010, when I walked the outflow channel with two refuge biologists, setting and checking small fish traps as part of a study tracking pupfish and dace abundance. We pushed through thick stands of native spikesedge and three-square bulrush, past leatherleaf ash trees and native willows, and saw little evidence of the previous agricultural development along our route. When we later returned to check the traps we found dace everywhere along the outflow channel and swarms of pupfish, which prefer slow-moving water, in the spring pool. Although some of the traps held crayfish and mosquitofish, the bass were gone, as was the salt cedar that once had lined the channel. It seemed that the restoration had worked pretty well, given Jackrabbit Spring's aquatic connection to sources of exotic species such as the red swamp crayfish.

The opportunity to restore Jackrabbit Spring came in 2005, after a human-caused wildfire burned 1,500 acres in the area and federal money from the Burned Area Environmental Rehabilitation and SNPLMA programs became available. During agricultural development the original channel had been modified for water diversion, and so the contractor, Otis Bay Ecological Consultants, removed berms and filled the impoundments with coarse sediment. Although the upper 1,500 feet of the channel had restored itself to "seminatural" conditions following the devastation of the 1970s, the natural geometry of the lower 1,500 feet of the channel had to be recreated, with a narrow, deep, and fast flow, to provide habitat for speckled dace. Two narrow culverts were replaced to allow upstream fish passage and prevent reestablishment of cattails, which favor crayfish. The contractor removed invasive plant species by hand cutting and careful application of herbicides, and recontoured the surrounding area to restore its natural topography. Finally, 250 acres were revegetated using either plants propagated from native seeds or cuttings collected at Ash Meadows, and a drip irrigation system was installed to facilitate plant establishment.

Although the long-term goal for a restoration project such as Jackrabbit Spring is, as Rob Andress says, "to get the system going and then let it create itself," it may be necessary to periodically control native species that crowd out other species. At Jackrabbit this may be happening with native willows, cattails, and bulrush; in some places the latter two over-shade the channel and form mats so thick that a tired biologist like me can lie on them and remain suspended two feet off the ground. And so even when restoration succeeds, work at a place like Jackrabbit Spring is never really done—while the biggest project, restoration of Carson Slough from its headwaters at Rogers, Fairbanks, and Longstreet springs to where it crosses the western boundary of the refuge, remains mostly a concept. The wet alkali meadows and peat beds that once covered Carson Slough took thousands of years to form, and to restore them will take more than simply "dechannelizing" the streams and reflooding the former meadows where the extinct Ash Meadows montane vole once lived. And although the vole's habitat in Carson Slough has not quite vanished, its recovery will extend across centuries or even millennia.

George Santayana once wrote that "beauty is a pledge of the possible." And because returning a place like Kings Pool or Jackrabbit Spring to some semblance of its natural condition is a pledge to the future, the work is beautiful in the full sense of the word. When I think about what has been accomplished at Ash Meadows; when I stand by the outflow channel of Jackrabbit Spring and watch a swirl of speckled dace or pupfish; or when I stoop to taste water flowing from School Spring and find no mosquitofish or red swamp crayfish, what I see is evidence that it is possible to heal ecosystems. When I walk along the newly restored channel below North and South Indian springs with Darrick Weissenfluh, the biologist who has overseen much of the restoration work at Warm Springs, and sense his visceral excitement, or hear him describe how his four-year-old daughter helped with the restoration by placing rocks in spring channels, I know that it is possible to offer a pledge to the future. When I hear Darrick say that visiting one of the Warm Springs restorations "is like going home," I know that good work can be done: a thin cascade of riffles and pools, mats of vibrant algae, darting pupfish, springsnails beneath pieces of native tufa, and native bunchgrasses lining the channel. And when I look out over Kings Pool and hear Don Sada describe how Ash Meadows used to be, I am heartened by the remarkable ability of ecosystems to heal, if given the proper opportunity. Restoration takes time and wisdom and determination, as well as resources, and although we cannot entirely recreate the past, we can work with the resilience of the natural world and create something that is beautiful, and mostly whole.

All of this is reason enough to warrant the money and effort necessary to restore Ash Meadows, but I believe that there is another crucial justification for the good work that is being practiced there. For me, places like School Spring and Jackrabbit Spring also stand as powerful metaphor: that it is possible to heal the human heart as well as the natural world. At Ash Meadows I have seen the worst of what people can do to ecosystems, but also the best. In doing so I have become more convinced that it is possible for humans to heal as well. At Ash Meadows the ecological realities of nouns such as "endurance," "resilience," and "restoration" also offer us a profound psychological allegory. Barry Lopez has written of the Grand Canyon: "The living of life, any life, involves great and private pain, much of which we share with no one. In places such as the Inner Gorge the pain trails away from us." Lopez wrote this passage in 1988, twenty-five years before he published the essay "Sliver of Sky," in which he made public the very private pain of his childhood sexual abuse and the story of how he eventually came to be healed. In "Sliver of Sky" Lopez described the importance of therapy in his healing process and how "a crucial component of recovery from trauma is learning to comprehend and accept the embrace of someone who has no specific knowledge of what happened to you, who is disinterested." But he also explained how, during the years of his "traumatic sexual abuse . . . the only relief I had was when I was confronted with the local, elemental forces of nature. . . . I took from these encounters a sense of what it might feel like to become fully alive. When I gazed up beneath a flock of homing birds or listened as the big winds swirled the dry leaves of eucalyptus trees or sat alone somewhere in a rarely traversed part of the Santa Monica Mountains, waiting for a glimpse of a coyote or brush rabbit, I would feel exhilaration. Encouragement."

Like Lopez, I suffered traumatic sexual abuse as a child. And like Lopez, I have found help in therapy, shelter and exhilaration in places like the Grand Canyon and Santa Monica Mountains. And more recently I have discovered an equal measure of encouragement and joy at Ash Meadows, where it is possible to walk through a once-blighted landscape and marvel at pupfish and naucorids, springsnails and riffle beetles. To confront such a contrast is to encounter hope and resilience: at Ash Meadows I can understand, emotionally, that it is possible to transcend the worst effects of the past. As with the ecosystems of Ash Meadows, trauma—delivered by my stepfather, rather than by bulldozers and water pumps—once left me stripped bare and devastated. In its aftermath nothing has ever been quite the same. The sadness and brutality of the past remains with me, just as the ecosystems of Ash Meadows still carry evidence of their dislocation and dissolution. But what has occurred at Ash Meadows during the last two decades also demonstrates that transcendence is possible: I shall be healed, much as Kings Pool and School Springs and Jackrabbit Springs have been healed.

———————

If the aquatic ecosystems of Ash Meadows can be restored by hard work, money, and the wise application of scientific knowledge, they only can be nourished with adequate water. The groundwater that feeds Ash Meadows is part of the same regional flow system that supplies Devils Hole, and excessive pumping could harm any of the restored sites on the refuge in the same way that it once affected Devils Hole. Hydrologists estimate that the annual groundwater yield, or recharge, of the Amargosa Desert hydrographic basin is 24,000 acre-feet, of which 17,000 acre-feet are discharged from Ash Meadows springs. If groundwater is to be managed sustainably this leaves 7,000 acre-feet for all other uses in the basin, most of which occurs in the Amargosa Farms area, home to Ponderosa Dairy, a concentrated animal feeding operation with over 9,000 cows. The dairy uses about 1,500 acre-feet of water per year, or about 20 percent of the available recharge in the basin. However, state-permitted water rights in the Amargosa Desert basin total 28,000 acre-feet per year, well in excess of its perennial yield. Data from the U.S. Geological Survey indicate that recent annual groundwater use in the Amargosa Desert basin has averaged around 12,000 to 15,000 acre-feet, mostly for irrigation, although in 1998 it ran to 22,000 acre-feet per year. If one does the simple math by adding average annual spring discharge (17,000) and groundwater withdrawal (13,500), the total of 30,500 acre-feet per year indicates that groundwater use in the basin has been exceeding recharge rates, a situation that has occurred chronically throughout the arid Southwest.

In places like Las Vegas Valley and Pahrump Valley excessive groundwater pumping has caused the water table to fall by 300 feet or more and dried artesian wells and springs. In these cases groundwater has become a nonrenewable resource and is being mined in much the same way that gold and oil are mined: the amount extracted represents a net loss of resource capital. If this is the situation in the Amargosa Desert then the basin's water table should be dropping. Tim Mayer, a hydrologist with the U.S. Fish and Wildlife Service, told me that data from monitored wells in the Amargosa Farms area indicate that "the decline [in groundwater levels] is real, and has been going on for some time"—a situation that may be connected to recent changes in discharge from Fairbanks, Longstreet, and Rogers springs in the northern part of Ash Meadows, which have been trending downward more than springs in other parts of the refuge. The decline in groundwater levels in monitored wells also is in general agreement with predictions generated by the U.S. Geological Survey's 2010 groundwater flow model for the Death Valley region. The model was developed during more than a decade of intensive research, in conjunction with feasibility studies for the Yucca Mountain Nuclear Waste Repository, which was to be sited about forty miles northwest of Ash Meadows.

Because groundwater use in the Amargosa Desert hydrographic basin was exceeding recharge and groundwater rights in the basin were severely over-allocated, in 2008 the Nevada state engineer issued Order #1197, stating that "any application to appropriate additional groundwater and any application to change the point of diversion of an existing ground-water right to a point of diversion closer to Devils Hole, described as being within a twenty-five mile radius from Devils Hole within the Amargosa Desert

Hydrographic Basin will be denied." Order #1197 had two immediate consequences for the area. First, no additional groundwater rights could be developed, which meant than no new wells (other than domestic ones) could be drilled. Second, no entity—say, the Ponderosa Dairy—could purchase water rights associated with an existing well and subsequently change the "point of diversion" by transferring the existing rights to a well closer to Devils Hole. The long-term impact of Order #1197 has been to limit unsustainable development of the Amargosa Desert area, an economic outcome similar to that imposed by the demise of Preferred Equities in the early 1980s, although on a smaller scale. Back then the Amargosa Valley Town Board incurred a sizeable bonded indebtedness to build the medical clinic, multipurpose room, and town hall that would be needed by the 30,000 anticipated residents of Calvada Lakes. When the fantastical development scheme evaporated in the metaphorical desert sun, so did the anticipated tax revenues, which would have repaid the debt incurred by the town board.

For many citizens of Nye County, Order #1197 was another episode in a storyline of economic disappointments extending from the 1976 Supreme Court *Cappaert* decision to the demise of Preferred Equities and creation of Ash Meadows National Wildlife Refuge in 1984. These events were related to the interconnected issues of ecological and economic sustainability; realities imposed by the desert's most precious limiting resource, water; and legal protection offered to Devils Hole and the area's endangered species. But the long tidal fetch of hydrology and history did not end with the Nevada state engineer's Order #1197, for in 2011 the Yucca Mountain Nuclear Waste Repository, which was to be built in Nye County, was defunded by Congress and the Obama administration. Although there were many reasons for the demise of the Yucca Mountain Project, concern about regional groundwater contamination from stored nuclear waste was one critical issue—hence the intensive hydrogeological research by the U.S. Geological Survey and development of its regional flow model. Whatever the environmental realities of the Yucca Mountain Project, public opinion in Nevada generally opposed the facility, while many people in Nye County supported it for economic reasons. Nye County has a poverty rate of 20.5 percent, as compared to a 12.9 percent rate for Nevada. There are few ways to earn a living in Nye County, a situation due partly to its aridity and limited groundwater, and partly to federal land ownership, which runs to 93 percent. Although many important economic activities take place on federal lands, including grazing, mining, timber harvesting, recreation, and (in the case of Nye County, which contains almost all of the Nevada

National Security Site), weapons testing, the tax-exempt status of federal property means that many of Nevada's rural counties experience chronic revenue shortfalls, which are only partly compensated for by federal land-based payments.

Nye County has been a focal point for the Sagebrush Rebellion, a western movement to curtail federal land ownership and management authority, and resentment in the county over the federal government's water policies runs high—particularly in relation to the U.S. National Park Service and Fish and Wildlife Service, which aggressively defend their water rights. It's no wonder, then, that Ed Goedhart, manager of the Ponderosa Dairy and former Nevada state legislator, told me that the U.S. Geological Survey's Death Valley regional flow model was "garbage," while Gary Hollis, a former Nye County commissioner, called it "a joke." Neither liked the science as they perceived it, and neither appreciated its implications for groundwater water withdrawals and economic development in Nye County. Both Hollis and Goedhart have clashed repeatedly with the federal government, in and out of court. Goedhart has been a particularly vocal critic of the federal government and Nevada State Order #1197. One hydrologist familiar with the Amargosa Desert basin told me that Goedhart claims to have purchased 7,000 acre-feet of water rights—basically all of the available recharge—and that he has been frustrated by his inability to transfer points of diversion for these rights to near the Ponderosa Dairy. Goedhart's dairy operation also has had difficulties with state and federal regulatory authorities, including a 1999 citation for illegally dumping 1.7 million gallons of wastewater into the Amargosa River and drilling an illegal well near the Ponderosa Dairy in 2006.

I've had several thought-provoking conversations with Sharon McKelvey, the Ash Meadows National Wildlife Refuge manager, but the most interesting one occurred early in 2012, when she told me that her "biggest challenge is to make us [Ash Meadows National Wildlife Refuge] relevant to Nye County," which she followed by saying that "every conflict I deal with is about water." Although I understand what McKelvey was getting at with the first part of her statement—that she wanted the people of Nye County to perceive the wildlife refuge as a beneficial economic and natural resource—Ash Meadows already is *very* relevant to Nye County, due to its reserved water rights and endangered species, and the ways in which these issues affect development. And because it seemed important to get a Nye

County perspective on Ash Meadows, I arranged to interview Gary Hollis, who was at the time a two-term county commissioner.

When I met up with Hollis at the Nye County government offices in Pahrump he was dressed more nicely than I—pressed jeans, tooled cowboy boots, striped button-down shirt, blue blazer with an American flag lapel pin, and Stetson hat. He led me to his office and asked his secretary to "please get the professor here a bottle of water." Although I was thirsty and appreciated his hospitality, I didn't want to be a "professor" to Hollis, any more than I wanted to be an environmental scientist, or more loosely, an "environmentalist." I did not want to carry the connotations associated with those terms during our talk; instead I just wanted to be Some Guy Interested in Water and Ash Meadows.

Gary looked to be in his early sixties, with slicked-back gray hair and a closely cropped, salt-and-pepper beard. He was stocky, with the look of someone who had spent much of his working life outside, and as we shook hands, I felt as though he easily could have reduced mine to a lump of mangled flesh and bone. His office was clean and unassuming, with iconic western art on the walls—one print of a lone cowboy sitting his horse, backlit by a blazing sunset, another of a stagecoach and team of galloping horses. There also was a large photograph of Yucca Mountain, which Hollis still felt could be the economic savior of Nye County. He leaned back in his chair, placed his boots on his desk, and began our conversation by saying, "I'm not an environmentalist, I'm a conservationist." I asked Hollis what he thought of Ash Meadows National Wildlife Refuge and water rights issues in the area, and for the most part I just let him go. As we talked, he sprinkled his commentary with sayings like, "Keep your friends close, your enemies closer," after which he paused and smiled, and offered up a qualifier: "I'm not saying that all federal agencies are my enemies, it's just that we often do not see eye-to-eye."

And he certainly was right. On almost every water-related issue, from hydrology to water rights to endangered species, Gary's viewpoint was contrary to the federal government's, or at least the portion of it represented by the U.S. Fish and Wildlife Service, National Park Service, and Geological Survey. He distrusted the Geological Survey's regional flow model, felt that wells in the Amargosa Farms area were "doing fine," and thought that interbasin transfer via deep aquifers was unlikely. He saw the Gravity Fault, which lies between Devils Hole and Ash Meadows, as an impermeable barrier, because "the water table is one hundred feet higher on the Devils Hole side, and what goes on in the Amargosa Farms area should not affect Ash

Meadows or Devils Hole, which is a problem with the U.S. Geological Survey's models." And if there was little movement of groundwater across the Gravity Fault, Hollis maintained that Order # 1197 should be amended to prohibit new wells only within a ten-mile radius of Devils Hole, instead of a twenty-five-mile radius. This would allow the Ponderosa Dairy and other agricultural developments in the Amargosa Farms area to purchase existing water rights outside of the much smaller exclusion zone and then move their points of diversion.

I asked Hollis what he thought of Ash Meadows National Wildlife Refuge, and if he saw it as benefitting Nye County. He thought for moment, took a sip of coffee, and replied, "No matter what happens, I just don't see it as an economic asset. Crystal Reservoir might be an exception, but they [the Fish and Wildlife Service] have banned bass fishing there." He went on to say that he'd like "the refuge to welcome Nye County, to work together to monitor wells on either side of the Gravity Fault. But right now, the USGS and Fish and Wildlife Service just don't want to know what's going on with the fault, and there's little trust on either side." Hollis felt that the 17,000 acre-feet per year allocated to Ash Meadows was "was probably too much," and that "rewatering Carson Slough was a mistake, because it just evaporates out there, and flows into California, which makes problems for me."

Although Gary maintained, "We're [Nye County] not against endangered species protection," he felt that the local governments were "not part of the listing and management process," and that "as an act of good faith the Fish and Wildlife Service should delist those pupfish that are doing well." He thought that the Devils Hole pupfish was being mismanaged, and that the U.S. National Park Service was "doing nothing but destroying those fish" by interfering too much with the population. "They're loving those fish to death. The fence around Devils Hole keeps nutrients out of the water, and the divers take pollutants in on their suits when they count the fish." He also felt that the Park Service should not have begun feeding the Devils Hole pupfish because "once you start feeding the fish, it's no longer the same fish"—a view partly consistent with the morphological response of Devils Hole pupfish to artificial refuges and Sean Lema's "organism-environment interdependency." But Hollis also believed that Devils Hole pupfish lived in "fractures in the ground" and that they (the Devils Hole, Ash Meadows Amargosa, and Warm Springs Amargosa pupfishes) were "all one fish," a view at odds with both genetic and morphological data, but one that has critical implications for the species' or subspecies' protection under the Endangered Species Act.

As Hollis talked I thought about the "same planet, different world" phenomenon, much as I had when I discussed issues related to the Owens pupfish with Dave Martin of the Los Angeles Department of Water and Power, Ceal Klingler, and others. I disagreed with Hollis's views on most everything—water rights and allocations, Ash Meadows, and endangered species—although his opinions on the Devils Hole pupfish did reflect, to some extent, my reservations about the Park Service's management policy. We saw the world, or at least that part of it represented by Ash Meadows, in vastly different ways, but my disagreement with him wasn't only a matter of values; scientific evidence also conflicted with his opinions on the Amargosa Desert basin's hydrology. Interbasin transfer via the deep carbonate aquifer is a very real and critical aspect of regional groundwater flow, and although the Gravity Fault needs more research the evidence suggests that it is not completely impermeable. What goes on at Amargosa Farms apparently affects Ash Meadows, and discharges from springs in the northern part of the refuge have been trending downward in recent years, in concert with decreases in the levels of some Amargosa Farms wells. Wayne Belcher, the USGS scientist who has spent more than fifteen years studying the hydrology of the Death Valley region, told me that although the geophysical evidence suggested that portions of the Gravity Fault did have low permeability, in other places groundwater levels were the same on either side of the fault—and that the one-hundred-foot difference cited by Hollis as evidence of the fault's impermeability mostly occurs in areas where there is a steep gradient in the aquifer.

And yet in spite of our differences, I liked Gary Hollis. I enjoyed hearing his views on Nye County, Ash Meadows, and water. I was sorry to hear that he later lost the 2012 election for county commissioner, and I'd buy him a beer if I had the chance, get him to tell me stories about working at an underground borax operation in Death Valley. He challenged my attitudes, made me reconsider why I saw Ash Meadows as I did, and I appreciated his dedication to providing water for the people of Nye County. And although Hollis's concerns sidestepped the issue of sustainable groundwater use, he did make an oblique but interesting reference to the problem during our conversation: "Nye County needs more water, but I don't have any place left to mine it." I don't know if he meant to imply that deep carbonate groundwater in Nye County is essentially a nonrenewable resource, given its residence time of 8,000 to 35,000 years, but that is the implication of "mine." He went on to add that one of the few unexploited groundwater sources in the area was on the Nevada National Security Site, formerly the

Nevada Test Site: "Here in Nye County, we have always been leaders in the defense of our country. Now that the area isn't being used for nuclear testing, we want access to some of the water. There are 90,000 acre-feet below Frenchman Flats [where above-ground nuclear detonations occurred during the 1950s]. I've put in an application for 14,000 acre-feet, but they turned it down. They don't want pumping because they're afraid of contaminated water—then clean it up, or compensate us."

I talked with Hollis for ninety minutes and then it was time to move on. I left feeling that I could sit down with him at a negotiating table if I had to and slog through the difficult business of compromising on issues where there was little common ground. It helped that he seemed more flexible than folks like Ed Goedhart, with whom I had once talked on the phone—a ten-minute rapid-fire Goedhart monolog and über free-market lecture on why the U.S. Geological Survey's models were wrong, and all government-held groundwater rights in the Amargosa Desert basin should be auctioned off to the highest bidder. Hollis seemed more open to listening and understood something about the necessity of compromise. He respected openness and directness, even from people he disagreed with; he and Sharon McKelvey had butted heads often, but he said, "That young lady who is the refuge manager—I can't say enough good things about her." And he admitted that, over the years "I've mellowed some. I am working with the government to set up a desert tortoise preserve at the base of the Spring Mountains, north of Pahrump. Fifteen years ago, I wouldn't have wanted anything to do with it, but now I'm willing to go along." And finally, as I was leaving his office, he told me pretty much the same thing that Sharon McKelvey had said: "Everything that I do is about water."

After the interview I drove toward Ash Meadows and found a place to camp in the open desert. As the deep night sky came on I wrote up my notes and thought about water, the relationship between values and ideology, and how science is perceived by the general public. Gary Hollis seemed open to negotiation, while Ed Goedhart appeared more intransigent, although my exposure to him had been mostly secondhand, as he never responded to my request for an interview after our phone conversation. I also wondered, though—in what ways would *I* be willing to compromise with folks in Nye County? Could we find any common ground, other than a vague appreciation for the landscape and a facile acknowledgment that it would be nice to get along, if only we could? One tangible area of agreement might involve concern about Las Vegas's plans to import groundwater from other regions of the state. But if it were within my power to do so would I ever agree to surrender any of Ash Meadows' water to agricultural development, refrain from restoring Carson Slough, or delist Ash Meadows' endangered species simply as "an act of good faith"? I cannot imagine conceding on any issue that imperiled the species of Ash Meadows or compromised the integrity of refuge, even if I were willing to listen to what Hollis and Goedhart might have to say—preferably over a beer or coffee rather than while facing one another across the negative space of a negotiating table. But it would be very difficult to develop an open and nonjudgmental dialog about Nye County's water, just as it has become almost impossible for many congressional Democrats and Republicans to listen to one another. Wayne Belcher of the U.S. Geological Survey once told me, "One thing I've learned through marriage counseling is to say that the other person always has a point." Belcher's principle may be wise, but the gulf between principle and practice is often great, especially when dealing with something as contentious as water in the arid West. As Gary Hollis told me, "Whiskey's for drinking, water's for fighting over."

One issue that I would never compromise on is how I view the integrity of the science that has gone into building the hydrographic models, the scientists who built them, or those who are charged with using the models' implications to enforce federal resource management policies. One of my concerns about the current state of political discourse is the willingness of many people to discount scientific research when the results disagree with their own viewpoints, or when they do not understand the science itself; too often, the data (and the motives of the scientists themselves) are viewed through the opaque lens of ideology. (See: Senator James Inhofe of Oklahoma or the Utah state legislature on climate change, the North Carolina state legislature on sea level rise projections, or young-earth creationists on radiometric dating.) There is a disturbing tendency among some people to hold science itself in contempt, rather than disagreeing about how to deal with its implications. To put it most charitably, Hollis and Goedhart are suspicious of the U.S. Geological Survey's motivations and the quality of its scientific research, but as Wayne Belcher told me, "I don't like sports metaphors, but we (the USGS) have 'no skin in the game.' Our job is to provide an interpretation of what we know about the flow system, using data and modeling. Our information goes to the policy makers, who make the decisions about water allocations."

It's not that the U.S. Geological Survey's Death Valley regional flow model is perfect—a point acknowledged by Tim Mayer and Wayne Belcher, PhD hydrologists who collectively have spent over twenty-five years studying the Amargosa Desert hydrographic basin. And so Belcher and other scientists are developing an "embedded model," one with higher resolution that incorporates more data on well pumpage, groundwater discharge, and isotopic signatures of spring water. It is even possible, although unlikely, that the current regional flow model is wrong in some details, but this should be sorted out with more research and the back-and-forth, critical approach of hypothesis testing and peer review. Instead, the main issue for me is how ideology distorts science and interferes with our understanding of the world. President Obama has written that "values are faithfully applied to the facts before us, while ideology overrides whatever facts call theory into question." Whatever one might think of Obama, his distinction between values and ideology is perceptive. I understand that my values differ from those of Gary Hollis and Ed Goedhart, and that we view Ash Meadows' water and endangered species in different ways. But what I cannot accept is the manner in which ideology acts as a selective filter on facts and scientific theory, and how knowledge can be sacrificed to preconceived ideas about how the world works. I never want to do this myself, or see it in other people. Tim Mayer of the U.S. Fish and Wildlife Service told me, "People like Goedhart dismiss the U.S. Geological Survey's flow model because it does not say what they want it to." And so I wonder if Gary Hollis's refusal to allow for interbasin groundwater transfer via the deep aquifer—a well-accepted scientific concept—has less to do with data and more with his reluctance to admit to its implications. As one person who is familiar with water issues in the Southwest observed, "It is extremely difficult to get people to change their ideology. Most folks just don't want to do that."

There was a lot to consider that night, and I didn't close my field notebook and turn off my headlamp until well after ten. As I lay in my sleeping bag I thought about Gary Hollis and Sharon McKelvey, and how they had told me much the same thing, which I might paraphrase as: "It all comes down to water." Yes. In Death Valley and the springs of Ash Meadows, in every place I have gone in this arid country, it is all about water. For the people of Pahrump and Amargosa Valley, for the U.S. Fish and Wildlife Service and National Park Service, for Gary Hollis and Sharon McElvey, for Jack Soules (RIP) and Don Sada, for the cows of the Ponderosa Dairy and the speckled dace of Jackrabbit Spring and the pupfish of Kings Pool, everything is about water. It is about the water that fell, mostly, thousands of years ago and now moves through the deep carbonate aquifer beneath the Amargosa Desert. It is about the water that rises to the desert's surface in a few precious places just to the east of the Gravity Fault, nourishing the plants and animals and microbes: the water of their necessity, the water of human desire, the water that flows for a little while before it sinks again into the desert. But then I realized that here in the Amargosa Desert, everything does not quite "come down to water"—at least not completely. For although Gary Hollis and Sharon McKelvey live in the same place and concern themselves with the same water they, and the constituencies they represent, confront one another from across an intellectual and emotional divide. And although I understand that while in one sense it certainly is true that for everyone and everything in this magnificent desert, all of "it" (life, work, conflict, comfort) does come down to water, out here it might be better to say, "It all comes down to how we think about water." And then I took a last drink from my bottle, and thought that it was good, and went to sleep.

Jeff Goldstein and I don wetsuits and snorkel gear, grab spearfishing guns, and slip into the outlet stream from Crystal Pool. We're after green sunfish— exotic predators that escaped from Crystal Reservoir by surmounting two fish barriers and swimming into Crystal Pool, where they can feast on pupfish. We slowly work our way upstream, carefully probing the tangled vegetation lining the channel, searching the eddies, checking beneath small logs and overhangs for large shadows or a flash of movement in the sun-brushed water. The morning drops away, and it is difficult to judge how long it takes us to complete our search, but eventually we reach a thick bolus of emergent vegetation blocking the stream. I grab handfuls of cattail and bulrush and pull myself forward, and after thirty feet of straining I suddenly break into the clear. The shallow channel drops away into Crystal Pool, into a broad and brilliant funnel of blue water and shimmering light. Beneath me, perhaps fifteen feet below the water's surface, is the main vent of Crystal Spring, a roiling vortex marked by swirls of golden-white sand. Waves of miniature dunes climb the gentle slopes of the pool, marching through wild algal gardens, their tangled dreadlocks streaming in the currents that rise from the vent. A thick spread of native springsnails dots the bottom of the pool, like tiny black beads scattered from 10,000 broken necklaces. Bits of vibrant green algae, cattail, and three-square bulrush float by; a lone grape leaf hangs suspended in the water, glimmering gold. Crystal Pool is all azure and aquamarine color, as brilliant as a sun-drenched Mediterranean shore, and I feel as though I am swimming in light as much water. The morning is numinous.

Crystal Pool is warm and comfortable, almost ninety degrees. The water that Jeff and I are swimming in may have fallen as rain or snow in the Spring

Mountains 10,000 years ago and then drifted through limestone fissures in the deep carbonate aquifer for millennia before rising into the presence of this day. And so I let my body hang suspended in Crystal Pool and drift, slowly and quietly, through time. As I float, I watch shoals of Ash Meadows Amargosa pupfish, mostly yellowish beige and small, swirl through the water. Larger pupfish, some a striking blue, patrol clumps of algae, harassing intruders and claiming bits of precious and productive space as their own. Jeff estimates that there are 1,000 to 2,000 pupfish in the pool, and they are everywhere—colonizing the shallows, rising through the water column, tugging at bits of algae. Although the scene is not completely Edenic—there are red swamp crayfish in the pool, and two green sunfish caught in the hoop trap secured to the far bank—it is wonderful to know that pupfish have returned to this place. For although in 1948 Robert Miller described the pupfish population in Crystal Pool as "large," and felt that "there is little likelihood that the population will become extirpated by man's interference," the pupfish soon were gone, their spring destroyed by pumping from a nearby well. In 1970 Clinton Lostetter of the U.S. Fish and Wildlife Service found no pupfish in Crystal Spring and gave what was left of the site a "low rating on list of desirable springs on Ash Meadows [sic], Inc. property." By destroying Crystal Spring it was as though people had demolished time itself, destroyed the 10,000-year-old water that flowed out of the Spring Mountains and annihilated a pupfish population whose lineage extended back millions of years, through the Ice Ages and into the deep reaches of the Pliocene and Miocene.

But now time has returned. I float in its substance, float in the good work done by the Fish and Wildlife Service and the Nature Conservancy, by Don Sada, Jim Deacon, Dave Livermore, and all of the other people who labored so hard and so long to rescue, protect, and restore Ash Meadows. Near the shallow end of Crystal Pool I take a deep breath, dive to the bottom, and grab a clump of cattail stalks to keep myself submerged. I hang there in the warm water, as quietly as possible, and splay out the fingers of my left hand in the welcoming sand. I feel its soft and sensuous texture, and as I do a small school of pupfish begin nibbling, ever so gently, on my fingers. I let them investigate for as long as I can, feeling the delicate brush of their tiny teeth on my skin, before I am out of breath. And so I release the cattails and float free, rising to the surface of Crystal Pool, through the ancient waters: rising into hope and joy, rising into the bright light of a shining day, rising into the beautiful now.

Exile and Loneliness

THE BLACK TOAD *(Bufo exsul)*

Till the landscape we have made reveals
to us the creatures we long for and must become.
—David Malouf, *An Imaginary Life*

Just beyond the dirt road's end, past the corral and stone fences, are the toads. They nestle among the wiry grasses and sedges along the drainage ditches or hang suspended in the shallow water, their snouts probing the dry air. During a quick, informal survey, I count more than one hundred; most are within five feet of water, although a few adventurous individuals have wandered, if toads can be said to wander, sixty feet from the nearest ditch. The toads come in a variety of sizes. Some are small toadlets, not more than three-quarters of an inch long; others, at almost two and one-half inches from the tip of their snout to their vent, are about as big as the species ever gets at this spring. The adults are beautifully and unusually colored—creamy-white bellies and throats marbled with a network of irregular black splotches; mostly black backs bisected by a broken line of creamy yellow and dotted with blotches of the same color; black limbs ringed by asymmetrical bands of pale yellow. To me they are decidedly "untoadlike," with a narrower head, fewer warts, and smaller glands than in the larger American toads that I find in the woods and ponds around Brockport. These toads are of the desert, and they cling to a thin world of water surrounded by a sprawl of dry scrub.

In the middle distance is a playa's dry white plain; beyond, a ragged ring of arid peaks, which climb toward 14,000 feet: the familiar, aching geometry of the Basin and Range country. The mountains frame a valley that is about twelve miles long and five miles wide. It has no downstream outlet to anywhere, and the toads that live in the valley, isolated as they are, are the only ones of their species. Their common name is descriptive enough—the

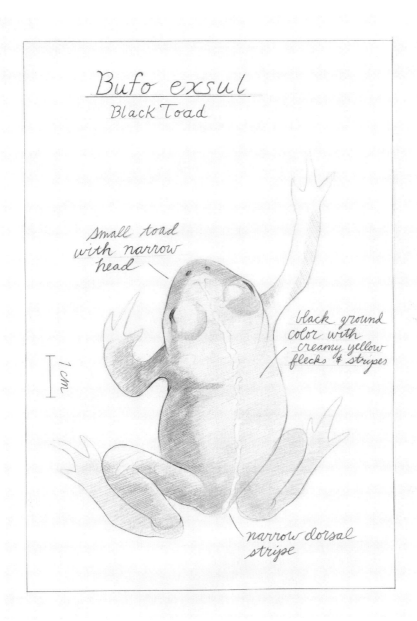

Bufo exsul
Black Toad

Small toad with narrow head

black ground color with creamy yellow flecks & stripes

1 cm

narrow dorsal stripe

Black toad (_Bufo exsul_)

black toad—but it's the binomial that pulls at my imagination: *Bufo exsul*, from the Latin for the "exiled toad," or alternatively, the "refugee toad."

I pick up an exiled toad and look into its eye, which has a horizontal black and elliptical pupil. The surrounding iris is also black, but flecked with splinters of gold, bright as pyrite. There's a whole world shining in that enigmatic eye, but it's one that is mostly closed to me, and so I place the toad, gently, back on the ground, then turn and survey its home. What a place: several springs and their small outlet streams at the western end of the valley that either disappear into the desert soil or flow into the toad-hostile, alkaline waters of the small and shallow lake in the center of the playa. That's it; there is nowhere else for these toads to hop, except into the dry and killing desert. The only way out of the valley requires miles of uphill travel, over passes ranging from 400 to 2,300 feet above the basin floor— doable for me, given some food and a few gallons of water, but inconceivable for a toad, with roughly 3 percent of my length, one one-thousandth of my mass, and skin that is, in this desert world, lethally permeable. I flop down on the ground and scan the horizon, trying for a toad's-eye view of the world. From my prone position, distances and elevations appear magnified. Before me is a thicket of grass and sedge, a rugged topography of tiny ridges and swales; beyond, the ground rises toward the impossibly steep and remote slopes of the White and Inyo Mountains. But as I contemplate toad views, I recall that toads see moving objects but not stationary ones, and so the toads around me probably do not, in any sense of the word, perceive the mountains that surround their springs. What, if anything, the toads actually sense about their spectacular home is beyond my knowing, but what I can understand is that from the perspective of toad time and toad distance, this valley is a very lonely place. The very qualities that draw me here, and to the Great Basin's larger world—heat and dryness, distance and emptiness—are the same qualities that transform the springs where black toads live into island prisons, more isolated and isolating than Devil's Island, Alcatraz, St. Helena, or the Château d'If.

I rise from my prone position, dust myself off, and note that when the angle of the desert light is just right, the toads seem to shine, small bits of animated obsidian scattered across the alkali ground.

Black toads occur naturally only in Deep Springs Valley, which lies fifteen air miles northeast of Big Pine in the Owens Valley. Within Deep Springs Valley, which is mostly arid desert scrub, black toads inhabit four spring systems; three of these are within two miles of one another in the south-eastern end of the valley. These three springs cluster around the shallow Deep Springs Lake, which in the warmer months is mostly dry playa. Another population of toads inhabits Antelope Springs, 3.3 miles from Deep Springs Lake. A few black toads occasionally have been reported from two other sites in Deep Springs Valley, and an introduced population once occurred at a flowing well in Saline Valley in Death Valley National Park, but apparently this population is now extinct. Thus the four springs in Deep Springs Valley—Corral, Buckhorn, Bog Mound, and Antelope—support the world's only black toads. These springs are the species' only country, its entire geographical and ecological capital. All told there might be forty to fifty acres of black toad habitat in the universe; George Myers, when he described the species in 1942, wrote that the black toad "has perhaps the most restricted range and fewest living representatives of any known amphibian." Although other amphibians, such as the Inyo Mountain slender salamander and the desert slender salamander, may have smaller or equally small ranges, the authors of a 2003 paper on black toads state that Meyers's "supposition still stands for anuran amphibians [frogs and toads]."

Whatever the exact extent of the black toad's habitat, its isolation is stunning. Stand at 5,000 feet, near Corral Springs, where black toads live, and take in the 360-degree view. Start your pivot by looking north at the great, rising sweep of the White Mountains as they climb through desert scrub, pinyon-juniper and bristlecone pine woodlands, and spare alpine tundra to over 14,000 feet. Rotate west, toward more mountains and West-gard Pass, a narrow slot cutting through a thick limestone rib at 7,271 feet that commonly is marked as the intersection of the White and Inyo Mountains. To the southwest are the Inyo Mountains, narrower and lower than the Whites but still rising to 11,000 feet. Continue your transit; directly to the south and east of the spring is a steep and fractured rock wall perhaps 800 feet high, home to roosting great horned owls but not toads. The wall, which is the lower part of the northeast arm of the Inyo Mountains, tracks the Deep Springs fault and the long axis of Deep Springs Valley into the far distance, where there are, of course, more mountains. From Corral Springs the easiest way out of Deep Springs Valley for anyone on two feet (or four legs) would be to follow the base of the Inyo Mountains north and east for about five miles before turning in a more easterly direction to cross Soldier Pass, which is only 400 feet above the valley floor. But beyond the divide is the waterless Soldier Pass Canyon and Eureka Valley—another dead-end basin, but even larger and more isolated than Deep Springs Valley. And so, having completed your pivot, and seen—imagined!—the great gathering of desert ranges and desert valleys stretching into a distance that in terms of visceral comprehension approaches the infinite, you understand how lyrically accurate George Meyers was when he wrote in his technical description, "*Exsul,* an 'exile' or 'castaway,' which *Bufo exsul* certainly is." For the black toads, there is no way out of Deep Springs Valley, and their nearest toad relatives are far, far away.

George Meyers based his description of the black toad on specimens taken (or, to avoid euphemisms, killed) in 1934 and 1937; the 1934 specimens were obtained by the indefatigable Carl Hubbs. When Hubbs visited Deep Springs Valley in 1934 he was searching for pupfishes. He found none, but came away from the valley with a series of toads that Meyers recognized as distinctive, primarily because of their striking black markings. Meyers described the black toad as "a localized derivative of *Bufo boreas* [the widely distributed western toad], closely similar to *B. b. nelsoni* [the Amargosa toad] in its small size, narrow head, and smoothness of skin." Meyers based his analysis on morphological characteristics, and his general conclusions about the black toad's evolutionary relationships have been corroborated by a 1973 study of proteins and recent mitochondrial DNA work, although some specialists recently have—confusingly—resurrected the genus name *Anaxyrus* for the black toad and many other species once placed in *Bufo.* (Because *Bufo* is still widely used and arguments about the merits of *Anaxyrus* versus *Bufo* have taken on the attributes of an academic cat fight [or toad fight, which also can be pretty vicious], I'll stick with *Bufo.*) In any event, the mitochondrial DNA study places the black toad within a lineage that includes the Amargosa toad; several populations of a subspecies of the western toad from southern California, *B. b. halophilus*; and more southerly populations of the Yosemite toad, *B. canorus.*

If these analyses are accurate then it is possible to think in a more detailed way about the black toad's isolation from others of its kind, an exile based not only on the characteristics of Deep Springs Valley, but also on the physical distance that separates *Bufo exsul* from its nearest relatives. Populations of western toads occur in Owens Valley, roughly twenty miles to the west, and Fish Lake Valley, Nevada, about thirty miles north of Deep Springs Valley; another, equally isolated western toad population inhabits Darwin Canyon in the Argus Mountains, seventy-five miles south of Deep Springs. The Yosemite toad, which presents a confusing geographic stew of mitochondrial DNA genotypes, occurs in the High Sierra, to the west and north of Bishop. The Amargosa toad, which since Meyers's time has been elevated to species rank and now is known as *Bufo nelsoni*, occurs in several springs and marshes along the Amargosa River north of Beatty, Nevada, eighty air miles or so to the southeast.

Of course, air miles are not the same thing as *Bufo* miles, even if one ignores the dry, rugged, and impossibly toad-hostile nature of the Basin and Range country, which toads cannot do. To properly contemplate the essence of toad miles, consider the permeability of a toad's skin, which drastically limits the time that it can spend away from water, and the relative weights of humans and toads. Although the skin of the black toad has more layers of keratin than does Inyo Mountains slender salamander skin, it still offers little barrier to evaporation. Place a toad (hopefully not *Bufo exsul*) in a 77°F environment with 25 percent humidity—conditions of a mild spring or fall day in Deep Springs Valley—and the toad will lose more than 40 percent of its body weight and die within two days. And what about toad miles? A large black toad weighs roughly 25 grams (one ounce), while a standard-issue adult male human without too much passion for pork cracklings and Doritos (for the purposes of this analysis, me) weighs in at close to 70,000 grams. Given this almost 3,000-fold mass difference, one human mile might be thought of as approximately 3,000 toad miles. But perhaps weight differences are misleading, and it might be better to think about toad distances by comparing the length of a human stride to that of a black toad hop. On flat ground my stride is close to one meter, or 39.4 inches, while the adult black toad hops I measured averaged about 1.7 inches. With this ratio of human stride length to black toad hop length, one human mile equals about twenty-three toad miles: much less than the mass-based comparison, but still a large difference, which would be magnified by the relationship between body size and the energetic demands of locomotion. This relationship is not linear; in the case of the 25-gram toad and 70,000-gram human, it takes about 12.5 times more energy to move a unit of toad weight over a given distance than to move the same unit of human weight. A final piece of information related to the relative difficulty of black toad locomotion is that frogs and toads are energetically less efficient at movement than are salamanders. Whether the relationship between human miles and toad miles is best thought of in terms of comparative body mass or stride/hop length, it takes a lot of energy for a black toad to move any substantial distance through its world.

If these numbers are too much of an abstraction, then stand near Bog Mound Springs just north of the Deep Springs Lake playa. Look northwest and uphill, toward Antelope Spring, which sits on an alluvial fan at the base of the White Mountains, 3.3 miles and 700 feet higher in elevation. From a black toad's point of view the two springs are at least seventy-six miles away, separated from one another by a waterless expanse of desert. Movement between the two springs must be an exceedingly rare event, as indicated by genetic analyses of fine-scale population structure in the black toad—although migration appears to be slightly more common downhill, from Antelope Spring to Bog Mound Springs, than in the opposite direction, which makes good toad-sense. Eric Simandle, who has studied the fine-scale genetic structure of black toad populations, wonders if major flood events sometimes wash toads downhill from Antelope Spring toward Deep Springs Lake, but floodwaters will never carry the toads uphill and out of Deep Springs Valley. The same genetic studies also suggest that black toads move more frequently between Bog Mound, Corral, and Buckhorn Springs than to Antelope Spring. The three springs, which are clustered around the northern and eastern end of Deep Springs Lake, are linked to one another by moister and more welcoming habitat, and none of their black toad populations are more than 1.5 miles from their nearest neighbors.

But it's that trek across inhospitable ground—to or away from Antelope Springs—that interests me most, because of what it suggests about the larger scale of the black toad's isolation. And so, to get a marginally better understanding of what a toad migration across arid ground entails, on a cool October day I trace a dry wash to Sams Spring, one drainage north of Antelope Spring. Black toads occasionally appear at Sams Spring, likely migrants from Antelope, and so I choose what looks to be the easiest route and count off 650 paces up a winding wash, which equals somewhere around 9.3 toad miles—quite a distance to hop through inhospitable territory, and an impressive journey for a highly aquatic animal. The inconsequential drainage is several feet deep and distinct at its mouth but quickly grows narrow and shallow before dissipating in bare gravel fifty yards or so shy of the dry creek bed below Sams Spring. Along the way I wind past mummified cow pies and several packrat nests, which suggest that water rarely flows down the wash. I step over several short toad barriers in the wash, small ledges and dams of rock mostly less than one foot high; they mean nothing to me but would require a taxing climb or detour for an emigrant toad. A scatter of Great Basin plants line the arroyo: Mormon tea, spiny hopsage, horsebrush, snakeweed, and cholla. This is a desert world, rather than a riparian one, and there is nothing in the wash to make a toad feel at home. There is no evidence of surface water other than the eroded network formed by the inconsequential drainage, although a kick of my boot reveals moist sand a few inches below the surface, residue from unusually heavy rains that soaked Deep Springs Valley a week before my visit. Of course, if a particularly adventurous and risk-prone black toad were to leave the security of Antelope Spring and venture up my little wash, it would probably do so on a rain-soaked night during one of those rare but massive frontal storms that sweep in off the Pacific Ocean, spill across the Sierra, and hit Deep Springs Valley before dissipating in the further reaches of the Great Basin.

As I traverse the wash leading toward Sams Spring I wonder what might impel a black toad to migrate away from Antelope Spring. Studies of another desert species, the red-spotted toad (*Bufo punctatus*), indicate that individuals living along intermittent streams are relatively sedentary as long as their breeding sites do not dry; they disperse up to one-half mile, mostly when these pools disappear. So, what kind of toad hunger would motivate black toads to hop away from the security of permanent water and all they know, rain or no rain, and move through alien country, sheltering in the moist sand or beneath a rock during the day, and seeking a refuge of distant water during the desert night? Although mark-recapture studies have found that temperate-zone toads may occasionally move up to 1.5 miles, toads rarely find their way home from distances greater than one mile, even in habitat much more welcoming than Great Basin desert scrub. Most aspiring black toad immigrants must perish, snatched by a hungry predator or more likely drying into a desiccated carcass well short of the nearest water, but some obviously make it from Antelope Springs to Sams Spring, far fewer down valley to Bog Mound Springs.

My stroll from Antelope to Sams Spring is short, but as I walk the distance opens before me and in my mind and heart I move beyond the local (here, in Deep Springs Valley) to the regional (from Deep Springs Valley to Owens Valley or the Amargosa River, and beyond). It's intellectually obvious that black toads aren't going to be leaving Deep Springs Valley any time soon. I've scanned the maps, read the technical papers, and understand enough about toad physiology to know this. But as I walk I also sense something visceral about the species' isolation. What brought the toads here was the wash of water that spread across the Great Basin during the Pleistocene glaciations, in much the same manner that pupfishes were brought to Salt Creek and Ash Meadows. What stranded them here was the ebb of the Pleistocene tide and how the country dried into stone and sand. And what now prevents the toads from leaving Deep Springs Valley is the physical hostility of the surrounding terrain and the country's compelling sweep of space, which demand the complete allegiance of black toads, as well as all the other aquatic creatures of the Basin and Range country.

Like many places in the Great Basin, Deep Springs Valley displays abundant geological evidence that during parts of the Pleistocene it was wetter and more toad friendly than it is today. Remnant beach terraces, some more than 300 feet above the present valley floor, indicate that Deep Springs Lake once filled much of the valley. Alluvial sediments originating in the White Mountains and deposited at Soldier Pass and other sites at the edge of Deep Springs Valley demonstrate that Pleistocene streams flowed east and southeast into Eureka Valley. These deposits are overlain by stream-transported Bishop ash erupted from the Long Valley Caldera, which means that the waters must have run until after the ash was deposited 760,000 years ago. This drainage system eventually was "defeated" by slippage along the active Deep Springs fault, which runs northeast along the base of the Inyo Mountains, but during the wet glacial periods of the early Pleistocene, Soldier Pass and Soldier Pass Canyon would have provided a route by which ancestral black toads could have colonized Deep Springs Valley.

Pluvial cycles in the Great Basin were complex, but whatever their timing flooding from glacial melting during the Pleistocene would have allowed toads and other water-dependent species to disperse over great distances, only to retreat into isolated pockets of habitat as the waters receded and the land dried into desert. The last Pleistocene lakes disappeared from Death Valley, Owens Valley, and nearby Fish Lake Valley in Nevada some 10,000–13,000 years ago, and it is reasonable to assume that Deep Springs Lake would have tracked a parallel course. Black toads have been isolated from other closely related lineages in the western toad group since at least that time and perhaps for much longer—ever since the Deep Springs fault defeated drainages leading out of Deep Springs Valley. Mitochondrial DNA sequence data suggest that the three major lineages in the western toad species group began splitting 1.4 to 0.66 million years ago, while divergence within these lineages began around 635,000 years ago. As the streams and lakes dried, ancestors of what we now call the black toad, western toad, Yosemite toad, and Amargosa toad would have hopped down their separate evolutionary paths, funneled into isolation by aridity and physiological constraints. If the physiological restrictions tying black toads to water are not quite as severe as those faced by pupfishes and springsnails, they remain an imperative that limits the toads' dispersal, and it is important to remember that black toads have never been seen more than sixty feet or so from water. And somewhere along the way, as Deep Springs Valley sank further into isolation, ancestors of *Bufo exsul* would have picked up the mutations that granted them their distinctive black markings. The toads would have clustered around the shrinking waters, withdrawing further and further into genetic divergence and exile, until they were left with only the four tiny islands of habitat that we know as Antelope, Bog Mound, Corral, and Buckhorn Springs, but which the black toads know as home.

Among toads that I am most familiar with—the American toad (*Bufo americanus*) in the eastern United States and red-spotted toad in the Southwest—amorous males attract females with high-pitched mating calls. On a cool night in April ephemeral breeding ponds around Brockport reverberate with the trills of American toads, which often are mixed with the cacophony of spring peeper advertisement calls, the more melodious toad trills providing a soothing counterpoint to the piercing racket of whistled *pings* thrown out by the tiny peepers. And in the desert it sometimes happens that after a long, dry day of spring hiking the first thing I will know of water will be the trills of red-spotted toads, their music drifting down a winding, narrow-walled canyon. Up to this point the streambed that I've been tracking has been nothing more than rock and sand, and empty basins lined with cracked clay, but gradually and surprisingly the canyon begins to gather a series of pools that grow larger and brighter as I walk those last few feet to rest. With the noise I make—the crunch of gravel underfoot, the creak of my pack as I throw it to the ground—the toads grow quiet. But as I settle down the males resume their insistent pleading and the canyon is again filled with toad song. In Deep Springs Valley, though, there are no choruses of black toad trills flung into the evening air, only a muttering of soft, high-pitched *clucks* or *plinks* given out by breeding males. Males produce these release calls when other males invade their space or attempt to mate with them. If an amorous male climbs onto the back of another male and grasps him in a mating embrace, the aggrieved male responds with a release call that must mean something like, "Get the —— off my back!" The sound made by a cluster of black toad males has been described as resembling "a distant flock of geese," but it reminds me more of a rotating flywheel, squeaky and badly in need of lubricant. Males of two other closely related species, the Amargosa toad and western toad, also lack a mating trill, although male Yosemite toads (*Bufo canorus*) produce a long, rapid musical trill, *canorus* meaning "tuneful."

Before I first visited Deep Springs Valley during the mating season, which runs from March through April, I imagined that the night air would be filled with trills, and so was disappointed that male black toads could manage nothing more than subdued *clucks*. I missed the music that I associate with spring along desert streams or in the wetlands near my New York home, but after coming into the silence of Deep Springs Valley, the reticence of the black toads now seems appropriate, and in keeping with the quality of the place.

It is good to visit the springs where the black toads live, hear the *clucks* and *plinks* of mating males, and see the long strings of eggs laid by the females. During breeding, quiet pools of shallow open water may be filled with clusters of mating, or amplexing, toads. In black toad amplexus, a male grasps a gravid female from behind, with his abdomen pressed against her back and his forelegs wrapped around her sides, just behind her forelegs. But black toad mating sometimes is less a quiet, intimate embrace than a chaotic free-for-all, because the object of one male's passion might also be an equally desirable object for other males—perhaps only one, but quite possibly two, three, four, five, or even fifteen competitors. An undisturbed pair might sit quietly in the water for up to twenty-seven hours, but at other times black toad mating may resemble a group of adrenaline-addled rugby players struggling for the ball, the amplexing pair knocked on their sides or backs, other males fighting to dislodge the (temporarily?) successful male, a confused swirl of black toad bodies spilling through the water, the struggle punctuated by staccato bursts of *clucks* when one male mistakenly grasps another male in the melee.

Males and females occasionally die during bouts of "multiple amplexus," but black toads are much more vulnerable to predation by birds, especially black-billed magpies and common ravens. Cynthia Kagarise Sherman, who studied the natural history and mating system of black toads in 1977 and 1978, found their carcasses beneath a magpie nest, "characteristically eviscerated, [with] one or both forelegs eaten, or else the back half of the body . . . removed," while ravens may have been responsible for "piles of 5–10 toads . . . shredded and ripped in half." The black toad's daily timing of mating activity, which switches from diurnal to nocturnal as the season progresses, may in part be an attempt to escape from diurnal predators such as magpies, which arrive in Deep Springs Valley in the spring. However, nocturnal mating does not save some toads from the beaks of ravens and magpies, and many other potential predators also occur in the Deep Springs area, including northern harriers, garter snakes, king snakes, long-tailed weasels, and coyotes.

Still, in October of a good year the short grass around mating sites is filled with metamorphosed toadlets, about three-quarters of an inch to one and one-quarter inch long from snout to vent. By November the year's crop of juvenile toads and the surviving adults have entered hibernation (or, as it is technically called in ectotherms, brummation), where they will remain for about four months before emerging into another desert spring.

Like the Inyo Mountains slender salamander and most pupfishes in the region, black toads have a very restricted distribution. But they have survived much in their time and should persevere if humans treat them properly and the four springs that they depend on do not fail due to climate change, an earthquake, or local increases in groundwater pumping. In spite of their limited range, black toads are not protected under the federal Endangered Species Act, although they are listed as a threatened, "fully protected" species by the state of California, and as such are safe from collection or intentional damage to their habitat. Three of the springs that harbor black toads—Corral, Buckhorn, and Bog Mound—are owned by Deep Springs College, a tiny school with about forty residents located seven miles north of Deep Springs Lake. The college, which runs a small cattle ranch, has worked with the California Department of Fish and Game to protect black toads on their property and has abandoned most agricultural operations in the toads' habitat, except for periodic cattle grazing and some water manipulations. However, black toads need open water in which to breed, and photographs from the 1960s and 1970s show that cattail and three-square bulrush have increased in parts of Antelope, Corral, and Buckhorn springs traditionally used as breeding sites by the toads. The toads' preference for open water is illustrated by an experiment conducted at Antelope Springs by a Deep Springs College faculty member, Amity Wilczek, and her students. Under the supervision of California Department of Fish and Game staff they established a series of experimental and control plots in an area with a heavy growth of three-square bulrush; the control plots had intact vegetation, while the bulrush was removed from the experimental plots. When I visited Antelope Springs in March of 2011 there were strings of toad eggs in the open water of the experimental plots but none in the thick mats of vegetation in control plots. Near another spring I also noticed that mating toads were congregating in a section of ditch that normally did not contain water and had little vegetation.

It would be relatively easy to clear aquatic plants from many of the springs, but California's 1960s-era regulations regarding fully protected species do not permit habitat manipulation, or incidental take, unless it is done by employees of the Department of Fish and Wildlife—and given the starvation funding for the agency and its overworked and underpaid employees, this has not always been easy to accomplish. The situation with the black toads and their habitat is eerily similar to the one involving Owens pupfish, Gary Giacomini, Steve Parmenter, and the ditch at Warm Springs in the Owens Valley. Students from Deep Springs College could clean the ditches easily, but the archaic "fully protected" designation is not flexible enough to permit this—another instance in which a well-intentioned law may in some situations harm the very species it was designed to protect. The difficulty of finding a legal way to use machines or people to clear the ditches of emergent vegetation probably means that periodic cattle grazing is a necessary but inefficient method of maintaining at least some of the open-water habitat that breeding toads require.

In spite of the difficulties of managing endangered-species habitat under California law, in the best of all possible worlds those interested in conserving black toads will find ways to maintain patches of open water where males and females can congregate in the spring—inefficiently, if the regulatory and legal environment is not changed, more effectively if it is. Hopefully, and no matter what type of future climate change brings to Deep Springs Valley, water will continue to flow from Corral, Buckhorn, Bog Mound, and Antelope springs; black toads will find enough habitat for making tadpoles and toadlets; and the species will flourish. But there is another plausible scenario for the black toads' future: in the worst of all possible worlds, which is identical to one that already has come to pass for hundreds of frog and toad species, the chytrid fungus *Batrachochytrium dendrobatidis*, or "Bd," will arrive in Deep Springs Valley. For black toads Bd could represent the antithesis to a Panglossian world of open water and vigorous spring flows, an amphibian annihilator in the guise of Yama, the Hindu god of death: "with fierce jaws and frowning fiercely, chosen as their lord by many ugly, fierce-faced hundreds of diseases." Although a lethal multitude of factors, from habitat loss to pesticides and increased ultraviolet light, has contributed to worldwide amphibian declines, Bd is often the main culprit. It is the ultimate "fierce-faced" disease, which has been described, without hyperbole, as "possibly the most deadly invasive species on the planet." It has been implicated in the decline of more than two hundred amphibian species and is responsible for the "the greatest loss of vertebrate biodiversity attributable to disease in recorded history." Bd has decimated frog and toad populations throughout much of the world, from Central and South America to Australia, the European Pyrenees, and western North America, and it could easily destroy a species such as the black toad, with its four vulnerable populations.

Although Bd has not (yet?) reached Deep Springs Valley it has penetrated the most remote parts of the High Sierra, less than thirty miles to the west, with devastating effects. In Kings Canyon and Sequoia National Parks, Sierra Nevada yellow-legged frogs (*Rana sierrae*) and mountain yellow-legged frogs (*Rana muscosa*) have vanished from more than 93 percent of their historic range, often within a year or two of Bd's appearance in their habitat. I hiked through much of this country during my teenage years—Milestone Basin, Sixty Lakes Basin, the Tablelands—and I can recall the constant "plop" of startled frogs as I wandered past the ponds and meandering streams that grace High Sierra meadows. No more. Now, on a bright July day, and in spite of their beautiful riot of wildflowers and rich green play of sedges, these meadows are diminished, as if some vital part of their essence had vanished with the frogs. Further north, in Yosemite National Park, surveys conducted in 1915 and repeated in 1992 showed that yellow-legged frogs had vanished from twelve of fourteen historic sites. But it's not only Sierra frog populations that are suffering; in Yosemite, western toads disappeared from seven of eight localities, while Yosemite toads vanished from six of thirteen sites. The same process has occurred in other protected high-mountain areas in western North America, such as Colorado's Rocky Mountain National Park, where western toads virtually disappeared between 1991 and 1999, as survival rates plummeted from 78 percent in 1991 to 3 percent in 1998. Such a history offers up nothing in the way of a hopeful future for frogs and toads unless one imagines that natural selection will allow a few individuals to found more resistant populations.

Bd works by attacking amphibian keratin, and although it occurs in the mouthparts of tadpoles, the fungus does not cause illness or mortality in pre-metamorphic amphibians. But when Bd infects the skin of adult amphibians it causes lesions, thickened epidermis, and death. Even after scientists understood Bd's role in amphibian population collapse, its mode of action remained unknown. However, it now seems that Bd kills adult amphibians by disrupting crucial skin functions, including maintenance of water and electrolyte balance and exchange of respiratory gasses. The degree to which amphibians interact with the environment via their highly permeable skin is greater than for other vertebrates, and so they are inordinately susceptible to any disease that disrupts physiological activities of normal skin.

A micrograph of amphibian skin infected with Bd shows a scatter of tiny circles spread throughout keratinized parts of the epidermis. The circles, or zoosporangia, are little more than ten micrometers across; about 10,000 of them laid end-to-end would fit in one centimeter. There may be a few tiny threadlike rhizoids spreading through the infected tissue, and with the proper preparation it is possible to see clusters of motile reproductive cells, or zoospores, within the zoosporangia. When zoospores are released from their parental sporangia they swim off to infect a new host, and so the disease can race quickly through an amphibian population. To my unpracticed eye it is difficult to look at micrographs of Bd and *see* death; it is such a tiny organism, although in its own way much fiercer than the animals I respect when my home range intersects theirs—brown bears, Mojave rattlesnakes, bark scorpions. Yama comes in many forms, I know, and some of them are almost infinitely small, but sharp canines, fangs, and stingers are more compelling than the minute, whitish gray circles I see in the black-and-white photographs published in the 1999 paper that first identified *Batrachochytrium dendrobatidis* as lethal to amphibians.

Once Bd reaches a population, the zoospores can easily swim from host to host. It's less clear how Bd spreads so quickly among populations, especially those in relatively pristine, isolated environments. Between 1987 and 2006 the front of Bd infection in Central America advanced from north to south at rates of up to twenty-five miles per year, while in the northern Andes Bd may have moved as much as 170 miles in a single year. Although rates estimated by large-scale studies are crude and smaller-scale studies suggest a much slower spread, chytrid fungus is very adept at colonizing new host populations. Locally, infected frogs or toads could easily transport the fungus as they hop from pond to pond. The Pacific treefrog (*Pseudacris regilla*), a small species, is one such vector. Native Pacific treefrogs are still abundant in the same High Sierra habitats that once supported yellow-legged frogs. Although they often harbor Bd they rarely die from the disease, and in laboratory studies they show less of the characteristic skin thickening that has killed so many yellow-legged frogs. Human agency must also play a role in the movement of Bd across longer distances, whether through the transport of animals for trade, or on the boot soles of an angler or hiker. In a laboratory setting Bd may survive in moist sand for up to three months, while after even three hours of drying bird feathers inoculated with Bd carried zoospores capable of founding new cultures. But whatever its mode of transport, Bd is very good at what it does—moving from place to place and killing amphibians.

One paper on *Batrachochytrium dendrobatidis* bears the title "Riding the Wave," the wave being its seemingly inexorable spread through Central and South America, a scorched-earth (or rather, scorched-water) march through the region's amphibian populations. And although Deep Springs Valley is an isolated place, I cannot stand by Corral Springs without considering the fate of yellow-legged frogs in the High Sierra and thinking that Bd's fungal wave—more like a tsunami—also could arrive *here*. Whether Bd finds its way into Deep Springs Valley on the feathers of a mallard or the hooves of cattle (or on my boots, for God's sake) it then could wreak havoc on the black toads, who have endured so much, for so long. Whatever hope I have that Bd will not play Yama for the black toads rises partly from Deep Springs Valley's isolation. There are relatively few human visitors to spread the disease, and no Pacific chorus frogs or introduced bullfrogs, another excellent vector. It might help, too, that Bd apparently kills best in cooler, moist environments, and for much of the year Deep Springs Valley is a hot, dry place. Water temperatures above 77°F inhibit Bd's growth, and studies on the Tarahumara frog (*Rana tarahumarae*), which occurs in southern Arizona and Sonora, Mexico, suggest that Bd's effects on frog populations are more severe when minimum water temperatures are less than 55°F. Water flowing from Corral Springs has a constant temperature of about 65°F, although away from the springhead it falls well below this value early in the breeding season, or prior to hibernation. On March mornings I have seen a thick skin of ice on sites where black toads will mate later in the day, and I imagine that once introduced to Deep Springs Valley, Bd would find enough cool water and vulnerable hosts to do quite well. In my more objective moments it is difficult to be optimistic about the future of *Bufo exsul*, but I do not want to cultivate despair. To paraphrase Emily Dickinson, "hope is the thing with warts," just as it is the tiny thing with fins, or the slender salamander drowsing away its days, deep within the Inyo Mountains.

––––––––––––

Autumn in Deep Springs Valley. I sit alone on a camp stool as my small fire dies down and the full night comes on. A great horned owl hoots from the cliffs behind camp; to the south is Corral Springs, which issues from the great wall along the eastern edge of the valley and flows toward the glimmering salt flats of Deep Springs Lake. Big-toothed sage, rabbitbrush, Russian thistle, bunchgrasses, barbed wires fences, alkali dirt, and piles of desiccated cow dung surround me. The night sky is huge and empty, the valley a bowl of silence held in the deepest stillness. I nurse my small glass of Scotch and look north, watch an occasional set of headlights ride Highway 168's long fall off Westgard Pass and speed eastward, into the blackness. The cars are too few and far away to bring me any noise and their silent passage, their absolute insistence on being somewhere other than here, helps fill the valley with a solitude as deep as the Pleistocene lake that once covered this place. A single light somewhere on a ridge high in the White Mountains winks off and then there are only the heavens, the quiet, and a thin drift of clouds "flowering / blue and mystical over the face of the stars." Beyond the embers of my fire there are black toads; beyond the toads, in other Great Basin valleys and mountains, are pupfishes and salamanders. All of these species and their scattered populations cling to their tiny islands, and I cling to them, to their essence and persistence, as much as I cling to the beautiful and wonderful geometry of this valley. I am alone here, but not at all lonely, and in this moment and place I am supremely happy, as settled and content as I have ever been.

It is just as the philosopher (Bruce Springsteen) has said: "We all carry a landscape within us." These internal landscapes are full of contradiction and complexity; they are alternately bright and dark, wild and settled, inchoate and sharply etched. They are the essence of who we are, and I believe that happiness, to the extent that it is possible in this world, most often comes when we encounter the congruence between the better parts of our internal landscape and the landscapes of the great world. In this congruence it is possible to feel at home and at peace: lock and key, enzyme and substrate, that often momentary but perfect fit between the external and internal worlds. Perhaps the best term to describe this relationship might be chemical valence: "The capacity of something to unite, react, or interact with something else." Depending upon who we are and where we are in our lives, we might discover this valence in a multitude of disparate places: at a NASCAR race, on the Upper West Side in Manhattan, while fly fishing from a small drift boat on the Yellowstone River, on an immaculate green golf course, while lying in bed with a lover or toweling a young child's head dry after an evening bath, or just sitting quietly with a good cup of tea and your dog as the morning comes on. The list of possible synchronicities between internal and external landscapes is endless, and sometimes it is impossible to understand the forms of congruence that bring happiness to others. I doubt that I will ever find much positive valence on the streets of Manhattan, and I know that it will never happen at a professional wrestling match, while many people would discover little valence here in Deep Springs Valley. We have our ways and our sympathies, and how others come into their own landscapes of desire may remain as puzzling to us as the theoretical physics of subatomic particles or the movements of the farthest stars. And of course, out of the reverse situation—a recognition of shared landscapes—come friends and lovers, and the most powerful antidotes to the loneliness we all must feel, sometimes and in some places.

In my life this sense of accordance, of belonging in and to something much greater than myself, has touched me most deeply and most often in the empty and open places of this world. For me the most compelling landscapes are those of the desert, western Great Plains, high mountains, and arctic tundra, the spare lands in which much of life has been stripped away by heat and dryness, cold and wind—environments in which living things search out the horizontal while the sky claims the vertical. I recall a passage from one of my favorite novels, David Malouf's *The Conversations at Curlow Creek*, which I have carried with me into the high desert. The book is set somewhere in the arid Outback of western New South Wales, and for a moment I switch on my headlamp and consider the following: "A high, wide emptiness that drew you on into an opening distance in yourself in which the questions that posed themselves had no easy sociable answer, concerned only yourself and what there was at last, or might be, between you and the harsh, unchanged and unchanging earth, and above, the unchanged and unchanging stars."

There may be times when it feels that the earth and stars never change, but here in Deep Springs Valley the evidence of the world says that they are anything but static. The stars move, the waters advance and recede, the mountains rise and then are buried in graves of their own debris. Stasis is very rarely a part of this country; instead, I think about Malouf's "high, wide emptiness" and how it draws me into an "opening distance" in myself, one that corresponds to the spatials of the Great Basin. I switch off my headlamp, take another sip of whiskey, and contemplate the dark spread of Deep Springs Valley. When this country is at its best and I am most receptive, I am drawn into ecstasy, into the sort of feeling that I get when listening to a beautiful piece of music or reading a wonderful poem. But in most cases it's not the entire song or poem that moves me most intensely, but rather a small section—say Clarence Clemons's saxophone solo on

Springsteen's "Jungleland," or more precisely and obscurely, the passage in Lanterna's "Luminous," which according to my MP3 player begins exactly two minutes and fifteen seconds into the song, and lasts for forty-five seconds. Or take one of my favorite poems, Theodore Roethke's "The Far Field"; much of it is good, but what pulls at my heart most strongly are just three of its 103 lines: "I learned not to fear infinity / The far field, the windy cliffs of forever / The dying of time in the white light of tomorrow." Music and mountains, poems and the great sprawl of the Great Basin—but there's a difference between my reaction to the Basin and Range landscape and to Clarence Clemons or Theodore Roethke, for the intense joy rising out of the synchronicity of musical notes or lines of poetry is ephemeral, while I can hold onto the intensity of the landscape for hours, track a primal euphoria every bit as wide and deep as the country itself. Just give me Deep Springs Valley on this night or the long slide of an empty road through the Basin and Range country on some high and bright vernal day, mountains rising all around and valleys beyond valleys. And so my love of this country, which rips my heart away, lets me grasp that opening distance in myself.

How did I come into my landscape aesthetic, and how did the landscape come into me? My attraction to the harshest and loneliest places developed slowly—or perhaps an incipient attraction was with me as a child, but it took me years to recognize its full depth and power. I do know that I discovered some vital and visceral connection when I was fourteen and first walked into the alpine expanse of the High Sierra, on the trail that climbed past Hamilton Lakes and over Kaweah Gap in Sequoia National Park. And three years later, when I went off to college in Arizona, I quickly recognized something compelling about the southwestern deserts, particularly the Grand Canyon and Slickrock country of Utah, although for a while I felt most secure in those lush pockets where there was water nearby and the green grace of cottonwoods. At first I didn't quite get the aesthetics of arid emptiness or feel completely at home there, a situation illustrated by an encounter I had in my early twenties when I was hitchhiking in southern Arizona and got stuck somewhere along a lonely stretch of Sonoran Desert between Organ Pipe Cactus National Monument and Tucson. I'd made the mistake of accepting a ride that dropped me off in the archetypal "middle of nowhere," where a rutted dirt road intersected the main highway. There was no reason for one of the rare cars headed eastward to slow down, and they blew by me at seventy or eighty miles per hour in a Doppler-like wash of air and noise. I had violated one of the cardinal precepts of hitchhiking: never put yourself in a place where drivers cannot evaluate the possibility

that you are on the lam from the nearest maximum security prison. I figured that I could easily end up spending the night where I was and so I
began seeking rides in either direction, in hope of getting somewhere, anywhere. After several hours of this back-and-forth begging an old rattletrap
Dodge Powerwagon slowed to a stop, and I had my ride to Tucson. The
driver was in his late fifties or early sixties, with deeply tanned, leathery
skin, wire-rimmed glasses, tousled gray hair, and dressed in dusty khakis.
He'd been down in the Pinacate Desert of Mexico, which is about as dry
and desolate as almost any place in the world, a landscape that he preferred
to the "lush" Sonoran Desert, with its thick stands of saguaros, cholla, and
organ pipe cacti. We talked for a while about landscapes of the Southwest
and I mentioned that I liked the country around Flagstaff, with its sheltering expanse of ponderosa pines. He glanced over at me, shook his head in
dismay, and said, "All those trees; they make a man feel like he's in jail." "All
those trees"—at the time I didn't understand what he meant, but now I do.
It's not that I dislike trees. Rather, I simply prefer them in small doses—a
tiny copse of white fir huddled in a north-facing slope somewhere in a high
desert mountain range, a vestige of the Pleistocene, or a single cottonwood
shading a small seep, deep within a sandstone alcove. . . .

And as I began my work as a field biologist—first in the southwestern
deserts, later in the alpine tundra and Canadian arctic—I came to understand that the same spare aesthetic that drew me to these places also drew
me to their animals and plants. I admired their toughness and tenacity, the
ways in which they clung to life, their ability to seek out the smallest islands
of grace in oceans of adversity—much like I did whenever my desired landscapes spoke most fiercely in the language of heat and cold, wind and water.
During my graduate work at Washington State University in the early 1980s
the physicality of shared experience, the ways in which so many of the animals and plants that I loved and studied sought their refuges and survived
where no living thing should survive, drew me deeply into environmental
physiology. And when I first read *The Theory of Island Biogeography*, by Robert MacArthur and E. O. Wilson, and the scientific papers spawned by their
monograph, I felt a compelling fascination with the graphs that plotted species richness against island area, those quantitative expressions of the landscape that I felt within me, and the landscapes that I was drawn to in the
larger world. Although I was not yet ready to confront, honestly and fully,
the forces that had shaped my attraction to the metaphorical aspects of islands and their inhabitants, I knew that there were islands everywhere and
sensed that the loneliness of isolated populations was my loneliness, too.

Later, I would consider how I had been affected by a complex mix of innate inclination and personal history: the thick childhood stew of my stepfather's alcoholism and sexual abuse, plus my small stature, the burdens that I felt so strongly throughout my high school years; the solace granted by books that I read during my adolescence (*Walden, Sand County Almanac, The Mountains of California, On the Loose*); and my early encounters with the wilderness of the High Sierra and California Coast Range. The warp and weft of nature and nurture, and their intricate interaction, the forces that shape who we are, and how we face the world. . . . In my twenties and thirties I kept a section in my journal entitled "Loneliness," where I collected quotations and my own thoughts dealing with isolation. I read Dostoevsky and Camus, *The Heart is a Lonely Hunter* and *The Sheltering Sky*, tried to find God several times but in the words of Gary Snyder "couldn't make Immortal." I came to believe (still do, on most days) that ultimately and existentially we are pretty much alone in this world, and that the only antidote to this isolation is love for others, and love for the landscapes of our desire: that congruence between the internal and external worlds, for hardscrabble deserts and the long roll of arctic tundra, for the drift of gray rain shrouds across the High Plains, for islands and their creatures, for the tender touch of my wife and the full presence of my children, for shared experience and the bonds of family and deep friendship. Perhaps these things have come too rarely in my life, but they still have come.

The point is that islands and the creatures that inhabit them resonate with me in some fundamental way. On islands, in islands, by islands—especially islands that are embraced by vastness, whether of water or earth—I feel an intense physical and aesthetic valence with the larger world, and am at home in a way described by David Malouf: "If the gods are there, it is because you have discovered them there, drawn them up out of your soul's need for them and dreamed them into the landscape to make it shine." It is the kind of feeling, of home and longing and recognition, that I once had on the summit of Te Manga, the highest point on Rarotonga in the Cook Islands of the South Pacific: a thin black spike of volcanic rock rising out of thick trees, with the emerald green ridges of an extinct caldera falling steeply away to the shores of the island. Beyond Rarotonga's wave-shrouded fringing reef was the full round ocean, an infinite sun-struck plane of the deepest blue, with a drift of cumulus on the farthest edge of the earth. And at my feet were springs of Polynesian blueberry, *Vaccinium cereum*: *Vaccinium* being a familiar genus of boreal and arctic realms, but *cereum* a species only of high-elevation cloud forests on Pacific islands, and so restricted to habitat islands within the volcanic islands that lay waiting, *out there*, just beyond the horizon's curve. Or to hear at the farthest wind-pounded edge of trees in the Canadian north the thin whistled song of a blackpoll warbler, a species at home in the boreal forest, with mile after endless mile of tundra spiraling away from the tiny island of spruce where some lone bird has found its refuge. Or, of course, to confront on their islands the rare species of this country, the pupfishes, black toad, and slender salamander—for what creates a more effective island than a trace of water in the desert, especially when incubated in rarity itself, the kind of rarity that speaks of extinction, the most powerful iteration of absolute loneliness?

And so I think of the last pair of great auks, strangled to death on a small island near Iceland in 1844; the last Tasmanian wolf perishing of exposure and neglect at the Hobart Zoo on September 7, 1936, after three years of solitary captivity; or the last dusky seaside sparrow dying in a captive breeding facility at Walt Disney World Resort on June 17, 1987, having lived on for fifteen months longer than any of his kin. In these extinctions there is a full measure of the loneliness that also pervades localized human extinctions: the last of the Greenland Vikings bleeding into an unknown end after the Black Death descended upon Europe and the supply ships failed to come; entire villages, destroyed by whatever particular acts of genocide have most recently poisoned our species; or Ishi, the last surviving member of the Yana people of California, who when asked his name replied, "I have none, because there were no people to name me." And on a much smaller and personal scale the kind of despairing isolation and extinction that we all might know but for some measure of chance and discipline, and a fortunate combination of neurotransmitters and personal history. Take for example my stepfather, who died of heart failure and alcoholism, absolutely alone in some seedy shithole of an apartment in Fort Wayne, Indiana, estranged from every last one of his friends and family. He spent the final twenty years of his life mostly in exile from northern California, where he was born and raised and once felt some comfort, drinking his way to his own extinction—and after his death he lay in his apartment for three days, until some passerby in the hallway happened to notice the stink of death seeping from his room, his last tiny island.

———————————

And so this is what I hope, and offer up as one more crucial value of rare and endangered species: that in addition to their intrinsic value, their right to exist independently of direct human concerns, and whatever their importance to ecosystem functioning, potential value to medicine, or worth in ecotourism dollars, they should be treasured for the very essence of their isolation and aloneness in the world. Hopefully, none of us need ever encounter the ultimate loneliness of Ishi, the last Vikings of Greenland, or my stepfather in Fort Wayne. But we still have our internal landscapes and personal islands, and to some degree all of us inhabit our own isolation, framed by personal history and circumstance (betrayal, financial distress, the loss of love and loved ones, the endless distance between desire and actuality, on and on). And of course there is the ultimate loneliness and inevitability of death. All of this is as much a part of the human condition as is its polar opposite, connection, and for me—and I would hope that for others, be they my archetypal waitress in Bishop and rancher in Lone Pine, or the wealthy condominium owner racing north on U.S. Highway 395, past Manzanar and on to a weekend of skiing at Mammoth Mountain—it is of some consolation to contemplate the landscapes of loneliness occupied by a rare species, particularly in the arid emptiness of the Great Basin, where we might encounter Robert Hass's "movement of grief / which has something in it of the desert's bareness / and of its distance." If only we might stop for a moment, and watch and listen, and *feel* something of what it might be like to be so alone, and like the black toad, so exiled by time and mountains and the drying of the earth. By doing so we then might understand the long view: that *we* are not alone, that these vulnerable yet tenacious creatures have gone on and may go on, their survival in many cases helped by humans with the upmost conviction and determination, even as we previously and perversely pushed them toward extinction. For me it is a great comfort to know that *we* can survive our loneliness, just as the black toad, Inyo Mountains slender salamander, and Salt Creek pupfish have survived in their loneliness. And it is wonderful to know that *we* can be saved from some measure of our loneliness, just as the Owens pupfish and Ash Meadows Amargosa pupfish have been pulled back from the brink of extinction. Out of these acts of knowing I believe, deeply and passionately, that it is possible to cultivate an encouragement that is of the greatest value to us all. We need our role models, our shared landscapes and reasons for hope, which for me are offered up more often by the natural world than by the evening news.

The fire at my feet has dwindled away, as has my whiskey, and on Highway 168 the last of the evening's distant headlights have disappeared. Deep

Springs Valley is still and cool and immense, the White and Inyo Mountains dark and massive, etched by the faint wash of starlight. The winds are calm. All of this emptiness and quiet is "a lightness, / a moveable island of joy," and the silence breaks across the heavens, breaks across time and life's great history, and the story of this country and its creatures: Paleozoic and Mesozoic, Miocene and Pliocene, Pleistocene and Recent. Emptiness and the great fetch of time flows out toward Ash Meadows, its drowsing pupfishes, and their precious islands of water: Devils Hole, Kings Pool, Jackrabbit Spring, School Spring. Death Valley and Owens Valley, too, have their drowsing pupfishes, which also have their tiny islands: Salt Creek and Cottonball Marsh, BLM Spring and Mule Spring. But in the Inyo Mountains the slender salamanders do not drowse; in the night, they rise from sleep and probe the thin threads of moist ground, wander through and beneath their tiny gardens of rock and sedge, willow and thistle. And close at hand, on the island that is Corral Springs, there will be toads, alive to the night, offering up their beautiful display of hope and tenacity to the waiting world.

The View from Telescope Peak

And yet this great wink of eternity.
—Hart Crane, "Voyages II"

I leave Mahogany Flat just after three in the morning, headed for Telescope Peak, the highest point in the Panamint Range, six and one-half miles to the south. It is late October in a year of early storms, and the night air is cool in my nose. The full moon is still high in the western sky, brilliant behind a field of broken clouds. For the most part I hike without a headlamp, climbing through open pinyon woodlands toward the broad ridge between Rogers and Bennett peaks. After months spent in this country, mostly in the lowlands, I want the long view. I want to stand on the summit of Telescope Peak and watch the sun rise over the great sweep of Basin and Range emptiness: west to the High Sierra, north toward the White Mountains, east past the Spring Mountains. I want to look down into the valleys, onto nations of pupfish and salamanders, toads and naucorids, and touch their compelling present—their isolation, their vulnerability, their determined persistence in this world. And because experience has taught me that spatial vastness brings with it a taste of temporal vastness, I hope that the view from Telescope Peak also will embrace time: the abyssal time of evolution, the shallow time of a historical, sometimes-ravaged past and an imagined future. I want the world in all of its "silence and intoxication / [to] give me a wafer of time; the flickering / and flashing embers of time."

I walk steadily, content with my movement and solitude, happy in the great quiet that embraces the Panamints. The dark, leavened by moonlight, is lovely and gentle. The angle of the trail is consistent but forgiving and I make good time, weaving in and out of shallow drainages as I round the east ridge of Rogers Peak and climb toward Arcane Meadows. I break into the open and see that—already—one of my expectations of this hike will not be met, for the great gulf of Death Valley, 9,000 feet below me, is filled with fine, gauzelike layers of stratocumulus. To the east, the high peaks of the Amargosa Range are islands in a sea of silvered cloud, and I understand that on this rising day I will not see Badwater, with its *Assiminea* snails, or Salt Creek, with its pupfish. To the west, Panamint Valley will vanish; to the northwest, Saline Valley will remain closed. I think that never before have I seen such an inversion in this country, and that it must be a rare phenomenon, but I don't know for certain. It's been more than three decades since I studied burros in the Panamints, and the years make me question my memory.

The temperatures are in the mid-thirties, perfect for good walking, and I fall into an easy rhythm that is broken only once, when I surprise a flock of quail. The birds explode off the trail and spin off into the darkness, disrupting my reverie and leaving me gasping for air, my heart racing. And then there are limber pine and the main crest of the Panamints, a broad open saddle marked by a stone cairn. I lay my pack at the base of the rocks and break for water and a snack. The moonlight is everywhere, laving the land in silver, blanketing the sagebrush slopes. The summit of Telescope Peak gleams in the distance, snow covered and drifting in and out of scattered clouds. At 4:30 I take up my pack and begin the long, gentle contour toward Telescope Peak. The trail is easy to follow without my headlamp, the rocks and thin roots of sagebrush layered in frost, glistening as though sprinkled with a dusting of tiny glass shards. Near the base of the final 1,500-foot climb I pass through a swirling band of heavy mist, and the air around me is suddenly as thick as Scottish fog. A few minutes later I break into the open and find crusted snow at my feet. The air chills. The moon slides toward the western mountains and darkness falls around me, the cold, crystalline sky a spindrift dance of stars. I look to the east, to the nascent dawn, then over the Spring Mountains, where I had hoped to find the soft, nacreous glow of Las Vegas, its lights and the thirst of 2 million people rising into the sky above Mount Charleston. But the quilt of clouds that cover Death Valley also shrouds the casinos and suburbs, golf courses and freeways, and there is only the faintest hint of light on the horizon.

My pace slows—I am not acclimated to the nearly 11,000 feet of elevation—as morning gathers over Death Valley and the Panamint Range. Dawn claims the trail, the buckwheat and gooseberry brushes, the gnarled bristlecone and limber pines, rimed in layers of snow and ice. The last few switchbacks take longer than they should, but I top out at 6:30, just before sunrise, and surrounding me is this great blessing of space. The mountains fall away in all directions: long ridge runs to the north and south, white salt-pan valleys to the east and west, sunk beneath clouds, desert ranges rising out of an ephemeral sea, its waves roiling into light. My thermometer reads twenty-one degrees and the bitter winds come on, slicing through my sweaty clothes and quickly chilling me. But I want to take in this country, absorb what I can of its essence: its time and aridity, and the presence of the animals that I have watched these last few months. And so I strip off my soaked t-shirt, throw on a dry one, and add all of the clothes that I have. I find a small alcove that faces southeast and shelters me from the worst of the wind, throw down a foam pad, and climb into my bivy sack. I open a thermos and pour myself a scalding cup of tea, feel its warmth slide into my core. Comfortable for the moment and ready to watch and listen, I settle into my perch and greet the rising day.

Symbolically and aesthetically, Las Vegas seems light-years away from Telescope Peak, yet it is what I think of as I huddle in my bivy sack and consider what I have seen at Devils Hole and Ash Meadows, by the banks of Salt Creek, along the narrow canyons of the Inyo Mountains, and in the broad basin of Deep Springs Valley. And oddly, what comes to mind is a marketing slogan embraced by the Las Vegas Convention and Visitors Authority: "What happens here, stays here." Like many marketing slogans, this one is patently false—say for the amorous conventioneer who visits the wrong prostitute, contracts gonorrhea, and infects his wife back home; the gambling addict who leaves Las Vegas with an extra ten thousand dollars of debt; or the "hospitality worker" who moved to Las Vegas in the early 2000s, purchased a home at the height of the housing bubble, lost his job, couldn't make the mortgage, watched his life slide into foreclosure, and left "Vegas" in search of economic salvation in some other Sun Belt city. And just as the conventioneer, gambling addict, and unemployed worker might export the consequences of "what happens here," Las Vegas's need for more water does not stay in Las Vegas. The binding curves of population growth, development, and drought mandate that Las Vegas must seek new sources of water beyond the declining supplies of local groundwater and Colorado River water. Las Vegas insists upon a particular presence, one predicated upon limitless growth and limitless water, and I fear that this inertial demand inevitably will harm the country and species that I love. And so the implications of the city's growing thirst are what I think of as morning spreads across the fields of layered cloud below me and opens up the long play of desert ranges, the Panamint, Funeral, Grapevine, Black, Owlshead, Argus, Inyo, and White mountains—all running toward the great horizon and vanishing into a guess of gray, their long and fractured ridges tracking the realm of possible futures.

––––––––––––––

Until the 1970s the Las Vegas Valley relied primarily on local groundwater. Although the metropolitan area still obtains about 10 percent of its water from local groundwater, the water table has sunk by over 300 feet since the early 1900s, due to withdrawals that consistently exceeded recharge. One consequence of groundwater mining has been land subsidence, which has exceeded six feet in some parts of Las Vegas Valley. Because local groundwater supplies no longer supported Las Vegas's growing population, in 1971 the Southern Nevada Water Project began importing water from Lake Mead on the Colorado River, which is now the city's primary water source. Nevada is entitled to 300,000 acre-feet of water per year from the Colorado River, but the Southern Nevada Water Authority (SNWA), which was created in 1991 to manage the region's water resources, understands that this will not be sufficient to meet the demand created by Las Vegas's exploding population, which climbed from about 273,000 in 1970 to slightly over 2 million in 2010. Although Las Vegas experienced negative growth during the recent economic recession, between 2000 and 2010 it grew by 41.8 percent, making it the third-fastest-growing metropolitan area in the country. Although population models embrace some degree of uncertainty, one recent projection anticipates that Las Vegas will quickly return to the growth rates of the early 2000s, and by 2041 will have a population in excess of 3 million. In 2009, the SNWA estimated that the Las Vegas Valley would require at least 186,000 acre-feet of additional water per year to meet increased demand, which could run to 350,000 acre-feet or more per year by 2060. In an over-allocated and arid world, this is a lot of water.

Las Vegas has exhausted its local groundwater supply, and the water it gets from somewhere else—mostly the Colorado River—will not be enough if its population continues to grow and climate change lowers precipitation in the upper Colorado River basin. In November of 2010, following a series of drought years, Lake Mead was at 39 percent of its storage capacity and its elevation had fallen to 1,082 feet, its lowest level since it was filled in the 1930s. Although Lake Mead's elevation increased to 1,114 feet by November of 2012, climate models predict future decreases in Colorado River flow of anywhere from 5 to 45 percent. It is a scenario perfectly illustrated by the ring staining the cliffs just upriver from Hoover Dam: a whitewashed vector of bleached stone that suggests one possible, drought-ridden future for Las Vegas. The declines in Lake Mead's storage began around 1999; if the trend continues and the lake's elevation falls below 1,050 feet, its two water intakes may become inoperative. So the SNWA is constructing a third water intake two and one-half miles off the current lake shore, "In order to address unprecedented drought conditions and provide long-term protection of Southern Nevada's primary water storage reservoir." But the recent drought is anything but "unprecedented." Major southwestern droughts occurred in the 1930s and 1950s, and more severe ones hammered the Colorado River Basin in the twelfth, sixteenth, and seventeenth centuries. One recent paper on stream-flow reconstructions for the Upper Colorado River Basin described "frequent past occurrences of flow lower than in 1999–2004." And so the SNWA's statement on drought conditions should have begun: "In order to address drought conditions typical of the Southwest."

Whatever its historical perspective, the SNWA understands that it needs to prepare for future droughts, which could be worse than those of the twentieth and early twenty-first century, even if language in its *Water Resource Plan 09* minimizes the possibility: "In the unlikely event that Lake Mead water levels reach a depth below 1,000 feet." The construction of a third water intake in Lake Mead is one aspect of the SNWA's plan for adapting to a drier, more populous future; decreasing per capita water use in the Las Vegas Valley is another. Since its formation in 1991, the SNWA also has aggressively pursued a series of conservation measures that have decreased the region's daily per capita water use from 350 gallons in 1990 to 222 gallons in 2011, with a target of 199 gallons by 2035: admirable, but still nothing like the daily per capita water use of 131 gallons in Tucson, Arizona.

The precious waters of the Colorado River are divided among seven states in the basin, including Nevada, by the 1922 Colorado River Compact. Each state uses its full allocation—or more accurately, over-allocation, because the compact was negotiated during a period coinciding with the Colorado's highest sustained flows between the year 1520 and the present. Given that the Colorado River is over-allocated and will likely experience a future decrease in flow, that Las Vegas will continue to grow, and that conservation measures will be insufficient to meet the deficit created by increased demand and decreased supply from current sources, the SNWA must look elsewhere for water. And although there has been fantastical talk of importing Mississippi River water, the more immediate option is to tap into groundwater in other parts of Nevada. The SNWA has pending or active applications in twenty-one basins in four counties, including Nye County. The largest of these include 137,000 acre-feet of groundwater rights in Spring, Delamar, Dry Lake, Cave, and Snake valleys, between seventy and two hundred miles northeast of Las Vegas. These rights consist primarily of "unappropriated" groundwater, plus some surface and groundwater rights purchased with ranch properties. Groundwater from the basins will be exported via a pipeline scheduled to come online in 2020, although the status of the entire project is threatened by the refusal of Utah's governor, Gary Herbert, to sign off on a deal to allocate groundwater from the Snake Valley, which straddles the high desert borderlands of the two states.

Of more immediate concern, at least from the standpoint of those rare, endemic, and threatened species of Ash Meadows and Death Valley that depend on aquatic habitats, are SNWA's plans to pump "unappropriated" (unappropriated by whom? humans? pupfish? springsnails?) groundwater in Tikaboo, Three Lakes, and Indian Springs valleys, which lie anywhere from twenty to eighty miles northwest of Las Vegas Valley. The SNWA has been granted 10,600 acre-feet per year of groundwater in Tikaboo and Three Lakes Valleys and has applied for another 16,000 acre-feet per year of groundwater in Indian Springs Valley. These hydrographic basins are part of the Death Valley regional groundwater flow system and lie upstream from Ash Meadows and Death Valley.

No one knows exactly how SNWA's planned groundwater withdrawals will affect the flow of springs required by the endemic and threatened species of Ash Meadows and Death Valley, but logic and the science of hydrology imply that there could be potentially severe impacts. Because planned withdrawals exceed recharge rates by at least 127 percent, groundwater levels in shallow-fill and deep carbonate aquifers undoubtedly would decrease, an effect that would be most pronounced near sources of pumping. But the declines eventually would spread throughout the region via the interconnected hydrological network, or as Wayne Belcher of the USGS says, "that whole interbasin flow thing." Some models developed by the USGS forecast groundwater declines of more than 700 feet near wells planned for Spring, Delamar, Dry Lake, Cave, and Snake valleys, with declines of ten feet or more just upstream from Ash Meadows. Groundwater pumping in Tikaboo, Three Lakes, and Indian Springs valleys, within the Death Valley regional flow system, potentially would have the most immediate and substantial impact on Ash Meadows—although Wayne Belcher feels that "these effects probably would not be felt for decades or more than a hundred years within the Death Valley regional flow system, and hundreds to perhaps thousands of years for pumping up north."

A week before climbing Telescope Peak, I visited with Zane Marshall, director of Environmental Resources for the Southern Nevada Water Authority. I'd first run into Zane at Devils Hole, where he was volunteering as a diver on the Park Service's semiannual pupfish count. He was busy with other things and we had not talked much, but as I watched him work and listened to his conversations with Park Service personnel and his fellow divers, I noticed his measured presence and careful approach to the counts. Zane obviously was concerned about the pupfish, and I figured that he would be a good person to talk with about the SNWA's plans for groundwater development in Nevada and their potential impacts on endangered species. We met in his tenth-floor corner office in the SNWA's high-rise headquarters, overlooking downtown Las Vegas. Zane was dressed casually, in slacks and a button-down Oxford shirt. He looked to be in his mid-thirties: fit, an ex-Marine with brush-cut hair, a wife, two young children, and a master's degree in biology from the University of Nevada, Las Vegas. He'd grown up in Las Vegas and got into the environmental field because as a kid he had loved "running around in the desert, chasing lizards." Along the way he had worked with Jim Deacon, the retired UNLV scientist who had done so much work on pupfish biology and labored tirelessly to protect Devils Hole and Ash Meadows. Deacon also was the lead author on a 2007 paper in the journal *BioScience* that criticized both the SNWA's plans to develop Nevada's groundwater resources and the logic of a worldview predicated upon the assumption that Las Vegas could expand its water-based carrying capacity and so continue to grow.

Like Dave Martin, the Los Angeles Water and Power ecologist whom I had interviewed about Owens pupfish, Zane saw no conflict between his training as a scientist and his work for the SNWA, which he felt "has a strong environmental ethic. The SNWA is in the business of sustainable resource development and is cognizant of the Endangered Species Act as a strategic component." He saw one of his most important roles as "getting the organization to understand the value of species, and how its water development plans can bring collateral benefits for them." When I asked Zane about the SNWA's plans for developing Nevada's groundwater, he replied that the organization is heavily committed to using "the best available science" for the project and adopting "a positive, proactive approach to endangered species protection." He felt that Jim Deacon's 2007 article was "interesting," but that it was a work of "advocacy based on outdated groundwater models."

I asked Zane if he thought that SNWA's groundwater withdrawals would negatively affect aquatic ecosystems and species. He thought for a few moments and replied, "We don't know exactly how the aquifer will respond to groundwater pumping. There could be impacts, but we have planned for an extensive monitoring and mitigation program to detect and then address any environmental consequences." He described the 2009 biological monitoring plan for the Spring Valley groundwater development, which could be the first part of the project to come on-line and would involve up to 60,000 acre-feet of pumping per year. The monitoring plan is a negotiated agreement between the SNWA and four federal resource management agencies: the Bureau of Indian Affairs, Fish and Wildlife Service, Bureau of Land Management, and National Park Service. Later, when I dug up the document, I read that its purpose was to establish a monitoring program that will "further the understanding of groundwater-influenced ecosystem dynamics and track biotic community responses to SNWA's groundwater withdrawal from the Spring Valley." The goals of the monitoring program were to "manage the development of groundwater by SNWA in the Spring Valley [hydrographic basin] in order to avoid unreasonable adverse effects to groundwater-influenced ecosystems [in] . . . those valleys adjacent to and down-gradient of Spring Valley . . . and avoid any impacts to groundwater-influenced ecosystems within the boundaries of Great Basin National Park." The language was superficially comforting: the federal government and SNWA agree to cooperate on tracking and mitigating effects of groundwater pumping. But what struck me most strongly, and left me with a disquiet that I still carry, is a phrase that Zane quoted to me from the document: that one of the goals of the monitoring plan is to "avoid unreasonable adverse effects."

What is unsettling about the term, as potentially commendable as it might be, is that it is not defined in any useful way. All the Spring Valley monitoring plan says about adverse effects is that one occurs "if an indicator or suite of indicators falls outside the acceptable range of variation," and that the "acceptable range of variation" for each environmental indicator will be determined by the biological working group, which includes one representative of the SNWA and each participating federal agency. The monitoring plan states that "at the present time, data are insufficient to determine indicator threshold levels," but what it does not explain is that defining the "acceptable range of variation" for any environmental indicator, say for the population of an endangered fish species, or water levels in monitoring wells, will depend upon an agency's values. Although the SNWA considers sustainable resource use in its planning, its primary institutional mission and values involve delivering adequate water to Las Vegas; these are very different from the mission and values of the National Park Service, which administers Great Basin National Park at the eastern edge of Spring Valley. The National Park Service Organic Act of 1916 established the fundamental role of the agency, which is "to conserve the scenery and the natural and historic objects and the wildlife therein and to provide for the enjoyment of the same in such manner and by such means as will leave them unimpaired for the enjoyment of future generations," a goal that could be compromised by groundwater pumping in Spring Valley. And the SNWA's mission also might conflict with those of the U.S. Fish and Wildlife Service, the agency charged with protecting the endangered Pahrump poolfish, which was transplanted to a Bureau of Land Management fish refuge in Spring Valley, or the twelve listed species at Ash Meadows National Wildlife Refuge.

No wonder that the biological monitoring plan for Spring Valley, which was negotiated under the auspices of the Bush administration, contained no clearly defined "unreasonable adverse effects" or "acceptable range[s] of variation." Voluntary agreement among the parties may well have been impossible, although the SNWA did enter into a 2006 memorandum of agreement with the U.S. Fish and Wildlife Service and several other entities concerning groundwater development in Coyote Spring Valley, in northeastern Clark County. The SNWA wanted to export 9,000 acre-feet of groundwater per year from the valley, which could affect flow in the Muddy River and spring systems in the Moapa Valley National Wildlife Refuge, home to the Moapa dace, a small endemic minnow. The SNWA's interest in Coyote Spring Valley's groundwater pales in comparison to that of Coyote Springs Investment, which hopes to build a 43,000-acre, 110,000-unit desert development in the upper Muddy River Valley—one that the corporation's website claims will be "defined by a continuous valley of green"—(Preferred Equities and Calvada Lakes, anyone?). However, SNWA's annual groundwater withdrawal of 9,000 acre-feet still represents a potential threat to the federally listed Moapa dace. Consequently, the Memorandum of Agreement Biological Opinion written by the U.S. Fish and Wildlife Service contained precise language describing "adverse effects" of the proposed pumping and explicit conservation measures to minimize impacts on the Moapa dace.

One argument against explicitly defining "unreasonable adverse effects" or "acceptable range[s] of variation" is that we do not yet have enough groundwater-pumping data or sufficient understanding of the aquatic ecosystems in places such as Spring Valley. Given our lack of knowledge, it would be foolish to arbitrarily decide on specific "unreasonable adverse effects" a decade or more in advance of the project. It would be better to wait, rely on an extensive monitoring system to determine the effects of pumping, and then use an adaptive management approach to adjust groundwater withdrawals. Perhaps. But there are two potential problems with this approach. One is what hydrologists John Bredehoeft and Timothy Durbin—the latter has consulted for the SNWA—have termed "the monitoring problem." This problem suggests that "there will be (1) a time lag between maximum impact and the stopping of pumping and (2) the maximum impact will be greater than what is observed when pumping is stopped." In other words, it might take a very long time for the system to recover after groundwater monitoring reveals the severity of the impact, even if pumping is dramatically reduced. The second problem is one of inertia. Once $3.2 billion dollars has been invested in a project (the estimated cost in 2009 of the SNWA's northern Nevada groundwater development project) and so many people (planners, developers, politicians, the citizens of Las Vegas) have become psychologically if not physically dependent on the anticipated water, in practice it would be very difficult to sit down at a negotiating table and define "reasonable" or "unreasonable" adverse effects. The decisions would no longer be about science; they would be controversial political and economic ones. Better, then, to struggle with the issues beforehand, as was done with Coyote Spring Valley groundwater and the Moapa dace.

The U.S. Fish and Wildlife Service and Park Service argued with the SNWA for years about the specifics of "unreasonable adverse effects" relative to the Spring Valley biological monitoring plan. The term needs to be explicitly defined, but one federal official familiar with the negotiations told me that the Fish and Wildlife Service and Park Service were "forced to accept it [the vague language about 'unreasonable adverse effects'] from the top." I know nothing about the dynamics of the negotiations surrounding the Spring Valley biological monitoring plan. Nor do I understand anything about the specific motivations and identities of "the top," whoever they might be. However, the language of the agreement, and the political influence apparently involved in the process, suggest that the mission of the SNWA, which is "to manage the region's water resources and develop solutions that will ensure adequate future water supplies for the Las Vegas Valley," might ultimately trump concerns about endangered species, whether in Spring Valley or Ash Meadows.

Realistically, the economic imperative of Las Vegas has the allegiance of too many powerful constituencies, and too few people want to confront the possibility of limiting growth in the Las Vegas Valley, no matter how much it exceeds its aquatic carrying capacity, or how its need for water ultimately affects the environment. In the same way, other cities in the arid West, say Phoenix or Los Angeles, have not truly dealt with their issues of growth and aquatic carrying capacity. For Las Vegas there always will be more water, somewhere: first the groundwater of rural Nevada, then (perhaps) the Columbia and Mississippi rivers. SNWA general manager Patricia Mullroy understands this logic and the limits to what can be done regionally, particularly in the face of climate change: "We can't conserve our way out of a massive Colorado River drought. We can't desalt our way out of a massive Colorado River drought. If the West is growing drier and the Midwest is growing wetter, I see that as an opportunity." In other words, there always will be water available for the right price, and the market can sidestep any notion of the common good.

Perhaps, though, there are solutions to Las Vegas's water problems that will not entail excessive environmental costs and harming the rare and endangered species of the region. Perhaps the effects of climate change will be less severe than predicted by most climate models and the flow of the Colorado River will increase. Perhaps the SNWA will manage its water resources even more efficiently and further reduce Las Vegas's water needs. And perhaps Nevada's water laws, which are among the strictest in the West, will prevent overpumping of groundwater in the northern part of the state. Jim Deacon's controversial 2007 *BioScience* article, "Fueling Population Growth in Las Vegas: How Large-Scale Groundwater Withdrawal Could Burn Regional Biodiversity," is an often-pessimistic look at how the city's future water needs could impact the environment, but it does offer hope that strict conservation and new technologies, combined with supplies of unexploited sources of water from reuse or recycling, could alleviate future shortages. The article also mentions that the Supreme Court's 1976 *Cappaert* decision and the Endangered Species Act protect species and ecosystems threatened by groundwater withdrawals; the Coyote Springs Memorandum of Agreement and the Biological Monitoring Plan for the Spring Valley Stipulation are not substitutes for, but the result of, legal protections guaranteed by *Cappaert* and the Endangered Species Act. And in the past endangered species have affected western water-development projects, as did the delta smelt in California and Columbia River salmon in the Pacific Northwest. But as one 1960s-era comic strip explained, an ultimate truth is a "5–4 decision in the Supreme Court," and the current 5–4 majority in the Supreme Court has a political agenda that easily could translate into a partial or complete reversal of *Cappaert* and changes in how the Endangered Species Act is interpreted. Or perhaps someday Congress will weaken the Endangered Species Act—in spite of the political support it enjoys—enough to allow unlimited groundwater mining, no matter what the environmental costs. The political constituencies of Ash Meadows Amargosa pupfish, Moapa dace, Pahrump poolfish, and Warm Springs naucorid are orders of magnitude less powerful than those of the Las Vegas gaming industry and developers, senators such as Harry Reid (who once had close financial ties with the Coyote Springs developer), and the inordinate influence wielded by Nevada's six Electoral College votes, given its status as a swing state.

No matter how genuine the environmental concerns of SNWA—and I do not doubt Zane Marshall's sincerity, or his view of SNWA's environmental ethic—the agency's bottom line is to deliver water to Las Vegas, whatever the cost in dollars and species. It's not that I think that the SNWA or its employees lack integrity, or that they are unconcerned about the environmental impacts of water development. It's simply that SNWA's ultimate responsibility is to provide water to Las Vegas. My pessimistic view is that the Endangered Species Act and the *Cappaert* decision will most likely stand, fully and completely, only if they do not derail the continued economic expansion of places such as Las Vegas. If this is so, perhaps the best chance for protecting the aquatic species and ecosystems of the region might involve a prolonged long-term economic downturn for Las Vegas, which is not something that I would ever hope for. In 2011, when Las Vegas's unemployment rate had reached 14 percent and its home foreclosure rate was five times the national average, Jim Deacon told me, "Las Vegas might not make it past this crash." Although the darkest days appear to have passed—in early 2013, unemployment rates in Las Vegas finally fell below 10 percent, and home-foreclosure rates were better than they once were—the spread of legalized gambling, climate change, and continued consumer uncertainty could compromise Las Vegas's future. But it is more likely that Las Vegas will continue to grow, and that the valley will greet its 3 millionth resident before 2050. If so, pressures on the region's water supplies and endangered species will become more severe.

Zane and I talked for a while about the likely water needs of Las Vegas and then transitioned to the subject of endangered species. He had volunteered for twelve years as a diver at Devils Hole, working on the semiannual pupfish counts, and was concerned about their fate. I asked him what the world would be like without Devils Hole pupfish: could he imagine such a place? He responded with an invocation for the future: "I have two little boys, and I would like them to see all that I have seen of the natural world, including pupfish. The world would be poorer without them." And when I followed up on his comment about children with my standard question about the worth of rare species, Zane responded much as other biologists I know would: "I believe that species like the Devils Hole pupfish have intrinsic value—they have a right to exist, and that we should protect them. I think, too, that we can learn a lot of lessons by studying how they respond to history." I didn't pursue what Zane meant by "respond to history," but for me the phrase encompassed both the last five decades of the species' population declines and our increasing involvement in its management, and the last 5 million years or more of its evolutionary past. The Parable of the Pupfish is profound but daunting in its complexity, an amalgam of genetic legacy, cycles of the earth and its climate, persistence and vulnerability, the precious presence of water in an arid world, the complexities of management, and the best and worst of human intent.

Toward the end of our interview I rose from my chair and walked over to Zane's office window, where I could look out over Las Vegas. Directly below the SNWA building was a tangled intersection of freeways—Interstate 15 tracking north toward Salt Lake City and south to Los Angeles; Interstate 515 and U.S. Highway 93, arcing southeast to Henderson and on to Boulder City and Hoover Dam; the western thrust of U.S. Highway 95, slicing through the suburbs before it bends north, toward the hinterlands of Ash Meadows and Death Valley. And beyond the freeways were the marches of North Las Vegas and the western suburbs, the sprawl of tract homes and strip malls and casinos and condominiums and industrial parks and just everything, filling the broad basin that holds Las Vegas. All of the buildings and roads were like some kind of stationary maelstrom spreading to the foot of the Sheep and Spring ranges, mountains rising seven thousand feet or more above the great nexus of people and concrete, tawny brown alluvial fans falling toward the developments, their steep slopes physical boundaries to a world seemingly without ecological or emotional constraints. It was late afternoon and the freeways were running thick with traffic, rivers of cars and trucks and buses rushing through the former desert, the exit ramps like eddies in the main hydrocarbon current, everyone and everything flowing into an uncertain future, a future that I would confront a week later on Telescope Peak, as the morning came on and its light spread over the arid lands. . . . And as I turned to take my leave I thought of water, and the lack of water, and the lost and lonely species, and how we shake the world with our careless needs, and our understandable but insistent desires.

I have come to Telescope Peak because I desire a physical and metaphorical vantage point from which I can look out upon the future. In my anticipation of this morning, I imagined an immaculate dawn and the type of limitless expanse so characteristic of this country. But the view given to me on this cold and windswept morning, as wraiths of mist swirl around me, is partly opaque. Eleven thousand feet below me, clouds fill Death Valley like some ephemeral shadow of ancient Lake Manly. Badwater and Salt Creek lie submerged beneath cloud Lake Manly's gray and drifting mists, which wash over the Black Range and Funeral Mountains. But as I look out past the 3,000-year-old bristlecone pines, those avatars of time, I understand that I could not have chosen a better morning for my walk, because the clouds work as perfect metaphor, and obscure my imagined futures. I have my suspicions about what this small corner of the Basin and Range might look like in forty years. I have my worries, my doubts about the fates of humans and pupfishes alike, but I do not know. It's not that all future scenarios are equally likely, or that probability, the statistics on population growth and water use, and well-crafted climate change models don't all point in the same direction. Rather, it's simply that the world is an immensely uncertain place. The vagaries of humans and nature are profound, and our ignorance runs deep. As an ecologist, as someone who loves information and believes, passionately, that science can help us anticipate and adapt to our possible futures, I still must accept what Charles Bock described as "the fragility of our capacity to know." The best that we can ever do, I think, is to embrace probability and uncertainty, and act with whatever wisdom and courage and humanity we can gather.

The future may be uncertain, but up on Telescope Peak I do know this: that the lives of Inyo Mountain slender salamanders, Owens pupfish, Salt Creek pupfish, Devils Hole pupfish, Amargosa pupfish, and black toads are worth every dollar and all of the compassion and energy we can muster in their defense. Their existence is worth insisting upon, even if it means that Las Vegas, Pahrump, and Amargosa Valley will be forced to acknowledge what the concept of human carrying capacity really means. I know this because I have watched these creatures move through their worlds. I have wandered through the parched and empty lands of the Basin and Range country, and seen how the pupfish and toads and salamanders survive on and in their islands of water. I have read the scientific papers and understand something of these creatures' genetics and physiology, their remarkable adaptations to a less than hospitable world, the ways in which they have traveled through time, the ways in which they are like us, and the ways in which they are wonderfully different. I know that there are good, pragmatic arguments for preserving these species, and all of the other rare species that inhabit this world—reasons that are in the best selfish, material interests of humans. These species may carry undiscovered genes and proteins that will help cure disease. In some cases they may provide services that help preserve and protect ecosystems that are important to humans. They certainly act as environmental sentinels, warning us of danger and foolishness, and suggesting how we might manage our world and water and future more wisely. And they also provide a window to the natural world, an understanding of how evolutionary, ecological, anatomical, and physiological systems work.

But it is not just a matter of cost-benefit analyses, of dollars and cents and balance sheets, bits of data and testable hypotheses. Beyond our pragmatic concerns there is what Joseph Wood Krutch realized as he listened to a chorus of peepers, that vernal avalanche of frog-song that rises into celebration during each northeastern spring: "we are all in this together." Yes. We are all is this together, "this" being public and personal history, the shit and sorrow of life, the painful trajectories of individuals and nations alike, but also the overwhelming joy and grace of this world. We desperately need all of the hope, all of the determined persistence and beauty that a Devils Hole pupfish or Inyo Mountains slender salamander can offer up, the ways in which they can help us endure. We need their beauty and otherness, their delicate and fragile strength. We need their allegiance to the physical conditions of this world, and to time, to the millions and millions of years that mark the vectors of their existence. We need the refuge species, the discards that ask for nothing more than the home that each and every one of us desires.

And just as protecting the existence of rare species is worth our money, time, and energy, the disappearance of the Tecopa pupfish, Ash Meadows poolfish, Ash Meadows montane vole, Vegas Valley leopard frog, and all of the other species that have been sacrificed to human greed, stupidity, ignorance, and desire demand all of our sorrow and contrition. "Natural" extinction is as much a part of the history of life as is the birth of new species, but there is a fundamental, aching difference between an extinction for which humans are responsible, and one due to forces beyond our control—a difference as morally distinct as the difference between a human death due to an accident, and one caused by individual culpability. The data on population growth, habitat loss, invasions by exotic species, and water consumption—what Gary Snyder calls "the steep climb / of everything, going up, / up"—tell a clear story about human-caused extinctions and the possible fate that awaits many of the earth's species, a fate depicted in numerous scientific papers, and poignantly described by the title of one recent article: "Can We Name Earth's Species Before They Go Extinct?" Yes: there are the papers and the numbers, but more fundamentally there are the ravaged alkali meadows, stripped of their vole nests; the bathhouse that marks the grave of a tiny fish; the desiccated springs, and the silence of their frogs. There are all of these things, in a world made poorer by loss and emptiness.

Up on Telescope Peak the day breaks against me, as it also breaks against the homes of the fugitive species: Kings Pool and Jackrabbit Spring, Devils Hole, Salt Creek and Cottonball Marsh, the canyons of the Inyo Mountains, BLM Spring, Deep Springs Valley. Light flows over this land, flows over all its magnificent and stunning life. And as it does I realize that I started out wanting to write a book about evolution and conservation, but that as I worked my way through this country, I found myself thinking more and more about beauty: its endless forms, its utility and necessity, the glittering fractals of its arid planes and desert species. I found myself thinking of these things, and of a line by George Eliot: "It would be like hearing the grass grow and the squirrel's heart beat, and we should die of that roar."

The morning comes on and as it does, I hear the roaring of the pupfish, the whisperings of slender salamanders, the heartbeats of black toads. The winds are up, pummeling my perch, spilling over the Panamints, tearing the heat from my body. I begin to shiver and know that it is time to leave. Downslope a flock of Clark's nutcrackers call. A band of finches crest the ridge and is gone, into the wild.

I rise, pack my gear, and head down Telescope Peak—warming quickly, the walking easy on this luminous morning: all things shining.

Epilogue

HOLD STEADY

Hold steady against the last 10 million years, the folding and faulting of desert ranges, the subsidence of valleys, the ebb and flow of ice and rain, the lava and ash, the Pliocene and Pleistocene. Forget the vanished mastodons and mammoths, cave bears and dire wolves, camels and giant ground sloths. Persevere against the great drought of the Holocene, the failing springs and rivers, the drying and dying plants. Hold steady against the hunters and gatherers, and later, the plows and pumps, the bulldozers and drainage ditches, the subdivisions and freeways. Endure, too, the crayfish and bass, the sunfish and bullfrog, the cow and burro, the cattail, salt cedar, and common reed. Hold steady against the collectors and farmers, the developers, those who would dismiss you, and those who will never care. Persist against flash floods and the shuddering earth, the chytrid fungus and parasitic worms and viral plagues. Hold steady in spite of your isolation, the loneliness of your lost lineages. Protect the last few of your kind, those who hide in rough canyons and tiny springs. And in the coming years, hold steady against our great and growing thirst. But mostly, hold steady against our ignorance, what we have not learned, and what we refuse to know. Hold steady against all of it, this great and terrible onslaught, now and forever more.

Amen.

Afterword

A plea: take care of these animals and their places. Obey the rules that protect them. Many activities that I describe in this book were done only with the permission of managing agencies such as the U.S. Fish and Wildlife Service and National Park Service, or in the presence of the biologists and managers charged with protecting these creatures and their habitats. If you do visit any of the places mentioned here, do so with respect and care. Seek permission when necessary, as with the springs where the black toad lives, which are owned by Deep Springs College. And if I do not mention specific localities, as with the Inyo Mountains slender salamander, don't ask for directions because I won't tell you: their habitats and populations are too fragile, and I suspect that unauthorized collecting may have severely damaged or extirpated several accessible populations. Practice the conservationist's analog of safe sex and do not spread STPs (stupidly transmitted pathogens). Clean your footwear thoroughly before traveling from one site to another, particularly in wetlands. Failing to do so could mean that you are the vector that moves an exotic snail—or worse yet, the spores of chytrid fungus, destroyer of frogs and toads—to a previously pristine spring. To help prevent the spread of chytrid fungus and other pathogens treat your footwear and any appropriate equipment beforehand with a dilute bleach solution. And (of course) join and donate to organizations fighting to preserve and protect endangered species and their habitats. These organizations almost always operate on very tight budgets and are constantly strapped for funds. They never have sufficient resources to do the work that they must do. My own small gesture of support for this cause has been to request that the University of North Carolina Press send half of any royalties from this book to the Friends of Ash Meadows National Wildlife Refuge, a nonprofit organization that supports the mission of this wonderful but woefully underfunded refuge. And I will do the same for any speaker's fees that may result from this book.

Since I finished the manuscript for this book, drought has deepened over California and the Intermountain West. In May 2014 the Sierra Nevada snowpack stood at 18 percent of normal, while Lake Mead's elevation fell to its lowest level since 1937. House Resolution 3964, which mandates that the California State Water Project and Central Valley Project be managed "without regard to the Endangered Species Act of 1973," passed the House of Representatives but stalled in the Senate. One sponsor of H.R. 3964, Devin Nunes, called the federally threatened delta smelt, which is endemic to the Sacramento–San Joaquin Delta, a "stupid little fish." The website of the House Natural Resources Committee described the water situation in California as a "man-made drought" even though 2013 precipitation in the state was the lowest in recorded history. The Southern Nevada Water Authority's plans to pipe groundwater from northern Nevada stalled in the courts, while an "emergency tunnel" at Lake Mead will link the uncompleted water intake with the oldest operative intake pipe.

The spring 2014 Devils Hole pupfish count was ninety-two, an encouraging increase from thirty-five in 2013. At the Ash Meadows Fish Conservation Facility, biologists raised twenty adults from sixty eggs collected after the dismal spring 2013 count, but the adults have not produced viable embryos. The Fish and Wildlife Service purchased a 400-acre parcel at Ash Meadows, reducing inholdings on the refuge to 261 acres, while restoration work continued in the Warm Springs complex. The owners of one inholding sued the U.S. government and refuge manager for diverting federally owned water, citing the "takings" clause of the Constitution, but the suit was dismissed. Both the refuge biologist and the refuge manager at Ash Meadows retired in 2014, but as of May 2014 the U.S. Fish and Wildlife Service had not committed to replacing the biologist—at a refuge with the highest density of endemic organisms in the United States and Canada.

I last visited the region in March of 2014 and saw thriving populations of Salt Creek, Ash Meadows Amargosa, and Warm Springs Amargosa pupfishes. Steve Parmenter tells me that the Owens pupfish is doing well at Mule Spring and BLM Spring but that they have not been reintroduced into Warm Springs. I heard black toads clucking away in Deep Springs Valley and found an abundance of Inyo Mountains slender salamanders at a newly discovered locality. In late March, biologists swabbed sixty-six black toads for chytrid fungus, but results of the tests are not yet known.

For now, the animals endure—in spite of drought, disease, and our shortsightedness.

Notes

INTRODUCTION

"God is in the details": attributed to Mies van der Rohe. http://architecture.about
.com/od/20thcenturytrends/a/Mies-Van-Der-Rohe-Quotes.htm (July 2, 2012)
"It is storming in the White Mountains": Rexroth, "Toward an Organic Philosophy,"
103.
"To consider what is appropriate": Illich, "The Wisdom of Leopold Kohr," n.p.
"No ideas but in things": W. C. Williams, "A Sort of a Song."
"Thus," says Tyndall: Rexroth, "Toward an Organic Philosophy," 104.

COLLECTING THE DEAD

Do you ever find yourself: Abraham Lincoln as quoted in Burlingame, *Lincoln*, 300.
This tiny gill-breathing snail: Sada, *Recovery Plan*.
part of the area's rich fauna: Hershler and Sada, "Springsnails of Ash Meadows."
Pyrgulopsis **is an old genus**: Hershler and Liu, "Ancient Vicariance."
when groundwater pumping dried Longstreet Spring: Sada and Vinyard,
"Anthropogenic Changes."
The Tecopa pupfish . . . occurred: Miller, *Cyprinodont Fishes*.
"white, barren alkali flat": ibid., 37.
The Tecopa pupfish was last seen: Miller et al., "Extinctions of Fishes."
Adult Tecopa pupfish: Miller, *Cyprinodont Fishes*.
104°F was "the second highest recorded temperature": ibid., 39.
Miller did not describe this species until 1984: Miller, "*Rhinichthys deaconi*."
The last known collection: Miller et al., "Extinctions of Fishes."
"two narrow streams of clear water": Frémont, *Report of the Exploring Expedition*,
266.
The Las Vegas dace probably persisted: Miller, "*Rhinichthys deaconi*."
Miller differentiated Las Vegas dace from: ibid.
"a delightful bathing place": Frémont, *Report of the Exploring Expedition*, 266.
The last Ash Meadows poolfish: Miller et al., "Extinctions of Fishes."
"Over the 6-year . . . greater numbers": Miller, *Cyprinodont Fishes*, 101.
Habitat alteration may have played: Miller et al., "Extinctions of Fishes."
Ash Meadows poolfish were small: Miller, *Cyprinodont Fishes*.

Empetrichthys **once ranged more widely**: Uyeno and Miller, "Relationships of *Empetrichthys erdisi*"; Smith et al., "Biogeography and Timing."

Empetrichthys latos pahrump **and** *Empetrichthys latos concavus*: Miller et al., "Extinctions of Fishes," 32–33.

groundwater withdrawals exceeded recharge: Comartin, "Development of a Flow Model," 1–2.

in the late 1960s biologists recognized: Deacon and Williams, "Retrospective Evaluation."

The extinct Pahrump poolfish subspecies: Miller, *Cyprinodont Fishes*.

The largest patch of habitat: Miller, *Cyprinodont Fishes*.

This species occurred: Gong, "*Rana fisheri.*"

"Our *R. fisheri* may go with the old springs gone": Wright and Wright, "Nevada Frog," 457.

These short-legged frogs: Gong, "*Rana fisheri.*"

northwestern populations of the Chiricahua leopard frog: Hekkala et al., "Resurrecting an Extinct Species."

a combination of groundwater pumping: Gong, "*Rana fisheri.*"

"a few semicroaks, which reminded me": Wright and Wright, "Nevada Frog," 456.

wet alkaline meadows: Bailey, "Revision of *Microtus.*"

"the big salt marsh below Watkins Ranch": ibid., 423.

"blackish, but with a few overhairs tipped with reddish": Hall, "Nevadan Races," 423.

Last located by W. C. Russell: ibid.; Sada, *Recovery Plan.*"

A CULTIVATION OF SLOWNESS
The Inyo Mountains Slender Salamander

almost no barrier: Spight, "Water Economy."

was not discovered until 1973: Marlow et al., "A New Salamander."

Its distribution, as far as is known: Yanev and Wake, "Genic Differentiation."

the family arose in eastern North America: Zheng and Wake, "Higher-Level Salamander Relationships."

some 80 million years ago: ibid., 502.

Within the genus *Batrachoseps*: material on *Batrachoseps* evolution is from Jockusch and Wake, "Falling Apart and Merging"; Elizabeth Jockusch, personal communication, April 10, 2012.

two finer divisions: Wake et al., "New Species of Salamander."

Species in the larger lineage: Jockusch and Wake, "Falling Apart and Merging."

a web-toed salamander in the genus *Hydromantes*: Ron Marlow, interview, December 5, 2010.

Mutational differences in the mitochondrial DNA: material from Jockusch and Wake, "Falling Apart and Merging"; Elizabeth Jockusch, interview, December 10, 2010; Elizabeth Jockusch, personal communication, April 10, 2012.

"has inherited California's complex geologic history": Elizabeth Jockusch, interview, December 10, 2010.

Large-scale uplift of the modern Sierra Nevada: Stock et al., "Pace of Landscape Evolution"; Wakabayashi and Sawyer, "Stream Incision." There is some debate about the timing and rate of Sierra Nevada uplift; for dissenting views, see Wernicke et al., "Origin of the High Mountains"; Mulch et al., "Hydrogen Isotopes."

Fossil trackways and skeletal material: Clark, "Fossil Plethodontid."

It wasn't until 3 to 4 million years ago: Phillips, "Geological and Hydrological History," 139; Bachman, "Pliocene-Pleistocene Break-up."

a complex series of glacial advances and retreats: Hill, "Geologic Story"; Elliot-Fisk, "Glacial Geomorphology."

ancient packrat middens, composed mostly of plant material: Grayson, *Desert's Past*, 115–53.

"resembl[ing] blocks of asphalt": Spaulding et al., "Packrat Middens," 60.

Members of the Manly Party: Grayson, *Desert's Past*, 115–16.

Packrat middens in the Panamint Mountains: Woodcock, "Late Pleistocene."

The most impressive of the recent eruptions occurred about 760,000 years ago: Phillips, "Geological and Hydrological History," 130; Hill, "Geologic Story," 52–58.

The early Holocene generally was cooler and moister: for information on Holocene climates in the Death Valley region see Grayson, *Desert's Past*, 92–153; LaMarche, "Holocene Climatic Variations"; Lowenstein, "Pleistocene Lakes."

thirty-five genera of mammals: Grayson, *Desert's Past*, 63.

Among the vanished species: ibid., 155–90.

aboriginal humans who arrived in the region: ibid., 235.

"just screwing around": Ron Marlow, interview, December 5, 2010.

a new species of slender salamander: Brame, "A New Species of *Batrachoseps*."

"It's just what they do": Robert Hansen, personal communication, November 16, 2010.

water loss approaches 30 percent: Ray, "Vital Limits."

Their resting metabolic rates are about 60 percent: Feder, "Integrating Ecology and Physiology"; Pough, "Advantages of Ectothermy."

65 percent of all salamander species: Pough, "Advantages of Ectothermy."

about 1.2 grams of food per year to survive: Fitzpatrick, "Energy Allocation."

A 3.3 gram masked shrew: Morrison, "Food Consumption."

rate of fifty beats per minute: Weitzel and Muler, "Effects of Temperature and Activity."

74 percent survived at room temperature: Feder, "Integrating Ecology and Physiology."

The percentage of food energy: Pough, "Advantages of Ectothermy"; Burton and Likens, "Energy Flow." Estimates for the percentage of food energy used by salamanders to add biomass vary somewhat between these two papers.

They would have surfaced along tiny streams: It also is possible that Inyo Mountains slender salamanders mate underground, but no one knows. Elizabeth Jockusch, personal communication, April 10, 2012.

the fifty acres of habitat that they have: Hansen and Wake, "*Batrachoseps campi*."

up to 10,000 per acre: Burton and Likens, "Salamander populations"; Burton and Likens, "Energy Flow."

"**Perhaps Inyo Mountains slender salamanders have survived**": David Wake, interview, September 15, 2010.

the smaller California slender salamander: Maiorana, "Size and Environmental Predictability."

clutch size in the Kern Plateau slender salamander: Wake et al., "New Species of Salamander"; Bury, "*Batrachoseps wrighti.*"

The Manzanar camp once held more than 10,000 "internees": U.S. National Park Service, "Manzanar."

SURVIVING AN ONSLAUGHT The Owens Pupfish

California Department of Fish and Game biologist: In 2013 the name of the California Department of Fish and Game was changed to the California Department of Fish and Wildlife. Because most all of the events described in this book occurred prior to 2013, I use the older name for the agency throughout the book.

"**I distinctly remember being scared to death**": Pister, "Species in a Bucket," 14; Miller and Pister, "Management of Owens Pupfish."

at least seven other fish extinctions: Sada and Vinyard, "Anthropogenic Changes," 277.

Its current annual discharge: U.S. Geological Survey, "Cattaraugus Creek." http://waterdata.usgs.gov/usa/nwis/uv?04213500; "Owens River at Keeler Bridge." http://ca.water.usgs.gov/owens/report/hydro_system_2surface.html (July 7, 2012)

choking clouds of arsenic- and salt-laden dust: Reheis, "Dust Deposition Downwind."

Although recent dust mitigation efforts: Great Basin Unified Air Pollution Control District, "Dust Control."

during the Pleistocene, when it covered: Orme and Orme, "Late Pleistocene Shorelines."

An early museum specimen of tui chub: Steve Parmenter, personal communication, October 1, 2012.

40,000 acres under cultivation: Reisner, *Cadillac Desert*, 59.

Los Angeles was growing rapidly: U.S. Census Bureau, "Population of Counties."

"**in abundance in all the shallower parts of the sloughs**": Kennedy, "A Possible Enemy," 180.

when Carl Hubbs visited the locality: Miller and Pister, " Management of Owens Pupfish."

Miller described the Owens pupfish: Miller, *Cyprinodont Fishes.*

Although Miller was pessimistic: material in this section from Miller and Pister, "Management of Owens Pupfish"; Phil Pister, interviews, September 21, 2010, and October 26, 2011; Pister, "Species in a Bucket."

"**lithologic, chemical, mineralogic, geophysical**": Jayko and Bacon, "Late Quaternary Shoreline Features," 203.

highstands, or deep-water events: Phillips, "Geological and Hydrological History," 139.

an event which may have occurred: Knott et al., "Reconstructing Late Pliocene," 23–34.

recognize four species of pupfish: Echelle, "Western North American Pupfish," 28.

the Owens pupfish is the most intrepid wanderer: Steve Parmenter, personal communication, October 1, 2012.

in theory these approaches: Anthony Echelle, personal communication, September 17, 2012; see also Hillis, Mable, and Moritz, "Molecular Systematics."

problems with actually applying them: Hillis, Mable, and Moritz, "Molecular Systematics," 534–39; Arbogast et al., "Estimating Divergence Times"; Ho and Larson, "Molecular Clocks."

A fossil pupfish from the Funeral Mountains: Miller, "Four New Species"; Miller, "Coevolution of Deserts and Fishes."

the western lineage of pupfish: Echelle, "Western North American Pupfish."

the oldest extant species: ibid.

no geological data supporting a direct connection: Knott et al., "Reconstructing Late Pliocene," 23–24.

mtDNA data for springsnails: Hershler and Liu, "Ancient Vicariance."

Although the Owens River may have been: Phillips, "Geological and Hydrological History"; see also Knott et al., "Reconstructing Late Pliocene."

"biogeographic enigma": Echelle, "Western North American Pupfish," 35.

drainage systems even reversed: Reheis et al., "Drainage Reversals in Mono Basin."

"It seems unlikely that fishes . . . such chaos": ibid., 1005; see also Phillips, "Geological and Hydrological History."

The surviving Owens pupfish: Information in this section comes from interviews with Steve Parmenter on October 1 and October 7, 2010, and March 12–13, 2011; Phil Pister reviewed this information.

"rare unto death": Quammen, Song of the Dodo, 275.

Gary was born and raised: Material in this section is mostly from an interview with Gary Giacomini on October 12, 2010; Steve Parmenter reviewed this section.

"if they fulfill . . . without their consent": U.S. Fish and Wildlife Service, "For Landowners."

there currently is no provision for such an agreement: Steve Parmenter, personal communication, October 21, 2012; Dawne Becker, personal communication, May 16, 2013.

Owens Valley region now delivers only 30 percent: Dave Martin, Los Angeles Department of Water and Power, interview, March 16, 2011.

These two court-mandated programs: Los Angeles Department of Water and Power, "Annual Owens Valley Report"; Inyo County Water Department, "Lower Owens River Project."

Dave's main task: Material in this section is based on interview with Dave Martin, Los Angeles Department of Water and Power, March 16, 2011.

This point was made to me by Ceal Klingler: Material beginning here, including quotations, is based on an interview with and emails from Ceal Klingler, March 17, 2012.

the roughly 200,000 acre-feet of water: Los Angeles Department of Water and Power news release. http://www.ladwpnews.com/go/doc/1475/1090271/Fact-Check-2011–2012-Owens-Valley-Operations-Plan (September 7, 2012).

the 387,000 acre-feet of water that the DWP planned to export: ibid.

"I'll go with the people": George H. W. Bush statement; see http://www.nfb.ca/film/being_caribou (September 6, 2012).

LA Aqueduct water for about $75 per acre-foot: Dave Martin, Los Angeles Department of Water and Power, interview, March 16, 2011.

"The only thing worse than the DWP": Phil Pister, interview, September 21, 2010.

"It would have no possible significance": Steve Parmenter, interview, October 12, 2010.

"leapfrogging": Miller and Pister, " Management of Owens Pupfish," 506.

"To see a world in a grain of sand": Blake, "Auguries of Innocence."

SOME FISH
The Salt Creek and Cottonball Marsh Pupfishes

The first specimens: Miller, "*Cyprinodon salinus*."

the salinity is about 50 percent that of seawater: Sada and Deacon, "Spatial and Temporal Variability."

About six miles away: LaBounty and Deacon, "*Cyprinodon milleri*."

The phylogenetic tree: Echelle, "Western North American Pupfish."

a 1993 study on allozymes: Echelle and Echelle, "Allozyme Perspective."

the more plausible hypothesis: Echelle, "Western North American Pupfish"; Anthony Echelle, personal communication July 20, 2012.

dating of lakeshore features: Knott et al., "Reconstructing Late Pliocene."

a freshwater lake up to one thousand feet deep: Phillips, "Geological and Hydrological History," 139.

Lake Manley disappeared around 120,000 years ago: ibid.

During this more recent period: Lowenstein, "Pleistocene Lakes"; Tim Lowenstein, personal communication, January 11, 2012.

Individuals from these two populations: Duvernell and Turner, "Evolutionary Genetics."

LaBounty and James Deacon, who in 1972 described: LaBounty and Deacon, "*Cyprinodon milleri*."

In New Mexico, genetically controlled: Lema, "Population Divergence."

During the summer, Salt Creek pupfish: Sada and Deacon, "Spatial and Temporal Variability."

The first mention of Cottonball Marsh pupfish: Hunt et al., *Hydrologic Basin, Death Valley*, 137.

Mitochondrial evidence suggests that *Cyprinodon*: Echelle et al., "Historical Biogeography."

"toughest fish in North America": Haney and Nordlie, "Influence of Salinity," 515.

Beavers, which never have to worry: Schmidt-Nielsen, *Animal Physiology*, 372.

a freshwater fish flushes excess fluids: Ibid., 317–20; Soltz and Naiman, *Native Fishes*.

In one experiment, Cottonball Marsh pupfish: Naiman et al., "Osmoregulation in Pupfish"; Steunkel and Hillyard, "Effects of Temperature and Salinity."

Humans can tolerate increases in plasma solute concentration: Bourque, "Central Mechanisms."

Experimental Salt Creek pupfish survived: Steunkel and Hillyard, "Effects of Temperature and Salinity."

Salinity values at Salt Creek: Sada and Deacon, "Spatial and Temporal Variability."

In the wild, some pupfish tolerate: Feldmeth, "Evolution of Thermal Tolerance"; Brown and Feldmeth, "Constant and Fluctuating Environments."

An example of this precise regulation: Feldmeth, "Evolution of Thermal Tolerance."

Pupfish living in shallow pools and marshes: Soltz and Naiman, *Native Fishes*.

experiments show that some adaptive change has occurred: Feldmeth, "Evolution of Thermal Tolerance."

Heat shock proteins serve as "molecular chaperones": Csermely and Yahara, "Heat Shock Proteins."

Amargosa pupfish do produce them: Sanders et al., "Specific Cross-reactivity."

the common killifish (*Fundulus heteroclitus*): Fangue et al., "Intraspecific Variation."

In another genus of closely related fish: Hightower et al., "Heat Shock Responses."

heat shock proteins are also found in the gills: Deane and Woo, "Gene Expression."

Because the water that feeds Salt Creek: Faunt et al., "Hydrology"; for a now-discredited hypothesis, see Jahren and Sanford, "Ground-Water is the Ultimate Source."

Some models suggest that unsustainable groundwater pumping: Deacon et al., "Fueling Population Growth."

although Native Americans once gathered them: Miller, "*Cyprinodon salinus*," 76.

"When we try to pick out anything": Muir, *My First Summer in the Sierra*, 157.

basic research on naked mole rats: Buffenstein, "Negligible Senescence."

naked mole rats also do not develop cancer: Selvanov et al., "Hypersensitivity to Contact Inhibition."

"Isn't it time we recognize that": Ackerman, "Another Species."

"anti-human sentiments are logically consistent with environmentalism": Woiceshyn, "Environmentalism and Endangered Species."

"Intrinsic value is a vaguely formulated concept": Maguire and Justus, "Intrinsic Value," 910.

Dr. Rob Roy Ramey II: Holthaus, "A Better Mousetrap," Ramey et al., "Genetic Relatedness."

"Ecologists have largely allowed economists": Leakey and Lewin, *The Sixth Extinction*, 126.

"Maybe it's not what the facts of the world point to": Moore, *Wild Comfort*, 74.

"the innumerable species inhabiting this world": Darwin, *Origin of Species*, 66.

A FRAGILE EXISTENCE
The Devils Hole Pupfish

"At the entrance to the valley": Johnson and Johnson, *Escape from Death Valley*, 160.

"On the second or third night": ibid.

Charles H. Gilbert, who described: Gilbert, "Fishes of Death Valley."

"remarkably abundant" fish vanished: Minckley et al., "Conservation and Management," 271.

"Ten young specimens from the 'Devil's Hole'": Gilbert, "Fishes of Death Valley," 233.

In 1930, Joseph Wales: Wales, "Biometrical Studies."

C. diabolis was a "dwarfed species": Miller, *Cyprinodont Fishes*, 83.

"a number of the characters": ibid.

"it might be argued that the fish": Wales, "Biometrical Studies," 68.

when President Harry Truman declared it: Deacon and Williams, "Legacy of the Devils Hole Pupfish," 71.

Miller made six visits to Devils Hole: Miller, *Cyprinodont Fishes*, 127.

"The entire existing population of this form": Sumner and Sargent, "Some Observations," 47.

The sediments that formed the rocks: Riggs and Deacon, "Devils Hole Story," 8–10.

Hydrologists know that water: ibid., 9–10.

the Gravity Fault: Faunt et al., "Hydrology," 154.

once supported twenty-nine plants and animals: U.S. Fish and Wildlife Service, "Desert National Wildlife Refuge Complex."

A counterclockwise drift and spiral: Belcher et al., "Saturated Zone Hydrology," 19.

a pit that formed about 60,000 years ago: Riggs and Deacon, "Devils Hole Story," 11.

mostly filamentous cyanobacteria and diatoms: Wilson and Blinn, "Food Web Structure," 186.

direct sunlight falls on the pool: ibid.

the total energy budget of this ecosystem: ibid., 195.

It falls about seventy-five vertical feet: Hillyard et al., "SOP VII—Devils Hole Pupfish."

"like being the first person to enter": Alan Riggs, interview, December 3, 2012.

"going back into the womb": James Deacon, interview, March 20, 2011.

the amount of oxygen-18 isotope they contain: Riggs and Deacon, "Devils Hole Story," 11–16.

a careful protocol: Hillyard et al., "SOP VII—Devils Hole Pupfish."

"is like swimming into the stillness": Zane Marshall, interview, September 25, 2012.

tally fish ranging from 12 to 40 millimeters: Kevin Wilson, personal communication, September 24, 2010.

the minimum count was only 127: Andersen and Deacon, "Population Size."

many of which looked "emaciated": Kevin Wilson, interview, October 1, 2012.

only to have it again fall: Kevin Wilson, personal communication, May 31, 2013.

Following the drowning: Silver, "Death at Devil's Hole."

a program costing $390,000: U.S. National Park Service, "Ecosystem Monitoring Plan."

intensive long-term ecological monitoring plan: ibid.

back in 1948 Miller and Hubbs: Hubbs and Miller, "Correlation between Fish Distribution."

these clays were not deposited: Hay et al., "Spring-Related Carbonate Rocks."

water levels in Devils Hole have not risen: Riggs and Deacon, "Devils Hole Story," 15.

no more than 11,500 years ago: Grayson, *The Desert's Past*, 235.

culturally important to the modern: Riggs and Deacon, "Devils Hole Story," 3.

between 200,000 and 600,000 years ago: Smith et al., "Biogeography and Timing"; Echelle, "Western North American Pupfish," 28.

"dating recent [speciation] events": Riggs and Deacon, "Devils Hole Story," 8.

a process called "lineage sorting": Echelle, "Western North American Pupfish," 35.

"a skylight to the water table": Riggs and Deacon, "Devils Hole Story," 1.

stream-of-consciousness riffs: see, for example, http://orgonepowerblessings
.blogspot.com/2009/07/dolphins-and-death-valley.html (February 6, 2014).

"Our blood is time": Michaels, "Miner's Pond," 63.

which average 92° Fahrenheit: Wilson and Blinn, "Food Web Structure," 189–90.

the lack of aggression: Soltz and Naiman, Native Fishes.

such as the thunderstorm: Wilson and Blinn, "Food Web Structure," 192.

when the primary producers in the Devils Hole: Riggs and Deacon, "Devils Hole
Story," 30–31.

To watch a video of the event: http://www.scientificamerican.com/article
.cfm?id=earthquake-at-devils-hole (December 12, 2012).

numbered 36dd: Dudley and Larson, Effects of Irrigation Pumping, 17.

when it was tested in the winter of 1968: Riggs and Deacon, "Devils Hole Story," 4.

"circumventing. . . . agency inertia and thereby starting a movement": Pister,
"Desert Fishes Council," 57.

in August 1971, the U.S. Department: Deacon and Williams, "Legacy of the Devils
Hole Pupfish," 79.

1908 U.S. Supreme Court decision: Abrams, "Implied Reservation."

Cappaert Enterprises appealed: Deacon and Williams, "Legacy of the Devils Hole
Pupfish," 79.

"We hold, therefore, that as of 1952": Riggs and Deacon, "Devils Hole Story," 7.

"cried out of relief": Phil Pister, interview, September 21, 2010.

"had begun the whole thing": ibid.

"conservationists will find": Abrams, "Implied Reservation," 50055.

Nye County commissioner Robert Rudd: Deacon and Williams, "Legacy of the
Devils Hole Pupfish," 80.

"There is an insecticide on the market": quoted in Deacon and Williams, "Legacy of
the Devils Hole Pupfish," 80.

In 1962 rotenone had been used: Holden, "Ghosts of the Green River."

In 1977 the court set this value at 2.7 feet: Deacon and Williams, "Legacy of the
Devils Hole Pupfish," 79.

By 1977, counts before and after: ibid., 226.

"larger than the maximum natural size": quoted in J. E. Williams, "Preserves and
Refuges," 179.

The Hoover Dam population: ibid., 177–79.

Two refuges with dimensions: Information on the refuges is from Karam, "Refuge
Management."

a graduate student, Abraham Karam: ibid., 41.

by 2005, 23 of 110 fish: Martin et al., "Shifts in the Gene Pool."

Although the 1980 recovery plan: U.S. Fish and Wildlife Service, "Devils Hole Pupfish
Recovery Plan."

Devils Hole pupfish possess unique genetic: Duvernell and Turner, "Evolutionary
Genetics"; Martin and Wilcox, "Evolutionary History."

its own evolutionary path for perhaps 20,000 years: This figure is from Martin
and Wilcox, "Evolutionary History," and is based on analysis of microsatellite
DNA markers. Analysis of mitochondrial DNA dates the origin of the *C. diabolis*
lineage at 200,000 to 600,000 years, well before the formation of Devils Hole
some 60,000 years ago. See Smith et al., "Biogeography and Timing," and Echelle,
"Western North American Pupfish," for mitochondrial DNA data, and Riggs and
Deacon, "Devils Hole Story," for Devils Hole formation.

do not display what is termed "reciprocal monophyly": Duvernelle and Turner,
"Evolutionary Genetics," 283.

"any species or subspecies of fish": U.S. Fish and Wildlife Service, "Endangered
Species Act, Section 3," http://www.fws.gov/endangered/laws-policies/section-3
.html (February 15, 2013).

One of his most interesting studies: Lema, "Population Divergence."

Amargosa pupfish raised: Lema and Nevitt, "Morphological Plasticity in Pupfish."

Robert Miller, who found some Amargosa pupfish: Miller, *Cyprinodont Fishes*, 35.

completed at a cost of 4.5 million dollars: Darrick Weissenfluh, personal
communication, November 19, 2012.

"we are never going to exactly recreate Devils Hole": ibid.

Andrew Martin's research: Martin et al., "Shifts in the Gene Pool."

As one of Martin's collaborators, Anthony Echelle: Anthony Echelle, personal
communication, October 24, 2012.

"abundance and magnitude of deleterious alleles": Martin et al., "Shifts in the Gene
Pool," 356.

Such an effort would involve: ibid.

"the National Park Service, Fish and Wildlife Service": Andrew Martin, interview,
November 16, 2012.

"I don't think we have time for that": ibid.

"the organism-environment interdependency": Sean Lema, personal
communication, November 16, 2012; Lema, "Organism-Environment
Interdependency."

"are going to move phenotypically": Sean Lema, personal communication,
November 16, 2012.

"Short term use of artificial refuges": Karam, "Refuge Management," 51.

another $250,000 for the Ash Meadows: Darrick Weissenfluh, personal
communication, September 30, 2013.

And as long as we are not: Rogers, "Animals and People."

"The structure of every living thing": Hass, ". . . white of forgetfulness, white of
safety," 323.

SWIMMING FROM THE RUINS
The Ash Meadows and Warm Springs Amargosa Pupfishes

at least twenty-nine species, subspecies, or varieties: U.S. Fish and Wildlife Service,
"Desert National Wildlife Refuge Complex"; Cristi Baldino, U.S. Fish and Wildlife
Service, personal communication, March 23, 2013.

the springs of Ash Meadows may be up to thirty thousand years old: Marshall et al., "Fluid Geochemistry," 200–201.

a process termed interbasin transfer: Belcher et al., "Interbasin Flow."

Ash Meadows has been well-watered: Hay et al., "Spring-Related Carbonate Rocks."

Genetic evidence suggests that the Amargosa pupfish: Echelle, "Western North American Pupfish," 28; Duvernell and Turner, "Evolutionary Genetics," 283; Martin and Wilcox, "Evolutionary History."

Miller, who described the Ash Meadows Amargosa pupfish: Miller, *Cyprinodont Fishes*, 44–47.

Miller distinguished the Warm Springs subspecies: ibid., 58–69.

to three endemic invertebrates: Weissenfluh, "Conservation of *Cyprinodon*."

one in South Indian Spring: Martin, "Conservation Genetics."

"similar to the Ash Meadows pupfish": Soltz and Naiman, *Native Fishes*, 17.

"the male process is absent": Polhemus and Polhemus, "*Ambrysus* Stål," 264.

the Nevares Spring naucorid: Whiteman and Sites, "Aquatic Insects."

"I didn't talk about springsnails": Don Sada, interview, November 15, 2012.

"a beautiful valley considerably lower": Johnson and Johnson, *Escape from Death Valley*, 160.

"in marshes along the irrigating ditches": Fisher, "Report on Birds," 19.

clay mining began there in 1917: Livingston and Nials, "Archaeological and Paleoenvironmental Investigations," 18.

when Robert Miller studied fish: Miller, *Cyprinodont Fishes*.

Major agricultural development at Ash Meadows: Deacon and Williams, "Legacy of the Devils Hole Pupfish."

To stand above Kings Pool: Photographs of Ash Meadows in the late 1960s are in Soltz and Naiman, *Native Fishes*, 64–69.

"9-percent additional load on the total discharge": Dudley and Larson, *Effects of Irrigation Pumping*, 40

"Because of the liberal estimates": ibid., 40.

"very high salinity—moderate sodium": ibid., 28–29.

"It is increasingly evident that the pupfish species": Lostetter, "Proposed Endangered Species," 2.

pupfish and dace habitat had decreased: Sada, *Recovery Plan*, 20.

"Most areas of botanical interest": Janice Beatley, unpublished memorandum, Ash Meadows National Wildlife Refuge headquarters files, Ash Meadows, NV.

irrigated land increased from 1,000 acres in the 1940s: Comartin, "Development of a Flow Model," 1.

The water table sank rapidly: Miller et al., "Extinctions of Fishes."

"the Interior Department will vigorously oppose": Pister, "The Desert Fishes Council," 61.

"just to save a few worthless fish": ibid.

"the safety of the Devils Hole pupfish": Deacon and Williams, "Legacy of the Devils Hole Pupfish," 82.

Preferred Equities and its president, Jack Soules: ibid., 82–86.

the agency "had to be dragged kicking and screaming": James Deacon, personal communication, March 2, 2011.

James Watt authorized emergency listing: Deacon and Williams, "Legacy of the Devils Hole Pupfish," 83.

"one of the most memorable projects": quotations from David Livermore, interview, January 30, 2013.

"it was devastated; no semblance": quotations from Don Sada, interview, November 15, 2012.

"in the corner of a bar": Cahalan, *Edward Abbey*, 101.

"All I can say is, keep fighting": postcard from Edward Abbey to Barbara Kelly, March 2, 1982.

"The whole thing was a dance": David Livermore, interview, January 30, 2013.

"because they knew where I was going": Sharon McKelvey, interview, March 9, 2012.

"what we create is definitely not": Rob Andress, interview, February 7, 2013.

Rob Andress estimates that the contractor's compensation: Rob Andress, personal communication, February 7, 2013.

the Southern Nevada Public Land Management Act (SNPLMA): U.S. Bureau of Land Management, "About SNPLMA."

The first restoration: information on the restoration of Ash Meadows springs primarily from Otis Bay, "Ecological Projects—Ash Meadows"; Wild Fish Habitat Initiative, "Jackrabbit Spring Restoration."

"to get the system going": Rob Andress, interview, February 7, 2013.

"beauty is a pledge of the possible": Santayana, *The Sense of Beauty*, 270.

"is like going home": Darrick Weissenfluh, interview, February 14, 2013.

"The living of life, any life": Lopez, *Crossing Open Ground*, 53.

"traumatic sexual abuse": Lopez, "Sliver of Sky," 46.

Hydrologists estimate that the annual groundwater yield: Moreo et al., "Estimated Ground-Water Withdrawals"; U.S. Fish and Wildlife Service, "Desert National Wildlife Refuge Complex," 4–22.

a concentrated animal feeding operation: Nevada State Environmental Commission, "Public Comments."

The dairy uses about 1,500 acre-feet of water: U.S. Fish and Wildlife Service, "Desert National Wildlife Refuge Complex," 4–23.

Amargosa Desert basin total 28,000 acre-feet per year: U.S. Fish and Wildlife Service, "Desert National Wildlife Refuge Complex," 4–23.

"the decline [in groundwater levels] is real": Tim Mayer, interview, January 7, 2013.

U.S. Geological Survey's 2010 groundwater flow model: Belcher and Sweetkind, *Death Valley Regional Groundwater*, 148–50, 324, plate 2.

the Nevada State Engineer issued Order #1197: State of Nevada, Department of Conservation and Natural Resources, "State Engineer Order #1197."

a sizeable bonded indebtedness: Deacon and Williams, "Legacy of the Devils Hole Pupfish," 84.

Nye County has a poverty rate of 20.5 percent: U.S. Census Bureau, "Quick Facts" http://quickfacts.census.gov/qfd/states/32/32023.html (April 3, 2013).

regional flow model was "garbage": Ed Goedhart, phone interview, January 2011.

a former Nye County commissioner, called it "a joke": Gary Hollis, interview, March
    9, 2012.
for illegally dumping 1.7 million gallons: Nevada State Environmental Commission,
    "Public Comments," 1.
an illegal well near the Ponderosa Dairy in 2006: ibid., 10.
her "biggest challenge is to make us": Sharon McKelvey, interview, March
    9, 2012.
When I met up with Hollis: All quotations by Gary Hollis from an interview on March
    9, 2012.
groundwater levels were the same on either side of the fault: Wayne Belcher,
    interview, September 24, 2012.
"One thing I've learned through marriage counseling": ibid.
As Gary Hollis said: Gary Hollis, interview, March 9, 2012. "Whiskey's for
    drinking, water's for fighting over" is attributed to Mark Twain, but there is no
    evidence that he actually said this: see Guy Rocha, "Myth #122," What Mark
    Twain Didn't Say." http://nsla.nevadaculture.org/index.php?option=com_
    content&task=view&id=803& Itemid=418 (June 3, 2013).
"I don't like sports metaphors": Wayne Belcher, interview, September 24, 2012.
"values are faithfully applied to the facts": Obama, *Audacity of Hope*, 59.
"People like Goedhart dismiss": Tim Mayer, interview, January 7, 2013.
"there is little likelihood that the population": Miller, *Cyprinodont Fishes*, 47.
a "low rating on list of desirable springs": Lostetter, "Proposed Endangered Species,"
    32.
the ten-thousand-year-old water: Marshall et al., "Fluid Geochemistry," 200.

EXILE AND LONELINESS   The Black Toad

I recall that toads see: Ewert, "Motion Perception."
forty to fifty acres: Wang, "Fine-Scale Genetic Structure."
"has perhaps the most restricted range": Meyers, "Black Toads," 13.
"supposition still stands": Murphy et al., "Population Status and Conservation."
"which *Bufo exsul* certainly is": Meyers, "Black Toads," 13.
Meyers based his description: ibid., 3.
evolutionary relationships have been corroborated: Goebel et al., "Mitochondrial
    DNA Evolution."
within a lineage that includes: ibid.
little barrier to evaporation: Schmidt-Nielsen, *Animal Physiology*, 324–26.
This relationship is not linear: Gatten et al., "Energetics at Rest."
Movement between the two springs: Wang, "Fine-Scale Genetic Structure";
    Simandle, "Population Structure and Conservation."
wash toads downhill: Eric Simandle, interview, March 27, 2012.
Studies of another toad: Tevis, "Unsuccessful Breeding."
temperate-zone toads may occasionally move: Bradford et al., "Habitat Patch
    Occupancy."
Alluvial sediments: Reheis and Sawyer, "Late Cenozoic History."

The last Pleistocene lakes: Lowenstein, "Pleistocene Lakes"; Marith Reheis, personal communication, March 7, 2012.

Mitochondrial DNA sequence data: Goebel et al., "Mitochondrial DNA."

Males produce these release calls: Kagarise Sherman, "Natural History and Mating System," 294.

Males of two other species: Wright and Wright, "Amargosa Toad"; Hammerson, Amphibians and Reptiles of Colorado.

male Yosemite toads: Kagarise Sherman, "Natural History and Mating System," 165.

An undisturbed pair: ibid., 314.

"characteristically eviscerated": ibid., 90.

Photographs from the 1960s: Murphy et al., "Population Status and Conservation"; Schuierer, "Natural History of Bufo exsul."

California's 1960s-era regulations: Steve Parmenter, personal communication, October 21, 2012; Dawne Becker, personal communication, May 16, 2013.

"with fierce jaws and frowning fiercely": Wood and Subrahmanyan, "From the Garuda Purana."

"possibly the most deadly invasive species": Rohr et al., "Evaluating the Links," 17436.

"the greatest loss of vertebrate biodiversity": Vrendenburg et al., "Dynamics of an Emerging Disease," 9689.

more than 93 percent of their historic range: ibid.

in Yosemite National Park: Drost and Fellers, "Collapse of a Regional Frog Fauna."

western toads virtually disappeared: Muths et al., "Amphibian Decline."

Bd works by attacking amphibian keratin: Briggs et al., "Enzootic and Epizootic Dynamics."

When zoospores are released: ibid.

in the 1999 paper: Longcore et al., "Batrachochytrium dendrobatidis."

Once Bd reaches a population: Lips et al., "Riding the Wave."

smaller-scale studies suggest a much slower: Vredenburg et al., "Dynamics of an Emerging Disease."

The Pacific treefrog: Reeder et al., "A Reservoir Species."

In a laboratory setting: Johnson and Speare, "Possible Modes of Dissemination."

One paper on Batrachochytrium: Lips et al., "Riding the Wave."

Water temperatures above 77°F: Forrest and Schlaepfer, "A Hot Bath."

"flowering / blue and mystical": Plath, "The Moon and the Yew Tree," 173.

as the philosopher (Bruce Springsteen) has said: "Ed Norton Interviews Bruce Springsteen on 'Darkness,'" Fresh Air, November 15, 2010. http://www.npr .org/2010/11/12/131272103/ed-norton-interviews-bruce-springsteen-on-darkness (June 10, 2012).

"A high, wide emptiness": Malouf, The Conversations at Curlow Creek, 59.

"I learned not to fear infinity": Roethke, "The Far Field," 194.

"couldn't make Immortal": Snyder, "Cold Mountain Poems #12," 48.

"If the gods are there": Malouf, An Imaginary Life, 2.

"I have none, because there were no people": A different version of this quotation is in Heizer and Kroeber, Ishi the Last Yahi, 99.

"movement of grief": Hass, "Variations on a Passage in Ed Abbey," 19.

"a lightness, / a moveable island of joy": Greger, "Crossing the Plains," 58.

THE VIEW FROM TELESCOPE PEAK

"silence and intoxication": Bracho, "Give Me, Earth, Your Night."

"What happens here": Benston, "Vegas Advertising."

Although the metropolitan area still obtains: Southern Nevada Water Authority, *Water Resource Plan 09*, 29.

water table has sunk: Pavelko et al., "Gambling with Water," 53.

in 1971 the Southern Nevada Water Project: ibid., 53.

currently is entitled to: Southern Nevada Water Authority, *Water Resource Plan 09*, 20.

Las Vegas's exploding population: U.S. Census Bureau, "Nevada: 2010, Population and Housing Units," Tables 4, 6. http://www.census.gov/prod/cen2010/cph-2-30 .pdf (June 15, 2013).

a population in excess of three million: Tra, "Executive Summary."

at least 186,000 acre-feet of additional water: Southern Nevada Water Authority, *Water Resource Plan 09*, 39–40.

Lake Mead was at 39 percent: U.S. Bureau of Reclamation, "Lake Mead Elevations," http://www.usbr.gov/lc/region/g4000/lakemead_bar.pdf (June 15, 2013)

the SNWA is constructing: Southern Nevada Water Authority, "Intake No. 3."

"frequent past occurrences of flow lower": Woodhouse et al., "Updated Streamflow Reconstructions," 13.

"In the unlikely event": Southern Nevada Water Authority, *Water Resource Plan 09*, 47.

SNWA has aggressively pursued: ibid., 15–19.

daily per capita water use of 131 gallons in Tucson, Arizona: Tucson City government, "About Tucson Water," http://cms3.tucsonaz.gov/water/about-us (June 15, 2013)

the compact was negotiated during: Woodhouse et al., "Updated Streamflow Reconstructions," 1.

there has been fantastical talk: Glennon, *Unquenchable*, 15–16.

tap into groundwater in other parts of Nevada: Southern Nevada Water Authority, *Water Resource Plan 09*, 28–33.

the refusal of Utah's governor: *Salt Lake City Tribune*, April 5, 2013: http://www.sltrib .com/csp/cms/sites/sltrib/pages/printerfriendly.csp?id=56108808 (June 16, 2013).

the SNWA has been granted: Southern Nevada Water Authority, *Water Resource Plan 09*, 31.

planned withdrawals exceed recharge rates: Deacon et al., "Fueling Population Growth."

declines of over 700 feet near wells: Bredehoeft and Durbin, "Groundwater Development."

"these effects probably would not be felt": Wayne Belcher, personal communication, April 10, 2013.

I visited with Zane Marshall: All Zane Marshall quotations from an interview conducted on October 14, 2010. Zane was very gracious in answering my questions, although in a personal communication on May 29, 2013, he expressed strong reservations about some of my views on the Southern Nevada Water Authority and effects of its planned groundwater development in northern Nevada.

"further the understanding of groundwater-influenced ecosystem": Biological Work Group, "Biological Monitoring Plan for the Spring Valley Stipulation," 1–1.

"manage the development of groundwater by SNWA": ibid., 1–1.

"avoid unreasonable adverse effects": ibid., 8–4.

"if an indicator or suite of indicators": ibid., 8–5.

"at the present time, data are insufficient": ibid., 8–4.

"to conserve the scenery and the natural and historic objects": U.S. National Park Service, "Organic Act of 1916."

Memorandum of Agreement with the U.S. Fish and Wildlife Service: U.S. Fish and Wildlife Service, "Proposed Coyote Springs Investment."

hopes to build a 43,000 acre, 110,000-unit desert development: U.S. Fish and Wildlife Service, "Record of Decision," 3.

"defined by a continuous valley of green": Coyote Springs Golf Club, http://www .coyotesprings.com/development.html (June 15, 2013).

"there will be (1) a time lag between": Bredehoeft and Durbin, "Groundwater Development," 512.

once $3.2 billion dollars: Southern Nevada Water Authority, "SNWA Summary of Cost Estimate for Clark."

one federal official familiar with the negotiations: This is one of the few places in the book where I quote an anonymous source. Although it would be preferable to identify the individual, he/she asked to remain anonymous, explaining the decision in the following way: "as public employees, we are not supposed to talk openly about such things, unless we are toeing the party line. I would be completely open, if I were in full agreement and really believed in these agreements [the Spring Valley Stipulation]—the official position."

"to manage the region's water resources and develop solutions": Southern Nevada Water Authority, "Mission."

"We can't conserve our way out of a massive Colorado River drought": P. Mulroy, quoted at http://www.treehugger.com/corporate-responsibility/nevada-water-authority-executive-proposes-high-stakes-mississippi-river-floodwater-diversion .html (June 15, 2013).

Jim Deacon's controversial 2007 *BioScience* article: Deacon et al., "Fueling Population Growth."

senators such as Harry Reid: Berzon, "Desert Developer's Woes."

when Las Vegas's unemployment rate had reached 14 percent: U.S. Department of Labor, Bureau of Labor Statistics. http://data.bls.gov/timeseries/ LAUMT32298203?data_tool=XGtable (June 15, 2013).

"the fragility of our capacity to know": Bock, Review of *About a Mountain*.

"we are all in this together": Krutch, *The Twelve Seasons*, 13.

"the steep climb / of everything": Snyder, "For the Children," 86.

"Can We Name Earth's Species Before They Go Extinct?": Costello et al., "Can We Name Earth's Species."

"hearing the grass grow and the squirrel's heart beat": Eliot, *Middlemarch*, 194.

all things shining: this line is from the final scene in Terrence Malick's movie, *The Thin Red Line*; it also is the name of a recent book by Hubert Dreyfus and Sean Dorrance Kelly.

Bibliography

Abrams, R. H. 1977. "Implied Reservation of Water Rights in the Aftermath of *Cappaert v. United States.*" *Environmental Law Reporter* 7: 50043–55.

Ackerman, F. N. 2010. "Another Species in Need." Letter to the editor, *New York Times Book Review*, November 7, 2010, BR6.

Andersen, M. E., and J. E. Deacon. 1991. "Population Size of Devils Hole Pupfish (*Cyprinodon diabolis*) Correlates with Water Level." *Copeia* 1991: 224–28.

Arbogast, B. S., et al. 2002. "Estimating Divergence Times from Molecular Data on Phylogenetic and Population Genetic Timescales." *Annual Review of Ecology and Systematics* 33: 707–40.

Auden, W. H. 2007. "First Things First." P. 245 in *Selected Poems*, 2nd ed., edited by E. Mendelson. Vintage, New York, NY.

Bachman, S. B. 1978. "Pliocene-Pleistocene Break-up of the Sierra Nevada: White-Inyo Mountains Block and Formation of Owens Valley." *Geology* 6: 461–63.

Bailey, V. 1900. "Revision of Voles of the North American Genus *Microtus.*" *North American Fauna* 17: 1–88.

Belcher, W. R., and D. S. Sweetkind. 2010. *Death Valley Regional Groundwater Flow System, Nevada and California: Hydrogeologic Framework and Transient Groundwater Flow Model.* U.S. Geological Survey Professional Paper 1711.

Belcher, W. R., et al. 2009. "Interbasin Flow in the Great Basin with Special Reference to the Southern Funeral Mountains and the Source of Furnace Creek Springs, Death Valley, California." *Journal of Hydrology* 369: 30–43.

Belcher, W. R., et al. 2012. "The Saturated Zone Hydrology of Yucca Mountain and the Surrounding Area, Southern Nevada and Adjacent Areas of California, USA." *Geological Society of America Memoir* 209: 1–71.

Benston, L. 2009. "Will Vegas Advertising That Worked Before, Work Again?" *Las Vegas Sun*, September 27, 2009. http://www.lasvegassun.com/news/2009/sep/27/will-vegas-advertising-worked-work-again/#axzz2WBYof4N4 (June 15, 2013).

Berzon, A. 2012. "Desert Developer's Woes Buffet Reid." *Wall Street Journal*, June 10, 2012. http://online.wsj.com/article/SB10001424052702303444204577458652541986234.html (June 15, 2013).

Beston, H. 1992. *The Outermost House: A Year of Life on the Great Beach of Cape Cod.* Henry Holt, New York, NY.

Biological Work Group. 2009. "Biological Monitoring Plan for the Spring Valley Stipulation." http://www.fws.gov/nevada/highlights/comment/spring_valley/

Biological_Monitoring_Plan_Spring_Valley_Stipulation_Feb_09.pdf (June 10, 2013).

Blake, William. 1968. "Auguries of Innocence." Pp. 193–94 in *A Concise Treasury of Great Poems*, edited by L. Untermeyer. Pocket Books, New York, NY.

Bock, C. 2010. Review of *About a Mountain*, by John D'Agata. *New York Times Book Review*, February 28, 2010.

Bourque, C. W. 2008. "Central Mechanisms of Osmosensation and Systemic Osmoregulation." *Nature Reviews Neuroscience* 9: 519–31.

Bracho, C. 2008. "Give Me, Earth, Your Night." P. 113 in *Firefly under the Tongue: Selected Poems of Coral Bracho*, translated by F. Gander. New Directions, New York, NY.

Bradford, D. F., et al. 2003. "Habitat Patch Occupancy by Toads (*Bufo punctatus*) in a Naturally Fragmented Desert Landscape." *Ecology* 84: 1012–23.

Brame, A. H., Jr. 1970. "A New Species of *Batrachoseps* (Slender Salamander) from the Desert of Southern California." Natural History Museum of Los Angeles County, *Contributions in Science* 200: 1–11.

Bredehoeft, J., and T. Durbin. 2009. "Groundwater Development: The Time to Full Capture Problem." *Groundwater* 47: 506–14.

Briggs, C. J., et al. 2010. "Enzootic and Epizootic Dynamics of the Chytrid Fungal Pathogen of Amphibians." *Proceedings of the National Academy of Sciences* 107: 9695–700.

Brown, J. R., and C. R. Feldmeth. 1971. "Evolution in Constant and Fluctuating Environments: Thermal Tolerances of Desert Pupfish (*Cyprinodon*)." *Evolution* 25: 390–98.

Buffenstein, R. 2008. "Negligible Senescence in the Longest Living Rodent, the Naked Mole-Rat: Insights from a Successfully Aging Species." *Journal of Comparative Physiology B* 178: 439–45.

Burlingame, M. 2012. *Lincoln: A Life*. Vol. 2. Johns Hopkins University Press, Baltimore, MD.

Burton, T. M., and G. E. Likens. 1975. "Salamander Populations and Biomass in the Hubbard Brook Experimental Forest, New Hampshire." *Copeia* 1975: 541–46.

———. 1975. "Energy Flow and Nutrient Cycling in Salamander Populations in the Hubbard Brook Experimental Forest, New Hampshire." *Ecology* 56: 1068–80.

Bury, R. B. 2012. "*Batrachoseps wrighti*." AmphibiaWeb: Information on Amphibian Biology and Conservation, Berkeley, California. http://amphibiaweb.org/cgi/amphib_query?where-genus=Batrachoseps&where-species=campi (August 31, 2012).

Cahalan, J. M. 2001. *Edward Abbey: A Life*. University of Arizona Press, Tucson, AZ.

Clark, J. M. 1985. "Fossil Plethodontid Salamanders from the Latest Miocene of California." *Journal of Herpetology* 19: 41–47.

Comartin, L. 2010. "Development of a Groundwater Flow Model of Pahrump Valley, Nye County, Nevada, and Inyo County, California, for Basin-Scale Water Resource Management." MS thesis, University of Nevada, Reno.

Costello, M., et al. 2013. "Can We Name Earth's Species before They Go Extinct?" *Science* 339: 413–16.

Crane, H. 1966. "Voyages II." P. 36 in *The Complete Poems and Selected Letters and Prose of Hart Crane*, edited by B. Weber. Anchor Books, Garden City, NY.

Csermely, P., and Y. Yahara. 2002. "Heat Shock Proteins." Pp. 65–75 in *Molecular Paths, Mechanisms and New Trends in Drug Research*, edited by G. Keri and I. Toth. Taylor & Francis, New York, NY.

Darwin, C. 1859. *The Origin of Species*. John Murray, London.

Deacon, J. E., et al. 2007. "Fueling Population Growth in Las Vegas: How Large-Scale Groundwater Withdrawal Could Burn Regional Biodiversity." *BioScience* 57: 688–98.

Deacon, J. E., and C. C. Williams. 1991. "Ash Meadows and the Legacy of the Devils Hole Pupfish." Pp. 69–91 in *Battle against Extinction: Native Fish Management in the American West*, edited by W. L. Minckley and J. E. Deacon. University of Arizona Press, Tucson, AZ.

Deacon, J. E., and J. E. Williams, 2011. "Retrospective Evaluation of the Effects of Human Disturbance and Goldfish Introduction on Endangered Pahrump Poolfish." *Western North American Naturalist* 70: 425–36.

Deane, E. E., and N. Y. S. Woo. 2004. "Differential Gene Expression Associated with Euryhalinity in Sea Bream (*Sparus sarba*)." *American Journal of Physiology: Regulatory, Integrative and Comparative Physiology* 287: R1054–63.

Drost, C. A., and G. M. Fellers. 1996. "Collapse of a Regional Frog Fauna in the Yosemite Area of the California Sierra Nevada, USA." *Conservation Biology* 10: 414–25.

Dudley, W. W., Jr., and D. Larson. 1976. *Effects of Irrigation Pumping on Desert Pupfish Habitats at Ash Meadows, Nye County, Nevada*. U.S. Geological Survey Professional Paper 927.

Duvernell, D. D., and B. J. Turner. 1998. "Evolutionary Genetics of Death Valley Pupfish Populations: Mitochondrial Sequence Variation and Population Structure. *Molecular Ecology* 7: 279–88.

Echelle, A. A. 2008. "The Western North American Pupfish Clade (Cyprinodontidae: *Cyprinodon*): Mitochondrial DNA and Divergence History." Pp. 27–38 in *Late Cenozoic Drainage History of the Southwestern Great Basin and Lower Colorado River Region: Geologic and Biotic Perspectives*, edited by M. C. Reheis, R. Hershler, and D. M. Miller. Geological Society of America Special Paper 439.

Echelle, A. A., and A. F. Echelle. 1993. "Allozyme Perspective on Mitochondrial DNA Variation and Evolution of the Death Valley Pupfishes (Cyprinodontidae: *Cyprinodon*)." *Copeia* 1993: 275–87.

Echelle, A. A., et al. 2005. "Historical Biogeography of the New-World Pupfish Genus *Cyprinodon* (Teleostei: Cyprinodontidae)." *Copeia* 2005: 320–39.

Eliot, G. 1994. *Middlemarch*. Edited by R. Ashton. Penguin Books, London.

Elliot-Fisk, D. L. 1987. "Glacial Geomorphology of the White Mountains, California, and Nevada: Establishment of a Glacial Chronology." *Physical Geography* 8: 299–323.

Ewert, J.-P. 2004. "Motion Perception Shapes the Visual World of Amphibians." Pp. 117–60 in *Complex Worlds from Simpler Nervous Systems*, edited by F. R. Prete. MIT Press, Cambridge, MA.

Fairchild, B. H. 1998. "Speaking the Names." P. 29 in *The Art of the Lathe*. Alice James Books, Farmington, ME.

Fangue, N. A., et al. 2006. "Intraspecific Variation in Thermal Tolerance and Heat Shock Protein Gene Expression in Common Killifish, *Fundulus heteroclitus*." *Journal of Experimental Biology* 209: 2859–72.

Faunt, C. C., et al. 2010. "Hydrology." Pp. 133–59 in *Death Valley Regional Groundwater Flow System, Nevada and California: Hydrogeologic Framework and Transient Groundwater Flow Model*, edited by W. R. Belcher and D. S. Sweetkind. U.S. Geological Survey Professional Paper 1711.

Feldmeth, C. R. 1981. "The Evolution of Thermal Tolerance in Desert Pupfish (Genus *Cyprinodon*)." Pp. 357–84 in *Fishes in North American Deserts*, edited by R. J. Naiman and D. L. Soltz. John Wiley, New York, NY.

Feder, M. E. 1983. "Integrating the Ecology and Physiology of Plethodontid Salamanders." *Herpetologica* 39: 291–310.

Fisher, A. K. 1893. "Report on Birds." In *The Death Valley Expedition: A Biological Survey of Parts of California, Nevada, Arizona, and Utah*, North American Fauna no. 7, part 2. Government Printing Office, Washington, D.C.

Fitzpatrick, C. 1973. "Energy Allocation in the Allegheny Mountain Salamander, *Desmognathus ochrophaeus*." *Ecological Monographs* 43: 43–58.

Forrest, M. J., and M. A. Schlaepfer. 2011. "Nothing That a Hot Bath Won't Cure: Infection Rates of Amphibian Chytrid Fungus Correlate Negatively with Water Temperature under Natural Condition." *PLoS One* 6(12): E28444.

Frémont, J. C. 1845. *Report of the Exploring Expedition to the Rocky Mountains in the Year 1842, and to Oregon and North California in the Years 1843–44*. U.S. Government House Doc. 166, Washington, D.C.

Gatten, R. E., et al. 1992. "Energetics at Rest and during Locomotion." Pp. 341–42 in *Environmental Physiology of Amphibians*, edited by M. E. Feder and W. W. Burger. University of Chicago Press, Chicago, IL.

Gilbert, C. H. 1893. "Report on the Fishes of the Death Valley Expedition Collected in Southern California and Nevada in 1891, with Descriptions of New Species." In *The Death Valley Expedition: A Biological Survey of Parts of California, Nevada, Arizona, and Utah*, North American Fauna no. 7, part 2. Government Printing Office, Washington, D.C.

Glennon, R. 2009. *Unquenchable: America's Water Crisis and What to Do about It*. Island Press, Washington, D.C.

Goebel, A. M., et al. 2009. "Mitochondrial DNA Evolution in the *Anaxyrus boreas* Group." *Molecular Phylogenetics and Evolution* 50: 209–25.

Gong, K. 2012. "*Rana fisheri*." AmphibiaWeb: Information on Amphibian Biology and Conservation, Berkeley, California. http://amphibiaweb.org/ (July 1, 2012).

Grayson, D. K. 1993. *The Desert's Past: A Natural Prehistory of the Great Basin*. Smithsonian Institution Press, Washington, D.C.

Great Basin Unified Air Pollution Control District. 2012. "Dust Control." http://www.gbuapcd.org/owenslake/Landsat/dustcontrolstatuscurrent.htm (December 14, 2012).

Greger, D. 1980. "Crossing the Plains." P. 58 in *Movable Islands*. Princeton University Press, Princeton, NJ.

Hall, E. R. "Nevadan Races of the *Microtus montanus* Group of Meadow Mice." *University of California Publications in Zoology* 40: 417–28.

Hammerson, G. A. 1999. *Amphibians and Reptiles of Colorado*, 2nd ed. University Press of Colorado and Colorado Division of Wildlife, Niwot, CO.

Haney, D. C., and F. Nordlie. 1997. "Influence of Environmental Salinity on Routine Metabolic Rate and Critical Oxygen Tension of *Cyprinodon variegatus*." *Physiological Zoology* 70: 511–18.

Hansen, R. W., and D. B. Wake. 2012. "*Batrachoseps campi*." AmphibiaWeb: Information on Amphibian Biology and Conservation, Berkeley, California. http://amphibiaweb.org/cgi/amphib_query?where-genus=Batrachoseps&where-species=campi (August 31, 2012).

Hass, R. 2011. "Variations on a Passage in Ed Abbey." Pp. 18–19 in *The Apple Trees at Olema: New and Selected Poems*. HarperCollins, New York, NY.

———. 2011. ". . . white of forgetfulness, white of safety." Pp. 322–23 in *The Apple Trees at Olema: New and Selected Poems*. HarperCollins, New York, NY.

Hay, R. L., et al. 1986. "Spring-Related Carbonate Rocks, Mg Clays, and Associated Minerals in Pliocene Deposits in the Amargosa Desert, Nevada and California." *Geological Society of America Bulletin* 97: 1488–1503.

Heizer, R. F., and T. Kroeber, eds. 1979. *Ishi the Last Yahi: A Documentary History*. University of California Press, Berkeley, CA.

Hekkala, E. R., et al. 2011. "Resurrecting an Extinct Species: Archival DNA, Taxonomy, and Conservation of the Vegas Valley Leopard Frog. *Conservation Genetics* 12: 1379–85.

Hershler, R., and H-P. Liu. 2008. "Ancient Vicariance and Recent Dispersal of Springsnails (Hydrobiidae: *Pyrgulopsis*) in the Death Valley System, California-Nevada." Pp. 91–101 in *Late Cenozoic Drainage History of the Southwestern Great Basin and Lower Colorado River Region: Geologic and Biotic Perspectives*, edited by M. C. Reheis, R. Hershler, and D. M. Miller. Geological Society of America Special Paper 439.

Hershler, R., and D. W. Sada. 1987. "Springsnails (Gastropoda: Hydrobiidae) of Ash Meadows, Amargosa Basin, California-Nevada." *Proceedings of the Biological Society of Washington* 100: 726–843.

Hightower, L. E., et al. 1991. "Heat Shock Responses of Closely Related Species of Tropical and Desert Fish." *American Zoologist* 39: 877–88.

Hill, M. 2000. "Geologic Story." Pp. 37–69 in *Sierra East: Edge of the Great Basin*, edited by G. Smith. University of California Press, Berkeley, CA.

Hillis, D. M., B. K. Mable, and C. Moritz. 1996. "Applications of Molecular Systematics." Pp. 515–43 in *Molecular Systematics*, 2d ed., edited by D. M. Hillis, C. Mortiz, and B. K. Mable. Sinauer Associates, Sunderland, MA.

Hillyard, S. D., et al. 2010. "SOP VII—Devils Hole Pupfish, Version 7.1." In U.S. National Park Service, *Devils Hole Long Term Ecosystem Monitoring Plan Environmental Assessment*.

Ho, S. Y., and G. Larson. 2006. "Molecular Clocks: When Times Are a-Changin'." *Trends in Genetics* 22: 79–83.

Holden, P. 1991. "Ghosts of the Green River: Impacts of Green River Poisoning on Management of Native Fishes." Pp. 43–54 in *Battle against Extinction: Native Fish*

Management in the American West, edited by W. L. Minckley and J. E. Deacon. University of Arizona Press, Tucson, AZ.

Holthaus, D. 2005. "Building a Better Mousetrap." *Westword*. http://www.westword .com/2005-01-20/news/building-a-better-mousetrap/ (September 10, 2013).

Hubbs, C. L., and R. R. Miller. 1948. "Correlation between Fish Distribution and Hydrographic History in the Desert Basins of the Western United States." Pp 17–166 in *The Great Basin, with Emphasis on Glacial and Postglacial Times*. University of Utah Bulletin 38, Biological Series, vol. 10, no. 7. University of Utah Press, Salt Lake City, UT.

Hunt, C. B., et al. 1966. *Hydrologic Basin, Death Valley, California*. U.S. Geological Survey Professional Paper 494-B.

Illich, I. 1996. "The Wisdom of Leopold Kohr." Fourteenth Annual E. F. Schumacher Lectures, Yale University, October 1994. http://neweconomicsinstitute.org/ publications/lectures/illich/ivan/the-wisdom-of-leopold-kohr (July 2, 2012).

Inyo County Water Department. 2012. "Lower Owens River Project." http://www .inyowater.org/LORP/ (July 8, 2012).

Jahren, A. H., and K. L. Sanford. 2002. "Ground-Water Is the Ultimate Source of the Salt Creek Pupfish Habitat, Death Valley, U.S.A." *Journal of Arid Environments* 51: 401–11.

Jayko, A. S., and S. N. Bacon. 2008. "Late Quaternary, MIS 6–8 Shoreline Features of Pluvial Owens Lake, Owens Valley, Eastern California: Implications for Paleohydrology of the Owens River System." Pp. 185–206 in *Late Cenozoic Drainage History of the Southwestern Great Basin and Lower Colorado River Region: Geologic and Biotic Perspectives*, edited by M. C. Reheis, R. Hershler, and D. M. Miller. Geological Society of America Special Paper 439.

Jockusch, E. L., and D. B. Wake. 2002. "Falling Apart and Merging: Diversification of Slender Salamanders (Plethodontidae: *Batrachoseps*) in the American West." *Biological Journal of the Linnean Society* 76: 361–91.

Johnson, L., and J. Johnson, eds. 1987. *Escape from Death Valley: As Told by William Lewis Manly and Other '49ers*. University of Nevada Press, Reno, NV.

Johnson, M. L., and R. Speare. 2005. "Possible Modes of Dissemination of the Amphibian Chytrid *Batrachochytrium dendrobatidis* in the Environment." *Disease of Aquatic Organisms* 65: 181–86.

Kagarise Sherman, C. K. 1980. "A Comparison of the Natural History and Mating System of Two Anurans: Yosemite Toads (*Bufo canorus*) and Black Toads (*Bufo exsul*)." PhD dissertation, University of Michigan, Ann Arbor.

Karam, A. P. 2005. "History and Development of Refuge Management for Devils Hole Pupfish (*Cyprinodon diabolis*) and an Ecological Comparison of Three Artificial Refuges. MS thesis, Southern Oregon University, Ashland, OR.

Kennedy, C. H. 1916. "A Possible Enemy of the Mosquito." *California Fish and Game* 2: 179–82.

Knott, J. R., et al. 2008. "Reconstructing Late Pliocene to Middle Pleistocene Death Valley Lakes and River Systems as a Test of Pupfish (Cyprinodontidae) Dispersal Hypotheses." Pp. 1–26 in *Late Cenozoic Drainage History of the Southwestern Great Basin and Lower Colorado River Region: Geologic and Biotic Perspectives*, edited by

M. C. Reheis, R. Hershler, and D. M. Miller. Geological Society of America Special Paper 439.

Krutch, J. W. 1970. *The Twelve Seasons*. Books for Libraries Press, Freeport, NY.

LaBounty, J. F., and J. E. Deacon. 1972. "*Cyprinodon milleri*, a New Species of Pupfish (Family Cyprinodontidae) from Death Valley, California." *Copeia* 1972: 769–80.

LaMarche, V. C., Jr. 1973. "Holocene Climatic Variations Inferred from Treeline Fluctuations in the White Mountains, California." *Journal of Quaternary Research* 3: 632–60.

Leakey, L., and R. Lewin. 1995. *The Sixth Extinction*. Weidenfeld & Nicholson, London.

Lema, S. C. 2014. "The Ethical Implications of Organism-Environment Interdependency." *Environmental Ethics 36*. In press.

———. 2006. "Population Divergence in Plasticity of the AVT System and Its Association with Aggressive Behaviors in a Death Valley Pupfish." *Hormones and Behavior* 50: 183–93.

Lema, S. C., and G. A. Nevitt. 2006. "Testing an Ecophysiological Mechanism of Morphological Plasticity in Pupfish and Its Relevance to Conservation Efforts for Endangered Devils Hole Pupfish." *Journal of Experimental Biology* 209: 3499–3509.

Lips, K. R., et al. 2009. "Riding the Wave: Reconciling the Roles of Disease and Climate Change in Amphibian Declines." *PLoS Biology* 6(3): 441–54.

Livingston, S. D., and F. L. Nials. 1990. "Archaeological and Paleoenvironmental Investigations in the Ash Meadows National Wildlife Refuge Nye County, Nevada." Quaternary Sciences Center, Desert Research Institute, Technical Report 70.

Longcore, J., et al. 1999. "*Batrachochytrium dendrobatidis* gen. et sp. nov., a Chytrid Pathogenic to Amphibians." *Mycologia* 91: 219–27.

Lopez, B. H. 1988. *Crossing Open Ground*. Charles Scribner's Sons, New York, NY.

———. 2013. "Sliver of Sky." *Harper's Magazine*, January 2013.

Los Angeles Department of Water and Power. 2011. "Los Angeles Department of Water and Power Annual Owens Valley Report," May 2011. http://www.inyowater .org/documents/OwensValleyReport2011.pdf (June 5, 2013).

Lostetter, C. H. 1970. "Summary Report of Proposed Endangered Species Acquisition for Department Task Force—Desert Pupfish." U.S. Department of Interior Fish and Wildlife Service.

Lowenstein, T. K. 2002. "Pleistocene Lakes and Paleoclimates (0 to 200 Ka) in Death Valley, California." Pp. 109–20 in *Great Basin Aquatic Systems History*, edited by R. Herschler, D. B. Madsen, and D. Currey. Smithsonian Contributions to the Earth Sciences 33.

Maguire, L. A., and J. Justus. 2008. "Why Intrinsic Value Is a Poor Basis for Conservation Decisions." *BioScience* 58: 910–11.

Maiorana, V. C. 1976. "Size and Environmental Predictability for Salamanders." *Evolution* 30: 599–613.

Malouf, D. 1996. *An Imaginary Life*. Vintage, New York, NY.

———. 1996. *The Conversations at Curlow Creek*. Vintage, New York, NY.

Marlow, R., et al. 1979. "A New Salamander, Genus *Batrachoseps*, from the Inyo Mountains of California, with a Discussion of Relationships in the Genus." Natural History Museum of Los Angeles County, *Contributions in Science* 308: 1–17.

Marshall, D. D., et al. 2012. "Fluid Geochemistry of Yucca Mountain and Vicinity." Pp. 143–218 in *Hydrology and Geochemistry of Yucca Mountain and Vicinity*, edited by J. S. Stuckless. *Geological Society of America Memoir* 209: 1–71.

Martin, A. P. 2010. "The Conservation Genetics of Ash Meadows Pupfish Populations. I. The Warm Springs Pupfish *Cyprinodon nevadensis pectoralis*." *Conservation Genetics* 11: 1847–57.

Martin, A. P., and J. L. Wilcox. 2004. "Evolutionary History of Ash Meadows Pupfish (Genus *Cyprinodon*) Populations Inferred Using Microsatellite Markers." *Conservation Genetics* 5: 769–82.

Martin, A. P., et al. 2012. "Dramatic Shifts in the Gene Pool of a Managed Population of an Endangered Species May Be Exacerbated by High Genetic Load." *Conservation Genetics* 13: 349–58.

Merwin, W. S. 1980. "The Well." P. 37 in *The Carrier of Ladders: Poems by W. S. Merwin*. Atheneum, New York, NY.

Meyers, G. S. 1942. "The Black Toads of Deep Springs Valley, Inyo County, California." Occasional Papers of the Museum of Zoology, University of Michigan, 460.

Michaels, A. 2001. "Miner's Pond." Pp. 55–63 in *Poems*. Alfred A. Knopf, New York, NY.

Miller, R. R. 1943. "*Cyprinodon salinus*, a New Species of Fish from Death Valley, California." *Copeia* 1943: 69–78.

———. 1945. "Four New Species of Fossil Cyprinodont Fishes from Eastern California." *Journal of the Washington Academy of Sciences* 35: 315–21.

———. 1948. *The Cyprinodont Fishes of the Death Valley System of Eastern California and Southwestern Nevada*. Miscellaneous Publications, Museum of Zoology, University of Michigan, 68.

———. 1981. "Coevolution of Deserts and Fishes." Pp. 39–94 in *Fishes in North American Deserts*, edited by R. J. Naimain and D. L. Soltz. John Wiley and Sons, New York, NY.

———. 1984. "*Rhinichthys deaconi*, a New Species of Dace (Pices: Cyprinidae) from Southern Nevada." Occasional Papers of the Museum of Zoology, University of Michigan, 707.

Miller, R. R., et al. 1989. "Extinctions of North American Fishes during the Past Century." *Fisheries* 14: 22–35.

Miller, R. R., and E. P. Pister. 1971. "Management of the Owens Pupfish, *Cyprinodon radiosus*, in Mono County, California." *Transactions of the American Fisheries Society* 100: 502–9.

Minckley, W. L., et al. 1991. "Conservation and Management of Short-Lived Fishes: The Cyprinodontidae." Pp. 247–98 in *Battle against Extinction: Native Fish Management in the American West*, edited by W. L. Minckley and J. E. Deacon. University of Arizona Press, Tucson, AZ.

Moore, K. D. 2010. *Wild Comfort: The Solace of Nature*. Trumpeter Books, Boston, MA.

Moreo, M. T., et al. 2003. "Estimated Ground-Water Withdrawals from the Death Valley Regional Flow System, Nevada and California, 1913–98." U.S. Geological Survey Water Resources Investigations Report 03-4245.

Morrison, P. R. 1957. "Food Consumption and Body Weight in the Masked and Short-Tail Shrews." *American Midland Naturalist* 57: 493–501.

Mueller, L. 1996. "The Need to Hold Still." Pp. 131–33 in *Alive Together*. Louisiana University Press, Baton Rouge, LA.

Muir, J. 1988. *My First Summer in the Sierra*. Sierra Club Books, San Francisco, CA.

Mulch, A., et al. 2006. "Hydrogen Isotopes in Eocene River Gravels and Paleoelevation of the Sierra Nevada." *Science* 87–89.

Murphy, J. F., et al. 2003. "Population Status and Conservation of the Black Toad, *Bufo exsul*." *Southwestern Naturalist* 48: 54–60.

Muths, E., et al. 2003. "Evidence for Disease-Related Amphibian Decline in Colorado." *Biological Conservation* 110: 357–65.

Naiman, R. J., et al. 1976. "Osmoregulation in the Death Valley Pupfish *Cyprinodon milleri* (Pices: Cyprinodontidae)." *Copeia* 1976: 807–10.

Neruda, P. 1990. "Ode to Salt." P. 367 in *Selected Odes*, translated by M. S. Peden. University of California Press, Berkeley, CA.

Nevada State Environmental Commission. 2009. "Public Comments Submitted to the State Environmental Commission (SEC) on Agenda Items 5 and 6, February 11, 2009, SEC Regulatory Hearing." http://www.sec.nv.gov/docs/comment_letters_all.pdf (April 2, 2013).

Obama, B. H. 2006. *The Audacity of Hope*. Crown/Three Rivers Press, New York, NY.

Orme, A. R., and A. J. Orme. 2008. "Late Pleistocene Shorelines of Owens Lake, California, and Their Hydroclimatic and Tectonic Implications." Pp. 207–25 in *Late Cenozoic Drainage History of the Southwestern Great Basin and Lower Colorado River Region: Geologic and Biotic Perspectives*, edited by M. C. Reheis, R. Hershler, and D. M. Miller. Geological Society of America Special Paper 439.

Otis Bay. N.d. "Ecological Projects—Ash Meadows." http://www.otisbay.com/projects/nevada/ashmeadows/ashmeadows.html (April 15, 2013).

Pavelko, M. T., et al. 1999. "Las Vegas, Nevada: Gambling with Water in the Desert." Pp. 49–64 in *Land Subsidence in the United States*, edited by D. Galloway, D. R. Jones, and S. E. Ingebritsen. U.S. Geological Survey Circular 1182.

Phillips, F. M. 2008. "Geological and Hydrological History of the Paleo-Owens River Drainage since the Late Miocene." Pp. 115–50 in *Late Cenozoic Drainage History of the Southwestern Great Basin and Lower Colorado River Region: Geologic and Biotic Perspectives*, edited by M. C. Reheis, R. Hershler, and D. M. Miller. Geological Society of America Special Paper 439.

Pister, E. P. 1991. "The Desert Fishes Council: Catalyst for Change." Pp. 55–68 in *Battle against Extinction: Native Fish Management in the American West*, edited by W. L. Minckley and J. E. Deacon. University of Arizona Press, Tucson, AZ.

———. 1993. "Species in a Bucket." *Natural History*, January 1993, 14.

Plath, S. 1961. "The Moon and the Yew Tree." Pp. 172–73 in *Sylvia Plath: The Collected Poems*, edited by T. Hughes. Quality Paperback Book Club, New York, NY.

Polhemus, J. T., and D. A. Polhemus. 1994. "A New Species of *Ambrysus* Stål from Ash Meadows, Nevada (Heteroptera: Naucoridae)." *Journal of the New York Entomological Society* 102: 261–65.

Pough, F. H. 1980. "The Advantages of Ectothermy for Tetrapods." *American Naturalist* 115: 92–112.

Quammen, D. 1996. *The Song of the Dodo: Island Biogeography in an Age of Extinction.* Scribner, New York, NY.

Ramey, R. R., II, et al. 2005. "Genetic Relatedness of the Preble's Meadow Jumping Mouse (*Zapus hudsonius preblei*) to Nearby Subspecies of *Z. hudsonius* as Inferred from Variation in Cranial Morphology, Mitochondrial DNA and Microsatellite DNA: Implications for Taxonomy and Conservation." *Animal Conservation* 8: 329–46.

Ray, C. 1958. "Vital Limits and Rates of Desiccation in Salamanders." *Ecology* 39: 75–83.

Reeder, N. M., et al. 2012. "A Reservoir Species for the Emerging Amphibian Pathogen *Batrachochytrium dendrobatidis* Thrives in a Landscape Decimated by Disease. *PLoS One* 7(3): E33567.

Reheis, M. C. 1997. "Dust Deposition Downwind of Owens (Dry) Lake, 1991–1994: Preliminary Findings." *Journal of Geophysical Research* 102: 25999–26008.

Reheis, M. C., and T. L. Sawyer. 1997. "Late Cenozoic History and Slip Rates of the Fish Lake Valley, Emigrant Peak, and Deep Springs Valley Fault Zones, Nevada and California." *Geological Society of America Bulletin* 109: 280–99.

Reheis, M. C., et al. 2002. "Drainage Reversals in Mono Basin during the Late Pliocene and Pleistocene." *Geological Society of America Bulletin* 114: 991–1006.

Reisner, M. 1993. *Cadillac Desert.* Penguin Books, New York, NY.

Rexroth, K. 1967. "Toward an Organic Philosophy." Pp. 101–4 in *The Collected Shorter Poems of Kenneth Rexroth.* New Directions Publishing Corporation, New York, NY.

Riggs, A. C., and J. E. Deacon. 2002. "Connectivity in Desert Ecosystems: The Devils Hole Story." Conference Proceedings, Spring-fed Wetlands: Important Scientific and Cultural Resources of the Intermountain Region. http://www.wetlands.dri.edu.

Rogers, P. 1997. "Animals and People: 'The Human Heart in Conflict with Itself.'" *Orion* 16(1) (Winter): 13–15.

Roethke, T. 1975. "The Far Field." Pp. 193–95 in *The Collected Poems of Theodore Roethke.* Doubleday, New York, NY.

Rohr, J. R., et al. 2008. "Evaluating the Links between Climate, Disease Spread, and Amphibian Declines." *Proceedings of the National Academy of Sciences* 105: 17436–41.

Sada, D. W. 1990. *Recovery Plan for the Endangered and Threatened Species of Ash Meadows, Nevada.* U.S. Fish and Wildlife Service, Reno, NV.

Sada, D. W., and J. E. Deacon. 1995. "Spatial and Temporal Variability of Pupfish (Genus *Cyprinodon*) Habitat and Populations at Salt Creek and Cottonball Marsh, Death Valley National Park, California." Report to U.S. National Park Service, Death Valley National Park, Coop Agreement No. 8000-2-9003.

Sada, D. W., and G. L. Vinyard. 2002. "Anthropogenic Changes in Biogeography of Great Basin Aquatic Biota." Pp. 277–93 in *Great Basin Aquatic Systems History*, edited by R. Hershler, D. B. Madsen, and D. Currey. Smithsonian Contributions to the Earth Sciences 33.

Sanders, B. M., et al. 1994. "Specific Cross-reactivity of Antibodies Raised against Two Major Stress Proteins, Stress 70 and Chaperonin 60, in Diverse Species." *Environmental Toxicology and Chemistry* 13: 1241–49.

Santayana, G. 1896. *The Sense of Beauty: Being the Outline of Aesthetic Theory*. Charles Scribner, New York, NY.

Schmidt-Nielsen, K. 1990. *Animal Physiology*. 4th ed. Cambridge University Press, New York, NY.

Schuierer, F. W. 1961. "Remarks upon the Natural History of *Bufo exsul* Myers, the Endemic Toad of Deep Springs Valley, Inyo County, California." *Herpetologica* 17: 260–66.

Selvanov, A., et al. 2009. "Hypersensitivity to Contact Inhibition Provides a Clue to Cancer Resistance of Naked Mole-Rat." *Proceedings of the National Academy of Sciences* 106: 19352–57.

Silver, K. 2005. "Death at Devil's Hole." *Las Vegas Life*, January.

Simandle, E. 2006. "Population Structure and Conservation of Two Rare Toad Species (*Bufo exsul* and *Bufo nelson*) in the Great Basin, USA." PhD dissertation, University of Nevada, Reno, Reno, NV.

Smith, G. R., et al. 2002. "Biogeography and Timing of Evolutionary Events among Great Basin Fishes." Pp. 175–234 in *Great Basin Aquatic Systems History*, edited by R. Hershler, D. B. Madsen, and D. Currey. Smithsonian Contributions to the Earth Sciences 33.

Snyder, G. 1969. Cold Mountain Poems #12. P. 36 in *Riprap and Cold Mountain Poems*. Four Seasons Foundation, San Francisco, CA.

———. 1974. "For the Children." P. 86 In *Turtle Island*. New Directions, New York, NY.

Soltz, D. L., and R. J. Naiman. 1978. *The Natural History of Native Fishes in the Death Valley System*. Special Publications of the Natural History Museum of Los Angeles County Science Series 30.

Southern Nevada Water Authority. 2009. *Water Resource Plan 09*. Las Vegas, NV.

———. 2011. "SNWA Summary of Cost Estimate for Clark, Lincoln, and White Pine Counties Groundwater Development Project, Submitted as SNWA Exhibit 195 to the Nevada State Engineer in Association with Hearings on SNWA's Groundwater Applications in the Spring, Delamar, Dry Lake, and Cave Valleys."

———. "Intake No. 3." http://www.snwa.com/about/regional_intake3.html (June 15, 2013).

———. "Mission." http://www.wuwc.org/html/members_snwa.html (June 15, 2013).

Spaulding, W. G., et al. 1990. "Packrat Middens: Their Composition and Methods of Analysis. Pp. 59–84 in *Packrat Middens: The Last 40,000 Years of Biotic Change*, edited by J. L. Betancourt et al. University of Arizona Press, Tucson, AZ.

Spight, T. M. 1968. "The Water Economy of Salamanders: Evaporative Water Loss." *Physiological Zoology* 41: 195–203.

State of Nevada, Nevada Division of Environmental Protection, Bureau of Water Pollution Control. 2013. http://ndep.nv.gov/bwpc/ponderosa.htm (April 2, 2013).

State of Nevada, Department of Conservation and Natural Resources. 2008. "State Engineer Order #1197." http://images.water.nv.gov/images/orders/1197o.pdf (April 3, 2013).

Steunkel, E. L., and S. D. Hillyard. 1981. "The Effects of Temperature and Salinity Acclimation on Metabolic Rate and Osmoregulation in the Pupfish *Cyprinodon salinus*." *Copeia* 1981: 411–17.

Stock, G. M., et al. 2004. "Pace of Landscape Evolution of the Sierra Nevada, California, Revealed by Cosmogenic Dating of Cave Sediments." *Geology* 32: 193–96.

Sumner, F. B., and M. C. Sargent. 1940. "Some Observations on the Physiology of Warm Springs Fishes." *Ecology* 21: 45–54.

Tevis, L., Jr. 1966. "Unsuccessful Breeding by Desert Toads (*Bufo punctatus*) at the Limit of Their Ecological Tolerance." *Ecology* 47: 766–75.

Tra, C. 2012. "Executive Summary. Population Forecasts: Long-Term Projections for Clark County, Nevada, 2012–2050." UNLV Center for Business & Economic Research, College of Business, University of Nevada Las Vegas. http://cber.unlv .edu/commentary/CBER-19June2012.pdf (June 15, 2013).

U.S. Bureau of Land Management. 2012. "About SNPLMA." http://www.blm.gov/ pgdata/content/nv/en/snplma.html (June 15, 2013).

U.S. Census Bureau. 2012. "Population of Counties by Decennial Census, 1900 to 1990." http://www.census.gov/population/cencounts/ca190090.txt (July 7, 2012).

U.S. Fish and Wildlife Service. 1980. "Devils Hole Pupfish Recovery Plan. Unpublished report, Portland, OR.

———. 2006. "Biological Opinion for the Proposed Coyote Springs Investment Development in Clark County, Nevada." Army Corps of Engineers Permit Application No. 200125042.

———. 2008. "Record of Decision for the Coyote Springs Investment Planned Development Project Multispecies Habitat Conservation Plan Environmental Impact Statement." http://www.fws.gov/nevada/highlights/comment/csi/ ROD_10–24–08.pdf (June 15, 2013).

———. 2009. "Desert National Wildlife Refuge Complex, Ash Meadows, Desert, Moapa Valley, and Pahranagat National Wildlife Refuges: Final Comprehensive Conservation Plan and Environmental Impact Statement, Clark, Lincoln, and Nye Counties, Nevada." http://www.fws.gov/desertcomplex/pdf/03_Final_CCP-EIS_ Intro-Ch1_20090814.pdf (April 2, 2013).

———. 2012. "For Landowners: Safe Harbor Agreements." http://www.fws.gov/ endangered/landowners/safe-harbor-agreements.html (July 8, 2012).

U.S. National Park Service. 2010. "Devils Hole Long Term Ecosystem Monitoring Plan Environmental Assessment." U.S. Department of the Interior, U.S. National Park Service, Death Valley National Park.

———. 2013. "Organic Act of 1916." http://www.nps.gov/grba/parkmgmt/organic-act-of-1916.htm (June 15, 2013).

———. 2012. "Manzanar National Historic Site: Japanese Americans at Manzanar." http://www.nps.gov/history/museum/exhibits/manz/campLife.html (August 31, 2102).

Uyeno, T., and R. R. Miller. 1962. "Relationships of *Empetrichthys erdisi*, a Pliocene Cyprinodontid Fish from California, with Remarks on the Fundulinae and Cyprinodontinae." *Copeia* 1962: 520–31.

Vrendenburg, V. T., et al. 2010. "Dynamics of an Emerging Disease Drive Large-Scale Amphibian Population Extinctions." *Proceedings of the National Academy of Sciences* 107: 9689–94.

Wakabayashi, J., and T. L. Sawyer. 2001. "Stream Incision, Tectonics, Uplift, and Evolution of Topography of the Sierra Nevada, California." *Journal of Geology* 109: 539–62.

Wake, D. B., et al. 2002. "New Species of Slender Salamander, Genus *Batrachoseps*, from the Southern Sierra Nevada of California." *Copeia* 2002: 1016–28.

Wales, J. H. 1930. "Biometrical Studies of Some Races of Cyprinodont Fishes from the Death Valley Region, with Description of *Cyprinodon diabolis* n. sp." *Copeia* 1930: 61–70.

Wang, I. J. 2009. "Fine-Scale Genetic Structure in a Desert Amphibian: Landscape Genetics of the Black Toad (*Bufo exsul*)." *Molecular Ecology* 18: 3847–56.

Weissenfluh, D. S. 2010. "Conservation of *Cyprinodon nevadensis pectoralis* and Three Endemic Aquatic Invertebrates in an Artificial Desert Spring Refuge Located in Ash Meadows National Wildlife Refuge, Nevada." MS thesis, Texas Tech University, Lubbock, TX.

Weitzel, G. J., and C. F. Muler. 1973. "Effects of Temperature and Activity on Heart Rates of *Plethodon cinereus*." *Journal of Herpetology* 7: 93–96.

Wernicke, B., et al. 1996. "Origin of the High Mountains in the Continents: The Southern Sierra Nevada." *Science* 271: 190–93.

Whiteman, N. K., and R. W. Sites. 2008. "Aquatic Insects as Umbrella Species for Ecosystem Protection in Death Valley National Park." *Journal of Insect Conservation* 12: 499–509.

Wild Fish Habitat Initiative. 2007. "Jackrabbit Spring Restoration at Ash Meadows National Wildlife Refuge." http://wildfish.montana.edu/cases/browse_details .asp?ProjectID=83 (April 2, 2013).

Williams, J. E. 1991. "Preserves and Refuges for Native Western Fishes: History and Management." Pp. 171–89 in *Battle against Extinction: Native Fish Management in the American West*, edited by W. L. Minckley and J. E. Deacon. University of Arizona Press, Tucson, AZ.

Williams, W. C. 1950. "A Sort of a Song." P. 7 in *The Collected Later Poems of William Carlos Williams*. New Directions Publishing Corporation, New York, NY.

Wilson, K. P., and D. W. Blinn. 2007. "Food Web Structure, Energetics, and Importance of Allochthonous Carbon in a Desert Cavernous Limnocrene: Devils Hole, Nevada." *Western North American Naturalist* 67: 185–98.

Woiceshyn, G. 1999. "Environmentalism, Eco-Terrorism and Endangered Species." *Capitalism Magazine*, January 25, 1999. http://capitalismmagazine.com/1999/01/ environmentalism-eco-terrorism-and-endangered-species/ (July 7, 2012).

Wood, W., and S. V. Subrahmanyan. "From the Garuda Purana." Quoted at http:// en.wikipedia.org/wiki/Yama_(Hinduism) (June 13, 2013).

Woodcock, D. 1986. "The Late Pleistocene of Death Valley: A Climatic Reconstruction Based on Macrofossil Data. *Paleogeography, Paleoclimatology, Paleoecology* 57: 273–83.

Woodhouse, C. A., et al. 2006. "Updated Streamflow Reconstructions for the Upper Colorado River Basin." *Water Resources Research* 42, W05415, doi 10.1029/2005WR004455.

Wright, A. H., and A. A. Wright. 1949. "Amargosa Toad." Pp. 154–61 in *Handbook of Frogs and Toads of the United States and Canada*. 3rd ed. Comstock Publishing Associates, Ithaca, NY.

———. 1949. "Nevada Frog." Pp. 454–59 in *Handbook of Frogs and Toads of the United States and Canada*. 3rd ed. Comstock Publishing Associates, Ithaca, NY.

Wrigley, R. 2006. "Skull of a Snowshoe Hare." Pp. 43–44 in *Earthly Meditations*. Penguin Books, New York, NY.

Yanev, K. P., and D. B. Wake. 1981. "Genic Differentiation in a Relict Desert Salamander, *Batrachoseps campi*." *Herpetologica* 37: 16–28.

Zheng, P., and D. Wake. 2009. "Higher-Level Salamander Relationships and Divergence Dates Inferred from Complete Mitochondrial Genomes." *Molecular Phylogenetics and Evolution* 52: 492–508.

Acknowledgments

Many, many people have helped with this project. For companionship in the field I am grateful to Martin Norment, Ralph Black, Steve Parmenter (thanks for those surprise Tecates after the long slog into Cottonball Marsh), Ceal Klingler, Darrick Weissenfluh, Jeff Goldstein, Amity Wilczek, and Dawne Becker. I am an avian ecologist by training and so at first was unfamiliar with much of the scientific, management, and historical terrain covered in this book. Many professionals helped me understand the research, submitted to interviews, graciously fielded my persistent questions, corrected my many mistakes, supplied important unpublished material, and vetted relevant passages in the book. These individuals helped make this a (hopefully) more accurate and better-crafted book; they include David Wake, Sean Lema, Elizabeth Jockusch, Tim Mayer, Wayne Belcher, Jim Deacon, Don Sada, Zane Marshall, Sharon McKelvey, Darrick Weissenfluh, Steve Parmenter, Phil Pister, Rob Andress, Andy Martin, Kevin Wilson, David Livermore, Peter Fame, Tim Lowenstein, Eric Simandle, Merith Reheis, Maria Dzul, Jennifer Back, Rey Sia, Tony Echelle, Richard Friese, Ceal Klingler, Jennifer Back, Cristi Baldino, Alan Riggs, Bailey Gaines, Dave Martin, and one anonymous federal scientist. In particular, I would like to thank Wayne Belcher for patiently answering my stream of questions about the hydrology of the Death Valley region. Gary Giacomini and Gary Hollis also graciously submitted to long interviews. As a matter of policy and ethics I gave every person quoted at any length the opportunity to comment on relevant passages in the manuscript so that I did not misrepresent their views; everyone except Gary Hollis responded to my offer. I made every attempt to accommodate any concerns expressed by my sources, but in a few cases the final manuscript differed from what they would have preferred. This was particularly true for Zane Marshall of the Southern Nevada Water Authority, whose view of groundwater development in northern Nevada and terms such as "unreasonable adverse effects" understandably differ from mine. Barbara Kelly supplied a copy of Ed Abbey's postcard about Ash Meadows. I also would like to thank some of the same individuals mentioned above, and others, for their careful, thoughtful readings of entire chapters (or more): Rafe Sagarin, Jim Deacon, Phil Pister, Steve Parmenter, Sean Lema, Margi Polland Fox, Ralph Black, Kevin Wilson, Dawne Becker, Cristi Baldino, Sharon McKelvey, Ceal Klingler, and one anonymous reviewer hired by the University of North Carolina Press, who provided a particularly thoughtful and detailed analysis of the manuscript. Of course, whatever the contributions by the many people mentioned above, any remaining errors are entirely my own.

Several organizations have supported my work. The College at Brockport, State University of New York, granted me a one-term sabbatical at the beginning of this project and provided several awards to cover travel expenses during my fieldwork. The U.S. Fish and Wildlife staff at Ash Meadows National Wildlife Refuge—Sharon McKelvey, Cristi Baldino, and Darrick Weissenfluh—helped tremendously with my project by letting me stay in the refuge bunkhouse for several weeks while I was volunteering at Ash Meadows, giving generously of their time and expertise, supplying important documents, and most important, allowing me to wander freely and visit many sensitive refuge sites on my own. Kevin Wilson of the U.S. National Park Service also went out of his way to facilitate my project and hosted me on several important visits to Devils Hole. Although Kevin and I may not (quite) see eye to eye on the best approach to managing the Devils Hole pupfish, I appreciate his willingness to assist my project, his thoughtful analysis of portions of the manuscript, and his dedication to studying and managing the aquatic ecosystems of Death Valley. The Andrews Experimental Forest in Blue River, Oregon, through its scholar-in-residence program, gave me a place to write and think about slender salamanders and pupfish during a pleasant and rainy week in November 2010. I particularly would like to thank Fred Swanson of the Andrews Experimental Forest, U.S. Forest Service, for nourishing "ecological" interactions between science and the arts. The interlibrary loan group of the Drake Library, College at Brockport, assisted with my research by tracking down innumerable books and articles. Sara Grillo helped assemble the notes and bibliography. Chris Carson, an associate professor in the Department of Art at the College at Brockport, created the sketches that grace this book.

In a number of ways *Relicts of a Beautiful Sea* has been a family affair. My son, Martin Norment, was a cheerful and energetic field companion on two research trips. (Martin, remember those ice-cold IPAs one March evening and the long view east from Marble Canyon to the Grapevine Mountains!) My daughter, Liza Norment, used her skills in geographic information systems to create the maps for this book. My sister and brother-in-law, Lisa and Paul Hendricks, commented thoughtfully on my writing and discussed with me a number of the ideas in this book. Finally, I would like to thank my wife, Melissa, for supporting my work. She has tolerated my many absences while in the field, constant early morning risings, and pupfish obsession. We are a one-car family, and during my sabbatical research, Melissa graciously agreed to my request to use our car for ten weeks, leaving her to bicycle to work and the store. Over the years we also have discussed many aspects of this project.

I also would like to gratefully thank the generations of biologists, resource managers, and conservation-minded people, living and deceased, who have done so much to protect the aquatic species and habitats of the Death Valley region. It would be impossible to name them all, but I would particularly like to acknowledge Carl Hubbs, Robert Rush Miller, and W. L. Minckley (all deceased), and Phil Pister, Jim Deacon, Steve Parmenter, Don Sada, Dave Livermore, Darrick Weissenfluh, Sharon McKelvey, and Cristi Baldino for their tireless work on behalf of the species and ecosystems that cannot advocate on their own behalf. Many of these people work or worked for state or federal government agencies and so belong to the much-maligned civil service sector. Yet I admire all of them (as well as others acknowledged earlier) for their passionate, competent, and energized devotion to their work and to the people, species, and ecosystems they serve. It took the determined efforts of many people and groups to save places such as Ash Meadows, but I would particularly like to acknowledge the work of two effective and determined nongovernmental organizations for their critical roles in the process: the Desert Fishes Council and the Nature Conservancy. Without them, there might not be an Ash Meadows National Wildlife Refuge, and I might be writing sorrowfully and in the past tense about species such as the Devils Hole pupfish.

Finally, I would like to thank the University of North Carolina Press for agreeing to publish my book, and for the generous help provided by its staff, including Heidi Perov, Susan Garrett, Dino Battista, Paula Wald, and Alison Shay. Liz Gray did an excellent job of copyediting the manuscript and making *Relicts of a Beautiful Sea* a better book. And I am particularly grateful to Joe Parsons, senior editor at UNC Press, for his continued support of my work, wise counsel, friendship, and great sense of humor.